OF EMPIRES AND CITIZENS

OF
EMPIRES
AND
CITIZENS

*Pro-American Democracy
or No Democracy at All?*

AMANEY A. JAMAL

PRINCETON UNIVERSITY PRESS
PRINCETON AND OXFORD

Library of Congress Cataloging-in-Publication Data
Jamal, Amaney A., 1970–
Of empires and citizens : pro-American democracy or no
democracy at all? / Amaney A. Jamal.
p. cm.
Includes bibliographical references and index.
ISBN 978-0-691-14964-6 (hardcover : alk. paper)—
ISBN 978-0-691-14965-3 (pbk. : alk. paper) 1. Democratization—Arab countries. 2. Islam and politics—Arab countries.
3. Democratization—Government policy—United States.
4. United States—Foreign relations—Arab countries. 5. Arab
countries—Foreign relations—United States. 6. Anti-
Americanism—Arab countries. 7. Arab countries—Politics
and government—1945– I. Title.
JQ1850.A91J348 2012
320.917′4927—dc23   2012008057

British Library Cataloging-in-Publication Data is available

This book has been composed in ITC Leagacy Serif Std

Printed on acid-free paper. ∞

Printed in the United States of America

1 3 5 7 9 10 8 6 4 2

CONTENTS

|||||||||||||||||||||||||||||||||||||||||||||||

List of Tables and Figures	ix
Preface	xi
Acknowledgments	xiii
A Note on Transliteration	xv

CHAPTER ONE
Introduction: Pro-American Democracy or No Democracy at All? — 1
The U.S. Strategic Approach to Democracy — 3
Revisiting the Classical Models: Theoretical Limitations — 12
Newer Democratization Debates — 12
Revisiting State and Society Relations in Clientelistic Settings: Real Congruence versus Contrived Congruence — 19
Empirical Realities: Jordan and Kuwait — 21
U.S. Dominance in the Arab World — 23
Anti-Americanism as the Independent Variable: Jordan and Kuwait — 29
Scope Condition, Case-Selection Strategy, Data, and Evidence — 34
Appendix: Human Development Index Scores and Jordan's Gross Domestic Product Growth Rate — 36

CHAPTER TWO
Becoming Jordan and Kuwait: The Making and Consolidating of U.S. Client Regimes — 38
Jordan's History of Clientelistic Dependence — 41
Post–World War II: Full Independence for Jordan but Continued Reliance on the British — 43
Economic Devastation after the First Gulf War — 46
Economic Progress and the Jordan-Israeli Peace Treaty, 1994 — 48
Continued Military and Economic Assistance: Increased Dependency — 52
Kuwait's History of Clientelistic Dependence — 54
The Iraqi Occupation of Kuwait and the Limits of Pan-Arabism — 57

CHAPTER THREE
Islamist Momentum in the Arab World: Jordan's Islamic Action Front and Kuwait's Islamic Constitutional Movement — 63
Islamists and Anti-American Positions across the Arab World — 64
The IAF and its Anti-American Positions — 66
IAF Support — 69

The 1994 Peace Treaty with Israel   73
Other Islamist Forces in Jordan   78
Regime-IAF Relations: Democracy in Retreat   79
U.S. Policy and Islamists: Pro-American Democracy or No Democracy
    at All?   86
Kuwait's Islamist Movement: A Pro-American Force   89
Islamists and Their Positions: Democratic Deepening in Kuwait   92
Democratic Successes and Advancements: Female Suffrage,
    Redistricting, and Succession   94
Regime-Islamist Relations in Kuwait   100

CHAPTER FOUR
Engaging the Regime through the Lens of the United States:
    Citizens' Political Preferences   103
Causal Logics Citizens Employ When Engaging Possibilities of Regime
    Change   104
Support for the Monarchy and U.S. Clientelism: Jordan   106
Support for the Monarchy and U.S. Clientelism: Kuwait   113
Supporting the Regime versus Supporting Democracy: Jordan   116
Supporting the Regime versus Supporting Democracy: Kuwait   121
The Geopolitics of Support for Shari'a: Different Islamic Worldviews in
    Jordan and Kuwait   128
Exploring Alternative Explanations   134
Conclusion   136
Appendix: Open-Ended Questionnaire Administered in Jordan, Kuwait,
    and Morocco   137

CHAPTER FIVE
Support for Democracy and Authoritarianism: The Geostrategic
    Utility of Cooperative Leadership   142
Jordanian and Kuwaiti Engagements with Security, Democracy, and
    Authoritarianism   144
Main Argument: Given Dependence on the United States, Opposition
    Opinion and Mobilization Strategies Matter   147
Islamism and Anti-Americanism   153
Anti-Americanism and Support for Democracy or Authoritarianism   155
Appendix: Macro-micro Synthesis—The Relationship between Attitudes
    and Regime Outcomes   166

CHAPTER SIX
Morocco: Support for the Status Quo   174
Moroccan International Clientelism   175
Islamist Positions in Morocco   177
Anti-American Sentiment   178

Islamist Popularity and Positions   180

Voices from within: Political Engagement and the Regime in Morocco   182

U.S. Responses to the Islamists in Morocco   190

CHAPTER SEVEN

Palestine and Saudi Arabia and the Limits of Democracy   191

Fatah's Decline and the Victory of Hamas   193

The U.S. Response to Hamas   198

Why Did the Palestinians Vote for Hamas?   199

Saudi Arabia and Its Status Quo Advantage   203

Islamist Positions in Saudi Arabia   208

Regime Responses, the Reform Movement, and the United States   211

The Role of the United States   214

Conclusion   219

Appendix: Questions from the PSR Poll   220

CHAPTER EIGHT

The Influence of International Context on Domestic-Level Models of Regime Transition and Democratic Consolidation   221

Theorizing about Nonclient Regimes   223

Egypt's Future Democratic Consolidation   224

The Clash of Civilizations and the Search for Liberal and Secular Democrats   227

Iran's Influence   231

Possible Paths Forward   232

Ignoring Arab Public Opinion and the Islamist Response   233

The Lesson of Latin America   238

Reassessing U.S. Policies in the Arab World   239

From Bush to Obama   241

Where Do We Go Next?   242

Bibliography   245

Index   267

TABLES AND FIGURES

||||||||||||||||||||||||||||||||||||||||||||||||||||||||||||||||||||||||||||||||||||||||||

TABLES

1.1 Freedom House scores	2
1.2 Total gross official development assistance from the United States across regions (in millions of dollars)	25
1.3 U.S. conflicts by region, 1990–2001	26
1.4 Human Development Index scores, 1980–2005	36
1.5 Jordan GDP growth rates	37
2.1 U.S. aid to Jordan	52
4.1 Jordanian regime supporters and opponents and national origin	107
4.2 Kuwaiti regime supporters and opponents	123
4.3 Support for Shari'a and security vulnerabilities	136
5.1 Logistic regression: Support for U.S. antiterrorism policies	152
5.2 OLS regression: Support for anti-Americanism	155
5.3 Jordan: OLS models on support for government and overt support for democracy	164
5.4 Kuwait: OLS models on support for government and overt support for democracy	165
7.1 Logistic regression: Support for Fatah	194
7.2 Evaluations of elections in the Arab world, 2005–6	195
7.3 Votes in the elections, 2005–6	198
8.1 Client states versus nonclient states	223

FIGURES

1.1 Middle East Human Development Indicators and Freedom House scores	3
1.2 Autonomous states and the relationship of state and society	20
1.3 Military personnel across time (excluding Iraq and Kuwait)	27
1.4 Military personnel across time (including Iraq and Kuwait)	28
1.5 Economic hierarchy across time	29
1.6 Jordanian and Kuwaiti attitudes toward the United States	34

4.1 Impact of attitudes toward Shari'a on attitudes toward the
  United States (pooled data: Jordan, Egypt, Palestine, and
  Lebanon)   130
5.1a Democracy is the best form of government (Jordan)   145
5.1b Democracy is the best form of government (Kuwait)   146
5.2 Support for strong leadership   147
5.3 The rights of the opposition   148
5.4 Proportion of respondents by country in the 2002 World
  Values Survey who express antidemocracy attitudes   167
5.5 Proportion below mean democracy support   168

PREFACE

‖‖‖‖‖‖‖‖‖‖‖‖‖‖‖‖‖‖‖‖‖‖‖‖‖‖‖‖‖‖‖‖‖‖

IN 2012, EVENTS IN THE ARAB WORLD ARE RAPIDLY UNFOLDING. PRESIDENT HUSNI Mubarak of Egypt has resigned and the Supreme Council of the Armed Forces, the military, has assumed power. Citizens are jubilant that a dictator of thirty years has been asked to step down—an outcome once considered unimaginable. Sticking to their protests in the face of threat and repression, the citizens of Egypt sent a sign that the ongoing living conditions—both economically and politically—were unacceptable. With a growing income gap, unemployment rates skyrocketing, and a youth population that knew nothing but Mubarak's rule, the population said *kifayeh* (enough)!

Yet what type of regime will replace Mubarak after (and if) the military steps down? This is the question that will occupy the minds of analysts, scholars, academics, and students of comparative and Middle East politics. Is Mubarak's exit the first stage of a democratic transition? Is it a final stage to military rule? Will there be substantial reforms? What will become of Egypt's notorious Emergency Laws? What role will the Muslim Brotherhood play? What will happen to the peace treaty with Israel? And will ties to the United States remain close? There are some glaringly clear reminders that the future of Egypt is of vital importance not only to the citizens of Egypt but also to regional and international actors as well.

As the events of the Arab Spring unfolded, it became increasingly clear that while the average citizen on the ground was demanding more democracy, more accountability, better economic opportunities, transparency, and a better life, the international order—chiefly that of the United States—was concerned about an Egyptian government that it could continue to work with. The international order had and has clear geostrategic interests in the area. The United States, through military and diplomatic channels, sent a message to Egyptians, including citizens, opposition movements, the regime in power, and to the regime yet to emerge: it is invested (and hopeful) in seeing a partner at the helm in Egypt.

What does this mean, however, for the future of democracy in Egypt? How do these geostrategic realities shape the ways in which citizens think about regime stability and democracy, and the role of the United States in their societies? And further, what do these negotiations mean for the future of democratic consolidation in Egypt and the Arab world more broadly?

This book addresses these questions by introducing the ways in which geostrategic, patron-client relations shape domestic-level negotiations about regime stability and prospects for democratization. While building on existing democratization theories and approaches, this book attempts to refine some of our understandings about democracy by linking the realities of the international order to domestic-level societal developments.

ACKNOWLEDGMENTS

THIS BOOK WOULD NOT HAVE BEEN POSSIBLE WITHOUT THE ALIGNMENT OF SO MANY factors. Family, friends, colleagues, workshops, and funding all contributed to this final product. I'm grateful to many, many people. First and foremost, I thank my colleague Atul Kohli for encouraging me to take on a topic that at first I felt was too big and ambitious. His very constructive feedback at the early stages of this project was invaluable. Three other colleagues were also instrumental to this project—Christina Davis, Irfan Nooruddin, and Ellen Lust. They read the manuscript more times than they actually cared to and listened to me complain about the project—and even when they didn't understand why I was complaining, they still listened. For that I am grateful.

Generous feedback from my colleagues at Princeton University benefited this project enormously. I thank Deborah Yashar, Mark Beissinger, Nancy Bermeo, Evan Lieberman, Grigo Pop-Eleches, Rafaela Dancygier, Dani Campello, Lynn White, Helen Milner, Chris Achen, Gary Bass, and Jonas Pontusson. Several other colleagues also provided insightful feedback: Lisa Anderson, David Laitin, Lisa Wedeen, Shibley Telhami, Mark Tessler, Tarek Masoud, and Jillian Schwedler all offered helpful comments and significant suggestions.

This project involved a massive data collection effort in three countries: Jordan, Morocco, and Kuwait. I worked with several research assistants, translators, transcribers, and data specialists, and I would like to thank Alex Kobishyn, Tim Shriver, Eman Jamal, Nariman Zarzour, Sami Hermez, Abdullah AlSharrah, Courtney Emerson, Urooj Raja, Jennifer Dennard, Souha Rasheed, Tonya Howe, Gail Buttorf, and Dana Weinstein; your research assistance was a tremendous help. A very special thanks goes to Princeton's Niehaus Center for Globalization and Governance's support of Raymond Hicks for his outstanding research work on this project. I also continue to be very grateful to Chuck Myers, who is just fabulous to work with, and the anonymous reviewers who gave very valuable comments.

My colleagues in the Middle East have been a tremendous asset to my ongoing fieldwork. I wish to thank Dr. Khalil Shikaki, Dr. Fares Braizat, Dr. Mohammed al-Masri and Dr. Ghanim al-Najjar for their ongoing support and assistance.

The book was also shaped by the talks I delivered at several institutions. I'm thankful for all my colleagues who asked me to deliver talks at the University of California–Berkeley, the University of Wisconsin–Madison, Harvard University, Princeton University, the University of Illinois–Urbana Champaign, the University of Minnesota, Boston College, Columbia University, the University of Michigan, the University of Pennsylvania, New York University, and Oxford University.

This project was well-funded and supported, and I am indebted to several organizations. In particular, I thank the Carnegie Scholars Program, the United States Institute of Peace, and Princeton University for providing the resources to complete this work.

Finally, the nurturing of this seven-year book project coincided with the growth of my four children. Asma started and finished college while I was working on this book. Lina finished her high school years and embarked for college. Ayah finished up elementary school and began middle school, and Maryam learned how to crawl, walk, talk and start preschool while Mom worked on the manuscript. When things got cluttered, they always kept me going. I thank my husband, Helmi, for his ongoing support and love. And finally, I thank my mother, Nidal Jamal, who continues to inspire me day in and day out.

A NOTE ON TRANSLITERATION

The Arabic is transliterated using the standards of the *International Journal of Middle East Studies*.

OF EMPIRES AND CITIZENS

CHAPTER ONE

Introduction

Pro-American Democracy or No Democracy at All?

Since the downfall of the Soviet Union, the world has witnessed a new wave of global democratization. Freedom House, which monitors democracy around the globe, reports that between 1994 and 2009, the number of electoral democracies increased from 69 out of 167 total states to 119 out of 192. Between 1994 and 2005, the number of "free" countries in the world similarly increased from 76 to 89, while the number of "partly free" countries decreased from 61 to 54, and the number of "not free" countries decreased from 54 to 49. On a seven-point scale, with seven being the most democratic, Eastern Europe improved both its political and civil liberties by a margin greater than three points. Other regions followed suit. Countries in Africa improved their scores by over one point, and even regions like Latin America, where political and civil liberties were already much better than in other regions, witnessed significant improvements (see table 1.1).

The Arab world stands apart from this trend. Political and civil liberty scores between 1989 and 2009 remained nearly constant, improving only marginally.[1] Even Russia, which slightly regressed in terms of its political and civil liberties and abounds with stories of rebounding oligarchy, did better in general on these scores than the Arab world. The Arab world witnessed further regressions in civil liberties—this despite progress along several pertinent modernization indicators including education, literacy, gross domestic product (GDP), life expectancy, health care, and human development (see fig. 1.1).[2]

This reality stands in sharp contrast to expectations. As countries in the Middle East modernized and grew economically, the common reasoning goes, they should have liberalized as well. And although current developments in

[1] My definition of the Arab world includes all Arab states in the Arab League: Algeria, Bahrain, Comoros, Djibouti, Egypt, Iraq, Jordan, Kuwait, Lebanon, Libya, Mauritania, Morocco, Oman, Palestine, Qatar, Saudi Arabia, Somalia, Sudan, Syria, Tunisia, the United Arab Emirates, and Yemen.

[2] See table 1.4 in this chapter's appendix for Human Development Index scores over time in Jordan, Morocco, Saudi Arabia, and Kuwait.

TABLE 1.1. Freedom House scores

Region	Political liberty			Civil liberty		
	1989	2009	Change	1989	2009	Change
East Asia	3.56	4.00	0.44	3.50	4.50	1.00
Latin America	5.35	5.68	0.32	5.13	5.45	0.32
South Asia	3.50	4.25	0.75	3.38	3.63	0.25
Middle East	2.15	2.08	−0.07	2.77	2.92	0.15
Former USSR*	3.79	3.36	−0.43	4.00	3.93	−0.07
Eastern Europe	2.25	5.50	3.25	2.75	5.71	2.96
Sub-Saharan Africa	2.09	3.55	1.47	2.67	3.83	1.16
Total (of regions)	3.28	4.15	0.87	3.52	4.37	0.85

Note: Data run from 1 (unfree) to 7 (free).
* Data are for 1991 rather than 1989.

Egypt, Yemen, Bahrain, and Tunisia are reasons for increasing levels of optimism, the Arab world in general continues to withstand demands for more democracy and to witness persistent levels of authoritarianism. Even while citizens have demonstrated a strong commitment to democracy, existing regimes don't appear to reflect the will of the people.

What accounts for this seeming paradox of continued economic development and persistent authoritarianism? The argument of this book is simple: one can't understand the lack of Arab democratic transitions—or the nature of future political liberalization and consolidation trajectories more generally—without taking into account U.S. entrenchment. In the Arab world, U.S. involvement has stifled indigenous democratization gains of the last several decades and levels of anti-Americanism have intersected with the growing influence of Islamism to stifle citizen democratic contestation across most Arab states.

Anti-Americanism, I argue, is the key variable. Too often absent from political science theoretical models on democratization and political development, it is the preeminent factor in shaping the everyday political engagements and negotiations of ordinary citizens in the region. Understanding state-society relations and the rationalizations citizens make about democracy and the geostrategic utility of existing less-democratic regimes requires us to understand how and why anti-Americanism has come to play a crucial role in the Arab region. Exploring this state of affairs, both in theory and on the ground, is the job of this book.

Specifically, this book explores Kuwait and Jordan as two states that have similar clientelistic ties to the United States. Both are monarchies holding parliamentary elections, and each has similar levels of support for its Islamist opposition movements (estimates in each country put levels of support be-

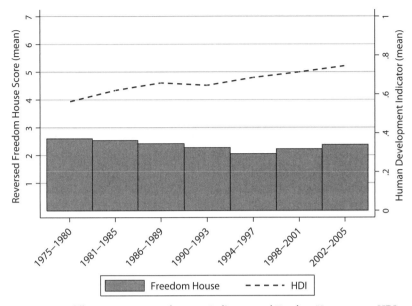

Figure 1.1. Middle East Human Development Indicators and Freedom House scores. HDI every five years (1975, 1980, etc.). FH score reversed (7 = most democratic).

tween 35 percent and 60 percent). But the two states vary in their levels of anti-American sentiment among these Islamist opposition forces (my key explanatory variable). This core difference reveals how concerns about a country's international relations shape state-society relations more broadly.

Although the book builds its argument by focusing on the cases of Kuwait and Jordan, it also draws on evidence from two other monarchies that have varying degrees of anti-American sentiment among their Islamist opposition as well: Morocco and Saudi Arabia. Further, I extend the findings to Palestine's democratic experience, which resulted in Hamas's parliamentary victory in 2006.

THE U.S. STRATEGIC APPROACH TO DEMOCRACY

Since the end of the Cold War, comparative politics has treated the role of the United States in the international context as one that monolithically generates democracy. As Samuel Huntington argues in *The Third Wave*, "External actors significantly helped third wave democratizations. Indeed, by the late 1980s the major sources of power and influence in the world [including the United States] were actively promoting liberalization and democratization."[3]

[3]Samuel Huntington, *The Third Wave: Democratization in the Late Twentieth Century* (Norman: University of Oklahoma Press, 1993), 93.

Studies of Latin America, the former Soviet Union, and Africa all emphasize the role the United States played in promoting democracy.[4]

Yet sometimes democracy may not suit the strategic interests of the United States. This is the case for the Arab world, a situation that has not been fully accounted for thus far in the political science literature. Studies looking at the involvement of international actors in the domestic politics of states have assumed that such involvement will result in more, not less democracy. This work assumes that the United States systematically and universally—and *not* strategically—promotes democracy across the globe, even in regions like the Arab world, where anti-American sentiment is rampant. In these settings, however, greater democratization could clearly bring groups unsympathetic to the United States into power, thus jeopardizing the interests of both the United States and the citizens of the region. The loss of patron support can result in several outcomes with devastating economic results, such as decreased access to resources in the form of aid, denial of access to external markets or preferential trade agreements, and even sanctions if the patron deems a governing authority a threat.

The Arab region is of fundamental importance to the United States, even as Arab states are highly reliant on the United States for security and economic aid.[5] Yet U.S. engagement with the region has been structured by strategies that have placed the interests of the United States above and beyond the daily welfare of Arab citizens. Four major interests shape U.S. involvement in the region today: access to oil, the containment of Iran, support for the state of Israel, and the limiting of Islamist strength and their access to power and weapons of mass destruction.[6] U.S. policies have been designed to secure these interests—not necessarily to increase democracy. As a result, the United States supports pro-American regimes, and most of these pro-American regimes happen to be authoritarian regimes that will

[4]See Huntington, *The Third Wave*; Marc Plattner, "The Democratic Moment," in *The Global Resurgence of Democracy*, ed. Larry Diamond and Marc Plattner (Baltimore: Johns Hopkins University Press, 1996), 36–48; Francis Fukuyama, *The End of History and the Last Man* (New York: Free Press, 1992); Steven Levitsky and Lucien Way, "International Linkage and Democratization," *Journal of Democracy* 16, no 3 (2005): 20–34; Robert Bates, "The Impulse to Reform," in *Economic Change and Political Liberalization in Sub-Saharan Africa*, ed. Jennifer Widner (Baltimore: Johns Hopkins University Press, 1994), 13–28; Kurt Weyland, *The Politics of Market Reform in Fragile Democracies* (Princeton, NJ: Princeton University Press, 2004); and Margaret Keck and Kathryn Sikkink, *Activists beyond Borders* (Ithaca, NY: Cornell University Press, 1998).

[5]See Sheila Caparico, "Foreign Aid for Promoting Democracy in the Middle East," *Middle East Journal* 56, no. 3 (2002): 379–95.

[6]See Marina Ottaway, *Promoting Democracy in the Middle East and the Problem of U.S. Credibility*, Carnegie Paper no. 35 (Washington, DC: Carnegie Endowment for International Peace, 2003); Marina Ottaway and Thomas Carothers, "Greater Middle East Initiative: Off to a False Start," Carnegie Policy Brief no. 29 (Washington, DC: Carnegie Endowment for International Peace, 2004); and Graham Fuller, *The Future of Political Islam* (New York: Palgrave Macmillan, 2003).

not only guarantee the United States access to Middle Eastern oil but also maintain peaceful relations with the state of Israel while simultaneously curbing the influence of Iran and Islamist movements.

In general, Islamist groups oppose these U.S. goals, and therefore it is in the interest of the United States and existing regime leaders to limit the ability of Islamists to influence policy—a reality not lost on ordinary citizens. In fact, citizens, especially those who hope to benefit from greater global economic integration, will prefer supporting the status quo rather than jeopardizing American patronage. Thus, given the conditions of U.S. entrenchment in the Arab region, indigenous demands for democracy will only grow and become sustained if the United States promises to honor the outcome of any democratic experiment, regardless of outcome. Conversely, demands for democracy will grow if democratic reformers are assured that Islamists won't jeopardize ties to the United States.[7] That the United States has demonstrated that it will only tolerate pro-American democratic outcomes while it simultaneously does very little to weaken anti-Americanism continues to influence debates about political liberalization and democratization. Put more simply, the United States will only tolerate friends in power and has done little to win friends from within these societies.

Would-be democratic reformers understand that a push toward democracy may result in bringing anti-American forces to power—which would mean jeopardizing U.S. patronage—and therefore prefer the status quo. The U.S. democracy promotion establishment has erroneously assumed that democracy promotion would by default also bring about pro-American attitudes—regardless of U.S. policies in the region. That citizens of the Arab world could come to appreciate the underpinnings of democracy while simultaneously harboring deep resentment toward the United States was an outcome that the United States had been less prepared for.

This explanation stands in sharp contrast to standard reasoning as it pertains to the Arab world. That reasoning advances two general explanations to account for the lack of Arab democratization, both of which focus

---

[7]Many scholars have noted that Islamists also see themselves as democratic reformers. See Jillian Schwedler, *Faith in Moderation: Islamist Parties in Jordan and Yemen* (New York: Cambridge University Press, 2007); Janine A. Clark, *Islam, Charity, and Activism: Middle-Class Networks and Social Welfare in Egypt, Jordan and Yemen* (Bloomington: Indiana University Press, 2003); Carrie Rosefsky, *Mobilizing Islam* (New York: Columbia University Press, 2002); Quinn Mecham, "Islamist Mobilization in Turkey: A Study in Vernacular Politics," *Political Science Quarterly* 118, no. 3 (2003): 526–27; Mona El-Ghobashy, "Constitutionalist Contention in Contemporary Egypt," *American Behavioral Scientist* 51, no. 11 (2008): 1590–1610; Lisa Wedeen, *Peripheral Visions: Publics, Power, and Performance in Yemen* (Chicago: University of Chicago Press, 2008); and Samer Shehata, "Inside an Egyptian Parliamentary Campaign," in *Political Participation in the Middle East*, ed. Ellen Lust-Okar and Saloua Zerhouni (Boulder, CO: Lynne Rienner, 2008), 95–120, as examples. In this manuscript, however, I use the term *democratic reformers* to signify non-Islamist democracy supporters.

on societal determinants of authoritarian tendencies. The first is grounded in political culture, the second in the region's political economy. Central to both approaches is the notion that Arab societies have not attained the levels of political and economic modernization that equip citizens with the requisite values and economic interests to pose significant challenges to existing authoritarian rule. Absent these by-products of modernization, citizens remain locked into supportive relations with their regimes.

Scholars and policy makers have systematically viewed political culture and economic development as central to citizen democratic contestation of existing regimes. Examples range from the feudal transition to democracy in England, to the third wave of democratization and the demise of the former Soviet Union. Because citizens had acquired new democratic values and had become more autonomous and empowered through economic development, the story goes, they could effectively assert significant pressure on existing regimes. Countries in the third and subsequent waves of democracy had another advantage: the United States had emerged successful from the Cold War and could now, without the threat of the Soviets, continue with its democracy agenda the world over.[8]

None of these theories, though, explains the lack of Arab democratization. The Arab world does not lack an appreciation of democratic values. Not only do the so-called Arab Spring protests of 2011 attest to the strong democratic current in the region but public opinion data from the region collected since the year 2000 also reveal overwhelming support for democracy. Polls across the region indicate that democracy enjoys support from close to 85 percent of the region's population.[9] Further, the recent wave of

[8]As Ronald Inglehart, *Culture Shift in Advanced Industrial Society* (Princeton, NJ: Princeton University Press, 1989), 22, notes, "The linkage between economic development and modern democracy is complex. Three factors seem particularly crucial: (a) the emergence of a politically powerful commercial-industrial bourgeoisie; (b) the development of preconditions that facilitate mass participation in politics; and (c) the development of mass support for democratic institutions and feelings of interpersonal trust that extend even to members of opposing parties." See also Christian Welzel and Ronald Inglehart, "The Role of Ordinary People in Democratization," *Journal of Democracy* 19, no. 1 (2008): 126–40.

[9]Polls across the region indicate that democracy enjoys considerable support. See Zogby International, *Arabs: What They Believe and What They Value Most* (Ithaca, NY: Zogby International, 2002; accessed at http://aai.3cdn.net/7b568f016f6ad3a301_b5m6be8kr.pdf); Pew Global Attitudes Project, *America's Image in the World* (Washington, DC: Pew Research Center, 2007; accessed at http://pewglobal.org/commentary/display.php?AnalysisID=1019); and Pew Global Attitudes Project, *Global Unease with Major World Powers: Rising Environmental Concern in 47-Nation Survey* (Washington, DC: Pew Research Center, 2007; accessed at http://pewglobal.org/reports/display.php?ReportID=256). Herein I use data from the Arab Barometer 2005-6 (principal investigators Mark Tessler and Amaney Jamal; accessed at http://www.arabbarometer.org/survey/survey.html) and the World Values Survey 2002 (accessed at http://www.wvsevsdb.com/wvs/WVSData.jsp).

protests across the region suggests that citizens long for more accountability, transparency, and representation—hallmarks of democracy.

Neither has the Arab world stagnated in its economic development. The many countries in the Arab world have gradually begun to enjoy greater economic growth, lower poverty rates, a more stable middle class, privatization and globalization, and greater rates of foreign direct investment (FDI).[10]

Existing Theories: Political Culture

It's worth first examining the two standard theories in greater depth before addressing the role that America has played in the lack of Arab democratization. First, renowned scholars in the field—including Gabriel Almond and Sidney Verba; Larry Diamond, Juan Linz, and Seymour Martin Lipset; Samuel Huntington; Ronald Inglehart; and Robert Putnam[11]—have linked modernization to values and orientations that would serve as democratic prerequisites. Through modernization, theories suggest, citizens would not only acquire better economic opportunities but would also develop the norms necessary for democracy.[12] That is, development encourages supportive democratic cultural orientations. Thus, economic development was deemed important to generating pertinent values useful to democratization.

The second theory highlights the importance of civil society for democracy. As societies develop, this line of reasoning goes, so too should their civil

---

[10]Jordan's plan, for example, included embarking on a process of trade and financial liberalization, as well as privatization; the nation has achieved economic growth at an annual average of 6 percent since 2004. Although the middle class has remained stable, Ibrahim Saif of the Center for Strategic Studies in Amman, Jordan, notes that the middle class has become less reliant on wages as its members have turned to increasing investment and self-employment opportunities. See chapter 2 for a more detailed discussion on Jordan's economic development trajectory. See also table 1.5 in this chapter's appendix for Jordan's GDP growth rates.

[11]Gabriel Almond and Sidney Verba, *The Civic Culture: Political Attitudes and Democracy in Five Nations* (Princeton, NJ: Princeton University Press, 1963); Larry Diamond, Juan Linz, and Seymour Martin Lipset, "What Makes for Democracy?" in *Politics in Developing Countries: Comparing Experiences with Democracy*, 2nd ed., ed. Larry Diamond, Juan Linz, and Seymour Martin Lipset (Boulder, CO: Lynne Rienner, 1995), 1–66; Huntington, *The Third Wave*; Inglehart, *Culture Shift in Advanced Industrial Society*; and Robert Putnam, *Making Democracy Work: Civic Traditions in Modern Italy* (Princeton, NJ: Princeton University Press, 1993).

[12]In a similar vein, Kiren Aziz Chaudhury, *The Price of Wealth: Economies and Institutions in the Middle East* (Ithaca, NY: Cornell University Press, 1997), addresses value changes linked to economic development that are important for the building of economic markets. Chaudhury highlights the importance of economic development for creating economic markets that are structured by market cultures. In such cultures, individualism is seen as an important norm that replaces precapitalist values. See also Albert Hirschman, *The Passions and the Interests: Political Arguments for Capitalism before Its Triumph* (Princeton, NJ: Princeton University Press, 1977), 30; and Stephen Holmes, "The Secret History of Self-Interest," in *Beyond Self-Interest*, ed. Jane Mansbridge (Chicago: University of Chicago Press, 1990), 267–86.

societies develop in ways that would make democracy a more viable outcome.[13] This scholarship examines the role of civic associations as schools for civic virtue and generators of social capital, and how they thus form major counterweights to existing authoritarian rulers.[14] Civil society can check the powers of the state, encourages citizen participation, helps the development of a democratic culture of tolerance and bargaining, generates new channels for representing interests, creates crosscutting cleavages, serves as forum for the retention of development of new political leaders, and allows for the enrichment and circulation of information to citizens. Thus, civil society has a vital role to play in shaping democratic attitudes and behaviors among populations. Where democratic contestation is weak or lacking, one plausible arena of exploration is civil society.[15] In the context of the Arab world, the region's political culture remains one key set of variables explaining the persistence of authoritarian rule.

A third theory suggests that the political culture of the region might be incompatible with democracy. In the context of the Arab world, this theme links the support for authoritarianism directly to Islam. The political culture of Islam, some argue, impedes the development of the prerequisites of modernization because Islam and democracy simply don't mix well.

This third line of argument maintains that, first, Muslims are more likely to accept the status quo, however disadvantageous it may be, as part of a doctrine of divine destiny.[16] That is, citizens of the Arab world are more likely to attribute their political situations to "Allah's way." Such adherence to the status quo bars any contestation of the established order. Second, as Huntington argues in his seminal work on the clash of civilizations, Islam and democracy are inherently incompatible because Islam, emphasizes the community over the individual and does not recognize the church-state divide. Individualism, Huntington maintains, is a key asset to liberal democratic orders. Third, as other scholars like Francis Fukuyama argue,[17] Islam poses a grave threat to liberal democracy because its doctrinal emphasis lacks a liberal democratic orientation. Fourth, Islam does not advocate political freedoms and in fact mobilizes people against democratic values.[18]

---

[13]Alexis de Toqueville, *Democracy in America*, ed. Richard D. Heffner (New York: New American Library, 1956).

[14]Putnam, *Making Democracy Work*.

[15]See Larry Diamond and Marc Plattner, "Introduction," in *The Global Resurgence of Democracy*, ed. Larry Diamond and Marc Plattner (Baltimore: John Hopkins University Press, 1989), ix–xxxiii.

[16]Elie Kedourie, *Democracy and Arab Political Culture* (Washington DC: Washington Institute for Near East Policy, 1992).

[17]Fukuyama, *The End of History and the Last Man*.

[18]As a result, a new body of scholarship has emerged to counter these assumptions, arguing that there are great possibilities for Islam and democracy. Scholars are pursuing several fruitful lines of inquiry. The first examines Islamic philosophical models—Shari'a, *fiqh*, and new

Fifth, Steven Fish finds that the status of women in Muslim societies hinders democracy.[19] Daniela Donno and Bruce Russett argue that the link between the inferior status of women and democracy is only substantiated in the Arab world.[20]

Following this logic, even if Arab societies are able to attain the necessary levels of modernization, Muslim societies are unlikely to appreciate and function within the norms of a democratic polity.

Existing Theories: Political Economy

Scholars have advanced two main formulations to explain how existing economic structures shape citizen support for their authoritarian regimes in the Arab world. The first is an extension of modernization theories. Because Arab societies have not developed economically, or because their economic trajectories have been marked by only slow progress, this line of reasoning goes, the Arab world has not developed autonomous middle-class groups that can place the necessary constraints on regimes.[21] Scholars who work on

ijtihād—and their effect on the compatibility of Islam with democracy at the theoretical level; see Khaled Abou El Fadl, *Islam and the Challenge of Democracy* (Princeton, NJ: Princeton University Press, 2003); and John Esposito and John Voll, *Islam and Democracy* (Oxford: Oxford University Press, 1996). A second line of argumentation posits that the writings of "progressive Muslims" offer much hope for democracy; see Abdelwahab El-Affendi, "The Elusive Reformation," *Journal of Democracy* 24, no. 2 (2003): 34–39; Lait Kubba, "Faith and Modernity," *Journal of Democracy* 14, no. 2 (2003): 45–49; Radwan Masmoudi, "The Silenced Majority," *Journal of Democracy* 14, no. 2 (2003): 40–44; Omid Safi, ed., *Progressive Muslims: On Justice, Gender and Pluralism* (Oxford: Oneworld, 2003); and Mark Tessler, "Islam and Democracy in the Middle East: The Impact of Religious Orientations on Attitudes toward Democracy in Four Arab Countries," *Comparative Politics* 34 (2002): 337-54. A third line of inquiry, based on new public opinion data, shows that Islamic religiosity and support for democracy are indeed compatible; see Tessler, *Islam and Democracy in the Middle East*; and Steven Hofmann, "Islam and Democracy: Micro-Level Indications of Compatibility," *Comparative Political Studies* 37, no. 6 (2004): 652-76.

[19]Steven Fish, "Islam and Authoritarianism," *World Politics* 55 (2002): 4–37.

[20]Daniela Donno and Bruce Russett, "Islam, Authoritarianism, and Female Empowerment: What Are the Linkages?" *World Politics* 56 (2004): 582–607. See also Amaney Jamal and Vickie Langohr, "Gender Status as an Impediment to Democracy in the Muslim World: What Does Gender Explain and Not Explain?" (unpublished manuscript, 2008) for a more careful discussion of the links among women's rights, democracy, and Islam. In short, we find little evidence to support the claim that there is a direct link between cultural predispositions about gender and levels of democracy.

[21]Guillermo O'Donnell and Phillipe Schmitter, *Transitions to Authoritarian Rule*, vol. 4, *Tentative Conclusions about Uncertain Democracies* (Baltimore: John Hopkins University Press, 1986); Dietrich Rueschemeyer, Evelyn Huber Stephens, and John Stephens, *Capitalist Development and Democracy* (Chicago: University of Chicago Press, 1992); Fukuyama, *The End of History and the Last Man*; Seymour Martin Lipset, "Some Social Requisites of Democracy," *American Political Science Review* 53, no. 1. (1959): 69-105; Lucien Pye, "Political Science and the Crisis of Authoritarianism," *American Political Science Review* 84 (1990): 3–19; Eva Bellin, *Stalled Democracy: Capital, Labor, and the Paradox of State-Sponsored Development* (Ithaca, NY: Cornell University Press, 2002); Kellee S.

the economic and political development of the Arab world, like Eva Bellin, Melanie Claire Cammett, Kiren Aziz Chaudhry, Jill Crystal, Pete Moore, and Benjamin Smith, have examined how existing business interests remain tied to the regimes in power.[22] This lack of business and middle-class autonomy, according to this theory, explains authoritarian persistence. Absent the development of independent economic interests separate from the regime, citizens remain bound in close supportive relations with these regimes, which further solidify authoritarian rule.

Scholars have also documented the growth of autonomous middle-class sectors as a key factor explaining the emergence of democracy across the globe. Barrington Moore and Samuel Huntington in particular have highlighted the importance of creating new economic forces in society through economic development.[23] This expanding middle class—businesspeople, professionals, shopkeepers, teachers, civil servants, managers, technicians, and clerical and sales workers—gradually began to see democracy as a means of securing their own interests. "Third wave movements for democratization," Huntington argues, "were not led by landlords, peasants, or (apart from Poland) industrial workers. In virtually every country the most active supporters of democratization came from the urban middle class."[24] Karl Deutsch, Samuel Huntington, Daniel Lerner, Charles Lindblom, and Seymour Lipset have each emphasized the crucial role played by the commercial-industrial elite in the emergence of democratic institutions.[25] The development of the

---

Tsai, "Capitalists without a Class: Political Diversity among Private Entrepreneurs," *Comparative Political Studies* 38, no. 9 (2005): 1130–58.

[22]Bellin, *Stalled Democracy*; Melanie Claire Cammett, *Globalization and Business Politics in Arab North Africa: A Comparative Perspective* (New York: Cambridge University Press, 2007); Chaudhry, *The Price of Wealth*; Jill Crystal, *Oil and Politics in the Gulf: Rulers and Merchants in Kuwait and Qatar* (New York: Cambridge University Press, 1995); Pete W. Moore, *Doing Business in the Middle East: Politics and Economic Crisis in Jordan and Kuwait*," Cambridge Middle East Studies (Cambridge: Cambridge University Press, 2004); and Benjamin Smith, *Hard Times in the Land of Plenty: Oil Politics in Iran and Indonesia* (Ithaca, NY: Cornell University Press, 2007).

[23]Barrington Moore, *Social Origins of Dictatorship and Democracy: Lord and Peasant in the Making of the Modern World* (Boston: Beacon, 1993); Huntington, *The Third Wave*. Extending his analysis to the third wave of democratization, Huntington identifies several independent variables that at their very essence again highlight the importance of political culture and economic development for forms of democratic contestation. First, he maintains that authoritarian regimes increasingly faced existing challenges when their societies had widely accepted democratic values. Second, he highlights the importance of economic development. In *The Third Wave*, 39, he notes that the ""unprecedented global economic growth of the 1960s, which raised living standards, increased education, and greatly expended the urban middle class in many countries," was vital to the third wave of democratization.

[24]Huntington, *The Third Wave*, 67.

[25]Karl W. Deutsch, "Social Mobilization and Political Development," *American Political Science Review* 55 (1961): 634–47; Samuel Huntington, *Political Order in Changing Societies* (New Haven, CT: Yale University Press, 1968); Huntington, *The Third Wave*; Daniel Lerner, *The Passing*

middle class, ending citizens' loyalty to authoritarian regimes, was vital, they argue, for democratic forms of contestation. While these theories have been built upon the Western experience in particular, scholars have applied these theories to the developing world.

The second line of argumentation looks to rentierism, or the dependence of states on rents derived from natural resources. States' abundance of wealth derived from oil or soft budgets (sources of revenue, like foreign aid) allows them to buy citizen acquiescence in the face of authoritarian rule.[26] Because they do not rely on taxes, rentier states remain above the concerns of citizens. Further, citizens who are recipients of rentier largesse are more likely to be supportive of their regimes. These citizens have exchanged their right to contestation for government services. Because citizens are pampered, they are more likely to support their regimes and less likely to engage in contested forms of participation.

Several countries of the Arab world could fall into this category, because either they possess massive resource wealth or they are the direct recipients of foreign aid.[27] The concentration of resources in the hands of government has allowed these regimes to offer services and deliver goods without any need for citizens to mobilize and demand those services. Hazem Beblawi argues that the state plays a crucial role in the rentier formulation, for it is the recipient and distributor of rents writ large. Because the society is a recipient of rents and not a payer of taxes, interest groups are less likely to take a particular interest in economic issues. Hence, society remains supportive of the regime and does not become an arena of contestation. Citizens don't need to contest the state, but instead lend it support because the state already distributes and offers goods and services.[28] In rentier states, citizens remain passive and compliant.

of Traditional Society (Glencoe, IL: Free Press, 1958), Charles Lindblom, *Politics and Markets: The World's Political Economic Systems* (New York: Basic Books, 1977); Seymour Martin Lipset, *Political Man: The Social Bases of Politics* (Garden City, NY: Doubleday, 1960).

[26]Lisa Anderson, "Peace and Democracy in the Middle East: The Constraints of Soft Budgets," *Journal of International Affairs* 49, no.1 (1995): 25–45; Eva Bellin, "The Politics of Profit in Tunisia: Utility of the Rentier Paradigm?" *World Development* 22, no. 3 (1994): 427; Michael Ross, "Does Oil Hinder Democracy?" *World Politics* 53, no. 3 (2001): 325–61.

[27]See Anderson, "Peace and Democracy in the Middle East."

[28]Hazem Beblawi, "The Rentier State in the Arab World," in *The Arab State*, ed. Giacomo Luciani (Berkeley and Los Angeles: University of California Press, 1990), 85–98; Lisa Anderson, "The State in the Middle East and North Africa," *Comparative Politics* 20, no. 1 (1997): 1–18; Chaudhry, *The Price of Wealth*; Bellin, "The Politics of Profit in Tunisia," 427; Gwenn Okruhlik, "Rentier Wealth, Unruly Law, and the Rise of the Opposition: The Political Economy of Rentier States," *Comparative Politics* 31, no. 3 (1999): 295–315; Ross, "Does Oil Hinder Democracy?"; Dirk Vandewalle, *Libya Since Independence: Oil and State-Building* (Ithaca, NY: Cornell University Press, 1998); Giacomo Luciani, "Allocation vs. Production States: A Theoretical Framework," in *The Arab State*, ed. Giacomo Luciani (Berkeley and Los Angeles: University of California Press, 1990), 65–84.

REVISITING THE CLASSICAL MODELS: THEORETICAL LIMITATIONS

These two prevailing models, the political and the economic—as appealing and neat as they may be—don't reflect the empirical realities on the ground in the Arab world. They also contain theoretical limitations, and are based on faulty assumptions. These bottom-up cultural and economic models of political change continue to occupy a significant place in studies of comparative politics and appeal to both policy makers and scholars of democracy. The appeal of these bottom-up models of democracy is a straightforward, accessible mechanism of cause and effect. If key democratic values and higher levels of education,[29] strong civic associations,[30] and viable economic structures can cause change favorable to democracy, then these changes can induce citizens to make democratic demands of their states. For example, societies might become more democratic through value change in favor of democracy, or a growing middle class could bargain for more democratic space.

Yet this equilibrium between a society and its political institutions relies on a major unexamined premise: existing political institutions derive the foundations of their legitimacy from their own societies. These theoretical approaches assume that states are autonomous, self-contained units legitimated by their societies, and thus likely to reflect the political preferences of their people. Ignoring the position of states in the larger international context, this view sees states as monolithically self-ruling and linked to their societies in a mutually reinforcing process that is shielded from external influence.[31] But in the real world, weaker states are dependent on more powerful states. Peripheral states not only derive legitimacy from their own people but also rely on winning the approbation of external patrons. Such winning then shapes domestic negotiations about regime type.

NEWER DEMOCRATIZATION DEBATES

Beginning in the first decade of the twenty-first century, a new wave of literature has emerged that examines transitions to democracy as a function of internal, domestic debates about redistribution of wealth and assets. These works focus on the internal negotiations that occur between elites and citizens about whether to expand the franchise, redistribute resources,

[29] See Lerner, *The Passing of Traditional Society*; Lipset, *Political Man*; Ronald Inglehart, *Modernization and Postmodernization* (Princeton, NJ: Princeton University Press, 1997); and Almond and Verba, *The Civic Culture*.

[30] Putnam, *Making Democracy Work*.

[31] For a discussion on liberal market reforms in the developing world, see Atul Kohli, "Democracy Amid Economic Orthodoxy: Trends in Developing Countries" *Third World Quarterly* 14, no. 4 (1993): 671.

and allow for mass representation. Carles Boix, as well as Darren Acemoglu and James Robinson, maintain that the balance of economic power between citizens and elites matters for democratic outcomes.[32] Levels of income inequality, they maintain, reduce the likelihood of a democratic bargain between society and the elite because the elite fear redistribution pressures. The more equal distribution of income induces democratization because the pressures for redistribution are markedly less. Boix further argues that mobile elite assets also facilitate democratization. When elites can remove their assets, his reasoning goes, they can shield those assets from becoming targets of redistribution.

Like Boix, and Acemoglu and Robinson,[33] and earlier work like Robert Dahl's *Polyarchy*, I find that democratic outcomes are contingent on internal negotiations between citizens and the elite.[34] In the same spirit, I maintain that citizens will continue to support the regime when it is economically beneficial to do so. The choice of political regime is a based on an individualized cost-benefit analysis that takes into account the possibilities of the opposition accessing power and influencing policies that may have redistributive effects. When opposition movements seizing or influencing power have significant costs, sectors of the society that benefit from less democracy will be less tolerant of democratization.

Yet, similar to the classical political culture and political economy formulas, these newer models pay inadequate attention to international context. In fact, they treat debates about redistribution as internally confined and state-contained. In several countries, especially those in the Arab world, debates about access to wealth and future economic progress are contingent on access to global markets, external patrons, and international aid. Domestic preferences for democracy are also influenced by the position of "globalization winners" who want to ensure continued access to global markets and guarantee that more democracy won't jeopardize such access.[35]

Given the centrality of mobile assets to these theories, we must reexamine our definition of mobile assets. Assets can travel across borders and

[32]Carles Boix, *Democracy and Redistribution* (Cambridge: Cambridge University Press, 2003); Darren Acemoglu and James Robinson, *The Economic Origins of Dictatorship and Democracy* (Cambridge: Cambridge University Press, 2005).

[33]This is not to say that ideology does not matter. However, as Acemoglu and Robinson, *The Economic Origins of Dictatorship and Democracy*, 42, maintain, "As long as one accepts the premise that the interests of individuals are partly about economic outcomes, our basic analysis remains unaltered."

[34]Robert Dahl, *Polyarchy* (New Haven, CT: Yale University Press, 1970).

[35]For a discussion on the ways in which globalization has created and engendered economic opportunities in Arab societies, see Henry Clement and Robert Springbord, *Globalization and the Politics of Development in the Middle East* (Cambridge: Cambridge University Press, 2001); Shana Cohen, *Searching for a Different Future: The Rise of a Global Middle Class in Morocco* (Durham, NC: Duke University Press, 2004); and Vali Nasr, *Forces of Fortune: The Rise of the New Muslim Middle Class and What It Will Mean for Our World* (New York: Free Press, 2009).

be protected from redistribution pressures insofar as the international order allows for such movement. In other words, if an external patron issues sanctions, freezes assets, or limits the movements of financial flows across borders, then this calls for a reexamination of the conditions under which assets can be considered mobile. Mobile assets are only as mobile as the international order permits them to be. Second, the empirical evidence doesn't line up as neatly against countries in the Middle East with regard to the ways that inequalities may structure domestic negotiations about democracy. For example, Gini coefficients, which measure levels of economic inequality, illustrate that Turkey (47) is worse off than Egypt (32) or Jordan (36), yet there is more democracy in Turkey. This is not to say that models of redistribution do not explain a good portion of variation in democratization outcomes. Rather, when we examine these models against the empirical record of the Middle East, the facts don't line up. The role of the international sphere on domestic political developments is a major omission in the aforementioned approaches.

Trade, Growth, Development, and Democratization

The international political economy (IPE) literature that overlaps with the fields of international relations and comparative politics is divided on whether there are democratization benefits from trade openness. Some scholars argue that trade and globalization enhance democracy in the developing world.[36] In fact, a number of studies show that economic globalization can be linked to normatively prized outcomes like human rights benefits in some places and times.[37] Ronald Rogowski finds a direct link between trade and democratic regimes in nineteenth-century England and ancient Greece.[38] Other scholars are more cautious about these causal claims. Acemoglu and Robinson, for example, argue that trade may enhance democratization but only if resources are distributed equally. Alícia Adserà and Carles Boix also caution that greater trade openness may harm democratic institutions, depending on the segments of society that benefit from

[36] See, for example, Barry Eichengreen and David Leblang, "Democracy and Globalization" (unpublished manuscript, Department of Political Science, University of Colorado–Boulder, 2007); Seymour Martin Lipset, "Some Social Requisites of Democracy," *American Political Science Review* 53, no. 1 (1959): 69–105; and J. Ernesto López-Córdoba and Christopher M. Meissner, "The Globalization of Trade and Democracy" (unpublished manuscript, 2005).

[37] See, for example, Emilie M. Hafner-Burton, "Trading Human Rights: How Preferential Trade Arrangements Influence Government Repression," *International Organization* 59, no. 3 (2005): 593–629; and David Richards, Ronald Gelleny, and David Sacko, "Money with a Mean Streak? Foreign Economic Penetration and Government Respect for Human Rights in Developing Countries," *International Study Quarterly* 45, no. 2 (2001): 219–39.

[38] Ronald Rogowski, *Commerce and Coalitions: How Trade Affects Domestic Political Alignments* (Princeton , NJ: Princeton University Press, 1989).

such openness.[39] In fact, beneficiaries of trade can be as narrow as specific firms only.[40] Helen Milner and Bumba Mukherjee find that the link between trade openness and democracy is quite weak,[41] and Atul Kohli echoes this finding.[42]

Even though the literature underscoring the influence of IPE on democracy yields mixed results, I offer yet two additional—and more serious—criticisms. IPE explanations ignore the ways that security considerations mediate the influence of trade, globalization, and aid on democracy. For example, in many countries in the Arab world, international actors—namely, the United States—are invested in regime stability and cooperative governments over democratization. Trade agreements, access to global markets, and aid are linked to a strategy of regime cooperation and durability and not necessarily transformation.[43] Second, scholars have assumed that trade follows a linear path: once countries engage in trade they continue doing so. If access to global markets is conditioned by patron-accommodation, however, then access to global trade, preferential agreements, and membership in trade organizations can be easily reversed. While IPE works on the Cold War have examined the close linkage between international security and international political economy,[44] newer post–Cold War works have not examined how security considerations condition the influence of trade on democratization. Indeed, trade can also be a security device in sustaining patron-client relations in the world order.

[39] Alícia Adserà and Carles Boix, "Trade, Democracy, and the Size of the Public Sector: The Political Underpinnings of Openness." *International Organization* 56, no. 2 (2002): 229–62.

[40] See, for example, Robert O. Keohane and Helen V. Milner, *Internationalizaton and Domestic Politics* (Cambridge: Cambridge University Press, 2005), which offers a detailed discussion on internationalization and sectoral gains from trade. Christina Davis, *Why Adjudicate? Enforcing Trade Rules in the WTO* (Princeton, NJ: Princeton University Press, 2012), also advances an argument about the ways in which certain domestic groups influence World Trade Organization dispute settlements.

[41] Helen V. Milner and Bumba Mukherjee, "Democratization and Economic Globalization," *Annual Review of Political Science* 12 (1999): 163–81.

[42] Atul Kohli, *State-Directed Development* (Cambridge: Cambridge University Press, 2004).

[43] Eva Bellin, "The Robustness of Authoritarianism in the Middle East: Exceptionalism in Comparative Perspective," *Comparative Politics* 36, no. 2 (2004): 139–57; Amaney Jamal and Irfan Nooruddin, "The Democratic Utility of Trust: A Cross-National Analysis." *Journal of Politics* 72, no. 1 (2010): 45–59.

[44] See Joanne Gowa, *Allies, Adversaries and International Trade* (Princeton, NJ: Princeton University Press, 1995); Benjamin Cohen, "The Revolution in Atlantic Economic Relations: A Bargain Comes Unstuck," in *The United States and Western Europe: Political, Economic, and Strategic Perspectives*, ed. Wolfram Hanrieder (Cambridge, MA: Winthrop, 1974), 106–33; Robert Gilpin, *U.S. Power and the Multinational Corporation* (New York: Basic Books, 1975); Robert O. Keohane and Joseph S. Nye Jr., eds., *Transnational Relations and World Politics* (Cambridge, MA: Harvard University Press, 1972); and Peter J. Katzenstein, ed., *Between Power and Plenty: Foreign Economic Policies of Advanced Industrial States* (Madison: University of Wisconsin Press, 1977).

Class and Those Who Stand to Benefit from Democracy

The literature underscoring societal pressures toward democratization based on Western experiences contains some conflicting accounts of not only the classes but also the class structure that results in more democratization. In studies of early Western feudal transitions to democracy, for instance, Moore and others emphasize the importance of the bourgeoisie in championing movements toward democratization. Moore's thesis became dominantly cited as the major intellectual work behind studies that advanced the importance of the middle class for democratization. Whether it was because the middle class was more educated and held the values of a democratic, cosmopolitan polity (see Huntington, Inglehart, et al.), whether it was because the middle class could buffer conflict between the poor and rich and keep transitions stable (Boix), or whether it was because the middle class had more to gain from democratization advancements (Moore), the development of an autonomous middle class became crucial—at least in theory—to the development of democracy. Acemoglu and Robinson argue that "almost all revolutionary movements were led by middle class actors and more important a number of challenges to the existing regime; for example the uprisings that helped induce the First Reform Act in Britain or those during the Paris Commune in France or the revolts of the Radical Party in Argentina were largely middle class movements."[45]

Yet the literature on comparative politics is still divided on the exact role of the middle class in democratization efforts. For example, Eva Bellin and Kellee Tsai, studying the Middle East and China, argue that the middle classes play key roles in sustaining existing authoritarian institutions because they benefit from authoritarian economic policies.[46] Other scholars of comparative development, like Dietrich Rueschmeyer, Evelyn Huber Stephens, and John Stephens, argue that the middle classes were important for democratic transitions.[47]

Although the literature is divided on the classes that mattered most for democratization and democratic consolidation, the categories of class have been treated in compartmentalized domains. Most of our existing formulations on class in comparative development paradigms rely on Marxist classifications of class that treat class in its relation to the domestic mode of production. Classes are structured more or less between the owners of capital and those

---

[45]Acemoglu and Robinson, *The Economic Origins of Dictatorship and Democracy*, 39. See also O'Donnell and Schmitter, "Tentative Conclusions about Uncertain Democracies," 50–52, on the crucial role of the middle class in contemporary democratization.

[46]Bellin, *Stalled Democracy*; Kellee S. Tsai, "Capitalists without a Class: Political Diversity among Private Entrepreneurs," *Comparative Political Studies* 38, no. 9 (2005): 1130–58.

[47]Dietrich Rueschmeyer, Evelyn Huber Stephens, and John Stephens, *Capitalist Development and Democracy* (Chicago: University of Chicago Press, 1992).

who sell their labor for capital. Yet in a globalized world order, these demarcations of class become more obscure. Today's domestic economies in Arab states rely on a host of factors that no longer neatly conform to simple "modes" of production. Foreign aid, global trade, remittances, labor flows, foreign direct investment, internet networks, and a host of other factors shape the economic standing of individuals within their societies.

As the reach of the global economy has increasingly penetrated domestic economies, classifying class interests becomes more difficult. For example, a poor farmer and a rich investor both might look favorably toward FDI initiatives that make possible more expedient forms of exports. Or a small business owner in a village and a wealthy business entrepreneur in a city might both stand to benefit from a more aggressive tourism program that will attract more annual visits.

Max Weber's formulation of "differentiated markets" is increasingly applicable to the ways that globalization shapes local class dynamics. While Weber is more concerned with introducing concepts like power and status linked to various market sectors, one's market position vis-à-vis globalization matters not only for status and power but also for income.[48] These status and power configurations can vary within class based on the ways in which members of various classes are linked to global markets.[49] There are winners

[48]For a discussion on sector-based (rather than income-based) class interests, see Carles Boix, *Democracy and Redistribution* (Cambridge: Cambridge University Press, 2003); Jeffry A. Frieden, "Invested Interests: The Politics of National Economic Policies in a World of Global Finance," *International Organization* 45 (1991): 425–51; James E. Alt and Michael Gilligan, "The Political Economy of Trading States: Factor Specificity, Collective Action Problems and Domestic Political Institutions," *Journal of Political Philosophy* 2, no. 2 (1994): 165–92; Michael Hiscox, "Class versus Industry Cleavages: Inter-industry Factor Mobility and the Politics of Trade," *International Organization* 55 (2001): 1–46; Peter Baldwin, *The Politics of Social Solidarity* (Cambridge: Cambridge University Press, 1990); and Isabela Mares, "Firms and the Welfare State: When, Why and How Does Social Policy Matter to Employers?" in *Varieties of Capitalism*, ed. Peter Hall and David Soskice (Oxford: Oxford University Press, 2001), 184–212. Sector-based class interests are a better study for considering the ways in which globalization patterns shape various domestic segments of different classes within societies. Yet even sectoral analysis needs to take into account the extent to which various sectors are integrated into the global economy. For example, two similar factories that produce the same exact product may have different interests based on their respective consumer bases (domestic vs. foreign).

[49]Max Weber, *From Max Weber: Essays in Sociology*, ed. Hans Heinrich Gerth, trans Hans Heinrich Gerth and C. Wright Mills (London: Routledge, 2009). Weber does not assume that all actors within a specific class share a common set of interests. He notes, "In our terminology, 'classes' are not communities; they merely represent possible, and frequent, bases for communal action. We may speak of a class when (1) a number of people have in common a specific causal component of their life changes, insofar as (2) this component is represented exclusively by economic interests in the possession of goods and opportunities for income, and (3) is represented under the conditions of the commodity of labor markets" (181). These points refer to a class situation that we may describe as the typical chance for a supply of goods, external living conditions, and personal life experiences, insofar as this chance is determined

and losers linked to global economic integration, and our conventional categories of class as a function of the "local" mode of production cannot distinctly capture individual preferences based on these categories alone.[50]

Toward a Model of Democratic Change in the Arab World

To return to the contribution of this book, I introduce the role of the patron, who, I argue, shapes these domestic strategic interactions—and may bolster the regime and ruling elite through rewards of economic assistance and access to global markets. Citizens who believe that the current regime has privileged and important relations with the external patron that help maintain stability and yield economic benefits may come to support a regime even when it is otherwise not in their apparent interest. The patron can also make acts of political contestation more costly by controlling these mechanisms. For example, the patron can sanction a country, denying it access to global markets, if its new regime—even a democratically elected one—does not conform to patron expectations.

Client Arab states that have remained authoritarian share two circumstances. The first is that the external patron, the United States, values friendly and cooperative alliances over democracy. The second is that existing regimes also value staying in power. These two factors at the societal level are constants that will induce change. My model stipulates that pressure to change the authoritarian status quo is facilitated when, all things being equal, antipatron forces grow or shrink and tip the balance closer to or farther from the patron. More specifically, when influential opposition movements become increasingly pro-patron, they reduce the fear that democracy will yield results that harm the patron-client relation. Conversely, when influential opposition movements become increasingly antipatron, they may overthrow the regime and risk hostile relations with the patron. In this latter scenario it is likely the case that the vast majority of citizens do not see themselves as beneficiaries of the patron-client relationship.

This dynamic may very well be one of the reasons why Egyptians decided to unseat Husni Mubarak. While the demonstrations in Egypt revealed that citizens were willing to protest against Mubarak, the United States demanded that the military not exercise violence against protesters,[51] sending

---

by the amount and kind of power, or lack of such, to dispose of goods or skills for the sake of income in a given economic order. For a more detailed discussion on market differentiation, see Weber, 182–83.

[50]See Theda Skocpol, *States and Social Revolutions: A Comparative Analysis of France, Russia, and China* (Cambridge: Cambridge University Press, 1979), on the ways in which transnational linkages shape class organizational capacity and behavior.

[51]A Muslim Brotherhood representative indicates that this U.S. signal was crucial for large-scale mobilization of protestors in the immediate days after the revolution began; personal interview with the author, March 2011.

an important signal to demonstrators that they would not be penalized for protesting against Mubarak. Further, the fact that the Egyptian military, a close U.S. ally, was willing to take over perhaps facilitated a more expeditious transition. Hence, it became clear to both Americans and Egyptians that Egypt would not lose ties to the United States as a result of Mubarak's removal.

Nevertheless, the contestation of the status quo in Egypt was a result of a growing segment of the population that found Mubarak's regime inefficient, abusive, and harmful to ordinary citizens. The Mubarak regime became increasingly corrupt, flaunting its corruption unapologetically, while a shrinking segment of the society benefited from the regime's economic policies. As the benefactors of the regime grew fewer, the majority of citizens began to see little utility in Mubarak. Even now, with Mubarak removed from power, a Pew Research Center poll finds that the majority of Egyptians would still like to maintain close ties to the United States.[52] This desire for close ties will certainly serve as an important dynamic in the future democratic trajectory of Egypt. Two factors will remain especially crucial as Egypt transitions. First, what role will the Egyptian military continue to play in Egypt? Given that the military is now the guarantor of strong ties to the United States, will citizens allow (or encourage) the military to continue to play an influential role to ensure Egypt's strong alliance? And second, what role will the Muslim Brotherhood play, or be allowed to play, in influencing Egypt's foreign relations? How will the fact that Islamists have secured over 65 percent of the vote influence the democratic trajectory in Egypt? If the Muslim Brotherhood is seen as possibly jeopardizing ties to the United States, this then may certainly harm the future of democracy in Egypt.

REVISITING STATE AND SOCIETY RELATIONS IN CLIENTELISTIC SETTINGS:
REAL CONGRUENCE VERSUS CONTRIVED CONGRUENCE

In client regimes, as most states in the Arab world are, the fundamental synthesis of state-society relations underlying both classical and newer models of democratization is radically altered (see fig. 1.2).[53] The client

[52]Pew Global Attitudes Project, *U.S. Wins No Friends, End of Treaty with Israel Sought* (Washington, DC: Pew Research Center, 2011.)

[53]Today, most Arab states in the region can be classified as clients of the United States. Regime clientelism, referring to the relationship that states have with external actors, is based on strategic alliances that mutually bolster the interests of both parties involved. This strategic relationship, however, takes place between strong and weak states. For modern developed countries, differences in state autonomy are used to categorize states as strong or weak. See Peter J. Katzenstein, *Between Power and Plenty: Foreign Economic Policies of Advanced Industrial States* (Madison: University of Wisconsin Press, 1977) and John Ikenberry, *Reasons of State: Oil Politics and the Capacities of American Government* (Ithaca, NY: Cornell University Press, 1988). Alvin Rubinstein, "Soviet Client States: From Empire to Common Wealth," *Orbis* 35, no. 1 (1991): 69, defines a client-state as a "regime that is under the protection of another. The rela-

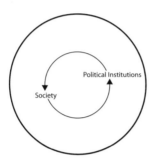

The Mutually Reinforcing Relationship between
Society and Political Institutions in
Autonomous States

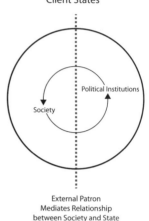

The Disrupted Relationship between
Society and Political Institutions in
Client States

Political Institutions

Society

Political Institutions

Society

External Patron
Mediates Relationship
between Society and State

Figure 1.2. Autonomous states and the relationship of state and society.

relationship diffuses direct accountability mechanisms between states and societies, disrupting the hypothesized mutually reinforcing impact of societies on institutions. States are not solely accountable to their citizens; they are also accountable to the external patron. This reality is not lost on ordinary citizens.

Three implications emerge from this analysis. First, client-patron relations disturb the feedback process between state and society. In client states, institutions are no longer solely expressions of society's preferences; in many cases, institutions reflect the preferences of the external power. As such, society's preferences and orientations in client states matter less for the durability and stability of existing institutions. Congruence between a society and its political institutions need not be the only reason a country shows

tionship is asymmetrical, but each party gains advantages from it; and as long as the benefits outweigh the costs, the relationship will be sustained." In general, however, the client is more "dependent" on the patron than the patron is on the client. Thus, the relationship is constituted by an unequal balance of power between patron and client. The patron has the ability to issue unilateral rewards for compliance and punishments for noncompliance. The dominant state ensures that clients are well protected and guarantees economic rewards and benefits. In return, the patron also secures its larger geostrategic goals. As Osita Afoaku, "U.S. Foreign Policy and Authoritarian Regimes," *Journal of Third World Studies* 17, no. 2 (2000): 59, notes, "While the impetus for international clientelism comes mainly from the foreign policy strategy of the big powers, the patron-client paradigm takes into account the client's needs which may be political, economic, military, or a combination of the above. This is in keeping with the principle of reciprocity that is necessary to sustain patron-client ties." See also Peter Gourevitch, "Squaring the Circle: The Domestic Sources of International Cooperation," *International Organization* 50, no. 2 (1996): 349–73.

remarkable authoritarian stability. Existing political institutions can derive their stability and durability from their patrons.

Second, client-patron relations hamper society's agency. Thus, society's preferences for more democracy need not induce greater demands on the state for political accountability because the state remains accountable to larger outside forces. A diffusion of the rentier effect and the emergence of new economic interests, for instance, need not result in direct contestation of the existing establishment. In societies that are already authoritarian, an increased appreciation of or desire for democracy need not result in democratic demands on the state.

This dynamic introduces a new layer of negotiation for citizens of client states. Democratic elements within a society will not push for more democracy if more democracy will bring to power forces hostile to the external patron. Democracy's potential to jeopardize the base of external support for the regime reduces the likelihood of contestation. Democratic orientations, new economic opportunities, and expanded civic qualities are not sufficient to structure societal demands for more democracy. Citizens must guarantee that their national well-being (the security and resource base of the nation) will not be jeopardized if they choose to exercise their newly acquired democratic civic worldviews.

Third, the durable stability that many Arab countries enjoy today reflects a contrived or manufactured congruence between citizens and their political institutions. In these clientelistic settings, society's preferences toward the status quo are not necessarily influenced by the "true" political orientations of citizens. Rather, citizens accept the status quo even while they recognize that is not necessarily ideal. In places like Jordan, citizens show remarkable levels of support for democracy alongside remarkable levels of support for the existing, nondemocratic political establishment. In clientelistic settings, the actual values of society matter less than the contrived values that are shaped by the status of a country as a client in the international order.

EMPIRICAL REALITIES: JORDAN AND KUWAIT

In the context of the Arab world, greater support for democracy has resulted in more democracy in Kuwait but not in Jordan.[54] Kuwait, a classic rentier state, has moved in a more solid democratic trajectory than has Jordan in

[54]Support for democracy is an attitudinal predisposition. Some analysts may question the usefulness of such support as a category worthy of scholarly attention. I offer two main reasons why studying support for democracy remains valuable to the field of comparative politics: First, it is important to understand whether members of society are first and foremost committed to the institutions of democracy. Understanding how citizens conceive of democracy and the degree to which they are dedicated to it as a doctrine are important should a political transition occur. Further, support for democracy remains one of the most robust measures of

the last several years, while Jordan since 1993 has witnessed significant democratic reversals. In the last several years, Kuwaiti citizens have increasingly been capable of holding their regime accountable.[55] This asymmetry offers a useful opportunity for analysis.

Three major accomplishments in the last several years highlight Kuwait's democratic successes. First, in 2005, women gained suffrage after extensive lobbying of their parliamentary representatives. Although a key supporter of such reforms, the regime could not impose its will until the parliament approved the reforms in 2005 with active influence from civil society. Second, when Shaykh Jaber al-Ahmad al-Sabah died in 2006 and it became clear that his successor, Shaykh Sa'ad al-Abdullah al-Salim, was not fit to assume the throne due to illness, Kuwait handled the succession crisis through constitutional channels. The Sabah family did not dictate the successor but instead allowed the head of parliament, as stipulated in the constitution, to begin a constitutional process to designate a successor. Third, in 2006, societal and parliamentary forces aligned with one another to press for significant electoral redistricting reforms that aimed to curb the overrepresentation of tribal and Bedouin forces in parliament.[56] These changes all occurred with active civil society involvement and parliamentary advocacy, despite Kuwait's position as a rentier state.

While Kuwait made significant advancements along its democratic trajectory, Jordan did not—despite strong notional support for democracy. And, in fact, most of the Arab world mirrors Jordan's "de-democratization" in the last ten to fifteen years. Jordan reversed its electoral law in 1993 to reduce the influence of opposition forces. It limited press freedoms as well as civil and political liberties more generally. And while support for democracy remains high in both polities, Jordanians also give more support to authoritarian practices than do Kuwaitis.

Why such asymmetry? Why would a population that simultaneously supports democracy also support authoritarian tendencies? Why do the citizens of the Arab world still profess support for regimes that have remained

---

democratic orientations in societies that are not democratic. Second, this then raises the question, what is the relationship between support for democracy and *actual* democracy? Amaney Jamal and Irfan Nooruddin, "The Democratic Utility of Trust: A Cross-National Analysis," *Journal of Politics* 72, no. 1 (2010): 45–59, have found that support for democracy maps onto other pertinent macrolevel democratic indicators across the globe; see figures 5.4 and 5.5 in the present volume. However, that support for democracy has not necessarily resulted in greater democratic gains in some countries is one of the key questions guiding the present study.

[55]According to Daniel Kaufmann, Aart Kraay, and Massimo Mastruzzi, "Governance Matters III: Governance Indicators for 1996, 1998, 2000, and 2002," *World Bank Economic Review* 18, no. 2 (2004): 253–87, in 1996 Jordan ranked 36 percent in the world on voice and accountability scores and in 2006 it fell to a rank of 29 percent. In 1996 Kuwait ranked 34 percent; in 2006 it ranked 39 percent.

[56]For a more detailed discussion of these reforms, see chapter 3.

authoritarian? Existing theoretical explanations offer us inadequate leverage to explain these empirical realities on the ground in the Arab world.

The given context of international hierarchy coupled with anti-American Islamist opposition movements has constrained the expression of desires for democracy across the Arab world. Examining Kuwait and Jordan will allow me to demonstrate how concerns about a country's international relations shape state-society relations more broadly.

U.S. DOMINANCE IN THE ARAB WORLD

The modern Arab world has consistently depended on external forces, whether through direct occupation, colonization, or client ties to superpowers. Because of this, according to Stephen Krasner, the Arab world can be classified as a region that is firmly embedded as a subordinate in an international hierarchical relationship.[57] Krasner elaborates, "Foreign actors . . . can use their material capabilities to dictate or coerce changes in the authority structures of a target; they can violate the . . . rule of nonintervention in the internal affairs of other states."[58] David Lake captures an extension of this definition when he describes the type of hierarchical relations between the United States and many other countries. Lake writes, "Hierarchy [between one state and another] exists when one actor, the dominant state, possesses authority over another actor, the subordinate state: Authority is never total . . . but varies in extent."[59] Both direct intervention and invitation can violate autonomy.[60] Thus, a weaker state, like many of those in the Arab world, can invite the United States to secure their interests, as do many of the states in the Gulf that rely on the United States for military security. In other cases, where countries in the Arab world do not conform to U.S. interests, as was the case under Saddam Hussein's Iraq, the United States has demonstrated the ability to intervene militarily. Economic sanctions are another tool that the United States has used against countries in the region.

---

[57] Stephen Krasner, *Sovereignty* (Princeton, NJ: Princeton University Press, 1989), 20.
[58] Ibid.
[59] David A. Lake, "Escape from the State of Nature: Authority and Hierarchy in World Politics," *International Security* 2, no.1 (2007): 56.
[60] Hierarchical relationships in the international order have been captured in various studies; see Lake, "Escape from the State of Nature"; Ian Clark, *The Hierarchy of States: Reform and Resistance in the International Order* (New York: Cambridge University Press, 1989); Robert W. Tucker, *The Inequality of Nations* (New York: Basic Books, 1977); Michael W. Doyle, *Empires* (Ithaca, NY: Cornell University Press, 1986); Craig Calhoun, Frederick Cooper, and Kevin W. Moore, eds., *Lessons of Empire: Imperial Histories and American Power* (New York: New Press, 2006); and Hendrik Spruyt, *Ending Empire: Contested Sovereignty and Territorial Partition* (Ithaca, NY: Cornell University Press, 2005).

Iran, Syria, Jordan, and the Palestinian Hamas-led government have all been on the receiving end of U.S. sanctions.

Over the last two decades, the Arab world has increasingly become a client of the United States, and its strategic utility to the United States continues to grow as well. The United States seeks to maintain regional stability, contain Iran, ensure Islamists do not seize power and terrorism does not spiral out of control, secure its access to oil, and protect the state of Israel. Thus, U.S. ties to existing Arab regimes first and foremost guarantee these strategic priorities for the United States. These objectives are also evident in its relations with Jordan and Kuwait.

A number of indicators substantiate the U.S. dominance of the Arab world. First, overall levels of U.S. official development assistance to all regions in the world from 1991 reveal that the Arab world is the largest recipient of aid from the United States. Even when we correct for Iraq, the Arab world exceeds Africa in its reliance on U.S. aid (see table 1.2). For the years 1991–2009, the Arab world received $69 billion in aid. Even excluding Iraq, the Arab world received $39.1 billion, an amount slightly below Africa's $39.9 billion.[61]

Second, Correlates of War data show that from 1990 to 2001 the United States has had more direct involvement in conflicts in the Middle East than any other region (see table 1.3). Because the data are only available to 2001, they exclude three notable things. First, the Iraq war is not captured here since it began in 2003. Second, the standoff with Mahmoud Ahmadinejad's Iran is also missing from this analysis. Third, the war in Afghanistan is grouped under Asia and not the Middle East. Had the wars in Afghanistan and Iraq and the current standoff with Iran been included in these scores, we would see even higher levels of U.S. involvement in conflicts in the Middle East.[62]

Lake's security and economic hierarchy measures also allow us to gain even more leverage on the extent to which the Arab world is a client of the United States.[63] While it is no easy task to measure the extent to which the United States influences another region, Lake skillfully creates two measures to capture the extent to which a hierarchical relationship exists between the United States and other countries. He conceptualizes two dimensions of dependence; one taps into security, and the other the economy. The degree

[61]Between 2001 and 2006 the per-capita aid in the Arab world was $16.41, compared to Africa at $3.89. It is also important to note here that these aid numbers are not driven by Egypt. For example, between 2001 and 2006 Egypt received close to $4 billion in U.S. aid while Jordan received close to $2.5 billion for the same time period. However, Jordan received more than Egypt on a per-capita basis.
[62]Correlates of War data codes U.S. involvement in conflicts in five different categories: (1) no militarized action; (2) threat to use force; (3) display of use of force; (4) use of force; (5) war.
[63]Lake, "Escape from the State of Nature."

TABLE 1.2. Total gross official development assistance from the United States across regions (in millions of dollars)

	1991–2009
Arab	$39,138.02
Iraq	$30,107.57
Africa	$39,992.65
Asia	$34,589.19
Eastern Europe	$12,410.04
Latin America	$28,352.34
Other	$9,506.40
Total	$194,096.21

Source: Organisation for Economic Co-operation and Development, OECD International Development Statistics; accessed December 2011 at http://lysander.sourceoecd.org/vl=92415576/cl=13/nw=1/rpsv/ij/oecdstats/16081110/v77n1/s4/p1.

to which a country can secure and economically sustain itself largely determines its levels of sovereignty.[64] Lake assesses security hierarchy via two measures. The first is the deployment of U.S. military forces from the dominant country into the weaker state. According to Lake, "Military troops enable a dominant state to influence the security policies of its subordinate. The dominant country can embroil the subordinate in foreign conflicts if it chooses; by launching attacks from the subordinate's territory, for instance, the dominant state automatically implicates the other in the conflict and makes it a target for retaliation by its antagonist, as in the case of the United States and Saudi Arabia in the 1990–91 Gulf War."[65]

Lake's second indicator of security hierarchy is the number of independent alliances that the subordinate state possesses. This measure doesn't work in the Arab world because the region's countries have virtually no independent alliances outside of the United States—and even the relations between Arab states and the United States are not structured around alliances

[64]Lake indicates that he follows common practice in international relations to tap into these two dimensions of sovereignty.

[65]Lake, "Escape from the State of Nature," 62. All measures are compiled for the United States and all other countries for which data are available from 1950 to 2000. Overseas troop deployments are reported by the U.S. Department of Defense. The measure is divided by population to adjust for differences in country size. See the data set at: http://weber.ucsd.edu/~dlake/data.html.

TABLE 1.3. U.S. conflicts by region, 1990–2001

	Number	Percent
The Americas	9	18.0%
Europe	11	22.0%
Africa	1	2.0%
Middle East	16	32.0%
Asia	13	26.0%
Total	50	100.0%

per se. Most Arab states that align with the United States possess "no other alliances outside the web of alliances held by that great power."[66]

Lake also captures economic hierarchy with two other measures. The first is the degree to which a country's monetary policy is autonomous.[67] The degree to which a country adjusts its exchange rate to that of the dominant country signifies its level of subordination.[68] The second indicator of economic hierarchy is relative trade dependence. The number of trading partners a country possesses signifies its degree of political autonomy, with more partners illustrating greater independence.[69] These two measures of security and economic hierarchy are designed to capture "not purely coercive relations between states, but rather, the authority, obligation, and legitimate coercion that are central to hierarchical relationships."[70]

Using these analytical measurements of the degree of international hierarchy between the United States and the Arab world, I extend Lake's data from 2000 to 2007.[71] Coinciding with the other tables gauging Arab depen-

[66]Lake, "Escape from the State of Nature," 63.

[67]This is determined by its exchange rate regime—how its currency is set relative to other currencies. A country can allow its currency to float against other currencies with its exchange rate being determined by financial markets. Second, a country can adjust its exchange rate to a single foreign anchor currency, most commonly the dollar or the Euro. By adjusting its exchange rate to an anchor currency the subordinate state indirectly imports or adopts the monetary policy of the dominant country. Third, a country can adopt the currency of a foreign state as its own—a process known as "dollarization."

[68]Lake relies on data from the International Monetary Fund (IMF). For the coding see Lake, "Escape from the State of Nature."

[69]Relative trade dependence is measured as each country's total trade with the United States divided by its own GDP, minus similar ratios for the other permanent members of the United Nations Security Council (China, France, Great Britain, and Russia).

[70]Lake, "Escape from the State of Nature," 68.

[71]The population and GDP data used to scale the troop data are from the World Penn Tables; see Alan Heston, Robert Summers, and Bettina Aten, Penn World Table Version 6.2, Center for International Comparisons of Production, Income and Prices at the University of Pennsylvania, September 2006. The trade data are from the IMF's Direction of Trade Data and

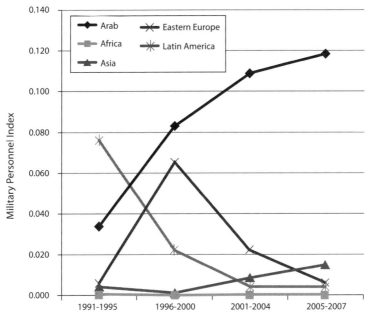

Figure 1.3. Military personnel across time (excluding Iraq and Kuwait).

dence on the United States, figures 1.3 and 1.4 show that the Arab world is highly dependent on the United States for its security. In fact, compared to other regions of the world, the Arab world has the largest percentage of U.S. troop deployments, even when Kuwait and Iraq are excluded. U.S. troops are located across the Arab region, from Qatar to Jordan, and from Egypt to Morocco. These numbers have risen annually since the early 1990s, signifying the strategic importance of the Arab world to the United States and illustrating the Arab world's dependence on America as well. The Arab world's economic dependence on the United States has also increased. Only Latin America is more economically dependent on the United States than the Arab world (see fig. 1.5), although Latin America is less dependent on the United States for its security needs (see fig. 1.4).

Three points about the Arab world's dependence on the United States stand out. First, it is the only region that depends on the United States in terms of both security and economic needs. According to Lake, "When both security and economic hierarchies exist between two polities, the relationship

the exchange rate data are from Kenneth Rogoff, Ethan O. Ilzetzki, and Carmen M. Reinhart, "Exchange Rate Arrangements into the 21st Century: Will the Anchor Currency Hold?" *Quarterly Journal of Economics* 119, no. 1 (2004): 1–48; see also http://www.economics.harvard.edu/faculty/rogoff/files/ERA_Background_Material.htm.

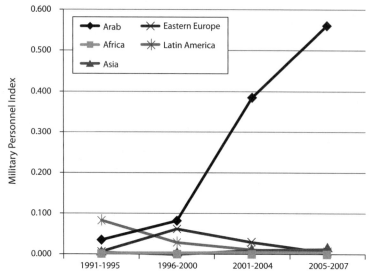

Figure 1.4. Military personnel across time (including Iraq and Kuwait).

becomes what is commonly known as either an informal empire or, at an extreme, empire."[72] Second, the data reveal that these patterns of dependence have been increasing over time; since the early 1990s, the United States has increasingly dominated the Arab world. Third, no other region in the world shows the remarkable levels of hierarchy between the Arab world and the United States in terms of its security and economic needs. In fact, most of the world has decreased its security dependency on the United States, while the Arab world today is more deeply entrenched in a hierarchical relationship with it. Arab "exceptionalism" may not be in its Islamic culture but instead may stem from the Arab world's subordinate location in the international system.

The given context of international hierarchy coupled with anti-American Islamist opposition movements has constrained the expression of desires for democracy across the Arab world. Examining Kuwait and Jordan—two similar clientelistic states that are both monarchies holding parliamentary elections, with similar levels of support for their Islamist opposition movements (estimates in each country put levels of support between 35 percent

[72] Lake, "Escape from the State of Nature," 61. According to Doyle, *Empires*, 12, *empire* means that one entity, "the dominant metropole, exerts political control over the internal and external policy—the effective sovereignty—of the other, the subordinate periphery." This is not the same as hegemony, where a very powerful state influences others around it but does not directly control others. See Joseph Nye, *Soft Power: The Means to Success in World Politics* (New York: Public Affairs, 2004), 135.

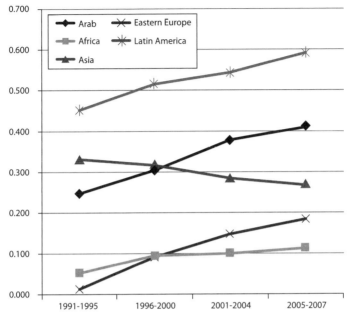

Figure 1.5. Economic hierarchy across time.

and 60 percent) but varying in the levels of anti-American sentiment among these Islamist opposition forces (my key explanatory variable)—will allow me to demonstrate how concerns about a country's international relations shape state-society relations more broadly. Although this book builds its argument by focusing on the cases of Kuwait and Jordan, it also draws on evidence from two other monarchies that have varying degrees of anti-American sentiment among their Islamist opposition: Morocco and Saudi Arabia. Further, the findings will also be extended to Palestine's democratic experience, which resulted in Hamas's parliamentary victory of 2006.

Anti-Americanism as the Independent Variable: Jordan and Kuwait

Citizen engagements with their regimes in the context of the Arab world are shaped by a two-level game.[73] Citizens take into account the preferences of the external patron in structuring their engagements with their regimes, and their attitudes toward their regimes are determined by international factors. The preferences of the patron matter for how citizens engage their regimes.

[73]See, for example, Robert Putnam, "Diplomacy and Domestic Politics: The Logic of Two-Level Games," *International Organization* 43, no. 2 (1998): 427–60; and Helen V. Milner, *Interests, Institutions, and Information* (Princeton, NJ: Princeton University Press, 1987).

Citizens base their intermediary preferences on their futures, assessing their marginal gains and losses based on the ways in which the global patron may respond to changes to the internal state context. Thus, some citizens stand to gain from a continuation of strong ties to the patron. Others have less to lose if ties are broken. According to Robert Putnam, "the two-level approach recognizes the inevitability of domestic conflict about what the 'national interest' requires."[74] Discussing trade agreements, Helen Milner maintains that because they have "*distributional consequences* . . . [c]ooperative agreements create winners and losers domestically; therefore they generate supporters and opponents."[75] Yotam Margalit similarly discusses the ways in which globalization creates winners and losers.[76] Adopting this logic of winners and losers, my argument posits that in the game of maintaining patron alliances there are indeed winners and there are losers (or those who have little to gain). This tension structures preferences about regime type. It's not so much that preferences are only about ideational affinities based on democratic or authoritarian preferences or, for that matter, secular and religious attachments. Rather, the regime in power—whether authoritarian or semidemocratic—receives support or opposition because of patron backing.

The theoretical framework I employ here is similar to Peter Gourevitch's "The Second Image Reversed,"[77] which draws both on dependency theories and Alexander Gerschenkron's formulations about the ways that the international system influences domestic politics. I especially draw on Gourevitch's assessment of regime types and the nature of coalitional partners that emerge from and dominate negotiations about regime outcomes. Gourevtich is correct to point out that "students of comparative politics treat domestic structure too much as an independent variable, underplaying the extent to which it and the international system interact."[78] Yet, as several authors point out, when the structure of the international order is systematic—or in the case of the Arab world, where most states are clients of the United States—there must emerge domestic-level factors that explain variations in regime outcomes or the nature of political engagement regarding regime outcomes in these regimes.

This study, therefore, advances that levels of anti-Americanism are a factor that also condition these types of domestic negotiations about regime

[74]Putnam, "Diplomacy and Domestic Politics," 460.

[75]Milner, *Interests, Institutions, and Information*, 9; emphasis in the original.

[76]See Yotam Margalit, "Commerce and Oppositions: The Political Responses of Globalization's Losers" (unpublished manuscript, 2010); and Rogowski, *Commerce and Coalitions*.

[77]Peter Gourevitch, "The Second Image Reversed," *International Organization* 32, no. 4 (1978): 881–912.

[78]Ibid., 900.

outcomes; indeed, anti-Americanism can shape the type of regimes that emerge and endure.[79] Building on theories of neodependency, it examines the ways that ordinary citizens, and not just the elite, respond to their peripheral location within the international system.[80] Further, it highlights the interactive effect of domestic and international factors on political development more generally.[81]

Specifically, Jordanian sectors invested in economic reform through closer ties to the United States and other Western countries are more likely to be supportive of the existing regime because they value the role the regime plays in securing relations with the United States and worry that a new democratically elected regime may not maintain such close ties with the United States. Strong ties to the United States have enhanced and potentially will continue to enhance Jordan's trajectory of economic

[79] Ideally, the research design at hand would allow us to look at states that are also not clients of the United States, but because most states in the region are U.S. clients this becomes increasingly more difficult. There are two countries that arguably are not U.S. clients: Syria and Tunisia. In Syria, it has been next to impossible to obtain the data that is needed for this project. Yet, my model will predict that in states that are not clients domestic-level factors will continue to structure debates about regime type. However, if there are growing segments of the opposition that wish to strengthen ties to the patron, then these factors may condition opposition strategies. As Tunisia consolidates its postrevolutionary rule the questions will certainly structure regime and opposition strategies.

[80] See Barbara Stallings, *Economic Dependency in Africa and Latin America* (Stanford, CA: Stanford University Press, 1972); Peter Evans, *Dependent Development: The Alliance of Multinational, State and Local Capital in Brazil* (Princeton, NJ: Princeton University Press, 1979); Fernando Henrique Cardoso, *Dependency and Development in Latin America* (Berkeley and Los Angeles: University of California Press, 1979); and Barbara Stallings and Robert Kaufman, eds., *Debt and Democracy in Latin America* (Boulder, CO: Westview, 1989).

[81] Several scholars have, however, examined the ways in which external factors like memberships in international and regional organizations and diffusion processes influence countries' democratic trajectories. See Daniel Brinks and Michael Coppedge, "Diffusion Is No Illusion: Neighbor Emulation in the Third Wave of Democracy," *Comparative Political Studies* 39, no. 4 (2006): 463–89; and Jon Pevehouse, *Democracy from Above: Regional Organization and Democratization* (Cambridge: Cambridge University Press, 2005). On the role of foreign aid and the effects on democratization, see Jon Pevehouse, "Democracy from the Outside In? International Organization and Democratization," *International Organization* 56, no. 3 (2002): 515–49; and Edward D. Mansfield, Helen V. Milner, and Peter B. Rosendorff, "Why Democracies Cooperate More: Electoral Control and International Trade Agreements," *International Organization* 56, no. 3 (2002): 477–513. On economic globalization and democratization, see Milner and Mukerjee, "Democratization and Economic Globalization"; Acemoglu and Robinson, *The Economic Origins of Dictatorship and Democracy*; Adserà and Boix, "Trade, Democracy, and the Size of the Public Sector"; Boix, *Democracy and Redistribution*; Carles Boix and Luis Garicano, "Democracy, Inequality, and Country-Specific Wealth" (unpublished manuscript, 2002); Eichengreen and Leblang, "Democracy and Globalization"; Nita Rudra, "Globalization and the Strengthening of Democracy in the Developing World," *American Journal of Political Science* 49 (2005): 704–30; and Keohane and Milner, *Internationalization*.

liberalization.[82] Further, these stable relations allow Jordan to maintain good ties to other Western countries (e.g., those of the European Union) as well. Those citizens most invested in economic reforms come from three different categories: middle- and upper-class citizens, who stand to gain from better economic conditions; store owners and shopkeepers, who believe that economic liberalization can bolster their standing; and educated younger citizens, who believe that greater economic liberalization will ultimately create more and better jobs. The potential for economic prosperity is, for these citizens, the growing hope that globalization can enhance the standing of the kingdom. For these potential winners of globalization, the eye is on global factors, including the role of the United States, for the dream of a better future.

Jordan also houses opponents to economic reform, although they do not oppose reforms because they believe that they are harmful to the kingdom. In fact, most Jordanians embrace the capitalist ethos of competitive markets. In 2002, 52 percent of Jordanians believed that international trade was good for their country. By 2007, that percentage had jumped to 72 percent. Trade is seen as vital to the kingdom's growth; thus, political stability and maintaining close ties to the United States are very important to realize these ambitions. Those who disagree believe economic reforms and liberalization today are part and parcel of a "Western agenda" that will further render Jordan reliant on external actors. Islamists and their supporters are therefore most skeptical of economic reform packages linked to the West. Globalization, they contend, is another form of neocolonialism.

Aside from Islamist objections to globalization, support for globalization remains significant in Jordan and elsewhere in the Arab and Muslim world. In 2007, positive evaluations of the free market were strong across the region, with 46 percent in Jordan, 65 percent in Kuwait, 66 percent in Palestine, and 66 percent in Morocco agreeing that such markets were good.[83]

---

[82]For a discussion on the economic determinants of regime support, see Susan C. Stokes, "Public Opinion of Market Reforms: A Framework," in *Public Support for Market Reforms in New Democracies*, ed. Susan C. Stokes (Cambridge: Cambridge University Press, 2001), 1–27.

[83]The Pew Global Attitudes Project, *World Publics Welcome Global Trade but Not Immigration: 47-Nation Pew Global Attitudes Survey* (Washington, DC: Pew Research Center, 2007), employs the following question wording:

(1) Please tell me whether you completely agree, mostly agree, mostly disagree or completely disagree with the following [statement]: a. Most people are better off in a free market economy, even though some people are rich and some are poor. (2) What do you think about the growing trade and business ties between (survey country) and other countries—do you think it is a very good thing, somewhat good, somewhat bad or a very bad thing for your country? (3) As I read a list of groups and organizations, for each, please tell me what kind of influence the group is having on the way things are going in (survey country). Is the influence of (read name) very good, somewhat good, somewhat bad, or very bad in (survey country): g. large companies from other countries?

International trade receives support from 72 percent in Jordan, 91 percent in Kuwait, 70 percent in Morocco, and 69 percent in Palestine. Even significant pluralities believed that the foreign companies have a positive impact in each of the countries. In Morocco, 72 percent of those surveyed supported this view, along with 68 percent of Kuwaitis, 59 percent of Jordanians, and 43 percent of Palestinians. These findings are substantiated by another survey conducted by the University of Maryland, which found that majorities in Egypt and the Palestinian Territories supported globalization for its potential positive results.[84]

In Jordan, citizens are cautious about the effects of democracy. Allowing more democracy could also allow anti-American movements like the Islamic Action Front (IAF) to seize greater power in ways that would undermine the patron-client relationship. If the IAF were to emerge triumphant, the United States would likely choose to sever ties with Jordan. Worse, the United States could sanction the state, harming the nation as a whole. Conversely, however, these same supporters of economic reform in Kuwait—those best positioned to benefit from greater economic global integration and advancement—are more likely to be less supportive of the Kuwaiti regime. This marked difference with Jordan is due to the fact that the Islamist opposition in Kuwait, the Islamic Constitutional Movement (ICM), is much less anti-American. Kuwaitis do not fear the implications of democracy the way the Jordanians do. In general, Kuwaitis are less anti-American than are Jordanians. These levels of anti-Americanism are exogenously structured, as I will discuss in chapter 3. During the First Gulf War (1990–91), the United States appeared as a liberator.[85] In Jordan, therefore, the IAF is better positioned to attract anti-American sympathizers to its doctrine (see fig. 1.6). When compared to Kuwaitis, Jordanians are less likely to believe U.S. democracy promotion initiatives are successful, less likely to believe most American are good people, and less likely to believe that U.S. culture has many positive attributes.

These findings are also evident in other client regimes in the Arab world. Moroccan, Palestinian, and Saudi Arabian citizens all balance their desire for democracy against the possible emergence of anti-American Islamist movements that may undermine the client status of their regimes with the United States. These factors are not at play in countries like Kuwait, Turkey, and Indonesia, all of which have more pro-American Islamist groups. This interaction between international structures and domestic conditions has stifled the democratization process in the Arab world. This is the central empirical finding of the book.

[84]See "Muslims Positive about Globalization, Trade," 2008 (accessed at http://worldpublic opinion.org/pipa/articles/brmiddleeastnafricara/index.php?nid=&id=&lb=brme).

[85]See Peter J. Katzenstein and Robert O. Keohane, eds., *Anti-Americanisms in World Politics* (Ithaca, NY: Cornell University Press, 2007).

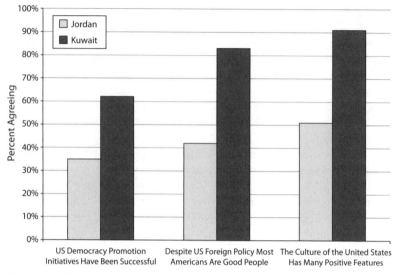

Figure 1.6. Jordanian and Kuwaiti attitudes toward the United States.

SCOPE CONDITION, CASE-SELECTION STRATEGY, DATA, AND EVIDENCE

While this book relies on the cases of Kuwait and Jordan to advance the microfoundations of its arguments, other cases are crucial for theoretical portability. Some readers will be concerned about the comparability of Kuwait and Jordan as two case studies. Although both states are monarchies, the two countries arguably fall into two different categories because of Kuwait's heavy reliance on oil. After all, Kuwait is an almost pure rentier state. I address this valid concern directly and throughout the book. First, I demonstrate that the rentier model does not explain the divergence in the dependent variable. Second, a similar rentier state—Saudi Arabia—shows almost reverse patterns from those of the Kuwaiti case because of the anti-Americanism of the opposition movements in Saudi Arabia. Third, I compare Jordan to other similar states that are not rentier states but have varying levels of anti-American opposition movements—namely, Morocco, Jordan, Palestine, Turkey, and Indonesia. Throughout the discussion of these case studies, I demonstrate that the chief factors that distinguish the countries of Kuwait and Jordan are not mediating the observed outcomes advanced in this study.

This book relies on multiple sources of information to substantiate the microfoundational claims advanced about citizen engagements and regime type. To substantiate my claims I rely on data from Kuwait, Jordan, and Palestine from surveys conducted in the first wave of the Arab Barometer and a set of 250 open-ended interviews conducted in Jordan, Morocco, and

Kuwait between 2005 and 2007. The open-ended interview material appears throughout the book to establish the causal logics citizens are employing when they discuss regime type and political processes linked to democratization. Although these interviews are not representative samples, they nevertheless examine predominant trends that emerged throughout the course of my research.[86] They show that winners of globalization are more cautious in pushing for more democracy because they are concerned about antipatron forces accessing power and disrupting the patron relationship. Thus, in client countries where anti-Americanism is high with organized groups to mobilize anti-American sentiment, debates about democratization will be more intense and constrained by concerns of stability.

Chapter 2 offers a detailed historical analysis of the emergence of regime clientelism in Jordan and Kuwait. Although Arab states have, to a large extent, been client regimes since their inception, their dependency on the United States has increased following the Cold War. Chapter 3 addresses how state and society—particularly Islamist opposition movements—deal with regime clientelism, especially the sources of anti-Americanism in Jordan, and especially among the IAF; I pay particular attention to the ways in which the regime and the United States have come to prioritize stability over democracy. Chapter 3 also examines regime and societal interactions in Kuwait with an emphasis on the recent democratic developments in the oil kingdom. The lack of anti-Americanism among the Kuwaiti opposition, especially among the ICM, has allowed for greater convergence between the democratic preferences of a society and its patron. Both chapters highlight how Arab regimes, Islamist opposition movements, and ordinary citizens continue to interact with one another through the prism of international dependency.

Using survey data from the Arab Barometer project, chapter 4 charts public opinion responses toward democracy and authoritarianism. Taking into account individual-level alternative hypotheses, this chapter illustrates that support for authoritarianism is also mediated by anti-American concerns. Even democratic citizens in Jordan will profess support for the regime in order to guarantee the patron-client relations so fundamental to Jordan's well-being. This delicate well-being could be jeopardized by anti-American elements entering the political process through more democratic means.

Teasing out the causal logics citizens offer for accepting or rejecting existing authoritarian realities, chapter 4 offers a more in-depth qualitative analysis of the impact of regime clientelism on the democratic predispositions and daily political negotiations of ordinary citizens. Relying on close to two hundred open-ended interviews with citizens in Jordan and Kuwait, this chapter also examines macrolevel alternative hypotheses assessing these attitudes and behaviors across both settings.

---

[86]Throughout the book, I will document the overall trends in percentage breakdowns. All coding was conducted using the qualitative software package NVIVO.

Chapter 5 demonstrates that different patterns of attitudes toward democracy and support for authoritarianism exist in Kuwait. Kuwaitis are far less likely to rationalize authoritarianism as strategically useful. This is because the Islamist opposition is not as anti-American as its counterpart in Jordan. As a result, Kuwait has moved along a more democratic trajectory. Kuwaitis can comfortably espouse democratic ideals and push for democratic reform, because existing opposition on the ground does not threaten its client status with the United States. This chapter further addresses alternative individual-level explanations on support for democracy and authoritarianism in Jordan and Kuwait.

Extending the analysis to Morocco, chapter 6 highlights how citizens across the North African monarchy rationalize authoritarianism through the prism of strategic utility to U.S. (and EU) ties. Chapter 7 extends the argument to Palestine and Saudi Arabia.

Finally, chapter 8 discusses how anti-Americanism continues to thwart the democratization trajectory in the Arab world. Anti-Americanism has often been seen as simply a problem relevant to East-West relations, terrorism, and the clash of civilizations. I maintain, however, that anti-Americanism has also stifled grassroots efforts toward democratization in the Arab world. The sheer dependence of the Arab world on U.S. patronage has meant that Arab citizens take their cues from the United States to secure the status quo. While the preference for democracy exists on the street, it needs to be fully endorsed by the patron. Anti-American forces have dampened U.S. enthusiasm for democracy, which in turn has stifled democratic demands from below. Given the fact that increasing international dependency has resulted in greater anti-Americanism, the democratic option remains all the more elusive today. This book shows that one of the key routes to democracy in the region will be to address the sources of anti-Americanism writ large.

APPENDIX: HUMAN DEVELOPMENT INDEX SCORES AND JORDAN'S GROSS DOMESTIC PRODUCT GROWTH RATE

TABLE 1.4. Human Development Index scores, 1980–2005

	1980	1985	1990	1995	2000	2005
Jordan	.647	.669	.684	.710	.751	.773
Morocco	.483	.519	.551	.581	.613	.646
Kuwait	.789	.794	—	.826	.855	.891
Saudi Arabia	.666	.684	.717	.748	.788	.812

Source: United Nations Human Development Index 1980–2011; accessed January 2012 at http://www.bloomberg.com/news/2011-11-02/human-development-index-trends-1980-2011-table-.

TABLE 1.5. Jordan GDP growth rates

	1997	1998	1999	2000	2001	2002	2003	2004	2005	2006
GDP growth rates in Jordan	4.2%	8.7%	1.4%	3.3%	4.3%	5.3%	6.4%	11.8%	11.5%	12.2%

Source: World Bank national accounts data and OECD National Accounts data files; accessed January 2012 at http://www.indexmundi.com/facts/jordan/gdp-growth#NY.GDP.MKTP.KD.ZG.

CHAPTER TWO

Becoming Jordan and Kuwait

The Making and Consolidating of U.S. Client Regimes

THE UNITED STATES EMERGED AS A KEY PLAYER IN THE ARAB WORLD AFTER THE SIGN-ing of the Eisenhower Doctrine of 1957. Although it had amicable relations with Arab countries before 1957, the United States deepened its connections to the region as a means of containing Soviet infiltration. For Jordan, this was important because of its buffer-state status between Israel and other, more hostile Arab countries like Iraq and Syria. U.S. interest in the Gulf region, which included Kuwait, was heightened by the need to protect access to oil and to prevent any hostile power from taking over these resources.[1] As Gary Sick points out, U.S. strategy in the Gulf has revolved around two themes: oil and containment. He writes, "the interests of the United States in the Persian Gulf region have been very simple and consistent: first, to ensure access by the industrialized world to the vast oil resources of the region; and second, to prevent any hostile power from acquiring political or military control over those resources. Throughout the Cold War, the most immediate threat was the Soviet Union; after the Soviet collapse, Iran and Iraq became the primary targets of U.S. containment efforts."[2] Because the

---

[1] According to David Lake's measures, Kuwait and Jordan are almost equally dependent on the United States economically. Between 2001 and 2004 Jordan's economic dependence on the United States is measured at 0.503 while Kuwait's economic dependence on the United States is at 0.439. This index (economic hierarchy) is the sum of the exchange rate regime index and the relative trade dependence index, divided by the score of the highest country value in 1995. Kuwait's security dependence on the United States during this time period is much higher than Jordan's. It has a value of 3.39, which means that Kuwait for 2001–4 had 3.39 times as many troops per population than did Panama in 1995, which was the highest value of military deployments at that time. Jordan's value is 0.002 for the period 2001–4.

[2] Gary Sick, "The United States in the Gulf: From Twin Pillars to Dual Containment," in *The Middle East and the United States: A Historical and Political Reassessment*, 4th ed., ed. David W. Lesch (Boulder, CO: Westview Press, 2007), 315. According to Sick, other objectives, such as preserving the stability and independence of the Gulf states or containing the threat of Islamic fundamentalism, were derivative concerns and were implicit in the two grand themes of oil and containment. Preoccupation with the security of Israel was a driving factor in U.S.-

Gulf countries were guaranteed security, the United States was also able to counter the influence of anti-American regimes. Both the United States and the Gulf states benefited from this clientelistic relationship.

The purpose of this chapter is twofold. The first goal is to demonstrate the making of client regimes in Jordan and Kuwait. According to David Lake's measures, both Kuwait and Jordan are embedded in a hierarchical relationship with the United States.[3] But the second, more important, goal is to illustrate how the end of the Cold War restructured the ways in which international hierarchy shifted debates about democratization at the domestic level. During the Cold War, the bipolar nature of the world order meant that if the United States were to lose its ally in Jordan, the Soviet Union would be able to step up on the back of a new regime. If the United States then decided to cut off economic and security ties to Jordan, Jordanians—especially those who benefited from greater ties to external patrons and the securities and protections of those patrons—might find comfort in the fact that the Soviet Union could play a role in continuing to secure Jordan's interests. Thus, those who resisted anti-American presence in the Arab world could launch their concerns more effectively because of an alternate patron—the Soviet Union—in the global order. Further, the existence of an alternative patron reduced the anxieties of those who benefited from patron backing. Arguably, the fact that there would be an alternate patron to continue protecting and supplying the client state with resources and security meant that regime transitions would still find potential alternate patron support. Thus, coup attempts were much more common during the Cold War period because those with economic interests that were linked to the regime did not feel they would sacrifice patron backing in the event of regime change. There would be another patron to step in and provide the assistance necessary to maintain state-business cohesion.

The Islamic Revolution in Iran was in part emboldened by the presence of the Soviet Union as a counterbalance to U.S. support of the Shah of Iran. In the post-Cold War era, as Islamism grew in strength—it, too, was seen as a potential threat—it could jeopardize international patronage. The argument advanced here is that in the unipolar global world order, anti-Americanism

---

Middle East policy for half a century, and developments in the Arab-Israeli arena sporadically influenced U.S. policies in the Persian Gulf. Especially after the end of the Cold War, the Israeli factor began to assume much greater importance in the formation of U.S. policy in the Gulf.

[3] Lake, "Escape from the State of Nature," 47–79. Economically, both countries are similarly dependent on the United States. The average score for each country between 1991 and 2007 is .44 Kuwait and .42 Jordan. Kuwait is more dependent on the United States in terms of security hierarchy, but this is more of a result of the fact that countries like Jordan and Saudi Arabia prefer to have troops stationed in neighboring countries rather than on their own soil.

became more costly for citizens in countries that were dependent on the United States for security and aid. Jeopardizing ties to the patron could mean the loss of both.

Further exacerbating the "cost" of anti-Americanism is that with the end of the Cold War, structural adjustment and privatization initiatives meant that Arab regimes would have to reduce their embeddedness in their own economies. Economic interest groups that had previously relied on regimes were forced to fend for themselves. This shift should have created more autonomy for business sectors. However, because globalization—that is, access to global markets, financial flows, aid, trade, free trade agreements, and other economic initiatives—was linked to the United States it then reinforced support for existing regimes, because these regimes were seen as guaranteeing access to the United States. In fact, many of these globalization "perks" were a result of strong security ties between patron and client. If the client chose to dishonor agreements with the patron, the patron could withdraw the support of trade and financial assistance. And even worse, were the client state to become hostile, the patron could unilaterally impose sanctions. Hence, those who stood to benefit from globalization found value in supporting the existing regime as a means of guaranteeing access to global markets—access secured by the patron. Thus, rather than induce autonomy among certain business sectors, globalization, with the conditions of a hegemonic world order, reinforced reliance on pro-patron authoritarian structures in societies that had influential antipatron movements.[4]

From the Eisenhower Doctrine emerged the Nixon Doctrine, which emphasized the twin goals of oil and containment. The Nixon Doctrine relied on two strategic states to accomplish these goals, Iran and Saudi Arabia, and thus it became known as the Twin Pillar Policy.[5] When the Shah of Iran's regime in Tehran fell in 1979, the United States and the rest of the Gulf region were left vulnerable to revolutionary Iran.[6] This heightened U.S. urgency to develop stronger and more durable ties with allies in the Gulf—namely, Saudi Arabia. With the Iran-Iraq War unfolding throughout much of the 1980s and the Iraqi occupation of Kuwait in 1990, the United States saw itself emerge as the chief patron of the Gulf region.

Today, all of the Arab Gulf states, including Kuwait, rely heavily on the United States for security.[7] Gary Sick puts it eloquently: "By the end of the

---

[4] Arguably a bipolar world order would have provided globalization beneficiaries more autonomy—since an alternate patron could step in and provide access to globalized markets and shield the client state from patron sanctions, for example.

[5] Sick, "The United States in the Gulf."

[6] Ibid.

[7] See F. Gregory Gause III, "From 'Over the Horizon' to 'Into the Backyard': The U.S.-Saudi Relationship in the Gulf," in *The Middle East and the United States: A Historical and Political Reassessment*, 4th ed., ed. David W. Lesch (Boulder, CO: Westview Press, 2007), 380–90; Shafeeq

twentieth century, the United States had become a Persian Gulf power in its own right. Its political, military, and economic footprint in the region was greater even than the governments of the region themselves. Its role as a security guarantor was not in doubt, and its prestige and influence were at their zenith."[8] The United States was the dominant force in the Gulf region, and all the Gulf countries turned to the United States for more security. This security was equally vital for their economic success, since without it all the oil reserves of the region were at risk.

Jordan's History of Clientelistic Dependence

If it weren't for the British, Transjordan would probably never have been created as an autonomous state. The British created Transjordan in 1921, and by 1928 it had become instrumental to peace and stability in the region. The British saw in Transjordan the opportunity to satisfy the ambitious desire of a Hashemite prince, Abdullah, while limiting tribal raids into the French mandates of Greater Syria. Thus, Transjordan's main function was to preserve the peace and stability of its northern border. Preserving peace and stability in the region would remain the goal of this desert kingdom well into the twentieth and twenty-first centuries. Today Jordan is a bastion of stability amid chaos. To the west, Jordan faces the turmoil in Palestine; to the East, Iraq; and to the north, Lebanon and Syria. Jordan has demonstrated remarkable durability.

William L. Cleveland captures the client status of Jordan well. "Because of the circumstances surrounding the establishment of Transjordan," he writes, "it is difficult to disagree with the statement that Transjordan was an artificial state created to accommodate the interests of a foreign power and itinerant prince in a search of a throne."[9] To remain on the good side of the British, Emir Abdullah had to deliver on the security interests of the Anglo and French empires. To this end, he established—with the help of the British—a military corporation called the Arab Legion, which would contain tribal violence and raids into neighboring territory. As Cleveland notes, "It was to prevent such raids as well as to bring order to the region that Abdullah was given his throne and provided with a British subsidy and

N. Ghabra, "Closing the Distance: Kuwait and the United States in the Persian Gulf," in *The Middle East and the United States: A Historical and Political Reassessment*, 4th ed., ed. David W. Lesch (Boulder, CO: Westview Press, 2007), 332–50; and Sick, "The United States in the Gulf."

[8]Sick, "The United States in the Gulf," 327. See also Adeed Dawisha, "The United States in the Middle East: The Gulf War and Its Aftermath," *Current History* 91, no. 561 (1992): 1–5.

[9]William L. Cleveland, *A History of the Modern Middle East* (Boulder, CO: Westview Press, 2004), 213.

the support of British civilian and military personnel."[10] When the British created Jordan, tribes with little or no loyalty to their new ruler dominated the territory, but with the backing of the British, Emir Abdullah quelled tribal violence and centralized his rule.[11]

In 1928, the British signed the Anglo-Transjordanian Agreement. As was the case with British agreements with Iraq and Egypt, British rule would remain indirect, but the British claimed the final word on matters relating to foreign relations, the armed forces, the budget, and all other essential government activities.[12] Although Emir Abdullah was not necessarily pleased with this dependent and compliant relationship, he understood that without the British he would have neither the territorial integrity of the state nor the resources to keep the state functioning—a pattern that each subsequent leader of Jordan would also understand. As Laurie A. Brand writes, "Because of its underdeveloped economic base and because of the role Transjordan was to play in British imperial designs, the Emirate's treasury depended upon an annual subsidy from England for survival."[13] After Jordan's recognition as a state in 1923, Emir Abdullah "remained heavily dependent on British support that had allowed him to survive the tribal revolts and attacks of the 1920s," notes Mansoor Moaddel, "and that kept his administration afloat despite the lack of taxable assets in Transjordan itself. Without Britain it is fair to judge that neither Abdullah nor Transjordan in its formative years would have survived."[14]

In return for Jordan's containment of tribal violence, the British provided an annual subsidy that allowed the Jordanians to both build the infrastructure of the state and support the Arab Legion. In 1921 British grants totaled £180,000. This economic aid, naturally, came with strings attached. Britain expected Abdullah to comply with its preferences and insisted that he expel political undesirables and eliminate the Department of Tribal Administration. When Abdullah hesitated to implement the British commands, a high-ranking British officer, Henry Cox, made it clear to him that Britain did not want to have to reconsider its stance on the whole issue of Trans-

[10]Ibid.

[11]Quintan Wiktorowicz, "Civil Society as Social Control: State Power in Jordan," *Comparative Politics* 33, no. 1 (2000): 51; Asher Susser, "The Jordanian Monarchy: The Hashemite Success Story," in *Middle East Monarchies,* ed. Joseph Kositner (Boulder, CO: Lynne Rienner, 2000), 90. See also Mohamad Ahmad Salah, *Athr al-Ma'awanāt al-Māliyya al-Brītāniyya fī al-Wad'a al-Mālī fī Sharq al-Urdun 1921–1925* [Effects of British Financial Assistance to the Financial Status of East Jordan 1921-1925], *Arab Journal for the Humanities* 80 (2002): n.p.

[12]Cleveland, *A History of the Modern Middle East,* 213.

[13]Laurie A. Brand, *Jordan's Inter-Arab Relations: The Political Economy of Alliance Making* (New York: Columbia University Press, 1995), 153.

[14]Mansoor Moaddel, "Religion and the State: The Singularity of the Jordanian Religious Experience," *International Journal of Politics, Culture, and Society* 15, no. 4 (2002): 530.

jordan. In other words, the British used their support for the kingdom as a means to coerce Abdullah to endorse their vision of rule. According to Philip Robins, "Abdullah well understood the implicit threat at the end."[15] He had no choice but to agree to Britain's conditions. The entire Transjordanian project relied on keeping its Western patron satisfied.[16]

Emir Abdullah's dependence on the British did not go without domestic opposition. Arab nationalists, especially those of the urban effendi class increasingly frustrated with Abdullah and his British connections, formed the Hizb al-Istiqlal (Independence Party).[17] The British had become nervous about the rhetoric of pan-Arabism. Because of Abdullah's reliance on the British, he was compelled, notes Moaddel, to "purge the Arab League and the Transjordan government . . . of most of the Arab nationalists whom Britain considered to be troublemakers."[18] As a result, Abdullah's pan-Arab reputation was scarred.[19] That reputation was further tarnished during World War II, when Abdullah sent his forces to fight with the British in Iraq. The Jordanian regime and its successive leaders would side with their patron, even if it meant opposing domestic opinion.[20] From the onset of the Jordanian project, it was clear that Jordan was first accountable to its external patron, and only then to its own citizens.[21]

POST–WORLD WAR II: FULL INDEPENDENCE FOR JORDAN BUT CONTINUED RELIANCE ON THE BRITISH

In 1946, Britain granted Transjordan independence, and Abdullah was elevated from emir to king.[22] On March 22, 1946, the new Anglo-Transjordanian Treaty was signed, with terms similar to those of older agreements. But now Transjordan was an independent country that would maintain peace and close friendship with the British. In a special annex to the agreement, the British would continue subsidizing the kingdom and supporting the Arab Legion. In return, Transjordan agreed to provide Britain with military facilities on its territory for the next twenty-five years.[23] According to Cleveland, "The awkward desert principality that had been created almost as an afterthought

---

[15]Philip Robins, *A History of Jordan* (Cambridge: Cambridge University Press, 2004), 30.
[16]Kamal Salabi, *The Modern History of Jordan* (London: I. B. Tauris, 1995), 104.
[17]Ibid.
[18]Moaddel, "Religion and the State," 531.
[19]Salabi, *The Modern History of Jordan*, 117.
[20]The obvious exception is the Gulf War of 1991.
[21]Salabi, *The Modern History of Jordan*, 152.
[22]Cleveland, *A History of the Modern Middle East*, 215.
[23]Salabi, *The Modern History of Jordan*, 153; Robins, *A History of Jordan*, 57.

of the post–World War I settlement became, in the years following World War II, a prominent military and diplomatic force in the region."[24]

Still exercising isolationism, the United States remained at a distance. In 1949, however, it established diplomatic relations with Amman. This was more a result of King Abdullah's emerging vulnerability in the region than of U.S. geostrategic interests. Leaders of other states, like King Faruq of Egypt and King Abdul Aziz of Saudi Arabia, ridiculed the artificiality underlying the Transjordanian project. King Abdullah sought closer ties with the Americans to increase his security, which resulted in greater diplomatic contacts between the two countries.[25] This relationship would grow in the following decades.

In 1951, King Abdullah was assassinated by a lone Palestinian gunman, and—despite his schizophrenia—Prince Talal, the son of Abdullah, was chosen by the British to succeed the throne. Prince Talal was chosen over Prince Nayef because the latter made the British and the Jordanian elite nervous. Some saw Prince Nayef's erratic and inconsistent behavior as threatening; he attempted to undermine British influence in Jordan and instigate a coup against the pro-British government at the time.[26] Prince Talal ruled Transjordan for nearly five years. In 1952, Talal's mental health deteriorated to such an extent that he was deposed in favor of his eldest son, Hussein, who assumed the throne on May 2, 1953.[27]

The transition between Abdullah and his grandson was smooth because the institutionalization of the political establishment had reached significant levels of success. A constitution was promulgated in 1952, and King Hussein attempted to allow the parliament a degree of autonomy. Soon, however, King Hussein realized that the sentiments of his population did not bode well for the clientelistic relationship with the British. Both the Palestinian and Transjordanian populations were desperately awaiting pan-Arab triumph—a vision that did not include the British. According to Kamal Salabi, support for Arab nationalism "was particularly the case among urban Transjordanians of the younger generation who had come to consider the monarchy rule as anachronistic, and many of whom were influenced by the Arab nationalist, Ba'thist, or communist political platforms."[28] Further discontent emerged in the ranks of the Arab Legion against British involvement. As a result, King Hussein reduced political liberties to guarantee the status quo. Without the support of the British, Hussein's rule would be in jeopardy.[29]

[24]Cleveland, *A History of the Modern Middle East*, 215.

[25]Robins, *A History of Jordan*, 58.

[26]Ibid., 77-78 and Robert Satloff, *From Abdullah to Hussein: Jordan in Transition*. New York: Oxford University Press, 1994.

[27]Robins, *A History of Jordan*, 78-87.

[28]Salabi, *The Modern History of Jordan*, 179-183 and Robins, *A History of Jordan*, 179.

[29]Salabi, *The Modern History of Jordan*, 179-183 and Robins, *A History of Jordan*.

Jordan found itself in a particularly vulnerable situation, somewhere between President Gamal Abdel Nasser's Egypt, with its triumphant message of nonalignment, and Iraq, which had entered into the Baghdad Pact with the United States in 1955. As Jordan contemplated joining the Baghdad Pact, fierce opposition and demonstrations emerged across the Hashemite kingdom, among Palestinians and Transjordanians alike. Most of the protesters took their cue from a communist/socialist vision combined with pan-Arab commitments. Citizens of Jordan preferred an alternate to the United States, which they saw as an imperialist, pro-Israeli force in the region. As long as the global context was confined to bipolar division, citizens could attempt to urge their leaders to alternate patrons. As a result of massive demonstrations, Jordan announced that it would no longer consider joining the Baghdad Pact.[30] The regime, however, would not stand idle as citizens attempted to redesign its clientelistic relationship with the United States, and it instituted a period of martial law following the demonstrations—a period that would last for the next three decades.[31]

Hussein's refusal to sign the pact buttressed his Arab nationalist credentials, and his 1956 dismissal of Glubb Basha—a British lieutenant-general and commander of the Arab Legion stationed in Jordan—won him even more support on the Arab street. But Hussein, despite being upset with Glubb, remained an Anglophile.[32] Enjoying spectacular legitimacy at home, Hussein backed Nasser in the 1956 war, and even argued for war with Israel. His prime minister at the time, Suleiman Nabulsi, resigned in protest. As Hussein toned down his rhetoric against Israel, Nabulsi reminded him of his obligations toward the British under the Anglo-Jordanian Treaty. The continuation of the British subsidy was vital for Jordanian longevity, Nabulsi argued, and Hussein shouldn't jeopardize the relationship for the cause of Arab nationalism.

Understanding the economic predicament of the Jordanian monarchy, Saudi Arabia, Egypt, and Syria pledged to subsidize the kingdom if Hussein broke ties with the British—which he did. Yet Saudi Arabia was the only country to pay the first part of its pledge, and the rest of the pledges never translated into actual cash flow. Hussein and Jordan were left feeling vulnerable, abandoned, and on the verge of economic crisis. Luckily for Jordan, the United States was in the process of unveiling the Eisenhower Doctrine of 1957. This doctrine allowed the U.S. president to assist with military and economic aid of any state directly threatened by communist expansion and aggression. According to Robins, "The announcement of the Eisenhower Doctrine seems immediately to have caught the king's eye, offering Hussein

[30]Robins, *A History of Jordan*, 91–92.
[31]Salabi, *The Modern History of Jordan*, 185–87.
[32]Robins, *A History of Jordan*, 93.

the chance to change his foreign policy orientation away from support for a has-been power [the British] and toward a superpower [the United States]."³³ King Hussein then approached the United States for a $30 million aid package, which replaced the British subsidy.

Jordan has remained a beneficiary of U.S. military cooperation and foreign economic assistance. The United States began providing Jordan with economic aid in 1951; in 1957, it began delivering military aid. From the 1950s through 2004, total U.S. aid to Jordan amounted to approximately $8 billion. According to the Congressional Research Service, "Levels of aid have fluctuated, increasing in response to threats faced by Jordan and decreasing during periods of political differences."³⁴ While the United States has looked out for Jordan's interests through this assistance, it has used such assistance as a means of both rewarding and punishing its client.

ECONOMIC DEVASTATION AFTER THE FIRST GULF WAR

By the early 1960s, Jordan was a firm U.S. client. Regional and economic crises only heightened Jordan's dependency on the United States. The 1970 Civil War in Jordan, the 1979 Islamic Revolution in Iran, the Iran-Iraq War starting in 1981, the Lebanese Civil War in the 1970s, and the Israeli invasion of Lebanon in 1982 all affected the regime's security and economy. Jordan clung to its patron for both military and financial support. The devastating economic bust of the late 1970s struck the region's oil revenues directly. By 1988, the Jordanian government had an operating budget deficit of close to 400 million Jordanian dinars, or close to 27 percent of its entire GDP.³⁵ A series of economic austerity measures were enacted that floated the Jordanian currency, reduced the size of the public sector, and increased the prices of basic foodstuffs.³⁶ These policies, however, resulted in massive protests, especially in Transjordanian strongholds like the city of Ma'an.³⁷ By the 1990s, Jordan's foreign debt had increased to $6.8 billion.³⁸

³³Ibid., 97

³⁴Jeremy M. Sharp, *Jordan: Background and U.S. Relations*, Congressional Research Service Report, October 17, 2008, 22.

³⁵Cleveland, *A History of the Modern Middle East*, 166.

³⁶Karen Pfeifer, "How Tunisia, Morocco, Jordan and Even Egypt Became IMF 'Success Stories' in the 1990's," *Middle East Report* 210 (1999): 23.

³⁷Curtis R. Ryan, "Jordan and the Rise and Fall of the Arab Cooperation Council," *Middle East Journal* 52, no. 3 (1998), 386.

³⁸Ibid. Jordan still faced dire economic conditions. Most important, the April riots were not really reflective of the perhaps "overemphasized Palestinian-East banker differences within Jordanian society but rather were instigated largely from within the East Bank community itself." James Phillips, *The U.S. Stake in Post-Hussein Jordan*, Executive Memorandum no. 574 (Washington, DC: Heritage Foundation, 1999; accessed at http://www.heritage.org/Research/Middle

Jordan's struggling economy would be dealt yet another significant blow when the kingdom sided with Iraq during the First Gulf War in 1991.[39] When King Hussein declined to join the Allied Coalition during Operations Desert Shield and Desert Storm, the kingdom suffered miserably, losing millions of dollars in U.S. aid.[40] The United States, along with Kuwait and Saudi Arabia, immediately suspended all aid packages to the kingdom. Compounding the situation, one of Jordan's largest trading partners at the time, Iraq, was burdened with United Nations sanctions that reduced Iraqi oil revenues, which cut into Iraqi imports from Jordan. The economic punishment of Jordan demonstrated the sheer magnitude of its reliance and dependence on external actors—namely, the United States.

After the fall of the Soviet Union, it became clear to domestic oppositions across the Arab world—especially those committed to leftist ideologies—that an alternate patron no longer existed. For many Arab societies, including Jordan, the days of pan-Arabism were over. Societies gradually began to see themselves more as national identities rather than pan-Arab. According to Malik Mufti, the tension between pan-Arabism and state loyalty saw the pendulum swing in favor of the latter.[41] Hence, Jordanian citizens gradually became more mindful of state interests and the national well-being of their country.[42] This realization came with yet another truth: many of the states were now fully and completely reliant on the United States, and Jordan was no exception.[43] The longevity and well-being of Jordan was contingent on sound relations with the United States.

The United States also emerged as the sole guarantor of Jordan's security. Although this reality was hard for many across the region to digest, the United States—having emerged triumphant from the Cold War—held the national well-being of Arab countries completely in its hands. The U.S. incursion into Iraq in 2003 again confirmed what citizens already knew: America could strike the region militarily if leaders deviated. Jordanian citizen concerns

---

East/EM574.cfm). As Joe Stork, "The Gulf War and the Arab World," *World Policy Journal* 8, no. 2 (1991): 396, notes, Iraq had emerged as Jordan's single most important trading partner; almost 75 percent of Jordan's industry was geared toward export to Iraq.

[39] Eliyahu Kanovsky, *The Middle East Economies: The Impact of Domestic and International Politics*, Mideast Security and Policy Studies no. 31. Ramat Gan, Israel: Begin-Sadat Center for Strategic Studies, Bar-Ilan University, 1997 (accessed at http://www.biu.ac.il/SOC/besa/publications/kanov/index.html).

[40] Direct aid was estimated at $55 million (not including military and other forms of aid). Martin Tolchin, "After the War, Congress Withholds $55 Million in Aid to Jordan," *New York Times*, March 23, 1991.

[41] Malik Mufti, "A King's Art: Dynastic Ambition and State Interest in Hussein's Jordan." *Diplomacy and Statecraft* 13, no. 3 (2002): 1–22.

[42] Dawisha, "The United States in the Middle East."

[43] Lamis Andoni, "King Abdullah: In His Father's Footsteps?" *Journal of Palestine Studies* 29, no. 3 (2000): 77–89.

about the risk of losing U.S. favor were heightened by the nature of anti-American opposition forces in the kingdom. If anti-American forces came to power, would the kingdom lose U.S. patronage? It is then curious that King Hussein would side with Iraq against the United States during the First Gulf War. Arguably, King Hussein was not hoping to lose U.S. patronage. Rather, he sent a clear signal to the United States and to his own people about the limits of opposing U.S. geostrategic preferences in the region. To the United States he sent a clear signal that his regime could fall if he sided against Iraq; to his own people he demonstrated that there were costs to opposing the patron. Thus, although there was a temporary rupture in U.S.-Jordanian ties during the war, perhaps the rupture strengthened the mechanisms of the two-level game at play. Citizens—especially those who stood to benefit from a more economically viable Jordan—would factor in concerns about anti-Americanism in their calculations about future democratic trajectories. Yet the debates also clearly illustrate that the balance is a delicate one. Had Hussein not sided with Iraq, this perhaps could have pushed the pendulum in a direction where citizens were willing to forsake U.S. patronage. This was not the case during the First Gulf War. Yet, the lessons from Egypt in 2011 are a clear reminder: when those who stand to benefit from U.S. patronage become a shrinking proportion of the population, the pendulum can swing. Thus, the client leader must continue to ensure that the benefits of the patron-client relationship are distributed to significant (though not necessarily overwhelming) portions of the population while simultaneously signaling his own vulnerability in the process. In the presence of anti-American sentiments, both the patron and globalization beneficiaries are more likely to rally their support for the client regime to maintain the status quo.

ECONOMIC PROGRESS AND THE JORDAN-ISRAELI PEACE TREATY, 1994

With the Palestinians already in direct negotiations with Israel, King Hussein saw an opportunity to sign a peace treaty with Israel that aimed to bring the Jordanian economy a much-needed influx of financial resources. And although significant pockets of Jordanians initially resisted normalization with Israel, the monarchy felt that stronger ties with Israel would be beneficial for their country as a whole.

Although the United States resumed its aid packages in 1991, Jordan had suffered economically between the years 1987 and 1991, when GDP had fallen by 21 percent per capita. This slowdown was followed by four years of rapid economic growth, where GDP per capita increased by 13 percent and the total GDP by 38 percent.[44] This growth was due to two main factors.

---

[44]International Monetary Fund, Statistics Department. *International Financial Statistics Yearbook 1996.* Washington, DC: International Monetary Fund, 1996, 465.

First, Jordan had been adopting economic austerity measures and cutting back governmental spending.[45] These decisions were beginning to pay off. Second, many of the Palestinians who left or were forced to leave Kuwait during the Gulf crisis brought their life savings with them to Amman. Estimates put refugee monies at $1.5 billion, most of which were invested in construction projects. Palestinian monies served as a massive infusion into the Jordanian economy, giving it a GDP of $5 billion in 1992.[46]

In 1992, however, official unemployment estimates stood between 15 percent and 20 percent—and unofficial estimates were much higher. Furthermore, the gap between the superrich and impoverished sectors was growing rapidly. As a result of signing the peace agreement, Jordan was considerably relieved of its debt burden. Following the cancellation of the $705 million debt to the United States, the United Kingdom canceled debts totaling $90 million; Germany, $53 million; and France, $4.5 million.[47] After the Treaty, Jordan benefited from an influx of money from the United States. Further, in 1996, the United States added Jordan to their major non-NATO ally agreement.

Strong relations with the United States have become the cornerstone of Jordan's vision for a better economic future. While King Hussein realized the importance of this relationship and moved cautiously to adopt it by such means as signing the peace treaty, his son King Abdullah II has wholeheartedly endorsed the vision. The United States thus emerged as Jordan's main economic and security backer. Without such support, Jordan's well-being could be jeopardized. According to Robins, "Abdullah has learnt the lesson of his father and great-grandfather before him that the swiftest and most effective way of aiding an ailing economy in Jordan is to seek strategic rents from abroad."[48] Thus, Abdullah immediately strengthened Jordan's ties to the United States and further linked the kingdom's fortunes to major international economic institutions, such as the International Monetary Fund (IMF) and the World Trade Organization.[49] As a result of Abdullah II's vision for greater economic development and integration into the global economy, Amman has become a site of investment and business relocation. Scrapping over one hundred laws on economic and trade regulation, Abdullah continues to foster economic growth and development.[50] Visitors

---

[45]Rex Brynen, "Economic Crisis and Post-rentier Democratization in the Arab World: The Case of Jordan." *Canadian Journal of Political Science* 25, no. 1 (1992): 69–97.

[46]Kanovsky, "The Middle East Economies."

[47]Ibid.

[48]Robins, *A History of Jordan*, 204.

[49]Curtis R. Ryan, " 'Jordan First': Jordan's Inter-Arab Relations and Foreign Policy under King Abdullah II," *Arab Studies Quarterly* 26, no. 3 (2004): 43–62.

[50]International Crisis Group, *The Challenge of Political Reform: Jordanian Democratisation and Regional Instability*, Middle East Briefing no. 10 (Amman, Jordan, and Brussels: International Crisis Group, 2003; accessed at http://www.crisisgroup.org/~/media/Files/Middle%20East%20

to Amman are shocked by the rapid pace of construction throughout the city. Not only do local investors from the Arab world—primarily from the Persian Gulf and other war-torn areas like Lebanon and Iraq—bring their investments to Jordan, but Western investment has grown as well.[51]

Abdullah's adamant support of the Americans following 9-11 and during the 2003 Iraq War has paid off. Jordan became the fourth country, after Canada, Mexico, and Israel, to sign a free trade agreement with the United States. The United States became Amman's largest trading partner, with almost a third of all of its trade exports in 2007 headed to the United States,[52] a marked increase from earlier years. (Textiles constitute the bulk of Jordanian exports to the United States.) The American Chamber of Commerce in Amman has calculated that the kingdom's exports to the United States increased by 453 percent between 2001 and 2005, while imports from the States grew by 18 percent year after year. Iraq is Jordan's second biggest export market, making up 11.3 percent of all exports, and the stability of that country rests overwhelmingly in the hands of the Americans.[53] Among Jordan's other key trading partners is another strong U.S. ally, Saudi Arabia; 80 percent of Jordanian imports come from Saudi Arabia's energy sector. Not only does Jordan overwhelmingly depend on the United States (and U.S. allies) for trade, but the Jordanian currency is strongly pegged to the American dollar.

These economic programs have been successful for the kingdom. Not only has Jordan's external debt decreased 75 percent since 1989 but its foreign currency reserves have also grown from less than $100 million in 1989 to slightly over $3.5 billion in 2002. These numbers have been vital in attracting foreign investment from Europe, the United States, Saudi Arabia, and Kuwait. The Jordanian stock exchange also did extremely well during this period, rising over 53 percent in 2002, with trading volume increasing by over 83 percent in 2001. These encouraging numbers are absolutely vital in terms of Jordan's future economic trajectory. Jordan's economy must continue growing at a rate of at least 6 percent per year if it is going to be able to absorb the 45,000–65,000 new workers that enter the Jordanian workforce annually.[54]

Jordan also experienced increasing levels of economic and military assistance. In 2003 and 2004, the country received substantially more economic

---

North%20Africa/Iran%20Gulf/Jordan/B010%20The%20Challenge%20of%20Political%20Reform%20Jordanian%20Democratisation%20and%20Regional%20Instability.pdf).

[51]Lionel Beehner, *The Effects of the Amman Bombings on U.S.-Jordanian Relations* (New York: Council on Foreign Relations, 2005; accesssed at http://www.cfr.org/publication/9200/).

[52]AME Info, "Jordan Looks Near and Far for Economic Growth," February 2007 (accessed at http://www.ameinfo.com/110694.html).

[53]Ibid.

[54]Bassem Awadallah, "Jordan's Economic Miracle," February 3, 2003 (accessed at http://www.jordanembassyus.org/new/events/event_02032003.htm).

and military aid than in earlier years. Total economic aid in 2003 (the year of the Iraqi invasion) stood at close to $1 billion, with military assistance at close to $600 million. In 2004, Jordan received $348 million in economic aid and an additional $204 million in military aid. Since 2000, Jordan has received a total of $2.78 billion in U.S. economic assistance, not including debt relief or military assistance (See table 2.1).[55]

Abdullah's policies have resulted in impressive growth rates. In 2007, the construction growth rate was at almost 8 percent[56]—facts and figures not lost on ordinary Jordanian citizens. They see that their country is growing and becoming more globally integrated, and they know that if they are not enjoying the fruits of the boom now, they may down the line. If anything, when they compare the economic boom of Amman with the devastation of neighboring Iraq, Palestine, and Lebanon, they see that they are better off than the rest. They also fully understand that their strong political and economic ties with the United States have allowed for the continued stability and economic growth. With increasing levels of security and economic growth, however, have also come increased levels of dependency and reliance on the United States. Virtually all barriers on goods traded between the United States and Jordan will have been eliminated by the end of 2011, thus giving U.S. exporters more incentives to export to the monarchy.[57]

After the events of 9-11, Jordan has also grown more dependent on the United States for security. As Abdullah turned to the United States to energize the Jordanian economy further, Amman also became more useful to the United States, providing intelligence on al-Qaeda after 9-11. Further, Jordan served as a key site from which the U.S. military could launch its devastating attack on Iraq in 2003. The United States organized a reduced debt-rescheduling timetable at the Paris Club for Jordan and then doubled its aid package between fiscal years 2002 and 2003. By the end of 2003, Jordan was the fourth largest recipient of U.S. aid worldwide, after Israel, Egypt, and Colombia. According to Robins, "Jordanian low-key, 'deniable,' yet extremely useful help to the American military in the eastern desert [during the 2003 Iraq war] has cemented the client relationship anew. Eight decades after its founding, Jordan's position now is eerily reminiscent of its position in the early years of its existence: A favored dependency of the regional superpower of the day."[58] Jordan is adamant about not repeating the mistake it committed during the First Gulf War, which was angering the United States after refusing to join the coalition against Iraq—a decision,

[55]Pierre Tristam, "Jordan: Country Profile," 2008 (accessed at http://middleeast.about.com/od/jordan/p/me071114.htm).

[56]U.S. Commercial Service, *Doing Business in Jordan: 2010 Country Commercial Guide for U.S. Companies* (Washington, DC: U.S. Department of Commerce, 2010; accessed at http://export.gov/jordan/doingbusinessinjordan/eg_jo_038317.asp).

[57]Ibid.

[58]Robins, *A History of Jordan*, 204.

TABLE 2.1. U.S. aid to Jordan

Year	Economic aid (in millions)	Military aid (in millions)
1992	30	20
1993	5	9
1994	9	9
1995	7.2	7.3
1996	702	30
1997	112.2	100
1998	150	75
1999	200*	120*
2000	200**	225**
2001	150	75
2002	150	75
2003	248 700***	198 406***
2004	248 100****	204

Sources: Bassem Awadallah, "Jordan's Economic Miracle," February 3, 2003 (accessed at http://www.jordanembassyus.org/new/events/event_02032003.htm); Embassy of the Hashemite Kingdom of Jordan, U.S.-Jordan Relations (Washington, DC: Embassy of the Hashemite Kingdom of Jordan; accessed at http://www.jordanembassyus.org/new/aboutjordan/uj1.shtml).
* In 1999, Jordan received an additional $50 million in economic assistance and $50 million in military assistance as part of the Wye Agreement Fund.
** In 2000, Jordan received an additional $50 million in economic assistance and $150 million in military assistance, satisfying the $300 million allocated for Jordan as part of the Wye Agreement Fund.
*** As part of FY 2003 emergency supplemental assistance.
**** As part of FY 2004 emergency supplemental assistance.

according to Curtis Ryan, that "still haunts Jordanian policy makers."[59] As a result, the Jordanian elite and citizens, especially those in globalized economic sectors, worry about such future ruptures.

CONTINUED MILITARY AND ECONOMIC ASSISTANCE: INCREASED DEPENDENCY

Although the monarchy tried to keep its support of the Americans a secret, satellite coverage along with leaks in the daily newspapers made it clear that the Americans were using Jordan's eastern border to launch the 2003 war

[59] Ryan, "'Jordan First.'"

into Iraq. Prime Minister Abul Ragheb denied this, but did acknowledge the presence of "hundreds" of troops, though other estimates put the number in the thousands.[60] Jordanian leaders maintained that the Americans were there to train Jordanians in how to operate Patriot Missile batteries. In reality, however, U.S. troops used the eastern border with Iraq to station Patriot Missile batteries to protect both Jordan and Israel, provide access routes into Iraq for American forces, and train Iraqi security forces.[61] According to Robert Bookmiller, "By lending support, both as an Arab and a Muslim voice, to American efforts in the war on terrorism [and Iraq], Jordan gained financial rewards and cemented a closer relationship with the Bush Administration."[62] The United States emerged as Jordan's closest partner.

The United States has also established permanent signals intelligence monitoring stations in Jordan. In 1995, the U.S. military had set up two airbases in Jordan, the Shahid Muwaffiq Airbase and the H-5 (Prince Hassan) Airbase, which house almost 1,200 personnel and thirty-four American F-15s and F-16s. Jordan not only granted access to the Americans before the Iraqi invasion but also allowed British and Australian personnel to enter the kingdom. On January 30, 2003, Jordan granted the United States blanket overflight rights, facilitating aircraft carrier strikes on Iraq from the eastern Mediterranean region.[63]

Since 2000, Jordan has received close to $1.9 billion in U.S. military aid; and used these monies to buy approximately eighty F-16 fighters and Black Hawk helicopters.[64] Jordan has also used U.S. military assistance grants to purchase advanced medium-range air-to-air missiles. In 2003, Jordan built its Special Operation Command and Anti-Terrorism Center to boost counterterrorism capabilities. Further, the United States is financing the building of the $99 million King Abdullah II Center for Special Operations Training, designed to beef up counterterrorism training. Jordan has emerged as a key country ensuring U.S. strategic interests in the region. For Jordan, the stronger ties to the United States have resulted in greater economic advancements, economic integration, and economic and security perquisites.

Although many have argued that the stability of the Hashemite regime results from the indispensability of the monarchy, most accounts focus on internal mechanisms that have produced this pro–status quo bias. Michael Fischbach has examined the role the monarchy played in co-opting the peasantry in the 1930s and 1950s, for instance, and Betty Anderson has

[60]Robert Bookmiller, "Abdullah's Jordan: America's Anxious Ally." *Alternatives: Turkish Journal of International Relations* 2, no. 2 (2003): 183.

[61]Ibid.

[62]Ibid., 191.

[63]William M. Arkin, "Keeping Secrets in Jordan," *Washington Post*, November 16, 2005 (accessed at http://www.informationclearinghouse.info/article11031.htm).

[64]Tristam, "Jordan: Country Profile."

looked at the welfare services distributed in exchange for tribal loyalty.[65] Others look toward the fear of future domestic tensions, either between Palestinians and Jordanians or from Islamist-secular tensions.[66] Although the monarchy has been vital in reducing tensions emerging from internal divisions, the pervasive and instrumental role played by the monarchy to secure national well-being via external actors is often missing from existing suppositions and analyses. Today, Jordan is completely reliant on the United States, just as the Hashemites have become indispensable to the Americans.[67]

KUWAIT'S HISTORY OF CLIENTELISTIC DEPENDENCE

Kuwait reportedly sits on 10 percent of the world's oil supply, and its dependence on the United States emerges solely from its strategic need to protect itself and its oil reserves from aggressive neighbors. The most imminent threat to Kuwait has come from its neighbor, Iraq. Maintaining that Kuwait is an Iraqi province, Iraq has threatened the country with military aggression. The British were instrumental in protecting Kuwait from Iraqi hostility throughout the early 1900s.[68] "Indeed," notes Mary Ann Tetreault, "the security of the nation was not problematic until the end of the nineteenth century."[69] Tensions with Iran and its revolutionary stance against pro-American Gulf regimes, combined with the tumultuous situation in Iraq after the 2003 U.S. invasion, are also of major concern to the Kuwaitis.[70] Situated among Saudi Arabia, Iraq, and Iran, Kuwait's small size and geographical location make it all the more vulnerable.[71] As Tetreault puts it, since the end of the nineteenth century, "survival has been a major concern of Kuwait's government and population."[72] That need has only been heightened with current destabilizations in the region.

[65] Michael Fischbach, *State, Society, and Life in Jordan* (Leiden, Netherlands: Brill, 2000), 177–78; Betty Anderson, *Nationalistic Voices in Jordan* (Austin: University of Texas Press, 2005).

[66] Laurie A. Brand, *Jordan's Inter-Arab Relations: The Political Economy of Alliance Making* (New York: Columbia University Press, 1995); Ellen Lust-Okar, "Elections under Authoritarianism: Preliminary Lessons from Jordan," *Democratization* 13, no. 3 (2006): 456–71.

[67] Fischbach, *State, Society, and Life in Jordan.*

[68] Mary Ann Tetreault, *Stories of Democracy: Politics and Society in Contemporary Kuwait* (New York: Columbia University Press, 2000), 70–71; Jill Crystal, *Oil and Politics in the Gulf: Rulers and Merchants in Kuwait and Qatar* (New York: Cambridge University Press, 1995).

[69] Mary Ann Tetreault, "Autonomy, Necessity and the Small State: Ruling Kuwait in the Twentieth Century," *International Organization* 31, no. 4 (1991): 567.

[70] Ibid., 566.

[71] Ghanim al-Najjar, *Challenges of Security Sector Governance in Kuwait.* Working Paper No. 142 (Geneva: Geneva Centre for the Democratic Control of Armed Forces, 2004; accessed at http://www.dcaf.ch/_docs/WP142.pdf).

[72] Tetreault, "Autonomy, Necessity and the Small State," 566.

Abdallah al-Sabah (r. 1950–65) oversaw the transformation of Kuwait into a wealthy oil-producing monarchy,[73] but before Kuwait's oil discoveries, it was a British protectorate. Under the guidelines of the protectorate agreement, Kuwait was allowed neither to permit foreign concessions within its territory nor to lease or lend land to any foreign power without British approval.[74] In return, the British protected Kuwait—especially from the aggression of neighboring Iraq.[75]

With the First Gulf War in 1991, the United States indisputably became the most important foreign power in the Gulf region, succeeding Great Britain, which had completed its disengagement from the region in the early 1970s.[76] But the firm alliance that has rendered Kuwait "dependent" on the United States as a client state took several years to solidify.[77] In 1961, Kuwait's political relationship with the United States involved little more that the operation of the U.S. consulate in Kuwait. More concerned with and focused on Iran and Saudi Arabia as part of its Twin Pillar security policy in the Gulf, the United States saw little benefit in Kuwait. The Kuwaitis, understanding their vulnerability as a small state among larger countries, relied for the most part on other Arab countries to secure their borders.[78] Thus for Kuwait, commitment to the pan-Arab causes, though fulfilling a patriotic obligation, was mandated by its security vulnerabilities. After all, it was other Arab countries, like Egypt and Saudi Arabia, that kept Iraq at bay in 1961 when it threatened to invade. As long as Kuwait was able to commit oil revenues to these pan-Arab causes, it could be guaranteed a certain level of protection.[79] These levels of security, however, would be shattered with the Iraqi occupation of 1990.

In the 1960s and '70s, Kuwait emerged as one of the most vocal and active participants in many of the pan-Arab causes, often at the price of distancing itself from the United States. It was active in the Office of the Boycott of the League of Arab States against Israel. Further, according to Shafeeq Ghabra, "When the United States suggested as its ambassador to Kuwait someone who worked as a counselor in Jerusalem, Kuwait refused to accept him."[80] Kuwait would not deal with anyone who had strong ties to Israel.

---

[73]Crystal, *Oil and Politics in the Gulf*, 64–65.

[74]Shafeeq N. Ghabra, "Closing the Distance: Kuwait and the United States in the Persian Gulf," in *The Middle East and the United States: A Historical and Political Reassessment*, 4th ed., ed. by David W. Lesch (Boulder, CO: Westview Press, 2007), 332.

[75]Al-Najjar, *Challenges of Security Sector Governance in Kuwait*.

[76]Crystal, *Oil and Politics in the Gulf*; Michael Herb, *All in the Family: Absolutisms, Revolution, and Democratic Prospects in the Middle Eastern Monarchies* (Albany: State University of New York Press, 1999), 78–79.

[77]Ghabra, "Closing the Distance."

[78]Ibid., 333.

[79]Tetreault, "Autonomy, Necessity and the Small State."

[80]Ghabra, "Closing the Distance," 310.

Other factors also served to distance the United States from Kuwait, including the actions of the Organization of the Petroleum Exporting Countries (OPEC) and its 1971 negotiations with U.S. companies over oil pricing. The 1973 Arab-Israeli conflict exacerbated tensions, resulting in OPEC further increasing oil prices. In addition to participating in such pan-Arab alliances, Kuwait also supported policies adopted by the nonaligned movement and the UN that were typically inimical to U.S. interests and wishes.

Nevertheless, Kuwait also had vested interests in maintaining cordial relations with the United States. Kuwait felt greater affinity with the West and the United States than with the Communist Soviet Union. Furthermore, Kuwait had made substantial investments in Europe and the United States. Despite the 1967 war, these investments paved the way in 1968 for the first official visit by a Kuwaiti to the United States. The Kuwaiti royal family had always desired closer relations with the United States, but the ongoing Arab-Israeli conflict thwarted those efforts. Hence, Kuwait developed a pattern of trying to remain silent about its strong and growing connections to the West while at the same time supporting pan-Arab issues. It did not advertise the fact that it sent most of its students to the United States for education and continued to channel billions of dollars in investments to the United States and western Europe. Kuwait was content with publicly scorning the United States for its pro-Israel policies while gradually benefiting from close ties to it.[81]

Yet the status quo in the Gulf could not be maintained. The 1979 Islamic Revolution in Iran undermined the Twin Pillar Policy the United States had advocated in the Gulf region. With the Iranian shah no longer in power to secure U.S. oil and containment interests in the Gulf, the United States only had Saudi Arabia to rely on. After the British withdrew in the 1970s, the Gulf region, especially with the growing influence of OPEC after the 1973 war, believed it could secure the region and its resources on its own. But the Soviet invasion of Afghanistan in 1979 and growing hostility between Iraq and Iran before the 1981 war led to the realization that the Gulf would need to rely on external partners for security.

Increased level of hostilities in the 1980s pushed many Gulf countries to forge closer relations with the United States, which were formalized through the Carter Doctrine—President Jimmy Carter's answer to the Nixon Doctrine. The provisions of this new doctrine stated that the "United States would not tolerate any attempt by an outside force to gain control of the Gulf region. The United States would use all means necessary, including military force to repel such an effort."[82] The doctrine highlighted the importance of the region's oil to the United States, especially given the fact that U.S. oil was diminishing as a percentage of world production. In 1938,

[81]Ghabra, "Closing the Distance."
[82]Ibid.

the United States had produced 62 percent of the world's oil, but by 1955, 80 percent of all new oil discoveries were in the Middle East. By 1962, the United States was importing two million barrels per day, and that figure more than doubled to five million barrels per day by 1973. In fact, two-thirds of the world's proven oil reserves are located in the region, emphasizing its exceptional strategic value. American demand for Middle Eastern oil continued to rise as oil discoveries in the United States declined.

The Iranian Revolution in 1979, along with the increased tension between Iraq and Iran, heightened the security vulnerabilities of the Gulf region. Although these increased hostilities pushed many Gulf countries to forge closer relations with the United States, these countries—including Kuwait—were fearful of domestic and regional reactions to those ties. As a result, Kuwait consistently opposed the pre-positioning of U.S. equipment and arms in the Gulf.[83] However, the ongoing tensions between Iran and Iraq pushed Kuwait to seek more visible assistance from the United States. Kuwait feared Iran's Islamic revolutionary stance and thus supported Iraq with logistics and aid. When Iran started attacking Kuwaiti oil tankers in 1985, it dealt the Kuwaiti economy a significant blow. Kuwaiti oil production fell from two million to 300,000 barrels a day. Thus, Kuwait turned to the United States for protection. President Ronald Reagan initially denied the request, and only after the Soviet Union agreed to fly its flags on Kuwaiti oil tankers did the United States reconsider its decision. Under the new agreement, the U.S. Navy escorted Kuwaiti oil tankers, with U.S. flags, until they were in Kuwaiti waters.[84] This operation was dubbed Operation Earnest Will.

Even though ties between the United States and Kuwait were becoming stronger, Kuwait was keen on keeping the mutually beneficial relationship a secret from its own citizens. During this period, Kuwait remained adamant about not allowing U.S. supplies or equipment on its territory. Even when the United States asked Kuwait for fuel to continue protecting Kuwaiti oil tankers, Kuwait rented other Gulf tankers to provide the fuel and would not allow the Americans on its territory. This pattern would change after the Iraqi occupation of 1990.[85]

THE IRAQI OCCUPATION OF KUWAIT AND THE LIMITS OF PAN-ARABISM

On August 2, 1990, Iraq invaded Kuwait. Before the invasion, Iraq had been issuing numerous complaints against the Kuwaitis over slant drilling for oil, border demarcations, and the sovereignty of the two islands of Bubiyan

---

[83]Ibid., 335.

[84]Ibid., 337.

[85]By 1990, however, Kuwait for the first time ever did allow the presence of a U.S. warship in its port. Ghabra, "Closing the Distance," 338; Sick, "The United States in the Gulf, " 319–20.

and Warba.[86] The Kuwaitis immediately turned to neighboring Saudi Arabia, hoping the larger monarchy would mediate the conflict; they also appealed to the Egyptians, believing that the Arab partners would show Saddam Hussein how unrealistic he had become. Yet, when all the partners met in July 1990 a disappointed Kuwait found itself on the defensive. The larger Arab mediators were devising plans for Kuwaiti concessions to Saddam to help appease the embattled leader after the devastating war with Iran. Once Iraq invaded Kuwait, it was clear to the Kuwaitis that their security needs necessitated the involvement of the United States.[87]

The Iraqis destroyed Kuwaiti buildings and industrial installations. Public and private offices, stores, hospitals, schools and homes were looted, and more than seven hundred oil wells were blown up. The war-related costs were enormous. On January 17, 1991, the United States took the offensive with a prolonged air campaign and a ground deployment that lasted only one hundred hours. On February 27, President George H. W. Bush declared the liberation of Kuwait and announced the cease-fire that would mark the end of the conflict.[88]

The war was tremendously costly for the tiny monarchy. Kuwait had to buy its security from the United States and other partners. The costs of Operations Desert Shield and Desert Storm were close to $16 billion. Kuwait also paid nearly $350 million a year for the costs incurred by the U.S. military. When the United States invaded Iraq in 2003, Kuwait had allowed close to 250,000 U.S. personnel and thousands of pieces of armor on its territory. It further allowed U.S. forces to use its Ali al-Salem and Ali al-Jaber airbases. In 2006 and 2007, Kuwait was expected to contribute $210 million for the burden-sharing support of U.S. troops in Kuwait.

After its liberation on February 26, 1991, Kuwait immediately signed a ten-year military defense treaty with the United States, the first of its kind with any Arab country.[89] In 2001, that defense treaty was renewed. These treaties allow the United States to pre-position weapons in Kuwait, train Kuwaiti forces, and conduct joint maneuvers with the Kuwaiti military. They also stipulate that the United States is Kuwait's major security guarantor, replacing the role once played by the British. In return, Kuwait was generous to the United States, allowing the largest U.S. military presence in the Gulf region to exist in its territory. Of the 300,000 U.S. troops in

[86]Ghabra, "Closing the Distance," 339.

[87]Mary Ann Tetreault, "Kuwait's Unhappy Anniversary," *Middle East Policy* 7, no. 3 (2000): 67–77 (accessed at http://www.thefreelibrary.com/KUWAIT'S+UNHAPPY+ANNIVERSARY .-a063564934); Crystal, *Oil and Politics in the Gulf*, 176.

[88]Ali Musallam, *The Iraqi Invasion of Kuwait: Saddam Hussein, His State, and International Politics* (New York: British Academic Press, 1996).

[89]Amin Saikal, "The United States and Persian Gulf Security," *World Policy Journal* 9, no. 3 (1992): 515–32. See also Dawisha, "The United States in the Middle East."

the Gulf region before the 2003 Iraqi invasion, 140,000 were stationed in Kuwait.[90] A related status of forces agreement provides that U.S. forces in Kuwait be subject to U.S. rather than Kuwaiti law.[91] The new defense treaty, signed in 2001, allows two U.S. airbases to remain in the monarchy almost at the expense of the Kuwaitis.[92] In 2006, Kuwait hosted as many as 90,000 U.S. troops. Camp 'Arifjan is a key staging facility for U.S. troops. In 2004 George W. Bush, demonstrating U.S. appreciation for Kuwait's co-operation, designated it a major non-NATO ally. In a reciprocal gesture, Kuwait committed $500 million to cover the reconstruction efforts in New Orleans after Hurricane Katrina devastated Louisiana.[93]

Kuwait has abandoned its earlier pan-Arabism. According to Ghabra, "Now that Kuwait stood in what it saw as the completely righteous position of a country dedicated to both pan-Arabism and the Palestinian cause only to be betrayed, it was now entitled to pursue its key foreign policy priorities with little care to other Arab issues. This meant that Kuwait was willing to embrace the United States more openly."[94] In fact, Kuwait permitted the United States to send troops based in Kuwait into Iraq during the 2003 war. After the Iraqi occupation, Kuwaitis were much more convinced that they must put their national priorities ahead of other pan-Arab issues. National issues started to take precedence over pan-Arab issues. As Gregory Gause puts it, "Citizens' interests [became] much more focused on their domestic agendas, rather than on glorious but impractical [pan]national agenda[s]."[95] Kuwait was "stung" by the failure of pan-Arabism to protect the country during the Iraqi occupation. Opposition and government supporters alike felt an emerging gratitude toward the American libera-tors.[96] Further, Kuwaitis felt little obligation toward one of the hottest pan-Arab issues—Palestine—especially after Yasir Arafat supported Saddam during the invasion. In 1994, Kuwait was crucial in persuading the other

[90]W. Andrew Terrill, "Kuwaiti National Security and the U.S.-Kuwaiti Strategic Relation-ship after Saddam," (Carlisle, PA: Strategic Studies Institute, September 2007; accessed at http://www.strategicstudiesinstitute.army.mil/pdffiles/pub788.pdf).

[91]Kenneth Katzmann, *Kuwait: Security, Reform, and U.S. Policy*, Congressional Research Ser-vice Report, July 5, 2006 (accessed at http://digital.library.unt.edu/govdocs/crs/permalink/meta-crs-9890:1).

[92]Karen Pfeifer, "Kuwait's Economic Quandary," *Middle East Report* 223 (2002): 10–13.

[93]Associated Press, "Kuwait to Give $500M for Katrina Relief," September 4, 2005 (accessed at http://www.foxnews.com/story/0,2933,168443,00.html).

[94]Ghabra, "Closing the Distance."

[95]F. Gregory Gause III, *Oil Monarchies: Domestic and Security Challenges in the Arab Gulf States* (New York: Council on Foreign Relations, 1994).

[96]Steve Yetiv, "Kuwait's Democratic Experiment in Its Broader International Context," *Middle East Journal* 56, no. 2 (2002): 257–62. As Gause, *Oil Monarchies*, 122, notes, "Kuwait, hav-ing suffered from military occupation, has developed a strong public consensus on the need for close military ties with the United States and other foreign powers, setting it apart from its neighbors."

Gulf monarchies to cease enforcement of the secondary and tertiary Arab boycotts of Israel.[97]

Kuwaiti foreign policy has become increasingly aligned with U.S. interests, a change observable in the patterns of UN voting in the past two decades. The Kuwait government continues to pay for all in-country military costs such as maintenance, food, and fuel, even allowing foreign companies to aid in the discovery of oil in the northern fields to intimately tie its security interests to the strategic interests of the United States and other foreign countries. U.S. equipment being deployed in postliberation Kuwait includes F/A-18C/D fighter bombers, M-1A2 Abrams tanks, armored personnel carriers, and Patriot and Hawk missiles. The United States hopes to standardize U.S. and Kuwaiti equipment while enhancing interoperability between the two nations. In 1999, Kuwait spent $3.3 billion dollars on military equipment from the United States;[98] in 2007, it was reported that the United States sold another $20 billion worth of military equipment to Saudi Arabia and five of its Gulf protectorates, including Kuwait; $13 billion worth of military equipment was supplied to Jordan and Egypt that same year.[99]

After 9-11, the relationship between the Kuwaitis and Americans grew even stronger. Kuwait invested in a public relations campaign to demonstrate its unwavering support for the United States.[100] Kuwait bolstered its efforts to protect U.S. forces in Kuwait and continues to work with the Americans in weeding out al-Qaeda suspects.[101] Since 9-11, Kuwait has also become more integrated into global economic institutions. In 1994, Kuwait became a founding member of the World Trade Organization. In February 2004, the United States and Kuwait signed a trade and investment framework agreement, often viewed as a prelude to a free trade agreement, which Kuwait has said it seeks.[102]

Kuwait has also been on a serious track to diversify its economy. On the advice of the IMF and World Bank, Kuwait began to encourage international investments throughout the 1990s. In 1995, it allowed foreign participants to buy shares in the Kuwaiti stock exchange.[103] Kuwait's direction of trade has also shifted in favor of the United States. The Kuwaiti dinar is

---

[97] Kenneth Katzman, *Kuwait: Security Reform and U.S. Policy*, Congressional Research Service Report, July 2006 (accessed at http://digital.library.unt.edu/govdocs/crs/permalink/meta-crs -9890:1).

[98] Pfeifer, "Kuwait's Economic Quandary."

[99] Patrick Martin, "Adding Fuel to the Mideast Fire: U.S. Unveils Huge Arms Package," August 1, 2007 (accessed at http://www.wsws.org/articles/2007/aug2007/mide-a01.shtml).

[100] Yetiv, "Kuwait's Democratic Experiment."

[101] Katzmann, "Kuwait: Security, Reform, and U.S. Policy."

[102] Ibid.

[103] Pfeifer, "Kuwait's Economic Quandary."

formally tied to several currencies, with the U.S. dollar being the primary currency, and interest rates in Kuwait now float directly with U.S. interests.[104] The United States has become the second-ranked purchaser of Kuwaiti exports, a shift from less that than 10 percent in the 1980s up to 20 percent in the 1990s.[105] Oil accounts for 90 to 95 percent of all Kuwait's exports but only around half of its GDP. Wholesale and retail trade, real estate, finance, construction, and business services account for the other three-fifths of Kuwait's GDP. Ten percent of Kuwait's revenue is channeled into the Future Generations Fund for the day when oil dries up. The bulk of this reserve is invested in the United States. With approximately 65 percent of the population under the age of twenty-five and close to 90 percent of employees in the private sector, creating jobs to absorb this youth bulge remains an immediate Kuwaiti priority. Kuwait hopes to attract foreign direct investment. In 2001, the Kuwaiti National Assembly passed the Foreign Direct Investment Act, which eased restrictions on foreign banks, provided long-term protection to foreign investors against nationalization or confiscation, and eliminated the requirement for foreign companies to have a Kuwaiti sponsor or partner. Kuwait has also started a program to privatize state-owned businesses and has witnessed significant growth in its GDP directly linked to oil markets.

The nonoil market has also played a significant role in diversifying the Kuwaiti economy. In 2002 this registered a rise in output to 6.2 percent from 4.0 percent a year earlier. Further, this sector's contribution to GDP rose from 54 percent to 57 percent. In 2004 Kuwait's GDP rose by 4.60 percent, in 2005 by another 6.80 percent, in 2006 by 8.30 percent, and in 2007 a very high 12.60 percent. Kuwait's current and future economic success is deeply linked to the United States. First, security agreements between the two nations provide the necessary protection to Kuwait's oil fields and secure its ability to export to world markets. Second, Kuwaiti efforts to build its nonoil sector are linked to enhancing relations with external partners—namely, the United States. Third, Kuwaiti investments are predominantly located in the United States and other Western countries, making Kuwait's current and future security and economic needs directly tied to that of the United States.[106]

Although Kuwait had struggled long and hard to avoid openly clientelistic engagement with the United States, the events surrounding Iraq's occupation of Kuwait pushed the country firmly into that role; citizens across

---

[104]National Bank of Kuwait, "Doing Business in Kuwait" (accessed at http://www.kuwait.nbk.com/investmentandbrokerage/researchandreports/doingbusinessinkuwait_en_gb.aspx).

[105]Pfeifer, "Kuwait's Economic Quandary."

[106]U.S. Central Intelligence Agency, *CIA World Fact Book: Kuwait* (accessed at https://www.cia.gov/library/publications/the-world-factbook/geos/ku.html); AME Info Services, "Kuwait: 2002 Economic Data" (accessed at http://www.ameinfo.com/25866.html).

the tiny kingdom exclaim their gratitude to the Americans. And unlike the citizens of Jordan, the citizens of Kuwait felt more reassured that there is little domestic opposition to the relationship their country has with the Americans. As such, the Kuwaitis are far less invested in securing the monarchy led by the al-Sabahs as a governing regime for the purpose of securing U.S. clientelistic access. They understand that any future regime would also honor the strong ties Kuwait has developed with the United States.

Chapter 3 examines the ways in which Islamist opposition movements have responded to the realities surrounding U.S. influence in the region. More specifically, it documents the Islamist pro-American turn in Kuwait in contrast to Islamism in Jordan.

Islamist Momentum in the Arab World

*Jordan's Islamic Action Front and Kuwait's Islamic
Constitutional Movement*

IN THE PAST THREE DECADES, MODERATE ISLAMIST MOVEMENTS HAVE INCREASINGLY galvanized the support of their populations, even as they remain a source of concern for many citizens, policy makers, and leaders. The popularity of their positions on anticolonialism, democratic and economic reforms, and their reconnection with core Islamic values has garnered much support for Islamist program initiatives. Islamists like the Jordanian Islamic Action Front (IAF) promise to improve the lives of ordinary citizens while simultaneously pointing out how the national agenda has been hijacked by a debilitated leader intimately linked to the United States and Israel. The IAF continues to promise independence from the United States. This message of independence finds mass support among observant and nonobservant Muslims alike. In Kuwait, the ICM enjoys a similarly strong base of support, but unlike the IAF, its focus remains primarily domestic and not international. The ICM advances a conservative Islamic doctrine, but serves as a pro-American force in Kuwait.

To better understand the anti-American positions of the IAF in contrast to the ICM, it is vital to understand the evolution of their programmatic initiatives in Jordan and Kuwait. This chapter first offers a general overview of Islamist positions vis-à-vis the United States in both Jordan and Kuwait. Second, it emphasizes the exogenous nature of anti-Americanism, arguing that it is a function of U.S. policies. I also show how international developments influenced Islamist stances relative to the United States. Jordan's dependency on the West, the continuation of the occupation of Palestinian lands by Israel, the Jordanian peace treaty with Israel, the so-called War on Terror, and the War on Iraq have further reinforced anti-U.S. sentiment among Jordan's Islamist opposition. In the Kuwaiti case, Saddam Hussein's occupation of Kuwait, U.S. liberation efforts, and the 2003 Iraq War have positively shaped Islamist opinion of the United States. Finally, the chapter posits that the democratic reversals in Jordan, which marked much of the

1990s and the early years of the twenty-first century, were directly linked to the fear of anti-U.S. opposition movements then gaining momentum. At the forefront of these movements was the IAF. Thus, Jordan's rationale for democratic reversals emerged from the goal of marginalizing anti-American forces in the kingdom. Jordan accomplished these reversals by maintaining parliamentary inefficacy and limiting both Islamist access to that institution and the freedoms of civil society more generally.

In Kuwait, the past two decades have been marked with increasing levels of democratization. Kuwaiti Islamists were not threats to democratic developments. Citizens in Kuwait galvanized their efforts to push for more democracy, often eliciting the support of Islamist groups. These democratic developments led to greater empowerment of the legislative body and increasing checks on the monarchy. The Kuwaiti Islamists were relatively pro-American, which is why they were not seen as threats to the Kuwaiti national well-being.

The chapter concludes with a discussion about the role regimes and the United States play in sustaining barriers to democracy in these settings. Both the Hashemites and the United States are satisfied with the authoritarian status quo in Jordan. While the United States has been lukewarm in its democratization efforts in Kuwait, it is more likely to demand greater democracy in that kingdom than it is in Jordan. This last section shows the ways in which the preferences of the regimes and the patron interact to shape debates about democratization at the domestic level.

Although this chapter does not deal with the issue of whether the Jordanian regime engineers or orchestrates the status quo in Jordan, it does argue that the regime benefits from the existence of Islamist movements. The monarchy is both threatened and bolstered because of the existing opposition. The monarchy has used the Islamist threat to its own advantage, signaling to the United States and other Western countries the need to stall democratization, which in turn continues to empower Islamists and increase anti-U.S. sentiment in the country and the region. And without an alteration of U.S. foreign policy, it appears support for the regime by the United States and those would-be Jordanian democrats will continue to persist.

ISLAMISTS AND ANTI-AMERICAN POSITIONS ACROSS THE ARAB WORLD

Since the inception of the Muslim Brotherhood by Hasan al-Banna in 1928, Islamist movements have directly challenged Western dominance in the Arab world.[1] The Brotherhood saw in itself the indigenous and authentic response to the social, economic, and political ills plaguing Arab society.

[1] Yvonne Yazbeck Haddad, "Islamist Perceptions of U.S. Policy in the Middle East," in *The Middle East and the United States: A Historical and Political Reassessment*, 4th ed., ed. David W. Lesch (Boulder, CO: Westview Press, 2007), 504–32.

Its desire to control the destiny of the Arab world found popular support across the region. The Brotherhood was appalled by the Western discourse that treated the Arab world as inferior and uncivilized, and thus deserving of Western forms of control. By embracing Islam the Arab world could not only reduce the influence of the West but could further develop and prosper in ways hindered by the Western presence. "Their goal," notes Yvonne Yazbeck Haddad, "was to initiate involvement in the unfolding history of the world, taking control of the lives of their constituency and participating in shaping the future."[2] At their core, Islamist movements aimed to redignify the Arab world from what they saw as an embarrassing trampling from the West. Very much invested in the discourse of self-determination, they also championed the Palestinian cause. Not only was Israel an unacceptable presence in the region, they maintained, but its existence should be a constant source of shame for Muslims everywhere.

Islamist movements have little faith or trust in the West, especially the United States. They point to a history of British colonialism, which culminated in the Sykes-Picot Agreement of 1916,[3] dividing the region into numerous states without regard for elite and citizen opinions. That the post–World War I Western powers sanctioned these divisions is another layer of Western disregard for Muslim heritage and society. Criticism of American support for the Israeli state, a centerpiece in Islamist platforms, also garners support from nationalist supporters. Further, U.S. support for oppressive and authoritarian regimes, coupled with the U.S. occupation of Iraq, has bolstered the credibility and legitimacy of Islamist movements across the region. Islamists believe that "Arab nations and peoples have continued to be subservient to foreign domination," which they describe as "a continuing predatory relationship."[4] Hence, one of the most basic popular Islamist stances in most countries in the Arab world is skepticism about regime ties to the United States. Islamists continue to reject "perceived U.S. schemes to bring the Muslim world under its cultural hegemony and to empower Israel over the Arabs and Muslims."[5] This is the most popular position of Islamist movements. The continued Israeli occupation and the U.S. incursion into Iraq remain points that galvanize much anger among the Arab masses and play into Islamist mobilization strategies. According to Graham Fuller, because the Arab world is operating in a negative international environment, these factors continue to bolster support for Islamism across the region.[6]

---

[2]Ibid., 506.

[3]As the Ottoman Empire was on the verge of collapse, negotiators François Georges-Picot and Sir Mark Sykes, in a secret agreement, divided the Middle East between France and England.

[4]Haddad, "Islamist Perceptions of U.S. Policy in the Middle East," 507.

[5]Ibid., 525.

[6]Graham E. Fuller, "Islamists in the Arab World: The Dance around Democracy," Carnegie Paper no. 49 (Washington, DC: Carnegie Endowment for International Peace, September 2004).

These anti-U.S. stances help mobilize the Islamist Jordanian street as well. Given the significant percentage of Jordanians of Palestinian origin and Jordan's proximity to Iraq, Jordanians are skeptical and even enraged by U.S. policies in the region. Indeed, several studies continue to demonstrate that a civilizational divide does not separate the Arab and Muslim worlds; rather, the fissure stems from U.S. policies in the region, and especially their perceived bias toward Israel.[7] In a 2003 survey, Shibley Telhami found that the vast majority of Arabs—59 percent in Lebanon, 79 percent in Egypt, 86 percent in the UAE, 91 percent in Morocco, 80 percent in Jordan, and 95 percent in Saudi Arabia—all had unfavorable opinions of the United States.[8] Foreign policy was the most cited reason for these opinions; 58 percent of the Lebanese, 46 percent of the Egyptians, 47 percent of people in the United Arab Emirates, 59 percent of the Moroccans, 58 percent of the Jordanians, and 67 percent of the Saudis stated unhappiness with U.S. foreign policies. A year earlier, a public opinion poll conducted by Gallup found that an overwhelming majority of citizens across the region denounced U.S. policies as "ruthless, aggressive, conceited, and arrogant."[9] These negative attitudes have increased since the United States has played a more assertive and unilateral role in the region after the fall of the Soviet Union.

The IAF and Its Anti-American Positions

In my open-ended interviews with citizens in Jordan, three different sets of issues characterized support for and opposition to the IAF.[10] Supporters of the IAF were more likely to reject the monarchy and the peace treaty with Israel, resent levels of political deliberalization and government corruption, and defend more Shari'a-oriented policies in the kingdom. Those less supportive of the IAF were more likely to validate the monarchy, corroborate the role of the United States and the peace treaty with Israel, and tolerate the antidemocratic practices of the regime.

[7]Shibley Telhami, "Arab Public Opinion on the United States and Iraq: Postwar Prospects for Changing Prewar Views" *Brookings Review* 21(2003): 24–27; Mohaned al-Hamdi and Mohamed Mostafa, "Political Islam, Clash of Civilization, U.S. Dominance and Arab Support of Attacks on American: A Test of a Hierarchical Model," *Studies in Conflict and Terrorism* 30, no. 8 (2007): 723–36; Mark Tessler, "Arab and Muslim Political Attitudes: Stereotypes and Evidence from Survey Research." *International Studies Perspectives* 4 (2003): 175–80; Marc Lynch, "Anti-Americanism in the Arab World," in *Anti-Americanism in World Politics*, ed. Peter J. Katzenstein and Robert O. Keohane (Ithaca, NY: Cornell University Press, 2007), 196–224; Ray Takeyh, "Uncle Sam in the Arab Street," *National Interest*, April 1, 2004 (accessed at http://www.allbusiness.com/government/3584148-1.html).

[8]Telhami, "Arab Public Opinion."

[9]Gallup Organization, *The 2002 Gallup Poll of the Islamic World* (Princeton, NJ: Gallup Organization, 2002).

[10]See chapter 4 for a detailed discussion of interviewee selection.

These clear divisions extend beyond the Palestinian/Jordanian cleavage and are increasingly structured around economic interests. Jordan's aspiring middle-class members, especially those who stand to benefit from greater global integration, are more likely to favor the status quo and the regime, while those less invested in globalization are more likely to support the IAF. This pattern holds among those of both Palestinian and Jordanian origin.[11] Jordanians hopeful that globalization can improve their daily lives were much more skeptical about the IAF's influence and worried that if it gained further power through democracy, the IAF could undermine the integration of Jordan into the world economy. Hence, my argument here is that the IAF serves as a vehicle to mobilize and galvanize mass popular discontent on issues that include foreign policy issues, among other things. The IAF is the most effective, best organized, and largest movement in Jordan. Thus, understanding the factors that structure its anti-American platforms is crucial when assessing its success in mobilizing significant sectors of the Jordanian population.

The IAF is a recent phenomenon. Until 1992, the organization was folded into the larger Jordanian Muslim Brotherhood, which has consistently criticized the role of the West in Jordan. In the late 1950s the Brotherhood was loud in voicing its criticism of the close relations its regime shared with the British. It was further frustrated by the regime's reliance on the British for security and military advice.[12] The Brotherhood denounced a U.S. aid offer in 1957 with the slogan, "No reconciliation [with Israel], no dollar, no atheism, and no imperialism."[13] When Jordan did not break ties with Egypt after the signing of the 1979 Camp David Accords, the Jordanian Muslim Brotherhood was infuriated.[14] These patterns among the Islamists have persisted, and in fact, anti-U.S. sentiment among Islamists has grown even more sharply as unpopular U.S. measures in the region persisted under the presidential administration of George W. Bush.

From its early inception, the Muslim Brotherhood in Jordan was committed to confronting the "Zionist enemy" in Palestine,[15] in which it did not

[11] For a discussion on how Jordanians of Palestinian descent find themselves mobilized behind the monarchy due to their economic interests, see Nicolas Pelham, "Jordan's Balancing Act," *Middle East Report Online*, February 22, 2011 (accessed at http://www.merip.org/mero/mero022211). Pelham notes that "the offspring of the Palestinian fighters who led the 1970 revolt against King Hussein now find themselves among the king's most ardent defenders. Having reinvented themselves as business men, they led a real estate boom in Amman, turning the Jordanian capital into the most populous Palestinian city in the world."

[12] Jillian Schwedler, *Faith in Moderation: Islamist Parties in Jordan and Yemen* (New York: Cambridge University Press, 2007).

[13] Nathan Brown, "Jordan and Its Islamic Movement: The Limits of Inclusion?" Carnegie Paper no. 74 (Washington, DC: Carnegie Endowment for International Peace, 2006).

[14] Quintan Wiktorowicz, "Islamists, the State and Cooperation," *Arab Studies Quarterly* 21, no. 4 (1999): 4–12.

[15] Schwedler, *Faith in Moderation*; Amnon Cohen, *Political Parties in the West Bank under the Jordanian Regime, 1949–1967* (Ithaca, NY: Cornell University Press. 1982); Marion Boulby, *The*

differ much from the larger Muslim Brotherhood operating in Egypt. While the Egyptian Brotherhood cast itself as an opposition movement to the regime, the Jordanian regime worked hard not to transform the Brotherhood into a "loyal" opposition, allowing it great freedoms and leeway. This strategy served two purposes. First, King Abdullah I did not want to see the Muslim Brotherhood gain momentum as an opposition movement similar to the Brotherhood in Egypt and elsewhere. Second, the regime also wanted to check the power of more pro-Arab and nationalist forces, including leftist and communist organizations. This tactic, employed regularly in Arab history (for example, Sadat in Egypt), allowed Islamists the platform to grow while denying secular, leftist, and communist opposition movements the same right. As a result, Islamist movements—including Jordan's—would become the central mouthpieces of anti-U.S. strategies across the region.

While most political organizations in Jordan were banned from 1957 to 1989, the regime allowed the Muslim Brotherhood considerable space to operate, disseminating educational programs to Islamize society. The Brotherhood used mosques as sites through which to get its message out and to mobilize its base. King Hussein even conceded the ministry of education to the Brotherhood, meaning that the Muslim Brotherhood not only worked closely with the regime but even saw itself as a strong ally, ridding Jordan of leftist, infidel, communist, and pro-Soviet entities.[16]

When King Hussein allowed for free and fair parliamentary elections in 1989, the Muslim Brotherhood had a comparative "mobilization" advantage over all other parties. As a result, it won 40 percent of the vote. After factoring in alliances and coalitions, it safely controlled a majority in the legislative body. The king rewarded the Brotherhood by giving its leaders dominant positions on his cabinet. The Brotherhood was handed the portfolios for the departments of health, social development, justice, Awqaf and Islamic affairs, and education. Although extremely important and influential, none of the portfolios involved the ability to influence foreign policy. The regime would not allow the Islamists a hand in international affairs.

While the Islamists celebrated their success, the regime had other plans. The successes of 1989 marked the beginning of the Brotherhood's gradual marginalization from the mainstream political process. In preparation for the peace treaty with Israel, King Hussein reorchestrated the political process to ensure a dilution of the Islamist influence.[17] Fearful of its astound-

Muslim Brotherhood and the Kings of Jordan, 1945–1993 (Lanham, MD: Rowman and Littlefield, 1999).

[16]Ellen Lust-Okar, *Structuring Conflict in the Arab World: Incumbents, Opponents, and Institutions* (New York: Cambridge University Press, 2007); Glenn E. Robinson, "Defensive Democratization in Jordan," *International Journal of Middle East Studies* 30, no. 3 (1998): 387–410.

[17]Laurie A. Brand, "The Effects of the Peace Process on Political Liberalization in Jordan," *Journal of Palestinian Studies* 28, no. 2 (1999): 52–67; Russell E. Lucas, *Institutions and the Politics*

ing victory in 1989, King Hussein moved to reduce the Brotherhood's influence by altering the electoral laws to weaken its presence in parliament. The electoral changes of 1993, which moved the system to a one person/one vote paradigm rather than list-proportional representation, accomplished precisely the intended outcome, and the 1993 parliament had much less Islamist representation; the IAF was only able to win seventeen of eighty seats. As a result of the government's marginalizing tactics, the IAF boycotted the 1997 elections. The elections of 2003 and 2007 witnessed the further marginalization of Islamists in parliamentary representation.

Though deliberate electoral manipulation and government harassment have reduced its formal political presence, the IAF continues to dominate Jordan's associational landscape. Its associational networks extend to schools, health care clinics, mosques, charitable societies, and women's associations.[18] An examination of IAF civil society influence, especially in the realm of professional associations, solidifies the notion that Islamists are a force to be reckoned with. Even while the government has limited the IAF's parliamentary influence, the group still dominates the associational terrain, sweeping elections year in and year out.[19] Its messages, ideologies, and anti-U.S. and anti-Israel platforms remain quite popular among many segments of Jordanian society.

IAF SUPPORT

The Jordanian-Israeli Peace Treaty (1994), the second Palestinian Intifada (2000–2005), the ongoing War on Terror (2001–), and the War in Iraq (2003–) have served to galvanize Jordanian public opinion against the United States. The IAF has been able to sway a significant percentage of the Jordanian population to its causes. And support for the Islamists in Jordan and elsewhere in the Arab world is significant—but difficult to gauge accurately because of the lack of transparent and open elections. Scholars place popular support for Islamists anywhere between 20 percent and 50 percent of the electorate.[20] In recent elections across the Arab world, Islamists clearly emerged as the major opposition forces. The Parti de la Justice et du Développement

---

of Survival in Jordan: Domestic Responses to External Challenges, 1988–2001, SUNY Series in Middle Eastern Studies (Albany: State University of New York Press, 2006).

[18]Wiktorowicz, "Islamists, the State and Cooperation"; Janine Clark, *Islam, Charity, and Activism: Middle-Class Networks and Social Welfare in Egypt, Jordan, and Yemen*, Indiana Series in the Middle East Studies (Bloomington: Indiana University Press, 2003); Schwedler, *Faith and Moderation*.

[19]Marc Lynch, *State Interests and Public Spheres: The International Politics of Jordan's Identity* (New York: Columbia University Press, 1999).

[20]Jillian Schwedler, "Democratization, Inclusion and the Moderation of Islamist Parties," *Development* 50, no. 1 (2007): 57, places support between 20 percent and 50 percent. F. Gregory Gause III, "Can Democracy Stop Terrorism?" *Foreign Affairs*, September–October 2005 (accessed at http://fullaccess.foreignaffairs.org/20050901faessay84506/f-gregory-gause-iii/can

(Justice and Development Party) in Morocco made remarkable gains in the 2002 elections, coming in third—right behind the long-institutionalized Socialist Union of Popular Forces and the Independence Party. In Bahrain, Islamists won a majority of the parliamentary seats that same year. In 2011, the party made significant gains in parliament, winning 107 of 395 seats. Yemen witnessed the Islamist Islah win of 46 of 301 seats, becoming the key opposition party there. In Kuwait and Jordan, Islamists continue as the key opposition blocs in each parliament.[21]

The Jordanian regime believes the IAF is a force to contend with. That the regime continues to liberalize and then deliberalize and look for ways to limit the influence of the Islamists in both parliament and civil society are yet additional reminders of the movement's potent influence. In 2007,[22] the IAF stated that it could easily win a majority under free and fair conditions.[23] This dominant influence of the IAF in the public sphere is echoed across Amman. Citizens and elites alike speak of the IAF's influence in the political and civic spheres, documented through my interviews in Jordan.

The political and civil elite in Jordan possess a clear understanding that the Islamists constitute a significant power base that garners legitimacy and respect among the citizens of the kingdom. Yet the reasons for the IAF's success are multifaceted. Coupled with the movement's smart organizational skills, a political environment of war and conflict has led directly to growing anti-U.S. sentiment. Civil society leaders further document other reasons for the IAF's strong presence. For example, the head of the al-Ramleh Society in Amman—a nongovernmental organization (NGO) established in 1971 to help promote human rights, educate the needy, and provide basic economic assistance—explained the overwhelming presence of the IAF in the Jordanian civic sphere and attributed IAF success to two factors. First, he felt its organizational abilities were far more effective than those of other groups. Other political parties did not target the grass roots the way the IAF did. Second, he believed that the overall political environment in Jordan wasn't hospitable to political parties in general, but that the Islamists had the advantage of mosques on their side.[24]

-democracy-stop-terrorism.html?mode=print), similarly attributes significant support to the Islamists.

[21]Gause, "Can Democracy Stop Terrorism?"

[22]The IAF demanded that Prime Minister Marouf al-Bakhit bring in international observers, a request the prime minister denied. The IAF fielded twenty-two candidates (down from thirty in 2003), and it only won six seats. The IAF blames the government for corrupt practices and electoral fraud. See Curtis R. Ryan, *Jordan: Islamic Action Front Presses for Role in Governing* (Washington, DC: Carnegie Endowment for International Peace, 2006; accessed at http://www.carnegieendowment.org/arb/?fa=show&article=20919).

[23]Brown, "Jordan and Its Islamic Movement," 12.

[24]Judy Barsalou, *Islamists at the Ballot Box: Findings from Egypt, Jordan, Kuwait, and Turkey*, United States Institute of Peace Special Report no. 144 (Washington, DC: United States Insti-

For the longest time Islamists could use the institution of the mosque as a site for political mobilization. The continuing weakness of other political parties allows the IAF to grow in strength and influence. By 1994, mosques had lost much of the autonomy they previously enjoyed. When it became apparent that Islamist sympathizers, imams, and IAF party members were using the mosques to mobilize popular sentiment against the treaty with Israel, the government circumscribed mosque autonomy. Since then the Jordanian government has placed greater restrictions on mosque activity. Imams have to have their sermons approved by government, and mosques are shut down between prayer times so that citizens don't use them as meeting arenas.[25] This technique has proven far more efficient, from a security perspective, than having to keep mosques under surveillance twenty-four hours a day; secret services need only monitor mosque activity during prayer times.

Across my interviews with elites in Jordan, it became clear that civil society leaders felt the IAF had appropriated major segments of the Jordanian street. Not only are the ideological underpinnings of the movements appealing, but some, like al-Urdun al-Jadid's Hussein Abu Rumman, attributed the movement's success to its ability to appeal to common citizens. "They can mobilize because they can communicate with the people," he said. At the Charitable Hashemite Organization, leaders there agreed: "Not only are [IAF members] well-organized but they know how to say the right slogans."[26] Enjoying widespread appeal and support, the IAF remains Jordan's most visible and recognized opposition movement.

Juxtaposed is the fear that such support might undermine Jordan's larger economic interests, especially as they relate to the United States. One leader of an international relief organization said, "I can't blame the government for removing democracy. The government has had to revoke these laws to control the Islamists." He went on to say, "Before we move on to demand more democracy we need to ensure that the economic well-being of Jordan is secure." This leader firmly believes in the benefits of globalization and stronger linkages to the United States. He worries that Islamists can harm these linkages. Other civic leaders committed to charity, democracy, and human rights shared these sentiments. Commented another leader, "Pan-Arabism is dead. Arab countries do nothing for Jordan. At least the G-8 countries try to help and the U.S. does a lot for us."[27]

tute of Peace, 2005 (accessed at http://www.usip.org/pubs/specialreports/sr144.html). Barsalou notes that due to Islamist organizational capital and the fact that they have relied on mosques for mobilizational purposes, Islamists have the most to gain from more liberalization.

[25]Nonetheless, 30 percent of Jordan's mosques escape government surveillance due to budgetary issues; anonymous civil society leader, interview with the author, summer 2005.

[26]Interview with the author, summer 2005.

[27]Interview with the author, summer 2005.

While conducting my interviews with elites and citizens alike in Jordan, I had expected to hear more concerns about the potential conservative ramifications of Islamist agendas, or worries that Islamic Shari'a doctrines would harm democracy. But these issues, although of concern to some, were not at the forefront of citizens' minds. In fact, I found significant support for the concept of Shari'a, although its multiple definitions are quite elastic. For example, the leader of the al-Ramleh Society went on to explain that he is not against Islam. "If we return to Islam," he noted, "it is compatible with democracy. Islam gives us the best of everything. If Islam is applied and it does not work, it is not about Islam, it is about its application." Again, this leader sees nothing inherently wrong with Islam; rather, the problem is with its application in the Islamist movements themselves and what he labels "irrational" understandings of Jordan's interests.[28]

The IAF has done little to quell the anxieties that are increasingly emerging among those who feel that the success and stability of Jordan rely on uncomfortably close relations with the United States. Although citizens across the kingdom resent the United States, middle- and upper-class citizens of the kingdom believe that greater prosperity for Jordan will arrive at the hands of stronger ties with the United States and the West. For its part, the IAF continues to inflame anxieties for many across the kingdom. In the 2007 parliamentary elections, Zaki Sa'ad, then general secretary of the IAF, said that his movement could win a significant percentage of parliamentary seats. Sa'ad was quoted in the *Washington Post* as saying that if his party were to win a significant number of seats, Jordan's relationship with the United States and Israel would change. He was unambiguous about the desire to revoke the peace treaty with Israel. He said, "We are clear. We reject this treaty because it is against Jordan's national interest. . . . We will ask for a referendum on it."[29] Not only did the IAF claim it would sever the treaty with Israel, but it also noted that it would distance Jordan from the United States. Further, the IAF has recently taken positions that are not popular with the United States. For example, it has increasingly embraced Palestine's Hamas and Lebanon's Hizbullah.[30]

Sa'ad, elected general secretary of the IAF in 2006, represents the more extreme faction within the IAF and has close relations with Hamas's Khalid Misha'al in Syria. In the same interview Sa'ad said, "We have a special feeling for Hamas in the face of the Zionist Project." Such statements find a consid-

[28]Interview with the author, summer 2005. I take up this theme about Shari'a understandings in more detail in chapter 4.

[29]David Williams, "Political Islam's Opportunity in Jordan," *Washington Post*, April 13, 2006 (accessed at http://www.washingtonpost.com/wp-dyn/content/article/2006/04/12/AR20060 41201897_pf.html).

[30]Hassan Barari, "Elections in Jordan: Poor Showing for Islamists," December 13, 2007 (accessed at http://www.ikhwanweb.com/Article.asp?ID=14866&SectionID=0).

erable audience in Jordan. The vast majority of Jordanians condemn Israel's policies in the West Bank and Gaza, and the considerable Palestinian constituency in Jordan also means that the IAF is popular among that group as well. An IAF leader put it to me this way: "We will support those who want to attack the Israeli military."[31] Yet, these statements and others by the IAF keep Jordanians who don't necessarily support the IAF feeling vulnerable.

THE 1994 PEACE TREATY WITH ISRAEL

The 1994 Jordanian Peace Treaty with Israel marked a major fissure in the relationship between the IAF and the Jordanian regime. Several factors arguably pushed Jordan into the U.S. camp and hence toward favoring the Treaty. Jordan was suffering the economic fallout of the post–Cold War era. Hit with economic crises linked to post–Cold War structural adjustment programs, Jordan was in search for quick fixes to an increasingly dismal situation. Further, Jordan was isolated and vulnerable. With growing political hostility in Iraq and Syria, and instability in Palestine, Jordan felt all the more insecure. Thus, it sought to solidify its relationship with the United States for primarily economic reasons, but for reasons of security as well.

As such, King Hussein became adamant about signing the peace treaty, expediting its passage with very little discussion. Both parliament and the cabinet were barred from any real policy-making roles. Neither body was informed of the details of the Washington Agreement, signed in July 1994, or the peace treaty of October 1994 until after they were signed.[32] The monarchy found support among tribal areas, business sectors, and military elites. The Islamists, along with the leftists and Arab nationalists, opposed the treaty. In their response, they formed the Committee for Resisting Submission and Normalization,[33] established on May 14, 1994, and consisting of

---

[31]Interview with the author, summer 2005.

[32]Russell Lucas, *Institutions and the Politics of Survival in Jordan: Domestic Responses to External Challenges, 1988–2001* (New York: State University of New York Press, 2006), 205.

[33]Since the peace treaty the IAF has mobilized against the regime, often serving as the major voice behind such national alliances as the Committee for Resisting Submission and Normalization and the Committee for Protecting the Country and for Antinormalization. Further, the IAF was the key player behind the Higher Committee for the Coordination of National Opposition Parties (HCCNOP). The committee, consisting of thirteen opposition parties, continues to voice its objection to the peace treaty with Israel and the decreasing levels of political freedoms in the kingdom. This alliance is seen as a somewhat formal break between the strong alliance of the Muslim Brotherhood and the regime. Not only does the HCCNOP demonstrate the increasing oppositional role the IAF plays in Jordan but indeed the alliance—with other opposition movements, several of which are leftist in orientation—also forces the IAF to advance common purposes like the peace treaty, and economic and political development; these themes are unlike an Islamic Shari'a agenda and keep the coalition intact.

eight opposition political parties. Its goal was and remains to ensure that relations with Israel are not normalized. It immediately began denouncing the Treaty and urged professional associations to blacklist members who had ties to Israel. Most associations complied.[34]

The IAF has been consistent in its policy preferences—especially those regarding Palestine, Israel, and the United States. It seeks the complete liberation of Palestine and the implementation of an Islamic state in Jordan. Although the parameters of what defines an Islamic government are malleable and often left to interpretation, the IAF's position on Palestine has remained more consistent. The group holds the position, as do many other Muslim opposition movements, that Palestine is Muslim land and therefore no one government can sign it away. According to Gudrun Krämer, the IAF has "called for jihad to liberate all of Palestine and condemned negotiations with the Zionist enemy as unacceptable under Islamic law. . . ."[35]

This antinormalization stance has persisted since the signing of the 1994 treaty with Israel and has been widely debated in parliament. In its electoral program (1993–97), the IAF declared, "Our struggle with the Jews is an ideological struggle . . . it's not based on a struggle about borders but rather it's about a struggle about existence." In this program, the IAF continued by saying, "Establishing any diplomatic or economic ties with [Israel] is submission to U.S. policy."[36] The same program outlines the IAF's strategy toward U.S. hegemony in the region by stating, "We reject U.S. hegemony in the region and our country . . . and ask to remove U.S. influence from Arab and Islamic lands."[37] These points were reiterated in its 1997–2003 program. In the 2003–7 program the same points were raised, but in addition the Iraq War of 2003 was mentioned. The IAF declared its opposition to the Iraqi occupation by stating that the occupation was an attempt "to remold the region politically and to change its Arab and Islamic identity to cohere with American and Zionist aspirations."[38] It went on to state, "We affirm the linkage between the Zionist Occupation of Palestine and the Anglo-American Occupation of Iraq. It is imperative that Arab and Islamic

[34]Janine A. Clark, "The Conditions of Islamist Moderation: Unpacking Cross-Ideological Cooperation in Jordan," *International Journal of Middle East Studies* 38 no. 4 (2006): 539–60; Lucas, *Institutions and the Politics of Survival in Jordan.*

[35]Gudrun Krämer, "Good Counsel to the King: The Islamist Opposition in Saudi Arabia, Jordan, and Morocco," in *Middle East Monarchies: The Challenge of Modernity*, ed. Joseph Kostiner (Boulder, CO: Lynne Rienner, 2000), 273.

[36]Jabhat al-'Amal al-Islāmī [Islamic Action Front], *Al-Barnāmij al-Intikhābī l-murashahīn Hizb Jabhat al-'Amal al-Islāmī (1993–1997)* [The Electoral Platform of the Islamic Action Front (1993–1997)] (Amman, Jordan: Jabhat al-'Amal al-Islāmī, 1993), 47.

[37]Ibid., 48.

[38]Jabhat al-'Amal al-Islāmī [Islamic Action Front], *Al-Barnāmij al-Intikhābī l-murashahīn Hizb Jabhat al-'Amal al-Islāmī (2003–2007)* [The Electoral Platform of the Islamic Action Front (2003–2007)] (Amman, Jordan: Jabhat al-'Amal al-Islāmī, 2003), 39.

positions become unified on these issues."[39] In its 2007–11 electoral program, the IAF repeated these points once again.[40] In fact, then-deputy of the IAF Abdallah al-'Akayilah's vow to resist normalization remained in effect. The regime's increasing repression of popular discontent also exacerbates resistance to the treaty.[41] This resistance embodies both the Jordanian and Palestinian elements of the IAF. The actual deliberations about the peace treaty, before it was signed, reveal that both Palestinians and Jordanians were divided on the best strategy to pursue vis-à-vis the agreement.[42] Jillian Schwedler argues that Palestinians in the IAF had been neither consistent nor cohesive in their opposition to Israel.[43] She finds that a major cleavage emerged among Palestinians, with refugees in 1948 exhibiting a more moderate desire to continue participation in the political process. The major divide revolved around whether the IAF should continue its participation in the legislative process if the treaty were signed. In the end, the IAF agreed to continue participation in the legislative branch while simultaneously stating their commitment to the Palestinian cause and opposition to the treaty. And although many lower-house IAF deputies continued expressing their opposition to the treaty, the parliament's proregime candidates endorsed it. Inside and outside parliament, the IAF continued to voice strong disapproval of normalization with Israel. That it continued to work in parliament also generated criticism from more hard-line Islamist leaders. In my interview with Islamist leader Layth Shubaylat,[44] for instance, he voiced strong criticism of the IAF, accusing it of being co-opted by the regime. He felt that the Jordanian-Israeli Peace Treaty had been "dictated to Jordan by the Americans" and it was therefore a duty of Jordanians to emphatically oppose the treaty. Shubaylat, like other members of the IAF, remains committed to antinormalization. In fact, in most of its election platforms, the IAF has referred to Israel consistently as the "Zionist enemy," demonstrating its disdain.[45]

The IAF continued to use parliament to object to the peace process by introducing legislation, forging alliances with other opposition movements, and remaining vocal about its opposition to the treaty. In May 1995, the opposition (including the IAF) succeeded in preventing the revocation of laws

[39]Ibid., 40.

[40]Jabhat al-'Amal al-Islāmī [Islamic Action Front], *Al-Barnāmij al-Intikhābī l-murashahīn Hizb Jabhat al-'Amal al-Islāmī (2007–2011)* [The Electoral Platform of the Islamic Action Front (2007–2011)] (Amman, Jordan: Jabhat al-'Amal al-Islāmī, 2007), 30–35.

[41]Russell Lucas, "Jordan: The Death of Normalization with Israel," *Middle East Journal* 58, no. 1 (2004): 93–111.

[42]Schwedler, *Faith and Moderation*.

[43]Ibid.

[44]Interview with the author, summer 2005.

[45]Brown, "Jordan and Its Islamic Movement"

forbidding the sale of land to Jews and boycotting the Jewish state. During that same year, when Israel announced the confiscation of lands in Arab East Jerusalem, parliament again voiced its concerns and called for a cancellation of the treaty. Parliament remains a key site of contestation of regime policy, and especially of policies linked to the Treaty. According to Marc Lynch, "[These] event[s] left a strong impression that an opposition consensus capable of overcoming regime commitments could be mobilized."[46]

Although the IAF and the opposition had few parliamentary successes, they were successful in blocking a January 1997 Israeli trade fair in Amman. The mobilization momentum behind the antinormalization forces worried the regime to the extent that it responded with further deliberalization. Laurie Brand documents this deliberalization as part and parcel of Jordan's initiation of the peace treaty. She notes that deliberalization began in 1991, when King Hussein dismissed Islamists from his cabinet and later used the electoral law of 1993 to reduce Islamist strength in parliament. As the conflict between regime and antiregime segments intensified, Hussein vowed to confront those who aimed to sabotage the peace treaty. In reality, however, he treaded carefully, keen not to completely dismiss or repress Islamists voices.

In stark contrast to his son, Hussein consistently made overtures to the opposition in order to preserve internal cohesion. He didn't appear to be willing to confront civil society with an iron fist, as Abdullah II has. When King Abdullah II assumed the reins of the monarchy, he was much less tolerant of antinormalization activity than was his father. He was also much more oppressive. Once he consolidated his base of rule, King Abdullah II further moved to reduce political and civil liberties across the Hashemite country. Civil society remained vigilant against normalization. When the much touted economic benefits of the peace process did not materialize, a growing segment of the Jordanian population showed its frustration with the treaty.

In the days preceding a major 1999 conference on antinormalization organized by the IAF and held in Amman, King Abdullah II moved to close the five main offices of Hamas there and arrested many of the Hamas leaders. He also placed increasing restrictions on the IAF. In response, the Islamists used the conference as a platform from which they urged the government to release Hamas officials and allow the Islamists to pursue their struggle against Israel. After calling on greater Arab solidarity to confront Israel, the United States, and Britain, the conference ended with Islamist leaders Ahmad 'Obaydat and Laith Shubaylat reminding members it was their national and religious duty to reject normalization with Israel.[47]

---

[46]Lynch, *State Interests and Public Spheres*, 209–11.

[47]Danishai Kornbluth, "Jordan and the Anti-Normalization Campaign, 1994-2001," *Terrorism and Political Violence* 14, no. 3, Autumn 2002.

The opposition and the regime continued to appeal to the sentiments of ordinary citizens. The regime emphasized security, stability, and economic progress, while the IAF called for the support of Palestine and Islam, and emphasized an anti-imperial stance. By the late 1990s, several factors tipped favor toward the Islamist camp. Since Hussein had signed the treaty with Israel, the peace process had been rocked by a series of problems. The Oslo peace process did little for Palestinian national aspirations. Yitzhak Rabin was assassinated. Israel was failing to honor several of its agreements with Jordan, especially on water issues and access to West Bank markets. Israeli voters picked Benjamin Netanyahu, a hawk, as prime minister. Finally, the attempted assassination on Hamas leader Khalid Misha'al in Amman exposed the vulnerability of Jordan's peace initiative. Jordanian citizens widely perceived that the signing of the agreements had enabled Israel to gather the necessary intelligence to target Misha'al. In effect, the peace treaty was seen as a means of giving Israel and the United States a free hand in Jordan, which played brilliantly into the hands of the Islamists.[48] Jordanian society increasingly became polarized between two camps: one proregime and pronormalization, the second more antiregime and antinormalization; little support fell in between.[49] The IAF has continued to profess that it would like to maintain U.S ties, as long as the United States treats Jordan with respect and dignity.

Opposition toward the peace treaty only intensified with the outbreak of the second Palestinian Intifada, or al Aqsa Intifada, in 2000. The IAF continued to call for a termination of the treaty with Israel and now publicly supported Hizbullah and Hamas. The regime's patience with the antinormalization movement reached its limit in 2001, when among the sixty-eight new names on the IAF's blacklist, which cataloged Jordanians engaged in normalized relationships with Israel, were prominent Jordanian regime leaders. State figures like Fayez Tarawnah, chief of the Royal Court, and former royal advisor 'Adnan Abu-'Odeh appeared. The IAF also released a statement that "this time around the masses will have no mercy on [the normalizers]." That the movement appeared to adopt or at least advocate violence against fellow Jordanians led the regime to confront them head on. Seven leaders of the antinormalization campaign were arrested in January 2001, including the secretary-general of the Jordanian Engineering Association, 'Ali Abu-Sukkar, who was convicted of incitement and of possession of explosives. He was later released in March of that same year.[50] In 2007, now-parliamentarian Abu-Sukkar was arrested again and sentenced to thirteen months in prison for visiting Abu Musa'ab al-Zarqawi's funeral and offering condolences to the family.

---

[48] Lynch, *State Interests and Public Spheres.*
[49] Ibid.
[50] Lucas, "Jordan: The Death of Normalization with Israel."

More recently, during the Spring 2011 Arab protests, the IAF has remained quite vocal in its opposition to the Israeli peace treaty. In March 2011, IAF deputy secretary-general Nimer al-Assaf stated, "We do not agree to the peace treaty with Israel simply because we do not feel that it is just."[51] About the presidency of Barack Obama, the head of the political office of the IAF, Zaki Bin Arshaid said, "America nowadays is working with the mentality of George W. Bush and all the promises of Obama to withdraw from Iraq or to close Guantanamo appeared to be public relation speeches which have no relation to truth, which makes us critical."[52] In a March 2010 interview, Dr. 'Abd al-Latif 'Arabiyat, founder of the IAF, established the regional affinities of the IAF with other causes. He dismissed concerns about the nature of the Hamas movement and argued that the "fight for their land against an occupation" was legitimate. He went on to say, "We support their goal and their cause." And about Iran, he questioned, "We don't approve of everything Tehran does, but still, what is the problem with Iran? We should oppose Iran for their nuclear program while we have Israel with hundred of bombs just across our border. Where is the logic of this?"[53] These regional stances, which clash with U.S. foreign policy, continue to serve as a source of concern.

This vigilant and diligent opposition to the peace treaty, the regime, and the United States has distanced some people from the IAF—especially those who stood to gain from increased economic global integration. Such staunch opposition also causes citizens to worry about the repercussions for Jordan if these opposition movements championed by the IAF gain a stronghold in the Jordanian parliament. This feeds into the sectors of the population that are proregime, less supportive of the IAF, less anti-American, and not vocally opposed to the peace treaty. At the same time, many citizens support the IAF, reject the peace treaty with Israel, profess more anti-American sentiments, and offer less support to the regime. This cleavage is further reinforced by the regime's position vis-à-vis its Islamist opposition—which, in turn, further polarizes the two camps.

OTHER ISLAMIST FORCES IN JORDAN

The reductions in liberties which primarily target the IAF are also designed to curb other smaller and more radical groups. Unlike the IAF, which merely seeks distance from the United States, these movements wish directly to

[51]Heather Murdock. "Muslim Brotherhood Sees Opportunity in Jordan." *Washington Times*, March 1, 2011.

[52]Zaki Bin Arshaid , interview with Walid al-Khatib (transcript), Center for Strategic Studies, Jordan, August 2010.

[53]'Abd al-Latif 'Arabiyat, interview with Walid al-Khatib (transcript), Center for Strategic Studies, Jordan, August 2010.

harm American interests by targeting government sites and American interests in the country. Take al-Zarqawi's al Tawḥid wal-Jihād movement, for
example, which claimed responsibility for the assassination of American
diplomat Laurence Foley on October 28, 2002. In 2004, it attempted to attack the U.S. embassy in Amman, and in 2005, it launched rocket attacks on
the port of 'Aqaba, targeting two U.S. naval vessels. More successful for al-
Zarqawi, however, were his disastrous attacks on three international hotels
in the heart of Amman—the Grand Hyatt, the Days Inn, and the Radisson
SAS. Iraqi intelligence officials had used Amman's American five-star hotels
for meetings during the Iraq War. The hotels were also signs both of greater
American penetration into and domination of Amman's capital. For radical Islamist groups like al-Zarqawi's jihad movement, these hotels would
become key targets for attacking American interests. In November 2005,
suicide bombers struck at all three hotels simultaneously, killing sixty-seven
Jordanians.[54]

Hizb ul-Tahrīr, another smaller radical Islamist movement, is committed
to the establishment of an Islamic caliphate administered under Shari'a.
Despite its small presence in Jordan, in March 2005 it delivered a letter to
parliament calling for the annulment of all political and economic agreements with Israel or face "Doom in the Hereafter."[55] The presence of these
movements has further allowed the regime to stall its democracy program.

REGIME-IAF RELATIONS: DEMOCRACY IN RETREAT

The Hashemite regime sells itself as the hope for Jordan's political and economic future. The king fashions himself as the leader who can get Jordan's
economic success right. He showcases his talents with the West while emphasizing that Jordan's survival relies on better economic improvements.[56]
The regime points out that the Islamists pose a serious threat to Jordan's new
vision for itself, which includes a commitment to enhance ties with Western
countries and bring the fruits of economic integration and globalization
to Jordan. To help the Jordanian project succeed, the regime has resorted
to tactics that include national projects like Jordan First, less tolerance

[54]Juan Cole, "A 'Shiite Crescent'? The Regional Impact of the Iraq War," *Current History* 105,
no. 687 (2006): 20–26; Schwedler, *Faith and Moderation*; and International Crisis Group Report, *Jordan's 9/11: Dealing with Jihadi Islamism*. Middle East Report no. 47 (Amman, Jordan,
and Brussels: International Crisis Group, 2004; accessed at http://www.crisisgroup.org/en/
regions/middle-east-north-africa/iraq-iran-gulf/jordan/047-jordans-9-11-dealing-with-jihadi
-islamism.aspx).

[55]International Crisis Group, *Jordan's 9/11*, 6.

[56]Scott Greenwood, "Jordan, the al-Aqsa Intifada and America's 'War on Terror,'" *Middle
East Policy* 10, no. 3 (2003): 90.

of antinormalization activity, and greater reductions of political liberties across the board.

Building National Consensus

The Jordanian regime has attempted to bolster its credibility and instrumentality for Jordan's future by building national consensus around its current policies, which include stronger relations with the United States and Israel. To do so, it has relied on a series of national projects implemented between 2002 and 2007 to mobilize mass sentiment around a Jordanian identity that places the concerns of Jordan above other nations—namely, Palestine and Iraq. In its packaging of national reforms, like the Jordan First campaign, the National Agenda, and the "We are all Jordan" slogan, it also emphasizes the ways in which groups that embrace non-Jordanian causes, like the Islamists, may harm the future development of Jordan. Not only do these national projects attempt to galvanize a national Jordanian consciousness that transcends internal cleavages but they also erect an "us versus them" dichotomy: the citizens of Jordan are either with the progress, reform, and change that will bring economic prosperity through normalization and stronger ties with the United States,[57] or they are for stagnation, instability, and war. On the side of progress, the regime is able to portray itself as a vulnerable entity undertaking important changes for the good of all Jordanian citizens. This image also helps solidify the regime's base of support.

The regime's reforms attempt to challenge Islamist messages that promise more economic justice. Directly competing against a major Islamist platform for greater economic equality, the king continues to promise a better economic future for all of Jordan. Of course, another source of fissure remains: foreign policy. The regime wants to enhance its international standing by continuing its strong alliance with the United States, part of which means maintaining the peace agreement with Israel.

The success of the regime's strategies relies on whether society will continue to allow the regime enough space to pursue its goals. By promising economic rewards in exchange for rejecting the Islamist platform, the king places himself squarely in confrontation with the Islamists. Thus far it appears that the regime has been able to win over a significant segment of the Jordanian population. Even those skeptical about the results of these globalized linkages remain compliant, worrying that the alternative is far more drastic for the kingdom than is the status quo.

The Jordanian regime has adopted three different yet complementary initiatives to enhance Jordanian national cohesion in the last decade: the

---

[57] Globalization successes are directly linked to the peace treaty with Israel. See Lamis Andoni, "Has Jordan Turned Its Back on Pan-Arabism?" *Middle East International* 573 (1998): 18–19.

Jordan First campaign, the National Agenda, and "We are all Jordan." While all three initiatives directly appeal to mass unity and prioritize the interests of Jordan above and beyond other regional issues like that of Palestine and Iraq, the National Agenda carries with it an additional appeal as well; it focuses on reform—and more specifically, economic reform—as extremely vital for the kingdom. Everything about the National Agenda is about the promise of reform, progress, and modernity. On its website, the National Agenda is referred to as "agenda al-watani" rather than the full Arabic term "Miythaq al-Watani." The use of the word *agenda*, an English word amid Arabic, signals the modernity of—as the tagline reads—"The Jordan we strive for." In other words, those who want positive change should endorse the regime's vision for the future. As the National Agenda report firmly states, "The ultimate purpose of the National Agenda is to achieve sustainable development through a transformation program that puts Jordan on a trajectory path toward fast economic growth and greater social inclusion, resulting in comprehensive strategies and initiatives developed to realize social, economic and political development, evaluate and monitor progress of its implementation according to detailed performance indicators."

The use of future payoff buzzwords like "sustainable development," "transformation program," "trajectory path toward fast economic growth," and "social, economic and political development" are all designed to convince Jordanians that the monarchy, and not the Islamists, knows the way to better their futures. The regime continues to package these national projects as part of a comprehensive reform effort that works to sell Jordan's regional security and potential for economic advancement to its citizens. With these initiatives, the king is calling on the people of Jordan to remain diligent in opposing forces that can thwart the national well-being of the country.[58]

This new social contract of reform not only promises Jordanians a better future but also allows the regime to exercise deliberalization for the purposes of the Jordanian national well-being. King Abdullah II has been quite successful in showcasing himself as the "reform-minded" leader. Even before his reform initiatives, he ascended the throne with a vision of moving Jordan expeditiously into the twenty-first century. Adopting technology across the kingdom, the king moved to digitalize Jordanian government offices and classrooms—even in rural areas, where people had never seen computers and where they still lack electricity. New bypass roads, bridges, and highways have emerged across Amman. Government offices have become more efficient, and the police now are much more accountable.

[58]For information on Jordan's national agenda, see National Agenda Steering Committee, *The National Agenda: The Jordan We Strive for 2006–2015* (Amman, Jordan: National Agenda Steering Committee, n.d.; accessed at http://www.nationalagenda.jo/Portals/0/EnglishBooklet.pdf).

These reform projects have received both support and criticism from Jordan's population. For example, citizens across Amman applauded the king's efforts—especially those among the growing younger generation and those of more middle- and upper-class backgrounds. They see in Abdullah the Jordanian future they long for. In the rural and more tribal areas, however, Abdullah's reforms have been received with less enthusiasm. In fact, these modernization efforts have further alienated the tribes, longtime reliable and compassionate supporters of the Hashemite monarchy. One such story was told to me. A frustrated woman in one of Jordan's tribal towns had lost the financial support her husband received from the monarchy. After her husband passed away, she had received no financial assistance, and she was deeply upset. Upon visiting her, King Abdullah II apologized and presented her with a computer as a gift. According to the person who told me the story, the woman did not know what to do with the computer, as she had never seen or operated one. It would have been more appropriate for the king to present her with a sheep, as was the custom. Such stories circulating in rural areas reveal the degree to which Jordanians, especially those in the tribal sectors, believe that King Abdullah II is out of touch with his constituents. Further, Abdullah II is also seen by many tribal groups in Ma'an, Karak, and Madaba, for example, as catering to Amman's urban middle- and upper-class sectors, most of whom are Palestinian, at the expense of the tribal base of support.

Further, citizen criticisms of the Jordan First campaign illustrate the differential responses to Abdullah's reforms and reveal a clear dichotomization of opinions. In general, there were those—both Palestinian and Jordanian—who worried about Jordanian commitments to fellow Arab and Muslim neighbors. To them, Jordan First was seen as a U.S./Israeli initiative to force Jordanians to abandon important national causes like Iraq and Palestine. Those of Jordanian origin were more likely to believe the reforms would unite Jordanians, although there were some in this camp who worried they would grant Palestinians additional rights, privileges, and benefits. Palestinians, especially those constituting the upper and middle classes, welcomed the reform initiatives, while working-class and refugee Palestinians viewed the reforms as a means of prioritizing all things Jordanian at the expense of everything Palestinian. They were more likely to see the reforms as a way of asserting Jordanian superiority and chauvinism while relegating Palestinians permanently to second-class citizenship. Further, there were those Jordanians and Palestinians, especially those who constituted the more educated and intellectual elite of Amman, who worried that the reforms might potentially create greater cleavages between Palestinians and Jordanians.

King Abdullah's strategy seeks to build consensus around his political and economic reforms by ensuring that all citizens remain invested in his reform initiatives. Hence, his privatization policies are most appealing to the

Palestinian business elite—but, by also giving former military folks a stake in private enterprise, he keeps the otherwise more marginal tribal elites on board, too. Although the Palestinian-Jordanian divide is not eliminated,[59] a new divide has been gradually solidified along the axis of economic opportunity. Some Jordanians see themselves as future beneficiaries of reform and development, while others imagine they have little to gain. In other words, the economic realities surrounding reform have induced a new cleavage in Jordan, one that potentially transcends the Jordanian-Palestinian divide.

Keeping the Islamists on Stage: A Strategic Choice?

The anti-American and anti-Israeli rhetoric of the IAF have served the regime in multiple ways. Primarily, the threat of the IAF has increased the strategic utility of the Hashemite monarchy to both the United States and Israel, and to segments of the Jordanian population. Further, the regime has been able to consolidate its base and reverse democratic liberties in the name of security and progress. The regime has attempted to deal with the Islamists in several ways, one of which is to give the IAF some leeway in the political sphere. It has allowed and continues to allow the Islamists space in which to mobilize and participate in the political process. Even in light of recent limitations of its freedoms, the IAF still enjoys considerable liberties when compared to Islamists elsewhere, as in neighboring Syria or even Egypt. By permitting Islamists the freedom to participate, the regime is still able to garner some (albeit dwindling) accountability from the Islamists while simultaneously showcasing Islamist strengths to society at large. In so doing the regime is able to monitor Islamist activity and suggest to supporters that Islamists constitute a dangerous threat. It is not clear whether this is the intended objective of the regime; nevertheless, it is certain that the king has been able to exploit the Islamist threat to bolster his standing with both the United States and with internal sympathizers.

In a speech delivered at Princeton University in February 2008, King Abdullah made it clear that the Islamists were divisive, jeopardizing not only his reform efforts but also peace and security in the entire region. Emphasizing the importance of American partnership for the development of the region, he said, "We must meet the expectations of this younger generation. In my region, we expect to need 200 million new jobs by 2020. Creating these opportunities will require investment and partnerships to develop new infrastructure, meet energy and water needs and improve public services and

---

[59]For example, Brand and Lust-Okar and have both carefully documented how the regime could easily flare up tensions between Palestinians and Jordanians when there was a possibility that broad coalitions could be formed to oppose the regime. See Laurie A. Brand, "Palestinians and Jordanians: A Crisis of Identity," *Journal of Palestine Studies* 24, no. 4 (1995): 46–61; and Lust-Okar, *Institutions and the Politics of Survival in Jordan*.

education. A strong Arab-American partnership must be created."[60] Having highlighted the importance of the United States for the future trajectory of the region, King Abdullah dropped the worrisome bombshell. Using the all-too-familiar binaries convincing to Western audiences—us versus them, evil versus good, progress and democracy versus stagnation and terrorism—the king delivered a powerful speech:

> I pose these questions for your consideration.... Will my region plunge into more chaos and violence, where extremism rules? Or will it be a peaceful, developing region? Will it be a region focused on conflicting radical ideologies fueled by manipulation of sectarian division? Or will it be a region reaping the benefits of globalization and strong global partnerships? Will it be a region that rejects Western alliances, perhaps violently, because they have become far too difficult to achieve? Or will it be a region that is a global partner in progress and prosperity with the West?[61]

Throughout the speech, King Abdullah systematically portrayed himself as the leader of peace and stability, a loyal ally to the United States. The alternative, in his view, is much worse. The alternative to "a peaceful, developing region" could be one fraught with "conflicting radical ideologies fueled by ... sectarian division." The threat of this alternative is a radical, violent attempt to destroy the hard work that Jordan and the United States have already accomplished.

King Abdullah continues to have authoritative discretion in all matters relating to governance. He alone appoints members of the upper house, has the ability to dismiss parliamentary members, and can pass temporary laws that further reduce the civil and political liberties of ordinary citizens. This trend has been exacerbated since 9-11 because the U.S. War on Terror has empowered the regime to assert itself. In Jordan, this war witnessed the passing of over one hundred temporary laws, all designed to curb political freedoms.[62] Targeting members of civil society organizations, many of these laws sought to quell mass displays and popular mobilization against the United States.[63] Jordan's professional associations, which have been vocal in their antinormalization and anti-U.S. pronouncements, have been frequent prey of government repression. The regime claimed that these associations were jeopardizing the country's ties to the United States, and in 2005 proposed to pass legislation limiting associational political activities.

[60]Speech given by King Abdullah at Princeton University, February 2008, webcast (accessed at http://wws.princeton.edu/webmedia/list_archives.xml?displayyear=2008).
[61]Ibid.
[62]See Jillian Schwedler, "Occupied Maan: Jordan's Closed Military Zone," *Middle East Report Online*, December 3, 2002 (accessed at http://www.merip.org/mero/mero120302).
[63]Marc Lynch, "No Jordan Option," *Middle East Report Online*, June 21, 2004 (accessed at http://www.merip.org/mero/mero062404).

The king even made it a crime to criticize Jordanian allies—including the United States.[64] Neither has the press been spared; its antinormalization rhetoric and criticisms of the regime have come under scrutiny, and press freedoms have been reduced.

King Abdullah's deliberalization policies have faced little contestation other than from the opposition movements themselves. King Abdullah has successfully made the case that Jordan's reform trajectory highly relies on greater acceptance from the West, and especially the United States. Ordinary Jordanians monitoring the situation believe that better ties with America can benefit the kingdom. Yet they also worry about the repercussions of aggravating the United States. Even those who believe closer U.S. ties are important see the United States as a regional powerhouse that does not hesitate to flex its muscles in the region. They are not without their reasons. The United States has dealt and is capable of dealing Jordan devastating blows—severing aid, limiting trade, placing sanctions, and even attempting to deploy troops. Lamis Andoni, a prominent reporter for the Al Jazeera TV network, expresses this sentiment: "Politically [since the peace treaty], Jordan is no longer in a position to take a stand that can even be perceived as obstructing U.S. interests in the region if it wants to guarantee a regional role and the flow of aid."[65]

The IAF further reinforces these concerns by trying to manipulate anti-U.S. sentiment on the ground. After Hamas won the elections in Palestine in 2006, the leader of the IAF's parliamentary bloc surprised Jordanians by going beyond the claim that under a fair law "Islamists in Jordan would obtain a majority" to assert that they "are prepared to assume control over the executive branch to realize the hopes of the people."[66] According to the IAF, "the hopes of the people" will be realized when ties with the United States and Israel are severed. The regime directly benefits from this vocal and significant opposition. If the Islamists were weaker, it is doubtful whether the regime would be able to garner the level of support that it does.[67] The strength of the IAF signals a security threat to the international order and an economic threat to the growing segment of Jordanian society invested in globalization. The regime gains support from a class of citizens that otherwise might pose the most serious challenge to the monarchy's rule. Given the

[64]See Robinson, "Defensive Democratization in Jordan"; Schwedler, "Occupied Maan"; and Curtis R. Ryan, "Jordan First: Jordan's Inter-Arab Relations and Foreign Policy under King Abdullah II," *Arab Studies Quartery* 26, no. 3 (2004): 43–62.

[65]Andoni, "Has Jordan Turned Its Back on Pan-Arabism?"

[66]Brown, "Jordan and Its Islamic Movement," 12.

[67]This formula works as long as the Islamists maintain anywhere between 35 percent and 60 percent support on the ground. Whether the regime intentionally allows the Islamists to gain and maintain such momentum or not is unclear. What is clear is that the regime has found a way to benefit from this status quo.

current political climate, a preference for the status quo translates into a preference for less democracy. Further, the United States has not staged a more vocal objection to Jordan's growing and increasingly repressive policies.

The regime emerges as the winner, representing itself to the Americans as a regime under threat—one that, if opened to full democracy, would be devoured by anti-U.S. forces. At the same time, it can represent itself to those awaiting the fruits of globalization as protecting their economic interests. Thus, Jordan has witnessed a liberalization trajectory accompanied by de-liberalization as well. In 1988, Jordan's Freedom House political rights score was a 6 and its civil liberties score was a 5. In 2011, thirteen years later, its scores are still 6 and 5, respectively. Arguably, therefore, though Jordan has witnessed significant political reforms in the last decade, these reforms have been accompanied by reversals as well.

U.S. POLICY AND ISLAMISTS: PRO-AMERICAN DEMOCRACY OR NO DEMOCRACY AT ALL?

The United States has historically taken a monolithic stance toward the Islamists of the Arab world. As early as 1993, the United States labeled Islamists as potential agents seeking to destabilize the entire Arab region. An address on May 18, 1993, by Martin Indyk, former U.S. assistant secretary of state for the Near East and North Africa, raised further concern about the future of the region; he referred to Islamists as "troublemakers" who can potentially create chaos in the Arab world. President Bill Clinton echoed these sentiments in his 1994 speech before the Jordanian parliament, a speech boycotted by the IAF. In the speech he laid out the U.S. perspective on politics in the Arab world: there were forces of tyranny (the Islamists) and forces of freedom (the United States) allied to authoritarian regimes.[68] It is this type of binarism that has structured U.S. dealings with Islamist groups across the region.

Although the United States continues to look for remedies to the Islamist problem, it has not been successful. Since 2003, several options—ranging from greater to less democracy, better economic opportunities, support of secular movements, support of liberal movements, and the direct curtailment of Islamist groups—have been floated.[69] The Greater Middle

---

[68]Haddad, "Islamist Perceptions of U.S. Policy in the Middle East," 518.

[69]As Mona Yacoubian, *Engaging Islamists and Promoting Democracy: A Preliminary Assessment*, United States Institute of Peace Special Report no. 190 (Washington, DC: United States Institute of Peace, 2007; accessed at http://www.usip.org/pubs/specialreports/sr190.html) notes, "The Islamists' successes stem from their effectiveness as vehicles for popular opposition. While liberal, secular opposition parties remain largely detached from much of the population, Islamists have developed vast and easily mobilized grassroots networks through charitable or-

East Initiative (2004) was designed to relieve political pressure in ways that would make Islamist messages less appealing and reduce anti-American sentiment. When it became clear that this tactic would result in significant parliamentary Islamist victories, the United States scrapped the strategy.[70] Those elections still ushered in a wave of Islamist victories, dubbed by many the "Islamist tsunami."[71]

That Islamist strength might jeopardize U.S. geostrategic interests is a concern shared in American policy and academic circles. Gregory Gause, for example, writes, "It is highly unlikely that democratically elected Arab governments would be as cooperative with the United States as the current authoritarian regimes." Free and fair democratic elections would likely bring to power "Islamist governments . . . less inclined to cooperate with the United States on important U.S. policy goals, including military basing rights in the region, peace with Israel and the war on terrorism."[72] However, without a major shift in policies it is still not clear whether this somewhat tacit approval of the status quo will create further anti-Americanism in the region.[73]

Since 2006, the democracy paradigm, it appears, has been abandoned in favor of a new strategy. The United States must find and support secular, prodemocracy, pro-U.S. movements that will counter the influence of the Islamists. But the number of such secular and liberal groups is limited. Nor is it clear whether secular movements will automatically embrace pro-West

---

ganizations and mosques. The leadership is often younger and more dynamic, with strong ties to the community, and the party organizations brim with energy and ideas, attracting those who are seeking change."

[70]For a critique of why the United States should not have abandoned elections, see Michele Dunne, "Getting Over the Fear of Arab Elections," *Daily Star* (Beirut), October 2, 2007.

[71]Gause, "Can Democracy Stop Terrorism?" Islamist movements in recent years have done remarkably well. In the 2002 Moroccan elections, the Justice and Development Party took 42 of the 325 seats, coming in third. The two long-established parties, the Socialist Union of Popular Forces and the Independence Party, won more seats: 50 and 48, respectively. In 2002, Islamists took nearly 50 percent of the seats in Bahrain (20 of 40 seats). In 2003, Islah, with its tribal alliance, took 46 of the 301 seats to form the opposition. In 2003 in Kuwait, Islamists won close to 35 percent of the seats. Even with all the restrictions in Jordan to dilute the voice of Islamists in the 2003 election they won 17 out of the 110 seats (with independents acquiring another 3 seats) to become the major opposition movement. In the municipal elections in Saudi Arabia, 6 of the 7 seats were won by Islamists affiliates. See also Marina Ottaway, *Democracy Promotion in the Middle East: Restoring Credibility*, Policy Brief no. 60 (Washington, DC: Carnegie Endowment for International Peace, 2008; accessed at http://www.carnegieendowment .org/files/pb_60_ottaway_final.pdf).

[72]Gause, "Can Democracy Stop Terrorism?" 69–70.

[73]Graham E. Fuller, *Islamists in the Arab World: The Dance around Democracy*, Carnegie Paper no. 49 (Washington, DC: Carnegie Endowment for International Peace, 2004); Ray Takeyah, "Uncle Sam in the Arab Street," *National Interest*, April 1, 2004 (accessed at http://www.allbusi ness.com/government/3584148-1.html).

liberal democratic values—or if such movements will openly align themselves to the United States.

For now, the most careful U.S. strategy is one that seeks to enhance economic development through globalization. Greater economic development may reduce the "audience effect" in the Arab world: if more citizens are invested in the economic trajectory of their countries, they may become less likely to endorse Islamist messages. According to Pete Moore, the Middle East Free Trade Agreements reflect the administration's belief that "freer trade is a low-cost silver bullet that can slay anti-American radicalism while delivering sustainable groups and securing regional peace."[74] For the United States, this is a useful strategy that allows it to pursue its existing unpopular political agendas in the region while simultaneously bringing the citizens of a country like Jordan directly onboard the economic globalization project. This strategy may work granted that larger sectors of society reap the benefits of these economic strategies. The more people become invested in the economic structures of their country, the more they will resist Islamist stances.

Although there is a growing sentiment in Washington, D.C., that the United States should embrace moderate Islamist groups as a means of countering the more radical tides, concerns remain about whether the Islamist movement in Jordan will attempt to strengthen its ties to Hamas, a prospect that would seem destructive to the peace treaty. And although East Bankers still dominate the IAF, it may be growing closer to Hamas—and, hence, becoming a thorn in the sides of the United States and supporters of Israel.[75] For their part, supporters of Israel worry about closer dialogue between the United States and Islamist movements. They believe that Western recognition of Islamist organizations anywhere, including the IAF, would only empower these movements against Israel.[76] The IAF in Jordan has similarly expressed its disdain for the United States and refuses to engage in any dialogue with it or other American organizations in Jordan, like the National Democratic Institute or the International Republican Institute. The IAF has maintained a tacit boycott of all U.S. organizations to protest U.S. policies in the region, even forbidding its members from traveling to the United States and thereby excluding them from study missions there. Further, low-level meetings between the United States and the IAF typically do not get beyond IAF statements of protest against U.S. policy.[77] The United

[74]Pete Moore, "The Newest Jordan: Free Trade, Peace and an Ace in the Hole," *Middle East Report Online*, June 26, 2003 (accessed at http://www.merip.org/mero/mero062603).

[75]Washington Institute for Near East Policy, *Hamas Weapons in Jordan: Implications for Islamists on the East Bank*, PolicyWatch no. 1098. (Washington, DC: Washington Institute for Near East Policy, 2006).

[76]U.S. State Department, *Middle East and North Africa Overview*, 2005 (accessed at http://www.state.gov/documents/organization/65472.pdf).

[77]Barsalou, *Islamists at the Ballot Box*; Yacoubian, "Engaging Islamists and Promoting Democracy."

States is moving cautiously in its reform efforts—demanding reform in education and more female representation in parliament, for example—but it is not pushing the political reform agenda stridently forward.

KUWAIT'S ISLAMIST MOVEMENT: A PRO-AMERICAN FORCE

In Kuwait, Islamists are generally more pro-American than their counterparts elsewhere, and their participation does not risk alienating the United States. In fact, most Kuwaitis welcomed increased levels of democracy despite the simultaneous increase in Islamist representation. That the Islamist program in Jordan is seen as more threatening than the Islamist program in Kuwait, while Kuwaiti Islamists remain more conservative than Jordan's Islamists, is due to the degree of anti-U.S. sentiment among the IAF in Jordan.

Kuwaiti Islamists were not always so pro-American. In fact, Kuwait's Muslim Brotherhood movement, established in 1952 as a branch of the larger Muslim Brotherhood, held many of the same anti-U.S. values of the larger party. By 1980, Islamist movements in Kuwait could be grouped along three main axes. Each Islamist group linked its organizational base to an association through which it launched its social and political platforms, the largest of which was the Muslim Brotherhood—rooted in the organization of the Social Reform Society. A second group, more traditional and Salafi in nature, linked its activities to the Heritage (al Turāth) organization. Third, the Cultural Social Society (Jami'yyat al-Thaqāfa al-Ijtima'iyya) encompassed the Shi'i Islamic community. Of the three movements, the Brotherhood had gained the most respect on the street, which translated into parliamentary representation from the early 1980s.[78]

Kuwait's Brotherhood maintained a close relationship with the al-Sabahs, and from its founding through the 1970s, it portrayed itself as the loyal opposition. The al-Sabahs, too, were invested in securing and strengthening ties to the Brotherhood. The monarchy in Kuwait, as in Jordan, saw the Brotherhood as a national ally against pan-Arab—and, especially, urban pan-Arab—voices. Kuwaiti Islamists could also be natural allies to the tribal or Bedouin sectors of society, sectors loyal to the monarchy.

Yet by the mid-1980s, the Brotherhood drew support from those same Bedouins, a shift facilitated by new redistricting laws adopted by the emir. In 1981, the Emir of Kuwait, Jaber III al-Ahmad al-Jaber al-Sabah, redistricted the country into twenty-five smaller regions to allow for greater tribal representation by bringing the Bedouin into the affairs of modern urban Kuwait. This process of what Shafeeq Ghabra calls "desertization" would help the regime further solidify its base and also bolster the Islamists, who

---

[78]Ellen Lust-Okar and Amaney Jamal, "Rulers and Rules: Reassessing the Influence of Regime Type on Electoral Law Formation," *Comparative Political Studies* 35, no. 3 (2002): 337–66.

would find natural allies among the more conservative Bedouin tribes. As Mary Ann Tetreault writes, "Tribal traditionalists who have benefited socially and politically from desertization also advocate state support of religiously sanctioned lifestyles and are among the strongest supporters of the regime."[79] New legislation to incorporate significant segments of the tribes as first-class citizens with full political voting rights accompanied the redistricting laws. These initiatives resulted in greater Islamist and tribal representation in parliament at the expense of the more urban and liberal sectors of Kuwait society.[80]

The Islamist groupings of the 1980s have persisted to the present, although these groups changed their names after the Iraqi invasion and liberation of Kuwait in 1990–91. Part of the reason for the change in name was rooted in a change of priorities. The Iraqi occupation had galvanized Kuwaiti political consciousness and solidarity. Further, it brought a younger generation into political awareness. Thus, the changes in Islamist strategies after the occupation would reflect a larger commitment to Kuwaiti, rather than pan-Arab, political life. Thus, the Muslim Brotherhood became the ICM, known by its Arabic acronym, HADAS. The Salafi movement became the Islamic Popular Alliance and then later Hizb al-Umma, while the Cultural Social Society became the Islamic National Alliance.

In 1991, the ICM was the most popular and influential of the Islamist groups and was still committed to an Islamist agenda. In that year, the ICM recommended the establishment of nongovernmental organization that could monitor Islamic relations in society, modeled after the morality police of Saudi Arabia. The government refused such an initiative, but the ICM continued to push for its conservative agenda. The ICM operated more like a political party and attracted a new generation of activists who were also highly political. Unlike other Islamist movements, however, and especially as a result of the Iraqi occupation, the ICM remained focused on domestic affairs.[81] Although

[79]Tetreault, "Kuwait's Unhappy Anniversary."

[80]Shafeeq N. Ghabra, "Balancing State and Society: The Islamic Movement in Kuwait," in *Revolutionaries and Reformers: Contemporary Islamist Movements in the Middle East*, ed. Barry Rubin (Albany: State University of New York Press, 2003), 105–24; Jill Crystal, *Oil and Politics in the Gulf: Rulers and Merchants in Kuwait and Qatar* (Cambridge: Cambridge University Press, 1995); Lust-Okar and Jamal, "Rulers and Rules"; Michael Herb, *All in the Family: Absolutisms, Revolution, and Democratic Prospects in the Middle Eastern Monarchies*, SUNY Series in Middle Eastern Studies (New York: State University of New York Press, 1999); Tetreault, "Kuwait's Unhappy Anniversary."

[81]As in Jordan, there are several other radical and smaller Islamist groups in Kuwait. Kuwait by and large and especially after 9-11 has been able to counter these movements. In 1992, radical Islamists were caught with explosives and weapons. These weapons were to be used to uphold strict Islamic interpretations. These more radical elements found, for example, the performance of the Romanian Circus insulting to Islamic morals due to the costumes of the

it was compassionate about issues like Palestine, it was also passionate about its own security.[82]

After the elections of 1992, where the Islamists did exceptionally well, the ICM and its allies enjoyed the largest bloc in parliament. Significantly, since the Iraq War the Islamists have used their parliamentary strength to advance sometimes unpopular domestic agendas, but not international platforms. With their outstanding showing in 1992, Islamists took on the more democratic and liberal opponents in parliament. With nineteen out of fifty seats, the group began demanding that Kuwait University (KU) adopt gender segregation laws.[83] Liberals were appalled. Not only did they see this as an attempt to regress Kuwaiti society to traditional standards of segregation but they also felt such legislation crystallized the Islamist agenda to spread their doctrine among the future generations. Democratic and liberal elements fought hard, but they couldn't defeat the legislation.[84] In 1996, parliament passed a law that called for KU to segregate its classrooms within five years, which later took effect.

The ICM has focused its energy on matters relating to Kuwaiti domestic politics, whereas in Jordan, the IAF has had to back away from conservative Islamic social agendas in order to establish alliances with more secular groups that support its foreign policy agenda. On Islamic issues, the ICM finds a natural ally with Bedouin tribal leaders, and on measures of government accountability, it finds support with the liberal opposition movement. A strategic movement in Kuwait, the ICM has built different coalitions on the policy debates that most concern it. Its coalition partners fluctuate depending on the issue at hand. As such, it finds a broad base of support. The Islamist bloc in Kuwait has continued to do well. Enjoying support from tribal sectors and a growing educated youth population, the Islamists have made impressive gains in parliamentary elections.[85] In 1996, it won 14 out of 50 seats; in 1999, it won 20 out of 50; and in 2003, it won an additional

---

performers, and they responded by opening fire at the performance. The government cracked down on such extremist elements.

[82]Nathan J. Brown, "Pushing toward Party Politics? Kuwait's Islamic Constitutional Movement," Carnegie Paper no. 79 (Washington, DC: Carnegie Endowment for International Peace, 2007).

[83]Mary Ann Tetreault and Haya al-Mughni, "Modernization and Its Discontents: State and Gender in Kuwait," *Middle East Journal* 49, no. 3 (1995):403–17; Jill Crystal and Abdallah al-Shayeji, "The Pro-Democratic Agenda in Kuwait: Structures and Contexts," in *Political Liberalization and Democratization in the Arab World*, vol. 2, *Comparative Experiences*, ed. Bahgat Korany, Rex Brynen, and Paul Noble (Boulder, CO: Lynne Rienner, 1998), 101–25; Ghabra, "Balancing State and Society."

[84]Mary Ann Tetreault, "Designer Democracy in Kuwait," *Current History* 96, no. 606 (1997): 36–39.

[85]Mary Ann Tetreault, "A Global Affairs Commentary: Frankenstein's Lament in Kuwait," November 29, 2001 (accessed at http://www.fpif.org/pdf/gac/0111kuwait.pdf).

seat. Finally, in 2006, it maintained its gains by winning another 21 of 50 seats.

ISLAMISTS AND THEIR POSITIONS: DEMOCRATIC DEEPENING IN KUWAIT

In Jordan, nearby wars inflamed anti-American sentiment. The War on Iraq in 2003 dealt the Jordanian population a tremendous blow, especially when it appeared that their monarch had aided the U.S. invasion. Kuwaiti responses were different. Whereas the First Gulf War moved the entire sector of Kuwaiti society firmly into the pro-American camp, the Second Gulf War deepened Kuwait's security dependence on the United States. The Islamists were no exception to this pattern. During Iraq's occupation of Kuwait, the entire society of Kuwait came to view both the pan-Arab movement and the larger Muslim Brotherhood movement with increasing suspicion and even disgust. These were the movements that were supposed to champion Arab and Muslim rights and dignity, but for the Kuwaitis they appeared to endorse an inhumane occupation. The ICM immediately distanced itself from the larger Muslim Brotherhood and embraced the United States out of both national loyalty and as a symbolic gesture to its constituency. Mosques became sites to foment support for the United States. In 2005, when Nabil al-'Awadi—an imam in the Southern region of al-Surrah—began preaching against the Americans in his Friday khutba, congregants cut him off. Congregants in other mosques who heard about the anti-American statements emanating from al-'Awadi's mosque also stood up to say, "O Allah, make Islam and America stronger."[86] An attack on the United States was seen by many as an attack on their Islam.

The ICM was appalled that the larger Muslim Brotherhood supported Saddam Hussein and disregarded Kuwaiti national ambitions during the entire occupation. The mainstream Muslim Brotherhood movement objected to U.S. intervention in the region, and especially in Iraq. For the ICM, it became a national obligation to support the Americans during the First Gulf War. Even after the war, the larger Brotherhood movement remained critical of the U.S. presence in Kuwait. According to Ismail Shati, a senior member of the ICM, when prominent Brotherhood branches visited Baghdad and issued statements condemning the U.S. presence in Kuwait in language that seemed to support Saddam Hussein, "the ICM had no other choice than to sever its ties to the larger Muslim Brotherhood movement."[87] Although the ICM remains committed to issues like Palestinian sover-

[86]"Report: Radical Kuwaiti Imams Drowned Out in Pro-American Protests by Local Worshippers." *Al-Siyasa*, July 9, 2005.

[87]Wendy Kristianasen, "We Don't Want to Box Islam In," *Le Monde*, June 4, 2002 (accessed at http://mondediplo.com/2002/06/04kuwait).

eignty, it nonetheless supports the role the United States plays in Kuwait. As Nasser al-San'a, a leader of the ICM who holds a seat in the Kuwaiti parliament, comments, "We have no problems with the U.S. We have no negative feelings about the presence of U.S. troops in Kuwait."[88]

National security remains the major concern of most Kuwaitis, and even Islamist candidates recognize the need for defense treaties with the allied powers—including the stationing of U.S. troops in Kuwait as a deterrent to would-be aggressors.[89] Most also support increased reliance on the joint military power of the Gulf Cooperation Council, despite the regional rivalries—especially with Saudi Arabia—that impede closer military coordination. Islamist candidates in general support expanding the Kuwaiti armed forces through foreign training programs and massive arms purchases. "After all, no one will defend us forever," notes the Islamist candidate Salah 'Abd al-Jaber.[90]

That the ICM values its security arrangements with the United States hasn't meant that the ICM remains uncritical of other Western policies. For example, many members of the ICM supported their government's ban on Danish goods after a controversy erupted over a cartoon published in Denmark in the fall of 2005, which depicted the Prophet Muhammad in disrespectful ways. ICM supporters in particular found the cartoons tasteless and insulting to Muslims.

ICM officials are also concerned that the United States continues to pressure the Kuwaiti regime to monitor Kuwaiti mosques. ICM officials point out that mosques in Kuwait—unlike in other Arab countries, including Jordan—can remain open in between prayer services; however, they worry that increasing U.S. pressure might induce the regime to restrict mosque activity. The ICM proudly states that unlike other Arab countries, Kuwait does not have a radicalizing tide that will undermine Kuwait's geopolitical standing. Many members of the ICM, like al-San'a, explain that the movement is concerned more about Kuwait's future economic trajectory than Islamic politicization. He spoke to me at length of the need for economic diversification and Kuwait's strategy to attract foreign direct investment. With the fall of Saddam, al-San'a was confident that Kuwait could excel in its economic reforms. He said, "It is like we have a car full of gas and good roads, and now it depends on the driver and how the driver decides to take the country."[91] Its objectives align well with other societal interests that seek to lead Kuwait out of oil dependency and to a more diversified economy.

Attitudes toward Hamas mark another point of distinction between the IAF and the ICM. While the IAF contains segments of what is seen as the

---

[88]Interview with the author, winter 2006.

[89]Kenneth R. Timmerman, "The Gulf Monarchies: Kuwait's Real Elections," *Middle East Quarterly* 3, no. 4 (1996): 53–58 (accessed at http://www.meforum.org/article/425).

[90]Ibid.

[91]Interview with the author, winter 2006.

Hamas wing, which has strong affinities to both Hamas in Palestine and Hizbullah in Lebanon, the ICM is more distanced from these two movements. Many in Kuwait's ICM feel that support for Hizbullah might empower Kuwait's Shi'i population. Further, some Kuwaitis believe that Hizbullah is a misguided movement. Several Kuwaitis felt that it was responsible for bringing Israel's wrath against Lebanon in 2006. Although there were many demonstrations in support of Hizbullah and Lebanon during the 2006 Israeli invasion, especially among Kuwait's Shi'i population, the mainstream press harshly criticized Hizbullah. The editor of Kuwait's *Arab Times* condemned Hizbullah in an editorial, saying, "Unfortunately we must admit that in such a war the only way to get rid of 'these irregular phenomena' is what Israel is doing."[92]

What support does exist in Kuwait for Hamas is more about supporting Fatah's opponent than Hamas itself. Many in Kuwait—even among the Islamist leadership—question Hamas's tactics vis-à-vis Israel and point out that the movement is doing the Palestinians more harm than good. Kuwaitis, though, took great pride in Hamas's electoral victory in 2006, tacitly applauding its gains because Hamas defeated Yasir Arafat's Fatah party; Kuwaitis viewed the victory as retribution for Arafat's support of Saddam during the Iraqi occupation. In general, however, Kuwaitis worried that movements like Hamas and Hizbullah were creating chaos in the Arab world. The Islamist movements have not necessarily condemned Hamas and Hizbullah, but neither have they embraced them. For now, the ICM appears to place its own nationalistic interests and goals to maintain a loyal constituency above other regional developments.

The ICM takes great pride in its "moderate" stances. As an ICM leader told me proudly, "the U.S. Ambassador to Kuwait commended the ICM and said that the Kuwaiti Islamic movement was the most advanced, the most integrated, and the most progressive in the Arab World."[93] This American endorsement of the ICM proves to many in the movement that the ICM is a model that should be emulated by other Islamist movements across the region.

Democratic Successes and Advancements: Female Suffrage, Redistricting, and Succession

Kuwait has seen significant, if not remarkable, political development since the Iraqi invasion of 1990; but, more important, these developments have been linked to further political liberalization since 2001. Unlike develop-

---

[92]Michael Rubin, "Iran against the Arabs," *Wall Street Journal*, July 19, 2006 (accessed at http://proquest.umi.com/pqdweb?did=1079537721&sid=1&Fmt=3&clientId=17210&RQT=309&VName=PQD).
[93]Interview with the author, winter 2006.

ments in Jordan, these liberalization gains have resulted in greater parliamentary strength. In fact, in 1988, Kuwait's Freedom House score was a 6 for political rights. By 2011, Kuwait's political rights score had improved to a 4—the best in the entire Arab world. This liberalization is due to a multitude of factors, including international pressure, regime commitment to change, and societal push for reform. Tellingly, the society galvanized to push for greater democratic openings in Kuwait without worrying about the overempowerment of the ICM or other Islamist movements. Although many people in the liberal camp explained that they felt Islamists might hold Kuwait back or take it down a more conservative path, these concerns did not necessitate the exclusion of the Islamists or thwart greater democratization. There was firm belief among liberals and democrats that democratic deepening was the proper route for Kuwait, and that Islamist stances would have to become more moderate if they were to remain viable political movements. In Kuwait, unlike in Jordan, liberals and democrats did not worry about the possibility of the ICM harming Kuwait's clientelistic status vis-à-vis the United States.

Three groundbreaking political developments in the last few years illustrate the conviction and willingness of civil society to press for more reforms through the legislative body: women's suffrage, the unseating of an emir, and a redistricting plan. The ICM has been a key force behind these democratization gains.

Female Suffrage

In May 2005, Kuwaiti women gained their right to suffrage. Although the emir had initiated legislation in 1999 to give women the right to vote, the parliament voted down the bill in that same year. Most tribal and Islamist members of parliament voted against the measure. Along with the international community, the emir supported women's suffrage, and since 1999 has repeatedly attempted to pass legislation in parliament, only to have it blocked by the Islamist-tribal coalition.[94] This coalition largely consisted of ICM and the Salafi movement. The Shi'is were much more in favor of women's suffrage.[95] Although it was unfortunate that women were consistently denied

---

[94] Adel Darwish, "Kuwait: Kuwait Goes to the Polls," *Middle East*, August–September 2003 (accessed at http://findarticles.com/p/articles/mi_m2742/is_337/ai_n25072206).

[95] Haya al-Mughni, *Women in Kuwait: The Politics of Gender* (London: Saqi, 2000), argues that there was another side to regime support for female suffrage that is due to the redistricting debates in parliament at the time. The regime, believing women would in general constitute a promonarchy and modern stance, attempted to dilute the influence of the opposition should the redistricting measures pass. Other concerns about female suffrage launched in other sectors of Kuwaiti society included the fact that women would become the majority of the electorate since men serving in the army were not entitled to vote. Women, if allowed to vote, would become the dominant voting constituency. Many conservative men feared that Kuwait would indeed become a country run by women. However, since the 2006 elections, it is clear that

the right to vote through legislative edict, the fact that parliament could veto an emiri decree is telling. Two decades earlier, the Emir of Kuwait, like the King of Jordan, could pass legislation bypassing parliament altogether. This was not the case in the postliberation phase. The Kuwaiti parliament had been empowered since the liberation phase.[96]

The multiple challenges women faced in demanding the right to vote were enumerated throughout my stay in Kuwait. Key female leaders in Kuwait—including Dr. Lubna al-Kazi, sociology professor at Kuwait University; Rola Dashti, the first elected woman of the Kuwait Economic Society; and Lulwa al-Mulla, secretary of the Women's Cultural and Social Society—explained to me the arduous path to legislative victory. Al-Mulla, outlining the ways women were excluded from participating in campaign events, was one of several women in Kuwait to push for greater equality. She and her colleagues would sit in cars outside male candidates' tents as a means of protesting the laws that forbade their participation.[97] Some male candidates welcomed their involvement, sending water and food to their cars as a sign of support. Others were less supportive and more confrontational.[98] From picketing courthouses, to staking out candidate tents, to finding male leaders to rally the *diwaniyyas* (meeting places), women remained vigilant in their pursuit of enfranchisement.

Despite setbacks, Kuwaiti women remained undeterred. Realizing that they had to win over those more conservative sectors, women actively engaged them and pushed for the reforms they needed. They took on parliamentary members to win over the support of tribal and Islamist elements. While the tribes remained quite stubborn in their stance against women's suffrage, al-Mulla says they made more headway with the Islamists. At the very minimum, they were able to neutralize the ability of Islamists to use "Islam" as the reason behind their oppression. Says al-Mulla, "We confronted them and asked them to tell us why Kuwaiti Islam was different than Egyptian Islam, or Palestinian Islam, or 'other Islams' where women could vote."[99] She says they had no good responses, and ultimately, they began supporting the tribes by claiming it was a cultural and traditional issue, grounds that had little Islamic backing. Al-Mulla and her organization did not stop with the lobbying of candidates, and other woman activists pressed on as well. They went through legal channels, attempting to

---

women are voting along issues not pertaining to gender per se. That not one single female candidate has made it to parliament in either 2006 or 2008 is demonstrative of this trend.

[96]Ghabra, "Balancing State and Society."

[97]Interview with the author, winter 2006.

[98]Mary Ann Tetreault, "Kuwait's Parliament Considers Women's Political Rights, Again," *Middle East Report Online*, September 2, 2004 (accessed at http://www.merip.org/mero/mero 090204).

[99]Interview with the author, winter 2006.

show the government the inhumane treatment of women. In fact, Rola al-Dashti repeatedly made the case that suffrage was a fundamental issue of human rights, and Lubna al-Kazi argued that these ideals did not conflict with Islamic norms.[100]

As pressure grew in support of female suffrage, the Islamist movement generally—and the ICM in particular—seemed to grow more divided on the issue of gendered political inclusion. By 2004, such divisions were public. Secretary General Badr al-Nashi publicly stated that he did not personally object to a woman's right to vote. Similar statements were made by Nasser al-San'a. Still, al-Nashi maintained that this was something the movement had to analyze and discuss further.[101] In May 2005, the parliament ratified by thirty-seven votes the law that would allow women the right to both vote and stand as candidates in elections.

While Kuwaiti women celebrated in the halls of the parliament, Islamists demanded that women participate within the confines of Islamic law. Thus, many Islamists begrudgingly supported the measure. Even those who were not happy and voted against it accepted the outcome. Said Nasser al-San'a, "because we value the democratic process, those who didn't want to see this legislation still accepted its outcome."[102] Nonetheless, al-San'a maintained that the movement would personally hold the prime minister accountable if women used their new rights to undermine the traditions and culture of Kuwait.

In the end, both female activists and the Islamist movement used the democratic process to advance their interests; each pursued competing agendas, yet all respected democratic contestation through the legislative body. Because the issue of women's suffrage was an internal matter of the state, and the Islamists were not seen as jeopardizing Kuwait's international standing, these spirited deliberations highlighted the success of democracy at the end.

The 2006 Succession: The Parliament Reigns

Kuwait's remarkable democratization successes extend to the succession crisis of 2006. On January 15, 2006, Shaykh Jaber al-Ahmad al-Sabah died after battling a long illness. Next in line was Crown Prince Shaykh Sa'ad al-Abdallah al-Salim, also very ill. Ample disagreement ensued in the ranks of the royal family about the next heir to the throne. Hence, the legislative branch assumed the responsibility of designating an heir when it invoked its constitutional right to replace an ineffective leader, Shaykh Sa'ad, with a

---

[100]Interviews with the author, winter 2006.
[101]Tetreault, "Kuwait's Parliament Considers Women's Political Rights, Again."
[102]Nasser al-San'a, interview with the author, winter 2006.

new prime minister, Shaykh Sabah al-Ahmad al-Jaber. Shaykh Sa'ad yielded to the parliamentary decision. Mary Ann Tetreault points out the clear significance of such a moment: "For the first time in an Arab monarchy, an elected body effectively deposed the monarch and empowered a new one."[103] This was not a traditional coup d'etat, nor a violent overthrow, but a peaceful transition of monarchical power in which the parliament played a crucial and vital role. The entirety of Kuwaiti society—liberals and conservatives, women's groups and Islamists alike—embraced this development as a democratic hallmark in Kuwait's history.[104] This peaceful transition, many Kuwaitis felt, was a triumph for democracy across the country.

Redistricting: Civil Society Galvanization

Since the desertization policies adopted in the 1980s, which gave the Bedouin sectors overrepresentation in parliament, liberals and other opposition movements have pushed for redistricting.[105] Small districts have favored the tribes and made it easier and more affordable for less popular parties and candidates to win seats. The platform presented by liberals included a conviction that larger districts would reduce the likelihood of corruption and vote-buying. The Islamists sided with the liberals in these demands. Like the liberals, the Islamists felt that they, too, would benefit from fairer districting. Further, both camps were convinced that larger districts would reduce the ability of the monarchy to support independent candidates in smaller districts. By limiting the role of the monarchy, new districting formulas would allow political parties to become more empowered. Thus, although both parties had competing domestic platforms, they worked with one another to enhance representation in Kuwait.[106] In another unique moment in Kuwait's history, Kuwait's liberal and Islamist oppositions struck an alliance to push redistricting.[107]

The regime was reluctant to consider redistricting demands. It did not want an overrepresentation of urban opposition members in parliament. The Islamists and the liberals had emerged as a cohesive voice in addressing government corruption in the legislative body, and redistricting would further empower these opposition voices. Demands for redistricting found

[103] Mary Ann Tetreault, "Three Emirs and a Tale of Two Transitions," *Middle East Report Online*, February 10, 2006 (accessed at http://www.merip.org/mero/mero021006).
[104] Ibid.
[105] The liberal Jamiyyat al-Kharejin was a vocal advocate of such redistribution reforms.
[106] Mary Ann Tetreault, "Women's Rights and the Meaning of Citizenship in Kuwait," *Middle East Report Online*, February 10, 2005 (accessed at http://www.merip.org/mero/mero021005).
[107] Brown, "Jordan and Its Islamic Movement"; Mary Ann Tetreault, "Kuwait's Annus Mirabilis," *Middle East Report Online*, September 7, 2006 (accessed at http://www.merip.org/mero/mero090706).

much support in parliament, however, with over twenty-nine ministers supporting the initiative. Fearing that things could get out of control and believing he could dilute the influence of parliament through new elections, the king shut down parliament in May 2006 and called for new elections that June. But the emir miscalculated; the new parliament brought a legislature even more committed to redistricting reforms.

Not only was there support for redistricting among the legislative body, but civil society also played a vital role. Citizens across Kuwait City mobilized to demand reforms. During the summer of 2006, demands intensified. Wearing orange shirts and caps and forming what would come to be known as the Orange Reform Movement, thousands of Kuwaiti citizens turned out in front of the legislative branch in support of the redistricting movements. In July 2006, Kuwait's redistricting laws were adopted, and it was agreed that they would apply to the next parliamentary elections, held in 2008.[108]

The debates about redistricting demonstrated not only the Islamists' ability to work effectively with others to push an agenda through parliament but also that society at large supported the agenda too, which would undermine the monarch's preferences. More important, the measure was a direct check on executive control. The citizens of Kuwait stood up. As a public forum, they maintained, parliament should represent citizen preferences and not solely serve as a vehicle that brings proregime segments to the fold. As such, the redistricting debates championed by the Islamists and the liberals enjoyed wide support from the populace as well. The society stood behind this initiative with little worry about any future consequences of overpowering parliament or weakening the regime. More democracy did not undermine Kuwait's sense of security.[109]

I further found among both elites and citizens the firm belief that democracy was essential to pursuing Kuwait's development trajectory. Many Kuwaiti elites see an important role for Kuwait to play in the Gulf economy. "We want to make Kuwait the financial hub of the Gulf. Why should Citigroup go to Dubai and not Kuwait?" Said Dr. Yousef al-Ebrahim, former minister of finance. He continued, "We need a group of policies to improve foreign investments and make Kuwait a financial hub. You have to invest in education, and training and how to be creative. This is the challenge. You need to change the role of government from managing the economy to regulating and monitoring, so more privatization. The government needs to build a regulatory framework, and progressive institutions to make sure that the private sector will achieve these national objectives. In this

[108]Ghanim al-Najjar, "Kuwait: Struggle over Parliament," *Arab Reform Bulletin* 4, no. 5 (2008; accessed at http://www.carnegieendowment.org/files/najjar_june06.pdf).
[109]Brown, "Jordan and Its Islamic Movement"; Tetreault, "Kuwait's Annus Mirabilis."

way, democracy can further the goals of Kuwait's economic trajectory."[110] Al-Ebrahim clearly believes democracy will benefit Kuwait. When pressed about democracy and potential fear of the Islamists, al-Ebrahim responded by saying, "I don't think their participation is bad. This is democracy. Let them participate and let them embrace the rules of the game. This is what democracy is about." Al-Ebrahim did not express any fear about increased Islamist participation. Former minister of information and former UN representative Mohammad Abbas Abulhassan agreed: "We should be aware that the terrorist challenge will not go away unless you treat your people with equal living, democracy granted, you provide them with all elements of good living." For Abulhassan, that is, democracy would continue to moderate Islamists.

<h3 style="text-align:center">REGIME-ISLAMIST RELATIONS IN KUWAIT</h3>

The Islamists in Kuwait continue to occupy an important, visible, and respected role in Kuwaiti politics. They are no longer strictly seen as the loyal opposition they were in the 1980s. The ICM is part of the opposition and has fashioned itself as a movement that embraces an Islamic conservative agenda while simultaneously working within the parameters of a democratic Kuwaiti society. Like other opposition groups, the movement respects the ruling family but will not hesitate to challenge it. Other opposition groups, like the liberals, often work with Islamists to form alliances necessary for parliamentary blocs. Islamists have been vital to Kuwait's democratic trajectory as advocates of democratic reform and will respect the outcomes of laws that they find undesirable, like female suffrage and banking policies that have not completely abolished interest (or *riba*). Across Kuwait, even among liberal forces, a consensus exists: Kuwait's Islamists must continue to participate in the democratic process. Kuwaiti society—its opposition movements and ordinary citizens alike, including those best positioned to benefit from increasing global ties and linkages—believe that further democracy will only strengthen the country.

Democracy in Kuwait will undermine neither U.S. nor Kuwaiti interests. The regime thus finds itself in a more difficult situation, unable to justify prolonged authoritarian entrenchment for national well-being as other Arab states do. The United States, once a strong advocate of democracy in postliberation Kuwait, has now taken a backseat. It neither vocally endorses nor condemns Kuwait's democratic trajectory. This could be a result of many factors. First, U.S. democracy efforts have proven unsuccessful elsewhere. Second, although Kuwait's Islamists remain committed to the

<hr/>
[110]Yousef al-Ebrahim, interview with the author, winter 2006.

United States, the United States could lose such impressive support if its policies in Iraq turn for the worse, or if its occupation drags on. Third, the United States has solicited Kuwait as a key partner in the War on Terror, the policies of which are hard to enforce while simultaneously calling for democracy, since many of these laws call for authoritarianism. Fourth, and perhaps most important, is the concern that if the United States were to embrace Kuwait's democratic gains it actually might be expected to do the same for other Gulf countries like Saudi Arabia, where anti-U.S. sentiment among opposition movements—and especially Islamists—is rampant. For the United States, then, it is far more advantageous to take a backseat, neither pressing nor hindering Kuwait's democratic agenda.

The ICM appears to be honoring the democratic pact. In 2006, it released a reform agenda that called for more effective popular participation. Its goals for Kuwait reflect the majority opinion of the citizens: greater economic development, more privatization, lesser reliance on oil, more accountability among government officials, and more stringent eschewal of corruption. In terms of its domestic reform agenda, the ICM mimics much of the rhetoric of other Islamist movements across the Arab world, addressing corruption and upholding more Shari'a-oriented policies. Unlike these Islamist groups, however, it does not profess an anti-U.S. agenda, thereby allowing itself greater leeway.[111] Instead, it speaks of its ambition to create a "constitutional monarchy" in Kuwait, one that resembles the British model. The ICM has also remained cautious, working gradually on its democracy agenda by forming strong alliances with other opposition movements, like the liberals and the nationalists. That these other opposition movements embrace the Islamists reflects the degree to which other groups deem the Islamists less threatening to Kuwait.[112]

Nor has Kuwait come under international pressure to do something about its Islamist movements. The United States has applauded Kuwait's Islamists as a model movement. As a result, Kuwait does not feel the need to appease its protector by reducing the rights of its Islamist groups. According to Nathan Brown, "international pressures have [not] led the Kuwaiti government to engage in the tool of harassment used in Jordan" against its Islamist groups.[113] Kuwaiti Islamists do not appear to threaten the United States or Israel, enabling society to demand more accountability in Kuwait than in Jordan. Significantly, domestic concerns about Shari'a and Islamization are topics that societies competently feel they can negotiate and deal with internally. Only when the international standing of the country is at risk do citizens rethink their democratization priorities.

---

[111] Brown, "Jordan and Its Islamic Movement"; interviews with the author, winter 2006.
[112] Brown, "Jordan and Its Islamic Movement"; interviews with the author, winter 2006.
[113] Brown, "Pushing Toward Party Politics?"

The different dynamics that structure Islamist political worldviews in Jordan and Kuwait affect the ways that citizens engage their regimes. The position of the Islamists vis-à-vis the United States—their respective countries' patron—is a paradigm that structures the daily interactions of citizens with their regime. In countries like Jordan, where Islamists are more threatening to U.S. interests, citizens cling to existing authority as a means of thwarting Islamist influence. In countries like Kuwait, where Islamists are not a threat, citizens are able to assign a much lower geostrategic utility to the monarchy for maintenance of the patron-client relationship. Kuwaitis, therefore, are more democratic than their Jordanian counterparts. Chapter 4 takes up this theme in more detail.

CHAPTER FOUR

Engaging the Regime through the Lens of the United States

Citizens' Political Preferences

THIS CHAPTER PROVIDES A DETAILED AND NUANCED ACCOUNT OF HOW ORDINARY CITI-
zens rationalize their political preferences. First, it will document the causal
logics citizens employ when supporting the monarchy in Jordan. It will illustrate how people who believe that the current regime has privileged and
important relations with the United States may come to support a regime
even when it is otherwise not in their apparent interest. This is so because
they fear the role anti-American Islamists may play in harming the relationship if they come to power. Furthermore, this chapter will demonstrate
that this is not the case in Kuwait, because the Islamist opposition is pro-
American. Second, this chapter will examine the ways citizens who oppose
the regime in Jordan cling to an elastic definition of Shari'a, one that seeks
to challenge the geopolitical status quo altogether.

This chapter relies on a series of open-ended interviews conducted by
two research teams in Jordan and Kuwait. The interviewees were selected
through a variety of techniques. Respondents were randomly approached
in coffee shops, taxis, hair salons, markets, malls, grocery stores, and on
university campuses. Using snowball sampling techniques, some respondents offered names of other potential participants. Each interview lasted
for sixty to ninety minutes, and most were conducted in Arabic. Targeted
sampling techniques were also employed to maximize socioeconomic, gender, and geographic diversity across each country. One hundred seven interviews were conducted in Jordan during the summer of 2005, and seventy-
one were conducted in Kuwait during the winter of 2006. It is important to
point out that these samples are *not* representative of the entire Jordanian
and Kuwaiti populations. However, what emerge from these interviews are
the commonalities in the strategic logics citizens employ when they assess
their engagements with existing regimes in each country.[1]

---

[1] See the structured interview questionnaire in this chapter's appendix.

CAUSAL LOGICS CITIZENS EMPLOY WHEN ENGAGING POSSIBILITIES
OF REGIME CHANGE

I divide this chapter into two sections. The first highlights the ways in which
Jordanian citizens engage international hierarchy and especially the role of
the United States in their country. In this section, I also capture the ways in
which citizens engage notions of regime change. I pay attention to the strategic choices citizens are making between their support of the status quo
and thoughts about democratization. I specifically highlight the ways citizens couch their responses to concerns about losing clientelistic access to
the United States as a result of anti-American Islamists playing a more predominant role in the political process. In the second section of the chapter,
I illustrate that citizens in Kuwait also have similar frameworks of engagement with U.S. clientelism, believing that they are better off with the U.S.
alliance than without. However, unlike their Jordanian counterparts, they
do not worry about Islamists—the main opposition movement—harming
the client relationship with the United States.

Reckoning with Clientelism

Jordanians and Kuwaitis count their blessings. In a region struck with terror, war, conflict, and insecurity, Jordan and Kuwait enjoy enviable levels of
tranquility. Both Jordanians and Kuwaitis understand the benefits of U.S.
patronage for this security. Although Kuwaitis and Jordanians value their
client relationship with the United States, Jordanians interviewed were in
general far more resentful of the client relationship than were the Kuwaitis.
While Kuwaitis viewed the Americans as liberators and protectors, Jordanians saw the United States as an imperial force, holding Jordan hostage to
its larger geostrategic plan to ensure Israel's survival above all else. In this
formula, then, the King of Jordan is instrumental in preserving ties with the
United States because the Islamists not only reject U.S. domination but also
are appalled that Jordan is used to protect Israel. Assessing the monarchy as
a strategic necessity for the alliance with the United States by no means implies tacit approval or enduring affinity. Some Jordanians are sympathetic
to the fragile and reliant role the Jordanian monarchy finds itself in vis-à-
vis America; this sympathy is particularly extended to King Abdullah, who
is often seen as a victim of American power. His love and care for Jordan
forces him to accept American terms. Other Jordanians are more skeptical
and resentful of the monarchy, believing that compliance is the price the
monarchy has paid to secure its interests and longevity. In other words, the
Jordanian monarchy and the United States are involved in a tightly knit
complicity. So interwoven is this agreement that citizens perceive no choice
but to accept it. Finally, there are those individuals in Jordan who believe

that the United States orchestrates Islamic radicalism to generate the outcome that is now apparent on the ground: approval for authoritarian rule at the expense of democratic contestation. That is, some Jordanian citizens believe that the United States and the monarchy engineer and foment anti-U.S. Islamist activism so that citizens will be afraid to demand more democracy lest these anti-American factions jeopardize the client relationship with the United States. Among these different response patterns in Jordan, however, was a noticeable convergence. In the end, whether the United States was a good or bad force, whether the monarchy was loving or self-centered, and whether the Islamists were justly anti-American or sponsored by the United States, citizens preferred maintaining the status quo rather than risk losing or jeopardizing the client relationship with the United States.

Support for the U.S. clientelistic relationship with Jordan by no means implies outright support for the U.S. government. Rather, Jordanians capably analyze the strategic benefits of strong ties with the United States. A 2003 poll, conducted in Jordan by the West Asia Center for Strategic Studies, found that although the majority of Jordanians were upset with U.S. policies in the region, with 25 percent believing the United States to be unjust and another 52 percent believing it to be an oppressive force in the Arab world, the vast majority of Jordanians believed that U.S. ties are good for Jordan. Eighty-six percent of Jordanians believed that the political and economic ties between Jordan and the United States were good for the country. In fact, 59 percent believed that the Jordanian government, along with civil society forces, should work to strengthen such ties. Anti-American sentiment on its own is not threatening to Jordanians; most citizens don't hold the United States in a positive light anyway. However, the willingness of some groups, like the Islamists, to operate against the United States worries citizens.

Kuwaitis similarly value the client relationship with the United States. Especially since the 1990 Iraqi invasion and occupation, Kuwaitis feel that they have a special relationship with the United States. Once hesitant to openly embrace the United States for fear that its pan-Arab credentials and its dedication to Palestine would be questioned, Kuwait now finds itself emancipated from these restrictions. According to Gregory Gause, "Kuwait, having suffered from military occupation, has developed a strong public consensus on the need for close military ties with the United States."[2]

In general, Kuwaitis embrace the alliance with the United States. However, many still express discomfort about the huge U.S. military presence in their territory, especially after the First Gulf War. Yet although Kuwaitis express such concerns, they are quickly dismissed; average Kuwaitis report

[2]F. Gregory Gause III, *Oil Monarchies: Domestic and Security Challenges in the Arab Gulf States* (New York: Council on Foreign Relations, 1994), 122.

not seeing U.S. ground troops on a daily basis. Kuwaitis seem content that the U.S. Army is far away, on remote desert bases. Further, the Kuwaitis interviewed spoke at length of regional security concerns, as Iran and Iraq remain countries that elevate levels of vulnerability. As a result, Kuwaitis feel blessed that the Americans look out for them. The difference between Jordanians and Kuwaitis resides in the degree to which they link support of the monarchy to maintaining strong ties to the United States. This factor is directly shaped by the anti-American nature of internal Islamist opposition movements in each country. Before capturing this latter theme, however, it is imperative to illustrate the ways in which Jordanian citizens, unlike Kuwaitis, link the U.S. client relationship to the monarchy.

The view that Arab citizens across the region place strong value on enhancing their economic standing through stronger ties to the West, and specifically the United States, has been documented in numerous surveys. The *Revisiting the Arab Street* report finds that majorities of citizens in Egypt, Jordan, and Lebanon have very positive assessments of economic bilateral ties with the United States. Almost 40 percent of Palestinians also perceive these ties in a positive light. The report also found that majorities of close to 50 percent in each country believed in strengthening further bilateral economic ties with the United States.[3]

These findings are echoed in the Pew Global Attitudes Surveys for 2007, where again the majority of citizens places a high premium on trade and business ties with external countries. Seventy-two percent of Jordanians believe that this is good for their country. Among those with strong viewpoints toward the United States, this number rose to 90 percent; 91 percent of Kuwaitis, 61 percent of Egyptians, 69 percent of Palestinians, and 71 percent of Moroccans also support the view that stronger ties with external countries are good for their countries. Those with more positive views of the United States were more likely to believe in such benefits across the board.[4]

Support for the Monarchy and U.S. Clientelism: Jordan

Jordanians are far more likely to be supportive of their monarchy even while they are critical of it. And although they are strong supporters of democracy, they are also more likely to be concerned about the appropriateness of democracy for Jordan. The Jordanians interviewed explicitly linked their levels of support for the regime and concerns about democracy to Islamist threats that may sabotage the client relationship Jordan enjoys with the United States. These were general response patterns that I found among support-

[3]Center for Strategic Studies in Jordan, *Revisiting the Arab Street: Research from Within*. Amman: Center for Strategic Studies in Jordan, 2005.

[4]Pew Global Attitudes Project, *America's Image in the World* (Washington, DC: Pew Research Center, 2007); accessed http://pewglobal.org/commentary/display.php?AnalysisID=1019.

TABLE 4.1. Jordanian regime supporters and opponents and national origin

	Regime supporters	Regime opponents	Total
Jordanian origin	$n = 20$	$n = 14$	$n = 34$
Palestinian origin	$n = 34$	$n = 38$	$n = 72$
	$n = 54$	$n = 52$	$n = 106$

ers of the monarchy, which also included Jordanian Palestinians. Often, support for the Jordanian monarchy is treated as a function of Jordanian-Jordanian support, while opposition to the monarchy is seen as emanating strictly from Palestinian-Jordanian quarters. This possible polarization is not substantiated by my qualitative data, nor is it substantiated in my quantitative findings (see chapter 5). Of the total sample of 106 Jordanian interviews with ordinary citizens, 59 interviewees were classified as supporters of the monarchy. Of the entire sample, 34 interviews (or 33 percent) were with people of Jordanian origin. Of this group, 20 (or 60 percent) were classified as promonarchy and 14 (or 40 percent) as antimonarchy. Seventy-two respondents (or 67 percent) reported that they were of Palestinian origin, and of this group, 34 (or 47 percent) were classified as promonarchy while another 38 (or 53 percent) were classified as anti-monarchy (see table 4.1).

It is also important to note that the overwhelming majority of those who identified themselves as monarchy supporters can be classified as working or living within economic sectors that stand to benefit from greater economic globalization. Of the 59 monarchy supporters, 11 are store owners who directly link their economic well-being to a Jordanian economy that will continue to grow. Nineteen individuals hold a bachelors degree or higher degree and thus occupy employment sectors that stand to benefit from greater economic global integration. These sectors include banking, tourism, services, and telecommunications. Seven supporters of the monarchy are also students vying for jobs in sectors that are strengthened by global linkages, and another five are women who are not employed but whose husbands are employed in sectors that benefit from greater access to globalization. Of the remaining 17 respondents, only three reported that their economic situations were very bad and would worsen in the years to come. The rest reported that they were very optimistic about their financial future. In fact, according to the Pew Global Attitudes surveys, citizens who felt optimistic about their economic standing were also more likely to have more favorable opinions of the United States: 69 percent of those with favorable opinions toward the United States had positive assessments of their economic situation, compared to 37 percent of those with less favorable attitudes toward the United States.[5]

[5] Ibid.

The majority of the 48 Jordanians who are classified as antimonarchy and more likely to support Islamism also tend to be located in economic sectors that do not stand to benefit from greater global economic integration. In fact, most of these supporters tended to be less optimistic about their economic futures. Seventy-seven percent of those with more favorable opinions toward the United States were optimistic about their economic futures, compared to a smaller optimistic group of 49 percent among those who were less favorable toward the United States. Often, members of this less optimistic group had acquired an undergraduate education but were unable to find suitable employment. Thirty-two of these individuals described their condition as "poor" or even "below poor." They work as taxi drivers, shop employees, vegetable vendors, hair stylists, secretaries, and assistants. Several of these respondents are poor students as well. Thus, support for the monarchy in Jordan is linked to the ways in which citizens reflect on their economic positions—and whether they believe the status quo can strengthen their economic standing. Arguably, for example, a taxi driver may not feel his job to be at risk from fluctuations in access to global markets. As one respondent put it, there will always be demands for taxis; when economic situations worsen, it means fewer people rely on or buy their own cars, and therefore dependence on taxis increases. These are the logics that citizens employ in order to embrace certain political actors in society. And these political commitments result in more or less support for the existing governing apparatus. These levels of regime support directly carry over to negotiations about democratization. Democratization no longer becomes solely a system of values and principles—it also becomes synonymous with an alteration of the status quo. This alteration can have direct economic benefits and losses depending on the ways in which citizens locate their economic interests vis-à-vis the United States. Seventy-three percent ($n = 43$) of monarchy supporters linked their support to the geostrategic utility of the Hashemite monarchy—its ability to maintain the client alliance with the United States. This group was more likely to worry about the appropriateness of democracy for Jordan even while they supported it. They were primarily concerned with Islamist extremism and how the United States would respond to it.

Jordanian Attitudes from Within: Linking Stability and Security to the United States and Monarchy

Jordanians both of Palestinian and Jordanian descent—but especially those who are committed to increasing levels of globalization as a means for further economic development—are very concerned about and invested in maintaining levels of security and stability. Take, for example, Bilal, an engineer with a very good job who praises the levels of stability his country enjoys. He says, "People come here from Saudi Arabia and Dubai. They respect the king because he keeps a peaceful country." Bilal believes that levels of stability in Jordan are quite commendable given the strife in neighboring countries. Not only is the king able to keep a peaceful country but, according to Bilal, "He knows how to keep good ties with the Americans." These good ties are seen as essential for Jordan's stability and security. This sentiment is echoed by Hamzeh, a Palestinian Jordanian. A cosmetic surgeon, he supports the monarchy because the king continuously works to secure the welfare of the kingdom. "Look," Hamzeh says convincingly, "we have peace and security." This is because the king "knows how to work with our allies [the United States] to protect us." When asked whether he thinks other Arab countries respect Jordan, this is what Hamzeh had to say: "All the Arab countries make us feel like we did something wrong because we have close ties with the Americans. They always place this guilt on us. But it should not be this way. We need to take care of ourselves and of this country, and we cannot worry about all the other countries. . . . Look, at least this country is now secure." In other words, Jordanians have to look after their own interests even if it means ignoring the anti-American preferences of nearby states.

Regional instability has dealt the Jordanian sense of security a tremendous blow. Jordanians feel extremely fortunate that, unlike Iraqis and Palestinians, they are safe and secure. Jordan, in its citizens' opinion, is much better off than its neighboring countries. These citizens also worry about the future of Syria, since that country has made enemies of the Americans. Lebanon, they point out, is also unstable, and Iran and Syria play significant roles in that country's political affairs. Take what Hashim, a corporate credit officer in one of Amman's largest banks, had to say: "Jordan has the most stability in the Arab world. . . . Look at Syria, Lebanon, Palestine, and Iraq. . . ." In Hashim's tone is both a sense of reassurance and of pride, but also of shame. He continues, "Jordan is the most stable country for reasons that everybody knows. The U.S. protects us." Like Bilal and Hamzeh, Hashim understands how important the United States is for Jordan's stability, but he is neither as enthusiastic nor as enthralled by this reality as they are. Hashim blatantly believes that the United States does not care for Jordan but instead prioritizes its own interests. In fact, he believes the United States "uses us as puppets." Further, Hashim believes both King Hussein and King Abdullah II of Jordan are important for this ongoing relationship with the Americans. He says, "Both our kings have been successful. And both kings know how to move the way the U.S. wants them to. They have to do this to survive." In Hashim's analysis is a sympathetic rationalization of the existing status quo. The Arab world, he tells us, is weak and lacks unity. His Jordanian leaders lack autonomy, but they are cognizant of this lack of autonomy; as a result, Jordan is that much more secure and stable. In other words, this leadership has been crucial to maintaining the status quo that ensures Jordan's stability.

Jordanian stability and security are important not only because the antithesis—war and conflict—is not desirable but also because it helps Jordan find a place in an increasingly globalized economy. Tariq, a museum director, is encouraged by the trajectory Jordan is taking: "King Abdullah is trying to find an economic place for Jordan in the world." Furthermore, Tariq adds that there is another strategic element to the U.S. client relationship—aid. "We get so much money from the U.S.," he says. Yet this strategic partnership has come at a tremendous cost for Jordan: "I think [President George W.] Bush told us, because sometimes we try to side with Iraq and Palestine, that we must say 'Jordan first' so we will not be enemies of the U.S.";[6] in other words, Tariq believes that Jordanians have had to distance themselves from regional conflicts they care about in order to secure their ties to the United States. Not only does the kingdom, then, defer to the Americans, but there is fear that the United States is also capable of enforcing its preferences on Jordan. Tariq worries that the United States can use its might to punish Jordan if Jordan does not agree to follow American preferences. In fact, he states, "America is not a peaceful country. France is more peaceful." He adds, "look at the U.S. military, half of it is always deployed outside the U.S." This is proof to Tariq that the United States is invested in interfering with the rest of the world. And while this factor annoys and angers him, he continues to be thankful that Jordan is peaceful, even if it means recognizing the role of the Americans. These levels of peace are guaranteed because "we are the puppet of the U.S. and they decide what we should do." This relationship with the Americans goes back to King Hussein, who "secured relations with the U.S. and made a base for them here." In other words, Jordan is firmly a satellite of the United States, and the former and existing monarchs are keys to maintaining the relationship.

Sami, a successful businessman of Palestinian origin, agrees with Tariq: the alliance with the United States not only breeds stability, but also the stability itself is vital for economic development. "King Abdullah has very good thoughts about the economy," notes Sami. "He is tremendously trying to fix it. In the next few years, the economy of our country will be great." Sami believes that King Abdullah is invested in maintaining these levels of security as necessary for the economic future of Jordan; this is why the king keeps strong ties with the United States. To preserve those ties, Jordan must

---

[6]The goal of the campaign was to galvanize Jordanian national priorities at the expense of other collective attachments. In other words, as was translated to me by citizens, it encouraged Jordanians to forget about other pressing issues like Palestine and Iraq and think instead about what was good for Jordan in the long run. To many Jordanians, that meant de facto acceptance of Jordan's status as a U.S. security client. The Jordan First initiative highlighted the prioritization of Jordan above all else (see chapter 3).

not have the same types of problems that challenge the region. "We are a peaceful country," Sami says. For him it is imperative that Jordan maintain these levels of peace and stability, which simultaneously shape and are shaped by the relationship with the United States. And although Sami understands that the United States is probably more interested in "Israel and getting oil in the Gulf," the relationship with the United States is Jordan's only hope for prosperity amid regional strife. "The king knows how to keep Jordan safe and growing through his ties to the U.S.," Sami firmly states.

Most Jordanians understand that strong ties with the Americans have come at the expense of pan-Arab dreams and have resulted in Jordan turning its back on its neighbors and even recognizing Israel before the institutionalization of a Palestinian state—sore points for many Jordanians. Yet, given the existing geopolitical realities of the region, they also believe that Jordanians do not have much of a choice. Samar, a USAID employee of Palestinian descent, shares Sami's sentiments. She supports neither Jordan's peace treaty with Israel nor the way the United States "encouraged" Jordan to sign the treaty; Samar says, though, that the treaty was important not only for peace but for prosperity, that "it helped the Jordanian economy and we benefited." Samar believes the United States has an ultimate objective in its relationship with Jordan: "[The Americans] want the Palestinians to stay in Jordan. So the U.S. has to stay nice to the king and the king listens to the U.S., so the Palestinians will stay in Jordan forever." Although she is deeply disappointed with this reality, she feels that she must accept the status quo—otherwise, things might be far more difficult than they are now. At least with the United States, Jordanians can hope for "stability and economic development," and these options are better than "war and poverty." Because no other leader "will listen to the U.S. the way the king does," Samar finds the geostrategic utility of the king crucial to maintaining Jordan's stable position in the Arab world.

Sana, a Palestinian Jordanian married to a restaurant owner, believes that there is a strong correlation between levels of peace and security and ties with the Americans. However, she also believes that the only reason Americans are interested in Jordan is because Jordan is stable and secure to begin with. "Look at all our neighbors, they are all suffering. We are the only stable country the U.S. can rely on." In other words, because Jordan is not anti-American, the Americans take care of Jordan. For Sana, then, anti-American forces must remain far removed from government, so that the alliance may be kept alive. This is very important, according to Sana, because not only does the United States look after Jordan, but other U.S. allies also "stay on good terms with Jordan and therefore Jordan can be secure and safe forever." She proudly states, "We are at peace with everyone. We do not go to war." She does not believe the United States is invested in Jordan for the sake of the Jordanians, however. Rather, the United States has strong

geostrategic interests in the alliance: "The USA does not care about the interest of Jordan. All they care about is their own benefits and interests. Their
strategy is to have peace with us, because we belong in the Middle East and
if they have a close ties with us, they can get into other countries in the Middle East." Sana obviously believes that the war in Iraq is a key reason for the
continued U.S. support of Jordan. Without the pro-American monarchy,
however, she wonders whether this relationship could or would persist. In
that sense, "King Abdullah keeps the good relations going with the Americans, and this is good for Jordan."

Sa'ad, a Palestinian investment manager, echoes many of these responses.
He believes that Jordan's stable comfort zone is a direct result of the monarchy's alliance with the United States. So secure is Jordan that it does not
need a military: "There is no need for the army, Jordan is in peace with the
USA and Israel and the rest of the world, so they have no one to fight back."
These good relations with everyone are a direct function of the king. Nader,
a Palestinian businessman in Amman, also endorses Sa'ad's point of view:
"Jordan is the safest country in the Middle East." These high levels of safety
exist because, Nader notes, the United States "wants a good relationship
with us" and because "our leadership knows how to constructively work
with the Americans."

That King Abdullah II, like his father King Hussein before him, is a smart
and shrewd leader who knows how to secure the interests of Jordan is a
theme that emerged throughout the interviews. Take Muhsin, an oncologi-
cal surgeon of Jordanian descent; he says, "Abdullah is a smart leader who
has great international skills." This is important to Muhsin, because Abdullah's father, Hussein, was just as savvy. And although Muhsin knows the
Americans have strategic reasons for the alliance with Jordan, "we rely on
them for economic and security help." This dependency is something the
kings understand, and they did everything to make sure Jordan remained a
viable country. Even today, Muhsin applauds the monarchy, saying, "Abdullah is trying to put Jordan on the map, through economic reform and tourism." The continuing development of Jordan calls for stability and security.

While some Jordanians feel that the alliance is based on mutual preferences, others are more skeptical and believe the United States, through its
might, dictates to Jordan the terms of the agreement. While some respondents see the kings as leaders cognizant of the limits of their autonomy,
others see them as stronger actors in the client formula. Finally, most people believe that there are strong geostrategic benefits to the alliance with
the United States, both in economic and security terms. Some were less
troubled by the costs of the alliance, however, while others felt more guilty.
Yet a consensus did emerge—the existing status quo of Jordan was a direct
function of the regime's alliance with the United States. In fact, without
that alliance, things could become considerably worse.

To protect the alliance, then, Jordanian citizens were more likely to lend their support to the monarchy because they worried about the impact of anti-American forces jeopardizing the relationship—even if this support stood in direct contradiction of their democratic ideals. The supporters quoted here, in addition to linking Jordanian stability to the monarchy via the Americans, are worried about Islamist anti-Western stances. They are not antidemocratic but are willing to compromise their democracy out of fear that Islamists will jeopardize the kingdom's existing beneficial relationship with the United States.

SUPPORT FOR THE MONARCHY AND U.S. CLIENTELISM: KUWAIT

Kuwaitis, like their Jordanian counterparts, recognize the importance of the U.S. client relationship to their overall levels of security and stability. Unlike the Jordanians, however, they are also much more likely to applaud that client relationship. A minority of citizens express concern about U.S. domination. Support for the United States comes with great pride, for if it weren't for the United States, Kuwait could have easily been subsumed in the turmoil and strife neighboring Iraq was inflicting in the Persian Gulf area more generally. This exogenous factor—positive U.S. interventionism—is crucial in explaining the pro-American viewpoints Kuwaitis have for the United States. In fact, as was highlighted in chapter 3, it is also why the ICM became more pro-American. Further, Kuwaitis feel exceptionally vulnerable given the size of their country amid regional heavyweights like Iran and Iraq. Kuwait's stability not only explains its enviable levels of prosperity; if Kuwait ever hopes to transition to a more diversified economy, it must remain stable and secure in order to attract foreign direct investment. Hence, the importance of the United States is even more vital. Unlike Jordanians, however, Kuwaitis do not view their monarchy as essential for maintaining the client relationship with the United States. In general, Kuwaitis are pro-American—even those who are leaders of the Islamist opposition movements. In my interviews, no fear emerged concerning anti-American leaders who could jeopardize the relationship with the United States.

These sentiments can be captured across Kuwait. Take Ali, a religious imam, for instance. He has no qualms about the strong relationship with the Americans. He says, "There is a need for the Americans, this is well understood by everyone." Ali worries about the ongoing unstable situation of Iraq and that hostile leaders there could have devastating effects on Kuwaiti security. These sentiments are reiterated by Ghada, a technical assistant, who also values the safety and security of her country. She likes not being worried, and she understands that the Americans "are important for that safety." Ghada, like the majority of Kuwaitis interviewed, did not link her support for the monarchy to the need to preserve strong ties to the United States.

Asma, a scientist, concurs. Like the majority of Kuwaitis interviewed, Asma worries about the security of Kuwait. She is worried that if U.S. forces leave Kuwait, "Iraq will attack us." Asma says that all Kuwaitis believe that the United States is vital for the security of Kuwait: "You find this opinion among Islamists, democrats, liberals, and others." However, like many Jordanians, Asma also believes the United States has larger geostrategic goals in the region and, to secure those goals, it plays all sides. For example, she says, the United States was supposed to be helping Iraq, but in the 1980s it was supplying arms to Iran through the contras. Although Asma believes that Americans "don't have to listen to anyone because they think they are superior," she also understands that these levels of superiority are a result of U.S. military might, which helps Kuwait. It is interesting to note that Asma makes no mention of the need to maintain these security arrangements with the United States through the monarchy.

Badr, a newspaper journalist, is, like Asma, critical of the United States, believing that it is responsible for the extremist Islamist elements in the region. He nevertheless believes the Americans are good for Kuwait. In fact, in his opinion, Kuwait is to blame for its occupation by Iraq. He says, "Why was it so easy for Iraq to conquer Kuwait? Because Kuwait was the only Gulf country that would not allow U.S. forces on its land prior to 1990. . . . Kuwait feels it paid for the price of pan-Arab slogans and was stabbed in the back. Then the Gulf War happened, and the Arabs did not stand with Kuwait." Although he did not support the 2003 war in Iraq, he believes that Saddam Hussein needed to be removed from power. He also issues a cautionary note to Bashar al-Assad, the president of Syria. "Bashar is an idiot," he says. "Fix yourself, because basically they will come and pummel you." In other words, although Badr feels safe and secure because the United States is on Kuwait's side—and further, he does not worry about such long-standing ties—he does feel the United States can alter leaderships in the region, as can Iraq. Badr believes that the United States is important for Kuwait's security; not once in the interview did he worry about Islamists sabotaging the Kuwaiti system or the alliance with the United States. Hence, Badr was able to talk about his democratic aspirations and his criticisms of the regime with ease.

Lulu echoes the sentiments of Badr and Asma. A bank employee, she feels that the relationship with the United States is important, despite her misgivings. It "bothers" her "to have any foreign presence in the Middle East." She wishes Kuwait could take care of itself, because the Americans are "not here for our good, but only for their own good. If we didn't have oil, they would not be here."

Yet even among those critical of the United States was a rationalizing logic justifying the acceptance of the Americans as Kuwaiti protectors. Eman, an economic analyst, also believes the Americans are in Kuwait "for their own agenda." But because Arabs turned their back on Kuwaitis, they were left with little choice. In fact, she says, American presence in Kuwait is "peaceful. It is good because our army is weak and it is necessary. We need [the Americans] for our safety." Eman does not believe in Arab nationalism and is adamant about saying that she sees herself as Muslim and Kuwaiti and not Arab. Since the First Gulf War she no longer follows news in Palestine, either. Explaining her disappointment with the Palestinian stance during the invasion, she goes on to say, "We feel for [the Palestinians], but I will not participate in any demonstrations for them. . . . It is different after the invasion."

Unlike Asma, Badr, and Eman, 'Awad, a successful oil businessman, does not think the United States has malignant intentions in the region. He is grateful to the United States because it secures the interests of Kuwait. Further, 'Awad believes the Americans actually care about Kuwait and they don't try to exploit the tiny kingdom. "The U.S. has opposed colonialism in Kuwait," he says. The Americans "did not come here to open markets. They did not come to occupy Kuwait. The presence of the U.S. is very positive." Like 'Awad, Basil, a Shari'a scholar, not only believes that the United States is a positive force, but he also applauds the levels of pragmatism that Kuwaitis enjoy in comparison to other Arabs. These levels of practical realism allow Kuwait to prosper as a nation under the protection of the United States. Basil views the Kuwaiti relationship with America as vital for the country's stability: "I have no problem with the U.S." He says that other Arabs should learn from Kuwaitis because Kuwaitis are more realistic. His support for the Americans derives not from an affinity with them but from a calculated concern: "[Arabs] should not fight the U.S. The U.S. is an elephant and the Arabs are ants, and if you keep hitting the elephant it will not change anything." If Basil were the leader of Kuwait, he would do the same as the al-Sabahs, he says: "I would bring them [Americans] into Kuwait." As he sees it, he United States is not a negative influence in the region. The Americans allow prayer, do not create checkpoints, and rule from afar. "At least they don't try to take away from us, like Saddam did."

Like Basil, Ghanim, a businessman, also believes Kuwaitis are far superior in their shrewdness when it comes to the United States. Kuwait has been able to secure its interests because it openly embraces the United States. In fact, Ghanim maintains, other Arab countries could learn a thing or two from Kuwait. He is thankful for the Americans' presence and sees no harm in it, saying that he "wishes they can stay forever." Further, Ghanim says with great pride that Kuwait is an example of a realistic and pragmatic country. Because Kuwait has accepted the presence of the United States, even its "colonial presence," Kuwait is much better off than other Arab countries. He argues, "The Arab world joked about us, saying that colonialism was bad, but it was the revolutionaries that tricked the Arabs saying colonialism must end, [and] they ended up worse than us." So although Ghanim believes the relationship with the United States borders on a colonialist relationship, he has no qualms about it. Further, he adds, there is no reason to be concerned because "U.S. troops do not negatively influence the country in any way."

A common theme emerged through both the Kuwaiti and Jordanian interviews: the United States was crucial to each country's security. Jordanians, though, were far more anxious about their anti-American Islamist groups—namely, the Islamic Action Front (IAF)—than were the Kuwaitis. As a result, Jordanians were less likely to embrace democracy and more likely to cling to the existing ruling status quo.

Supporting the Regime versus Supporting Democracy: Jordan

Anxiety about the Islamists in Jordan emerges as a direct result of a perceived inability to handle the country's external affairs in a way that would satisfy the Americans. This is not because the opposition movement is Islamist but more because it is anti-American. Although some Jordanians flat out disagree with Islamist political goals on domestic issues like conservative social policies, others are more accepting of and sympathetic to the Islamist domestic and regional agenda, especially insofar as Palestine, Hamas, and Hizbullah are concerned. In fact, vast majorities of Jordanians believe Hamas and Hizbullah are legitimate resistance movements; according to a Center for Strategic Studies (CSS) poll conducted in 2005, 73 percent see Hamas as legitimate, and 64 percent Hizbullah. These figures, however, are significantly lower than a previous CSS poll conducted in 2004, where 87 percent of Jordanians supported Hamas and another 84 percent supported Hizbullah.

Yet levels of support for Hamas and Hizbullah as legitimate resistance movements did not extend to the IAF in Jordan. After all, citizens rationalize that Hizbullah and Hamas fight to liberate their lands. Further, many Jordanians worry that support for democracy could empower Islamists to resist the United States in ways that would undermine levels of peace and security in the kingdom. Take the same Jordanians above who vowed support for the monarchy; here they rationalize their support for the regime as a means of countering the influence of anti-American Islamists. Bilal, for example, worries about the Islamists who use the name of Islam "to do bad things. They are not invested in the present day. Their thinking of Islam is not positive all the time. They do some good things like they try to stop the war between Israel and Palestine which is good. But they also want to stop our ties to the U.S. which will be very bad." Bilal understands what democracy is, and he is fully aware that Jordan is not a democracy. He wishes that Jordan could be more democratic, but he also knows that it has to "worry about its security first."

Hamzeh is more straightforward. He explains that he wishes Jordan were more ideal as a country. There is a lot of corruption and poverty, and the monarchy does not rule by democratic procedures. A physician, he is well-versed in democratic discourse, but he also says, "Democracy cannot be compatible when you have extremists on the ground who want to fight anything that is West." This, he argues, will "spin" Jordan out of control. Hamzeh is willing to compromise his democratic ideals for security. Hashim joins Hamzeh and Bilal: "Anything that is too extreme is not good." He takes issue with the way Islamist movements fight the United States and target innocent civilians, arguing, "It's wrong because you can't kill people in Islam without a reason, but the extremists use religion as a tool which is wrong. Unless they're fighting for their country, like Palestine, I can't see any justification. . . . It hurts Islam and hurts our [national] interests." He goes on to ask, "what will happen to us, if the U.S. strikes back?" Hashim understands what democracy means, and under different conditions he would support "letting people rule themselves." He also believes that democracy can create more equality "and put people at the same level"; yet, some groups will "use democracy to harm the country as a whole."

Nadir, a student, believes that among the greatest qualities of the monarchy under both Hussein and Abdullah is the relation they fostered with other countries, especially the United States. He is a strong supporter of democracy, but he says he has no problem with the monarchy as long as it keeps things "going well internationally." Although he flatly says, "Jordan is not democratic," he goes on to point out, "One of the things that is going extremely well for Jordan is the level of safety the kingdom enjoys. Jordan is the safest country in the Middle East." Nadir explains that he fears Islamists because they are so focused on the Day of Judgment. In other words, they could cost the country greatly because they don't value the present as much as the Day of Judgment. And because they misinterpret Islam to justify their actions, he worries that the consequences for a country like Jordan can be severe.

Other Jordanians, like Tariq, only wish that the Islamists really could understand Islam better. He condemns their uncompassionate behavior, arguing, "They are hard Muslims with no compassion. . . . All they want is to fight the Americans and the Jews. This is nonsense!" Tariq then goes on to explain that these Islamists are so narrow-minded that they don't even understand the prophetic ways. The Prophet said, "You can't sleep in your bed if you hear that your neighbor is hungry, even if your neighbor is Jewish." Tariq longs for that type of Islamic compassion rather than what he considers the radicalism he sees today. However, Tariq has difficulty "blaming" the Islamists for their own inadequacies. Unlike the Jordanians who see the Islamists as homegrown problems that societies must contend with, Tariq sees Islamists as creations of the United States. In fact, he believes the United States is behind this tarnishing of Islam: "Osama bin Laden started out as a good Muslim, then he was funded by the U.S. to fight Russia. Everything he became is because of the U.S." Tariq wonders whether the radicalization of Islamists is the ultimate objective of the U.S. government, in order "to keep Muslim societies nondemocratic and held hostage to the Islamist extremist messages." In other words, Tariq wonders whether the internal negotiations regarding democracy highlighted above aren't directly manufactured by the United States—considering Islamist anti-American positions.

Samia, another well-off student, worries about extremism in Jordan but cautions that Jordanian Islamists have no reason to be anti-American and worries about their influence in Jordan. Although she fully accepts the roles that Hamas and Hizbullah play in liberating their countries, the IAF, she argues, is not justified. She is also not against Islamic Shari'a. In fact, she says, if Shari'a were implemented, "People will be happier; fairness and equality will exist; and the country will progress like the Islamic world was progressing back in the day." But now that can't happen for multiple reasons. As she talks, she first points out the Jordanian progression is linked to an international design that dictates to Jordan the terms of the progress. Jordan's client status means that Jordan "must listen to the U.S." And these Islamist movements "won't know how to listen to the U.S., because they only thing they know how to do is make objections to the U.S." This dynamic, Samia argues, will end up "hurting Islam more and destroying Jordan." Samia, like Tariq, and Nadir, above, remains committed to the monarchy. Samia is thankful to the monarchy for keeping a grip on these potentially "radical" elements in society, radical elements that will destroy not only Islam but the country as well. She is not happy with her decision of having to "resort to monarchical rule" to protect the interests of her country and herself; however, although she understands that Jordan is not a democracy, the king plays an "important role in preserving the peace especially when these groups will cause our country to fall apart."

Sami is all for democracy. He believes "democracy is about freedom of opinion," yet he worries whether it is good for Jordan. He argues that Jordan needs to develop economically, and these developments are contingent on strong ties with the United States. Sami also worries that Islamists will jeopardize U.S. ties. If democracy will bring to power individuals who will "resort to extremism to reach their goals, even inhumane ways against the West," then they will have no country. In other words, Jordan needs to ensure its survivability before it can advance democracy. Islamists can bring the wrath of the Americans to Jordan. Therefore, although he supports democracy, he also wants to empower the existing regime to do something about the Islamists, even if it is "nondemocratic." He feels the monarchy is the best form of leadership to see Jordan through economic development; hence, it must be empowered to continue this mission. In Sami's assessment, "Jordan cannot afford everything to be democratic."

Sana not only believes that the Islamists might cause harm to the West in ways that would jeopardize U.S. ability to take care of Jordan; she also simply believes the United States would respond negatively to Islamists having real democratic power in Jordan. Sana says, "We are the only country in the Middle East without problems with the United States. If we will elect Islamists it will appear that we are terrorists. It will be a black dot on Jordan." This black dot, she worries, will provoke the Americans against Jordan. In a sense, she shares the concerns that the Americans would have: "look, [the Islamists] are extreme in our own country and try to impose their ideas on their own people. Imagine what they would do if they had power to engage other countries?" In other words, Sana worries that Islamists would use their power to alienate allies and create more enemies. She argues that because Islamists are "not applying Islam in the right way" they are perhaps better off with dictatorship. Democracy can be an "inapplicable theory" and will "cause potential harm." The Arab world is already struggling and can't afford irresponsible leadership. She understands that the region already suffers from "colonialism, occupation and war." In a sense, she admires King Hussein for his ability to "build the country" in a region full of conflict and strife. Not any leader could manage to "navigate the mines" of the region the way he did; "[h]e worked really hard because he cared about the civilians." In fact, Sana goes on to explain that his open cooperation with the United States was because of his strong commitment to Jordan and its people.

Like Sana, Samar believes the Islamists will pose a threat for the United States and Israel, and like Tariq, she also believes that this carefully orchestrated scheme has effectively produced its desired result, "to keep the Arab world backward." Although she longs for the "glory days of Islam, where Muslims led good lives . . . not the terrorism and extremism you see today," she worries about these radicals in Jordan. Samar wishes that more Islamists would be invested in teaching and spreading the word of "true" Islam, and not become the "scary, complicated, and complex" groups who want to organize attacks: "They turn off the people." If these Islamist groups want to really fight the enemy, then why, she asks, do they target "innocent people"? These tactics hurt their interests. She believes a Jordan ruled by Shari'a would not only be democratic but would also return the true message of Islam to the real Muslims "who are democratic." However, Samar goes on to say, "Israel and the U.S. will not allow it." She feels the United States and

Israel keep these anti-Western, radical Islamist movements alive so that Arab societies like Jordan can never democratize. That way, the status quo, which serves "Israeli and American interests," can "always be maintained through the king." Because she does not trust either the Americans or "their agents," the Islamists, Samar believes that Jordanians have no other choice but to support the monarchy. Samar convincingly argues that Jordan is not a democracy: "Democracy is the ability to choose one's own leader. Not somebody born in the right family." Yet, the monarchy serves this "vital interest and it is an embattled country that needs to cater to Israeli and American interests."

Similarly, Sa'ad understands full well that the monarchy in Jordan is not democratic. "The monarchy means no democracy," Sa'ad notes. "Once a person is ruling, he should not rule forever. He needs to be changed. It should be like Britain. The monarchy is there with no effect, and the prime minister should be in control." The problem with Jordan's monarchy is that "[b]oth the father and son are puppets for America, they do what the USA wants them to do." Nonetheless—and however disgusted with the relationship he may be—Sa'ad has a tone of support and sympathy for the monarchy: "This country was made out of nothing. It's a desertlike country and the economy is really bad." In other words, how else could Jordan survive? He does not support Islamist groups because while "they think they are doing the right thing" they are in fact "after fame and symbols." He thinks anti-West groups are wrong, and that people like Osama bin Laden can "cause suffering for the entire population." Although most groups do not support Islamist extremism, Sa'ad worries about how the United States was able to blame "entire societies" for the acts of a few. So in this formulation, it becomes even more important for Muslims to make sure Islamist groups don't attack the West.

Sa'ad believes that there is no democracy in Jordan. "No, the king changes the government whenever he wants. This government is an autocracy and not a democracy; I believe it's an autocracy because it's ruled by one person." In fact, Sa'ad says rather bitterly, "The regime pretends like they hear the people, but they really do not do anything that the people ask them to do—the only people they listen to are the Americans and the Israelis." While Sa'ad understands his government as "autocrat[ic]," he also believes the monarchy is essential for the current international status quo. The United States might indeed "[look] after the interest of Jordan," but it does so only in the "short term." According to Sa'ad and others like him, "if Jordan does anything wrong, or goes against the will of the USA, they [the United States] will go against us. They really look after their own benefits; they benefit from our geographic location, and how we surround other counties that interest them like Israel, Iraq, and Syria—it's really not because they care about us or love us." For Sa'ad, then, Jordan needs to make sure that no forces go against the United States in the meantime: "The monarchy will maintain the relationship."

Muhsin is adamant about Islamists not governing the country. He is not too worried about the Islamists' socially conservative agenda, but he is worried about the political ramifications. He says, "When Islam was first created hundreds of years ago, the Arab world dominated the European and Christian worlds. Things have flipped today and we are behind and dominated. We have to learn how to cope with this. Islamists can't cope with this. If we listen to the Islamists, they will destroy us. We will fall even more behind. Do they have knowledge in politics or international relations? This does not mean we should disengage from Islam but we must think reasonably." Muhsin says that political Islamist groups, especially those with militant tendencies, "are not acceptable." He worries about the IAF, pointing out that although some of their leaders are not militant, others are. Furthermore, these Islamist groups have the potential to "scare the crap out of the people. They tried to sneak in chemical weapons into our country and have links with al-Qaeda. They scared the hell out of everyone." And although Muhsin professes himself a democrat, he understands the strategic importance of supporting the existing monarchy. In order to prove that there is nothing inherently undemocratic about Muslim culture, he elaborates. "Look," he says, "a democracy means people governing people. I support democracy and not a dictatorship. [However,] we are a long way from democracy here in the Middle East today. But we weren't always against democracy. If you go back, after the Prophet died, his successor was chosen by the people; the leaders in the early Islamic period were elected, and it's part of our religion. Islam never said *dictatorship*, nor did it call for rigid rules. Islam is in tune with living." But because the Islamists don't seem to understand Islam— they are "extremists and will hurt our interests with the U.S."—Mushin concludes "we can't call for democracy." Further, he worries that these groups will come to power with little knowledge about international matters. "We need groups who can actually represent us internationally. . . . We have a long way to go," he adds. Muhsin thinks King Abdullah is a smart leader and especially prudent in his international skills, "like his father." Abdullah is trying to put Jordan on the map, and he is invested in improving the economy through tourism. Muhsin is no fool: "The U.S. has strategic interests in Jordan and we rely on the U.S. for economic and security help. Both Hussein and Abdullah have had very strong relations with the U.S."

SUPPORTING THE REGIME VERSUS SUPPORTING DEMOCRACY: KUWAIT

Like the Jordanians, Kuwaitis also felt that the client relationship with the United States was beneficial to its security. Unlike the Jordanians, however, the vast majority of Kuwaitis I spoke with did not have outright negative opinions of the United States; the Americans were seen as liberators and protectors. And although Kuwaitis keenly tied their security interests to those of the Americans, they believe the United States to be a less belligerent force in the region. The patron-client relationship, they maintained, was essential given the instability in neighboring Iran and Iraq. Kuwaitis were further comforted by the fact that its opposition groups, including the Islamist opposition, are pro-American. Furthermore, Kuwaitis were not worried that Islamists would jeopardize the current relationship the kingdom has with the United States. In fact, most Kuwaitis maintained that the Islamists are modern, are not anti-West, and accept the national priorities of Kuwait. Because of this understanding, Kuwaitis were more likely to demand more accountable and democratic forms of governance, and they were also more likely to ask that the existing monarchy be held to democratic procedures and norms. Notably, Kuwaitis were more likely to be worried about the influence Islamists could potentially have on internal—rather than external/international—politics. Some Kuwaitis had little tolerance for the ICM or Salafi conservative interpretations of Islam. Nevertheless, a consensus emerged among those committed to democracy: Islamist conservatism should not preclude their participation in domestic politics. The democratic process, they maintained, necessitates involvement of all groups and sectors. Finally, among those who did support the monarchy, it was rare to find that security concerns were a driving force for their support of the monarchy. Support of the al-Sabahs was rarely linked to geostrategic considerations, as they were in Jordan. Rather, love for al-Sabah revolved around his kindness, generosity, and other actions and credentials far removed from maintaining the alliance with the United States. Because Kuwaitis are not threatened by anti-U.S. opposition movements that might jeopardize the client relationship the way Jordanians are, the quality of their engagement vis-à-vis the regime is more likely structured by local issues and concerns rather than international ones. Hence, Kuwaitis were less likely to be supportive of the regime and more likely to uphold their democratic ideals. Democracy, according to Kuwaitis, will not jeopardize the well-being of Kuwait as a nation.

Kuwaiti Attitudes from Within

These general sentiments of Kuwaitis are captured in the in-depth interviews with ordinary Kuwaiti citizens. Of the 71 interviews conducted in Kuwait, 24 (33 percent) were proregime and pro–status quo, while 47 (67 percent) were more critical of the regime and were in favor of increasing democratic reforms (see table 4.2).

Ali is a regime supporter who does not link his support to countering the anti-U.S. influence of the Islamists, as his counterparts in Jordan do. Rather, Ali told us he loves the Emir al-Sabah because "the emir takes the

TABLE 4.2. Kuwaiti regime supporters and opponents

Regime supporters	Regime opponents	Total
$n = 24$	$n = 47$	$n = 71$

time to talk to the people and go out and meet with them." Personally, Ali has met the emir four or five times. This, Ali argues, means that the "rulers are already accountable to the citizens." He says the monarchy tries to be democratic, and indeed, "compared to all the other Islamic and Arab countries in the region," it is most democratic. He goes on to explain that the relationship with the United States is very important, especially given the unstable situation in Iraq. "There is a need for the Americans, [and] this is well-understood by everyone." Ali believes that the Islamists of Kuwait pose no threat to the United States' or Kuwait's national integrity. In fact, he says, "there are the ideologues who have hijacked Islam and made it a terrorist religion. And there are those who operate for the love of Islam and what it stands for. In Kuwait, the Islamists represent the latter tendency." The Islamists in Kuwait are seen as loving groups of people who will not cause harm to anyone.

This sentiment about Islamists was captured among regime supporters and democratic enthusiasts alike. Asma, for example, is a strong supporter of democracy. She would like to see more accountability between the regime and the people. She also wouldn't mind if the parliament reflected the interests of Kuwaitis more generally, as well. Like the majority of Kuwaitis interviewed, Asma worries about the security of Kuwait. However, she makes no mention of the need to maintain these security arrangements with the United States through the monarchy. She does not fear that anti-U.S. forces will threaten the security of Kuwait. Therefore, Asma is able to call for more democracy and work toward more accountable government.

Although the majority of Kuwaitis I interviewed did not believe the Islamists posed an external threat to the security arrangements with the United States, some still did not have a strong desire to see Islamists gain more strength. 'Awad, for example, feels that the Islamists in Kuwait are all promonarchy forces. In fact, 'Awad, a strong democrat, believes the al-Sabahs bolster the influence of the tribes and Islamists so that they can stay in control of Kuwait. He is annoyed that the Islamists and tribal elements have such large representation in the Kuwaiti parliament. Since 1991, Islamists have enjoyed a significant plurality of seats, winning close to 40 percent of the vote. This involvement by the monarchy in parliamentary affairs is antidemocratic, 'Awad maintains. His concerns with and criticisms of the Islamists have more to do with their function as an arm of the regime rather than a threat to the security arrangements of the regime. 'Awad is not worried that his democratic engagement and his demands for more leadership accountability might threaten ties with the Americans.

At the conclusion of the interview, 'Awad said he felt good about a few democratic developments in Kuwait, including women's right to vote. He believes Kuwait is moving along a democratic trajectory, especially in light of the succession after the emir's death in 2006: "The way they went according to the constitution was very positive, and it showed that the ruling family had to abide by it just like the society." 'Awad is committed to the democratic process in Kuwait.

Badr works for a left-leaning opposition newspaper in Kuwait. He believes that the constitution needs to grant more democratic rights, and that democracy needs to progress in society by the implementation of the constitution. He is proud of the fact that his newspaper is the only one to document human rights abuses in Kuwait. Although he has little tolerance for the conservative messages Islamists espouse on issues of gender equality—and in many cases Kuwaiti Islamists are more conservative than others in the region—he feels that they must be represented if Kuwait is to be a true democracy. He does not feel that any of their ideas are dangerous; they are simply too conservative.

Badr feels that the Islamists have a strong influence in society because Shaykh Sa'ad allowed them more leeway to counter the influence of the leftists. However, he says, "we must keep pushing for democracy, because democracy will bring everyone to work together, even if it also brings the Islamists to power." And although he disagrees with the policies of the Muslim Brotherhood/ICM in Kuwait, he is pleased that they play the game correctly; they play within the system and do not try to sabotage Kuwait: "The Muslim Brotherhood in Kuwait has encouraged political participation within the system. Other groups in other countries are against the system and they do not encourage political participation." Badr is happy with democratic developments in Kuwait. He is pleased that there is outspoken resistance to the monarchy, even from the political Islamist groups. "They used to be more shy and the young people want to go out and be loud. This is all positive," Badr notes.

Badr is dedicated to ensuring that Kuwait becomes a parliamentary democracy. He is upset that Shaykh Sa'ad appeared to be rejecting the constitution by dissolving the parliament a couple of times. "He turned parliament into a weak body with no real legislative role. It became simply an advisory council." Badr says that if it were not for the "strong voice of the citizens of Kuwait," then the progovernment members of parliament at the time would have allowed the constitution to fall. He is hopeful that Sabah al-Ahmad will respect the democratic constitutional process more than his predecessor because it was indeed the constitution that ensured his own succession.

Badr is also committed to the security of Kuwait through the Americans and not once in the interview was he worried about the Islamists sabotaging the Kuwaiti system or the alliance with the United States. Hence, Badr was able to talk enthusiastically and with ease about his democratic aspirations and his criticisms of the regime.

Badr's sentiments are shared by Basil. Basil is a scholar of Shari'a law, and he works for the ministry of the interior as a security guard. Basil began his interview by saying, "Shari'a is life, but is not understood. Because it is not understood, it can kill innocent people." He worries that terrorists are hijacking Shari'a. Basil is keen to distinguish between the type of Shari'a he wants for Kuwait and that of the terrorists: "We want it to be according to the Shari'a, but we want it to be done justly. But if it is going to cause problems with the people or the country then I do not want it." Basil is proud that Kuwait's Islam is different than others. It is not violent or anti–United States. Further, he says Kuwaiti society values security, and as such, they are for "peace with the Jews."

He is happy that Islamists in Kuwait don't use their mosques to preach hate against U.S. and Arab leaders. He believes Islam should be political but it must be led by educated individuals who will not cause harm to the people. "The implementation of the role of mosques is often wrong in the Arab world, they brainwash like the Germans did." Basil views the Kuwaiti relationship with the United States as vital for the country's stability: "I have no problem with the U.S."

Basil is very uncomfortable, however, with movements that use Islam to justify their hatred toward the United States. He says that even when we look at Islam there is no contradiction between being a strong advocate of Islam and being pro-American. In fact, he says the Americans are "our brothers." He then proceeded to give examples from the Quran: "The Quran says that Muslims can learn from the devil, so why can we not learn from the U.S.? I am not saying that the U.S. is a devil, but we need to keep cooperating and learning from them." In the Quran, Basil tells us, is an *āyah* (verse) that says a "very strong nation will rise that will be just." For Basil, this strong nation that will rise and preach justice is the United States. For most other Islamist groups, the nation that will rise and be just is the new Islamic state, yet to be created. If he were the leader of Kuwait, he would do the same as the al-Sabahs, he says: "I would bring them [the United States] into Kuwait."

Basil believes that other Arab countries deserve their lack of development. Those other Arabs are too invested in "war and blowing people up." He also feels that other countries hate Kuwait because they think that Kuwait is the one that brought the United States into the Middle East. "They think we are sinners," he says. Basil would like to see Kuwait move toward more democracy and believes that all groups are moving in that direction.

More important, Basil is able to evaluate his monarchy on its democratic performance and not its geostrategic importance.

Like other Kuwaitis, Basim is not worried about the consequences of increasing levels of democracy. He sees democracy as a way of improving things in the monarchy. He notes that the Constitution "was placed in 1961, and it has not progressed and they have not yet amended it." He does not like the fact that there are no political parties. Further, "there is a lot of corruption in the government." He wonders about whether the al-Sabahs "know what they are doing and if they are good for Kuwait. They don't have a real plan." According to Basim, one of the problems facing Kuwait is that the Islamists are too conservative. "If we had more democracy, other political parties would be able to counter their influence. Otherwise," he says, "they pose no other risks." About the United States, he says, "we have an agreement between Kuwait and the U.S. I don't have a problem with it. I support it." Basim, along with several other Kuwaitis interviewed, does not juxtapose his support for democracy to concerns that Islamists may jeopardize the client relationship with the United States.

Eman, like Basim, is a strong advocate of democracy and says she will continue to accept the al-Sabahs "as long as they work with parliament." She would like the parliament to ensure the rule of the majority. As the system stands now, the viewpoints of the people are not necessarily reflected. In order to do so, the al-Sabahs need to work with the parliament and the parliament needs to represent the peoples' wishes more effectively. Eman is not worried about the potential influence of Islamists in parliament or in international affairs. She thinks most of the Islamists in Kuwait "are not extreme. They are involved in charities and helping the poor. They are more humanitarian than other Islamists elsewhere." As such, Eman is not worried about their involvement in political life.

Ghada is a supporter of the monarchy, but her support extends to the al-Sabahs for reasons other than security. She values the monarchy because it has done so much good for the country. She recalls when Shaykh Jaber al-Ahmad al-Sabah passed away. "When he died, we wept because it was like he was part of the family. He made a lot of changes for the country. He was a very social person, and there were times when he was in good health, he would go and shake hands with normal people." Ghada goes on to tell a story. When she was younger, her grandfather came home and told her family that they would not believe who rode in his truck. She said that a passenger got in his truck and was asking him about his life, and what he thought about the things that were happening in Kuwait, and if he was happy with the emir—and it ended up being him. "He was a very humble man, and liked to be with the regular people."

Ghada is very content with her lifestyle in Kuwait. She feels Kuwait approaches the ideal: "Free health care, no taxes, free education, the working laws are excellent." For Ghada there is no need to demand more democracy, because she has everything she needs. Her support for the existing monarchy is not structured by security vulnerabilities and worries about U.S. patronage. Like many other Kuwaitis, Ghada believes that Islamist opposition in Kuwait is moderate and pro-American. She feels that Islamic movements in Kuwait come in all varieties. Some are moderate, some fanatic, but a lot are liberal. In that sense she feels strongly that they are entitled to their opinions. Further, Ghada indeed values the safety and security of her country. She values living in a safe place and not being worried, and she understands that the "Americans are important for that safety." Again, Ghada's support for the monarchy was not influenced by concerns about the Islamists harming Kuwait's relationship with the United States.

Ghanim, too, is very prodemocracy and offers concrete ways to improve the status of democracy in Kuwait. He wants to see a legislative body that is more accountable to its citizens. Ghanim does not worry that democracy will harm the security position of Kuwait, nor does he feel Islamists might pose any internal threat to international affairs. However, he is not particularly fond of the Islamists or the Bedu (Bedouin tribes). Ghanim is worried about the influence of the Bedu and Islamists in society, but he does not oppose their participation. In fact, he thinks their participation in parliament might be a good thing because that way "the government can control their voice and ideas." Ghanim is a strong advocate of democracy and argues that democracy "needs to protect human rights; it should be about participation of the society and the rule of the majority. . . . The ruling family is not democratic and the emir has the final power," he says. Although parliament is good, he worries that the emir "has all the money so he can back people and buy interests and this defeats the purpose of a national assembly." Ghanim would like to see the royal family more transparent and accountable.

Lina, like Ghanim, does not like Islamist groups and does not agree with them, but also thinks that they must be a part of democracy. She doesn't like what they try to do when they come to power, but she believes that this is part of the democratic process. She really takes issue with their conservatism, however, and is appalled that they try to enforce their conservative values in parliament. Before the Kuwaiti liberation from Iraq in 1991, Lina says, the Islamists were "very provocative. They were anti-American and they would call for jihad. But after the liberation, they stopped these messages." Further, she points out that the events of 9-11 also showed the Islamists how damaging Afghani extremism was. The Taliban and al-Qaeda "were out of control and were proud of their extremism. They wanted to destroy the West but the U.S. responded" with war. Lina goes on to say, "After 9-11 then, Islamic movements wanted to distance themselves from the terrorists. This was very positive for Kuwait and it brings political stability." Because of this political stability, Kuwait could focus on issues of female voting and succession—both considered to be democratic triumphs in the past few years. Lina maintains a strong commitment to democracy and argues there is "room for more of it." Lina continues to demand more democracy and unlike her Jordanian counterparts is not concerned that more democracy can endanger Kuwaiti ties to the Americans.

Finally, and like Lina, Lulu is no fan of Islamist movements because they are conservative and have the potential to move Kuwait backward on the modernization front. However, she maintains their right to exist. Lulu is committed to the democratic value of representation: "Any political idea should exist, whether it is Islamic, conservative, or liberal." She feels the Islamist movements in Kuwait have had a positive impact in some areas. "They have a lot of passion and help others in society." In fact, she says, "I wish that the West would hear more about the activities that the Islamist groups do for their society, for their culture, and for people in need." Lulu does not believe the Islamists in Kuwait pose a threat to the Americans.

She believes the Kuwaiti government provides for its citizens, but it is not an ideal government. "The government is trying to move toward more democracy, but it is not democratic yet," she notes. She is happy that women were just given the right to vote, but she would like to see fewer government appointments and more parliamentary autonomy. Again, like most of the Kuwaitis I spoke to, Lulu was able to call for more democracy based on her democratic convictions without having to worry about the potential security ramifications of Islamists coming to power. Unlike Jordanians, Kuwaitis were far less likely to be supportive of the existing regime out of fears revolving around security and stability.

The Geopolitics of Support for Shariʿa: Different Islamic Worldviews in Jordan and Kuwait

Jordanians were equally divided in their support of and opposition to the regime. While supporters were more likely to be invested in the status quo, believing that economically they would benefit most from it and understanding that the status quo could only be sustained by the United States, those who opposed the regime were more likely to resist the status quo along with U.S. patrimonial dictates. Regime opponents in general had less to lose. They were stuck in dead-end jobs earning no more than 100 JDs ($150.00) a month as clerks, shopkeepers, or taxi drivers, for example. In many cases these individuals worked hard to move upward on the social mobility ladder and were unable to find suitable employment opportunities. With financial burdens worsening, these individuals were outraged by the injustice they perceived as infesting their society. They were more likely to talk about justice, calling for a regime that didn't squander the wealth of the population and international forces, like the United States, that could be a fair arbiter of democratic norms across the globe. They attributed the deteriorating living standards in Jordan to a U.S. government–Jordanian monarchy conspiracy that oppresses people in order to secure geostrategic priorities in the region—particularly full support of Israel, full access to oil, and a defeat of Islam. Eighty-seven percent of Jordanians in a World Public Opinion poll believe that the primary U.S. goal in the region is maintaining control of oil. Another 80 percent believe the United States has the geostrategic goal of weakening and dividing Islam.[7] In this formulation, the "puppet" regime in Jordan serves U.S. interests at the expense of citizens and Islam. Therefore, among opponents, there was only one way to shift this reality: to reify Islam and remove Jordan from the client relationship with the United States.

In conversations and interviews with citizens across Jordan and Kuwait, an important variation emerged in how citizens thought about Shari'a. Slightly more than 80 percent of Jordanians who opposed the regime were overwhelmingly doing so by supporting an Islamic state as a means of furthering their anti-American agenda. Jordanians were also far more likely to believe that Shari'a and democracy were not only compatible but also that Shari'a was the true road to democracy. The discourse of Shari'a, they thought, would also remove Jordan from its clientelistic status. This is substantiated in other research conducted across the region as well. In pooled data from four Arab countries—Jordan, Egypt, Palestine, and Lebanon—those citizens who have negative opinions of the United States are more likely to support Shari'a as a system of governance (see fig. 4.1).

Across Jordan not only was there much more support for Shari'a than there was in Kuwait, but in Jordan it was more readily a tool of the opposition. Political Islam, Shari'a, "just and true democracy," regime change, and anti-U.S. stances were all part of the same discourse—one that opposed the existing status quo. What is more compelling is that these understandings of Shari'a for many Jordanians are deemed compatible with support for democracy. According to the Arab Barometer national survey, a full 87 percent of Jordanians who believe that a system governed by Islamic law is a suitable form of government for Jordan also believe that democracy is the best form of government, period. In fact, in Jordanian circles across Amman, Zarqaa, Madaba, Ma'an, and 'Aqaba, conversations about politics turn on the utility of Islam to the betterment of existing circumstances. In Islam, some argue, true democracy, true justice, and true dignity would emerge. Citizens

---

[7] Kull, Steven. "Can Obama Restore the U.S. Image in the Middle East?" *Harvard International Review*, December 19, 2008 (accessed at http://hir.harvard.edu/can-obama-restore-the-us-image-in-the-middle-east).

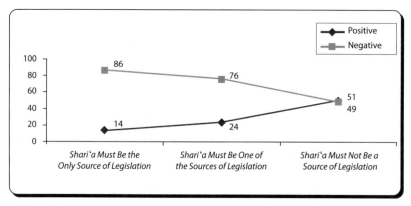

Figure 4.1. Impact of attitudes toward Shari'a on attitudes toward the United States (pooled data: Jordan, Egypt, Palestine, and Lebanon). Source: Center for Strategic Studies in Jordan, *Revisiting the Arab Street: Research from Within* (Amman: Center for Strategic Studies in Jordan, 2005).

expressed a deep and strong attachment to their religion. Through the Islamic understandings of the "just society," Islam serves as template for efficacy, integrity, pride, and esteem. Shari'a removes individuals from what is perceived as the embarrassing reliance on and domination of the United States. True independence and autonomy are a prerequisite to real democracy.

Thus, for Jordanians opposed to the status quo, Islam becomes a mechanism to distance these citizens from Western forms of democracy and from the United States. Take Linda for example, a store clerk in one of Amman's trendy malls. Not only does she believe that the current government is corrupt and ineffective but also that the only reason the regime remains in power is because it plays a vital role: to secure U.S. geostrategic interests in the region. She questions how America promotes democracy in the Arab world. She believes it offers more talk than substance: "The U.S. pretends it wants democracy, but it is not for the people." The real democracy, she maintains, "is in Islam." She further believes that the United States is not fair and continues to destroy the region: "The U.S. destroys us economically, emotionally, and with war, and calls us terrorists in the process." An Islamic state, for Linda, is the solution. "If we were to follow Shari'a, we would be the happiest people, because we have the best religion."

Miriam, a college student, also strongly opposes the regime and is a strong advocate of Shari'a. Yet, she commented, "It should be applied the right way, because this is an Islamic and Arab country." In her tone is a strong nationalistic sentiment, one designed to differentiate the Arab and Islamic world from the West. Miriam believes that Arabs and Muslims have the right to fight for their rights. The problem, according to Miriam, is "not that Muslims and Arabs are not democratic, as the U.S. would have the world believe," but that since they have suffered the most from oppressive U.S. policies in the region, these policies have "radicalized people to fight for their rights." In other words, the Muslim world has no other option than to pursue the path that it is currently following. She believes that her country is held hostage by the United States: "We listen and are ruled by the U.S. If we were to follow the way of Islam, things would be different." Here, Miriam directly positions Islam as a means of countering U.S. hegemony in her country.

These echoes of U.S. intervention are captured among opposition voices to the monarchy. The citizens believe that they are occupied by a U.S. empire that seeks complete domination. Mazin, a retired army member, believes the United States is in fact guilty of promoting Islamist extremism across the region; he states, "The U.S. created groups like al-Qa'eda." Further, he argues that the Islamists are empowered because of U.S. and Israeli policies in the region. "When the U.S. gives a green light to Israel to oppress Palestinians," Mazin notes, "of course hatred and extremism will grow." This is all to satisfy U.S. geostrategic interests. "The U.S. will keep oppressing us for their interests, which includes oil and Israel. Do you think the U.S. would care if we exported bananas? No!" In order to satisfy Israel, Mazin goes on to say, the United States forces Jordan to keep hold of the Palestinians. He believes the United States needs a compliant Jordanian regime to host the millions of Palestinians who might want to return to Palestine: "The U.S. pressured Jordan to take all the Palestinians, or they said they would find a new king for Jordan." Thus, the United States is used to getting its way in the region. Today, Mazin says Jordan is stable, but it's because the "Jordanians conduct the business of the Americans and Israelis." This, for Mazin, is embarrassing; he believes that Shari'a will "solve all the problems in the region." According to Mazin, the citizens of Jordan suffer because they are not ruled by Shari'a. True Shari'a would release them from this burden with the United States. However, he cautions, "The U.S. will make this hard for us. We are trying to break this huge mountain with a small hammer. But with time," he tells me, "more people will embrace Islam and we will improve our situation."

Lina, a consultant, shares this view of Islam as an empowering force that can counter U.S. dominance. "If we were to follow Islam correctly," she says, "we would be the most advanced country and have the strongest influence and presence." True democracy is in Islam: "The fetus before it is born already has democratic rights in Islam." She considers Jordan's complicity with the United States a tarnish on Jordan's overall standing in the world. "There are countries that don't respect us, because they consider us to be a smaller America." Mervat, a housewife, like Lina and Mazin, is convinced that Islam is the solution. She says, "Shari'a is everything to me." And she is a strong advocate of political Islamic groups. An ideal government is one where "there is a connection between the government and the people and not the government and the U.S."

Conquest and subordination loom large in the minds of those who advance an Islamic model of governance in Jordan. For them Islam inspires change, hope, and faith in a future that is not about defeat. These more malleable and elastic definitions of Shari'a enable an alternative structure, indeed an alternative reality; at its core is democratic justice. As Mustafa, a retired civil servant, argues, "Look at our history; we had the best leaders who were religious. . . . If you take the core principles of Islam and apply them, they are indeed democratic." He continues, "Islam should be applied in Jordan. But the U.S. tells us we can't have Islam. Why? The U.S. says Islam is not just. Look at Islamic rule: even at the time of the Prophet there was a Jewish person who was poor, and the Prophet said we must feed him. Neighbors were taken care of regardless of their religion." Mustafa believes the United States is denying Jordan true democracy by denying it Islam.

Across Jordan, many people felt that true democracy, given contextual realities, could only emerge through Islam. Said Layth, "When we apply Islam, our democracy will be better than theirs [the United States']." Among these opposition voices, the United States was seen a hypocritical force, not only "help[ing] Israel and destroy[ing] our lives" but "encourag[ing] and pay[ing] for such behavior." Layth continues, saying, "We pray one day the U.S. will be just, but it is not." Leila concurs, believing that the United States, because it is an unjust power, will not allow the Arab world to be democratic. She believes U.S. dominance has led to extremism. People in the West, she says, are not extreme because they live in free societies; "[b]ut if we are democratic, this government will be changed and the U.S. does not want that. Therefore, we will have no democracy. . . . If we have an Islamic state we will have human rights and justice. These days the government and the U.S. don't want Islam and they don't want democracy." This sentiment is reiterated by others.

Sharing these sentiments is Bassim, who works two jobs and can barely make ends meet. A father of four, he says, "The U.S. and the Jordanian government fear our religion [of Islam]. They both know that the people of Jordan will accept no other system than an Islamic system. In this day and age, democracy will allow us to criticize the king, but it will not allow us to support Islam. Shari'a is a political liability." True democracy, Bassim maintains, will emerge with a true Islamic state: "without Islam there can be no democracy." He goes on to say, "We need leaders to stand up to the United States and Israel, because they do not respect the people of this region." He is upset that the current government in Jordan is such a weak force in the world: "Jordan today lives off hand-me-downs and loans from the international community." Bassim believes this is a U.S. design to "keep the people impoverished so we're always thinking of our next meal and not more important things like politics."

Kuwaiti engagements with Shari'a were different than those in Jordan. Two sources of variation structure the differences. First, Shari'a was not overwhelmingly a discourse of the opposition. Both regime supporters and opponents wanted some role for Shari'a, but they called for measured influence. Second, the discourse of Shari'a in Kuwait did not encompass an anti-U.S., anti-clientelism stance but instead focused on domestic issues. Thus, while Jordanian citizens opposed to the status quo appropriated Shari'a doctrine as a means of standing up against the United States, Kuwaitis believed that Shari'a should play some role in governance but certainly should not be the only source of legislation in the Kingdom.

Ahmad says, "It should be used as a guideline. . . . If we were to follow it 100 percent we would go back a hundred years." Mahmoud concurs: "Kuwait should not be ruled by Shari'a, but it has to be considered in the laws, because this is an Islamic country." Munira also shows her cautious support for the doctrine, saying, "We would like Shari'a, but we have to consider that times have changed. Today we live in a modern world." Lujain, however, says, "I am against Shari'a because I feel that I would be forced to follow laws that I do not believe in."

Many in Kuwait look to Iran and Saudi Arabia as poor examples of Islamic states, and wonder whether Kuwait can escape such a model of Islamic governance. Says Mustafa, "I don't want to live in a country like Iran or Saudi Arabia, where people take advantage of Islam to rule." Nonetheless, some support Shari'a out of conservative values, seeing Shari'a as a means of avoiding problems that liberal democracies in the West have to contend with. Omer says, "If we had Shari'a, then we would save ourselves from dealing with the issues that the U.S. and Europe are dealing with. I don't want Kuwait to have to address issues of same-sex marriage and out-of-wedlock births. This is not normal for us." While many looked to Saudi Arabia as a bad example of a Shari'a state, several looked to other countries outside the Arab world as positive examples. "Look at Malaysia," said Nadia, "they have democracy and respect for Islam." Salwa believes Islam is compatible with democracy as long as it understands the boundaries of democracy. She, too, is a supporter of liberal democracy and wants to ensure that religion doesn't infringe on individual liberties. Sami concurs, arguing that a liberal democracy is "superior to a *shura-* [consensus-] based Islamic democracy." And Wajdy worries about Islamic governance. He believes Islam is just, but he also believes that it requires a level of sophistication and understanding. "If people were well-read, then yes, we could have an Islamic democracy. . . . You need to educate people's minds about Islam and democracy first. That's why there is nothing better than a democracy." For Wajdy, democracy is a simpler, more clear-cut political system that can potentially appeal to everyone. Basil agrees, saying, "Shari'a is life but it is misunderstood. Because it is not understood it can kill innocent people. It can be interpreted in too many different ways." Therefore, for Basil, an Islamic government is too risky.

Even where I found significant support for Shari'a, it was measured and always linked to a domestic agenda. The main points of contestation revolved around interpretations of conservative versus liberal democracy. For example, liberals like Bassim worry about Islamic laws reducing individual liberties. He does not think that Shari'a should be part of the government. He is happy, though, that the civil laws do not offend the Islamic religion. And Eman says that although she would like Shari'a to rule Kuwait, it would directly contradict liberal democratic values and that's the direction in which she would like Kuwait to move.

Juxtaposed to these responses were those that supported Shari'a. It is noteworthy here to point out that supporters of Shari'a were not necessarily opponents of the regime, nor did they see Shari'a as a road map to independence and autonomy. Anti-Americanism was not structuring their political engagements and appropriations of Shari'a principles. Where there was support, it was normally grounded in social conservatism. Take Linda in Kuwait: she would like Shari'a to rule, because Islamic law would protect society. She does not want to live in a democracy that would end up legalizing abortion. She goes on to say, "Gambling and wasting money or valuables for no reason is not right. Drinking alcohol and getting into a car accident and killing an innocent person is not right. Islam wants us to stay away from these things because of our own good." Muhsin doesn't want Shari'a per se but is sympathetic to the doctrine; he, too, talks about a socially conservative agenda for Kuwait without "gambling, prostitution, and alcohol."

However conservative or liberal these Kuwaiti responses were, they focused on domestic issues and the pros and cons of the doctrine as they apply to the country. Unlike Jordan, where Shari'a was seen as a nationalist vehicle toward autonomy and self-determination, in Kuwait it was evaluated on its conservative or liberal merits. And whereas Jordanians saw in Shari'a the true path to autonomy from the United States, Kuwaitis in their democratic engagements were not looking to subvert the realities of regime clientelism in the ways Jordanians were.

EXPLORING ALTERNATIVE EXPLANATIONS

While it may be tempting to attribute the sources of variation that emerge between Jordanian and Kuwaiti patterns of political engagement solely to the Palestinian-Jordanian cleavage in Jordan, both my qualitative and quantitative data show that this is not the case. The Palestinian-Jordanian cleavage was not significant in any of the quantitative models that we will examine in chapter 5. Further, in the qualitative evidence, Palestinians, especially those who constitute the middle class, are as likely to be supportive of the regime as their Jordanian counterparts. In fact, it is the business class that is invested in stronger ties to the United States, the global community, and by default the peace treaty with Israel. As Laurie Brand says, "Certainly the business community (both Palestinian and Transjordanian) has been one of the most enthusiastic backers of the [peace] process; supporters of the peace process hope that it will result in greater foreign investment in Jordan."[8] King Abdullah continues to arduously work to remove the parameters of the traditional cleavage. First, his marrying Queen Rania, a Palestinian, has been a huge victory for Palestinians in Jordan who absolutely adore the queen. Further, some of Abdullah's most respected and trusted advisors are Palestinian. For example, in 2007, Farouk Kasrawi and Bassem Awadallah, prominent Palestinians, had the king's ear on decisive economic and political matters. King Abdullah continues to augment a unified Jordanian identity crucial for its progress toward its development trajectory. Many Palestinians are lending support to Abdullah's messages and goals as well. New economic realities guided by globalization have transcended the traditional Palestinian-Jordanian divide.

A second explanation would have it that Kuwaitis are more critical of their regime because they can "afford" to be more critical. After all, their country is an oil-rich state that will be well off regardless of any new leadership. Although this logic seems plausible, it certainly does not appear to carry water. First, this line of logic directly contradicts rentier formulations. Citizens in resource-rich states shouldn't be contesting regime authority. Second—and more important—if this logic were correct, we would expect to see active democratic contestation in all resource-rich countries, where citizens could "afford" to depose the existing rule. I maintain that citizens are cognizant of the fact that resources alone can't provide wealth and comfort; in the end, these resources need to be exported to the international community. International boycotts and sanctions can render the richest oil states obsolete. Witness Iraq under Saddam. Resources alone are not sufficient to protect a country economically if the wrong leadership emerges and/or remains in power. Thus, citizens of resource-rich states are not equally enthusiastic about democracy. For example, Saudis are much more reluctant about democracy than are their Kuwaiti counterparts, given the dynamics of Islamic opposition in that country. In fact, oil-rich states rely on access to foreign markets, and such reliance keeps these states vulnerable to international pressures.

A third explanation would postulate that fear of regime change in Jordan is driven by Islamist support for Shari'a rather than Islamist levels of anti-Americanism. I offer two key points of evidence to discredit this valid alternative explanation. First, in Jordan citizens were asked on the Arab Ba-

[8]Laurie A. Brand, "Palestinians and Jordanians: A Crisis of Identity." *International Journal of Middle Eastern Studies* 24, no. 4 (1995): 46–61.

TABLE 4.3. Support for Shari'a and security vulnerabilities

	Compromise human rights for security (support)	Compromise human rights for security (do not support)
Support Islamic parliamentary system	42.52% $n = 128$	57.48% $n = 173$
Do not support Islamic parliamentary system	33.45% $n = 186$	66.55% $n = 370$

Source: Arab Barometer 2005–6, accessed January 2007 at http://www.arabbarometer.org/survey/survey.html.

Note: Pearson chi2 (1) = 6.9226 Pr = 0.009.

rometer to evaluate the following statement: "The government should implement only the laws of the Shari'a." A clear majority in Jordan supported this statement, with 87 percent agreeing. Initially, Shari'a does not appear to be a polarizing issue in the context of Jordan and thus cannot explain the polarization behind support for the status quo. However, I conduct bivariate analysis to further examine this important alternative explanation. Via the Arab Barometer we asked a set of questions to tap into support for Shari'a-oriented policies. One of these questions is as follows: "To what extent is a parliamentary system of government suitable where only Islamic political parties and factions compete in elections"? Thirty-five percent of Jordanians find such a system suitable. If concerns about Shari'a do indeed mediate concerns about the Islamists, we would expect that those people who do not support this statement to be more vulnerable and hence more likely to support the compromising of human rights for purposes of security and stability. Table 4.3 shows that this is not the case. In fact, those members of society who do support an Islamic parliamentary system are more likely to do away with human rights for purposes of security than those who not. Thus, vulnerabilities are not mediated for concerns about support for Islamic Shari'a.

CONCLUSION

Clear differences emerge between Jordanian and Kuwaiti assessments of the geostrategic utility of the monarchy. In both societies, there was ample acceptance of the idea that the clientelistic relationship was beneficial for security, stability, and—in the case of Jordan—economic well-being. Although Kuwaitis were more likely to see the United States as a benevolent force, the people of both states used the status quo as a template to frame their understanding of national and individual well-being. However, differences emerged between Jordanians and Kuwaitis regarding the ways the client relationship structured levels of engagement with their regimes. Because Kuwaitis saw Islamist opposition as more pro-American and not a threat to the patron-client relationship, they were able to assess their leadership in terms of its performance—the services it fulfills, its connection with and attitudes toward the citizenry, and other democratic criteria—rather than regional political stability. Although some Kuwaitis were bothered by the conservative power Islamists asserted through their parliamentary participation, none were worried about Islamists jeopardizing their relationship with the United States, as was the case in Jordan.

Jordanians, on the other hand, were far more likely to link their support for King Abdullah II to security and stability concerns. They worry that the anti-American Islamists, if given democratic rights, may jeopardize the relationship with the United States and Israel. Hence, although supportive of democracy, Jordanians are more cautious about its suitability for Jordan. They prioritize security and worry that democracy may have profoundly negative effects. In many of the interviews, another common theme emerged: Jordanian commitments to Islam involved a liberation worldview, one that would rid Jordan of U.S. clientelism. This was not the case in Kuwait. There, Islamic engagements were centered on domestic issues revolving around liberal and conservative domestic agendas.

Chapter 5 offers further quantitative evidence to the bolster the arguments advanced in this chapter. Chapter 6 and chapter 7 explore how regime clientelism has structured state-society relations in other Arab countries by examining patterns that emerge in Morocco, Palestine, and Saudi Arabia.

APPENDIX: OPEN-ENDED QUESTIONNAIRE ADMINISTERED IN
JORDAN, KUWAIT, AND MOROCCO

Please tell me a little about yourself.

1. What do you do for a living? How long you have lived here? What education do you have? Are you married? Do you have children? How old are you?
2. If married, what does your spouse do? If not married, can you tell me a little about your parents?
3. On the whole, are you satisfied with your life these days? What are some things that you are really satisfied with? What are some things that can be better? (What are some serious problems that you face? What are the causes of these problems? What can be done to help resolve these problems?)
4. Generally speaking, do you think that people can be trusted in your country? How about in your neighborhood?

5. Do you think people care about other people in your country?
6. If you were to have an important and immediate economic problem and your were in desperate need of funds, to whom would you resort?
7. If you were to have conflict with someone in your neighborhood who was clearly overstepping his/her boundaries what would you do? (After response—if the answer is not "court": Would you consider taking the person to court?)
8. If a government office promised you something and did not deliver what would you do? Would you seek the help through a *wasta*?[9]
9. If a police officer treated you with disrespect what would you do? Would you file an official complaint?
10. If you are applying for a job do you think your merit is enough to obtain that job?
11. Do you purchase lottery tickets? (Measure of Islamic observance.)

Now I would like to discuss matters of religion with you.

1. On the whole would you consider yourself a religious person? What does "a religious person" mean to you? What ideals and values does a religious person hold? Do you hold those values?
2. What does Shari'a mean to you?
3. Do you think your country should be ruled by Shari'a?
4. Do you think Islam in your country is different than other types of Islam that exist in other places like Egypt or Saudi Arabia?
5. What about political Islamic groups? What do you think of these groups?
6. Some people in the West refer to Islamist groups as extremist. What do you think?
7. Do you think Islamist groups in your country are anti-West? Anti–United States?
8. Are there extremist elements in this society? What is your opinion of them?
9. Do you pray? Fast? Attend mosque? (How often?)
10. Do you belong to any Islamic association or organization?
11. Do you think Islam and democracy are compatible?

What is your economic situation?

1. On the whole how would you evaluate your economic situation these days?
2. Do you think you have good opportunities in your country? Why or why not?

---

[9]The term *wasta* refers to using one's personal connections or "pull" to get something accomplished.

3. Do you think your country's economic standing will improve in the next several years? Why or why not?
4. On average what is your monthly income?
5. In the past year have you needed to take a loan?
6. Are you and/or your spouse currently employed?
7. Do you worry about job security?

Now I would like to ask you about your overall ideas on government.

1. In an ideal world, what would be your ideal form of government?
2. What roles and functions should this ideal form of government play?
3. What does democracy mean to you?
4. In this regard do you think your country has an ideal government? Is it democratic? Would you like to see more democracy?

What are your evaluations of government in your country?

1. How would you evaluate the educational system and institutions in your country?
2. Does the government offer you any services? What type? What is your evaluation of these services?
3. What type of services would you like the government to provide?
4. How would you evaluate the parliament?
5. How would you evaluate the army?
6. How would you evaluate the monarchy? (Modified according to country.)
   A. [Previous monarch] and [current monarch] have both ruled in the last decade; how would you compare the two?
   B. Are there things you particularly like about [current monarch's] rule? Are there things you don't like?
7. How would you evaluate the police?
8. How would you evaluate political parties? Can you name a few?
9. How would you evaluate the [chief Islamist party in your country]? Further, how would you evaluate the [chief secular party]?
10. People often say that corruption is widespread in your country. Do you believe this is true?
11. If yes, has corruption personally hurt your opportunities? How has it affected you or others you know?
14. People often say that *wasta*s are important. Do you think they are important?
   A. If yes, what is your opinion about *wasta*s? Are they good or bad?
   B. What is your opinion of the Makhzen? Does it operate in the interests of all people? (Morocco only)

17. People often say that the family you come from matters. Do you think this is true?
   A. If yes, how does your family matter?
   B. If yes, has this hurt or helped your opportunities in your country?
20. Do government officials care about people like you? Why or why not?
21. Do you think the voices of the people are heard? Why or why not?
22. People often say that there are only two classes in your country, the rich and the poor. Do you think this is true?
23. People often say that people in your country don't care about local political affairs. Do you think this is true? Why or why not?
24. People often say that citizens fear the regime in your country. Do you think this is true? How about you—do you fear the regime?
25. What do you think about the policies of Morocco in the Western Sahara? Do you support the government's role? (Morocco only)
26. What do you think about the government's recent efforts to counter human rights abuses in your country?
27. Which political leaders do you support the most? Which political leaders do you feel are just?
28. What about the court system—is it just?
29. Are the laws of your country fair?
30. Are the laws of your country applied to everyone?
31. Are you Arab or Berber? If Berber, do you think this has hindered your opportunities in Morocco? (Morocco only)
32. To what extent would you say there is an Arab/Berber divide or cleavage? What are the immediate effects, if any, of this ongoing cleavage? (Morocco only)

Questions on gender

1. Do you think women are treated fairly in your country?
2. Do you think women would make good political leaders?
3. What is your opinion on
  — the Moudawana reforms?[10] (Morocco)
  — honor killings? (Jordan)
  — women's right to vote? (Kuwait)

Questions on national/Arab pride

1. Are you proud to be [nationality]?
2. What identity matters most to you: (a) Muslim/Christian (religious), (b) Arab, or (c) [nationality]?

[10]The Moudawana is the Moroccan Family Code, which in part addresses women's rights.

3. Would you consider leaving your country?
4. Do you think your country has reached its potential?
5. What are some serious problems facing your country?
   A. What are the causes of these problems?
   B. What can be done to help resolve these problems?
8. People often say that the Arab world should be farther ahead than it is now. Do you think this is true?
   A. If so, why do you think the Arab world lags behind the rest of the world?
10. Do you think other Arab countries respect your country?
11. What do you think of the U.S. role in your country?
12. Do you think the United States looks after the interests of your country? Why or why not? Do you think the United States cares about democracy in your country?
13. What about the Europeans? Do you think France looks out for the interests of your country? What about Spain? Why or why not? Which Western power do you think has been the kindest to your country? Which Western power has not been so kind?
14. Do you follow the events in Palestine? What do you think about the ongoing conflict? What about Iraq?

Questions on civic and local participation

1. In your free time what do you do?
2. Do you socialize a lot?
3. Do you participate in any local associations? What types?
4. Do you watch TV? If so, what type of programs do you watch?
5. Do you watch Al Jazeera? Do you like it? Why?

Questions on political participation

1. Did you vote in the last election? If yes, whom did you vote for? What were the factors that influenced the way you voted?
2. If you did not vote, why not?
3. Are you planning to vote in the upcoming elections? If so, whom do you plan to vote for?
4. Would you like to participate more in political life? In what ways?

CHAPTER FIVE

Support for Democracy and Authoritarianism

The Geostrategic Utility of Cooperative Leadership

WHILE CITIZENS ACROSS THE ARAB WORLD SUPPORT DEMOCRACY AND AGREE THAT IT is the most suitable form of governance to advance the human condition, I have found Jordanians far more hesitant to embrace it than their Kuwaiti counterparts as a reformist doctrine. Jordanians are more likely to bracket democracy for a larger, more important goal: maintaining the national well-being of the entire country. This, Jordanians explain to me, is contingent upon Jordan's close ties with the United States, a relationship that could be jeopardized if Jordan were to empower forces unfriendly to the United States. Hence, for Jordanians, the existing monarchy serves a vital geostrategic role in securing the ongoing relationship with the United States; further democracy might weaken the monarchy in ways that could jeopardize this relationship. Kuwaitis also highlight the crucial role of the clientelistic relationship with the United States for maintaining the country's security. In Kuwait, however, citizens are not as concerned about losing clientelistic favor and benefits in the pursuit of democracy.

This chapter relies on survey data collected across the Arab world. The four sources of data I use in my analysis of the Jordanian case come from the 2001 World Values Survey data,[1] Mark Tessler's 2004 public opinion poll,[2] Mark Tessler and Amaney Jamal's 2005-6 Arab Barometer survey,[3] and a 2007 Pew Global Attitudes survey.[4] My analysis of the Kuwaiti case relies on three sources of data: Tessler and Jamal's 2005 Kuwait survey,[5] Tessler and Jamal's Arab Barometer survey administered in late 2006,[6] and the 2007 Pew

[1] N = 1000; principle investgator, Ronald Inglehart.
[2] N = 1000; principle investgator, Mark Tessler.
[3] N = 1000; principle investgators, Mark Tessler and Amaney Jamal
[4] Pew Global Attitudes Project, *America's Image in the World*. Washington, DC: Pew Research Center, 2007 (accessed at http://pewglobal.org/commentary/display.php?AnalysisID=1019).
[5] N = 750; principal investigators, Mark Tessler and Amaney Jamal.
[6] See this chapter's appendix for Arab Barometer sampling methods for Jordan and Kuwait.

Global Attitudes 2007 survey.[7] This chapter complements the qualitative data presented in chapter 4.

This chapter will offer quantitative support to the causal logics citizens employ when engaging democracy, authoritarianism, regime stability, and transition in Jordan and Kuwait. Because the argument advanced in this book is multi-layered, this chapter attempts to unpack the argument incrementally. I offer an empirical strategy that gradually addresses the microfoundations of my argument. This argument can be sketched briefly as follows: Citizens in client states (especially those who value access to global economic markets) will want to ensure stable ties to the patron in the event of transition. Therefore, citizens living in countries with organized anti-American opposition movements that have considerable constituency basis will be more likely to favor less democracy to ensure that anti-American forces don't harm relations with the United States. Ultimately, then, citizens in client states with similarly large opposition movements that are less anti-American will more likely favor democratization because the changes in regime will not jeopardize relations with their patron.

In order to gain empirical leverage on the causal logics citizens employ in Jordan and Kuwait about the nature of the suitability of the existing regime, this chapter will first illustrate the high priority citizens place on regional stability. Arguably, these levels of stability are a function of maintaining strong ties with the patron, the United States. Second, this chapter will then examine the value citizens place on free trade and access to global markets. Through multivariate analysis, I will demonstrate that citizens who value economic globalization also tend to have more favorable opinions of U.S. policy. That is, favorable opinions about the United States are directly linked to citizen economic interests in both Kuwait and Jordan. Third, I then demonstrate that there is a divergence in the nature of Islamism in the two countries when it comes to levels of anti-Americanism. Islamist supporters in Jordan are far more anti-American than Islamist supporters in Kuwait. Fourth, and finally, I argue that this variation in the nature of anti-Americanism among Islamist opposition movements shapes the ways in which citizens engage democracy and their own regimes in the two countries.

Notable variation emerges between Jordan and Kuwait. More specifically, citizens who stand to benefit from greater economic globalization will support less democracy and more authoritarianism when anti-Americanism among the organized Islamist opposition is strong. Conversely, those who are more anti-American would like to see more democracy and less authoritarianism. They would like to see a change in the status quo, and they don't leverage their political engagements through the lens of U.S. patrimony. This,

[7]Pew Global Attitudes Project, *America's Image*.

I argue, will be the dynamic shaping political engagement in Jordan. Ideological affinities to democracy are not sufficient to override the pressing
need to maintain stability. In Kuwait, however, given the fact that the Islamist opposition is not anti-American, political engagement is not structured around concerns of opposition movements harming relations with
the client. Therefore, in this case, citizens in Kuwait, who are more pro-
American, are also more likely to be democratic. Here, I maintain, citizens
are able to engage their political ideals. Those who are more pro-American
are also more democratic. This chapter concludes with a discussion about
the attitudinal verses behavioral consequences of my findings. The data
I present here is attitudinal and not behavioral, and therefore, a legitimate
question arises: to what extent can the evidence I present here explain behavioral and macrolevel outcomes? I address this valid concern in the chapter appendix.

JORDANIAN AND KUWAITI ENGAGEMENTS WITH SECURITY,
DEMOCRACY, AND AUTHORITARIANISM

Across Jordan and Kuwait, citizens place a high premium on security and
stability. Given the turmoil and strife in the region, both Kuwaiti and Jordanian citizens consider themselves fortunate to live in countries that are
secure and stable. Not only do security and stability guarantee that citizens
can live without war but they also mean that each country can continue to
benefit from its client relationship with the United States. Of course, the
client relationship itself brings these countries more security, and these levels of security are absolutely vital for further global economic integration,
attracting foreign direct investment, expanding tourism in each country,
and—in the case of Kuwait—diversifying the economy so that it is not only
reliant on resource wealth.

When asked to describe the number one priority for their countries in
the next ten years, a majority in both Kuwait and Jordan cited "maintaining
order" as the clear goal. Other response options included giving people a
larger say in government affairs, reducing foreign influence, reducing rising
prices, protecting freedom of speech, and fighting corruption. Fifty percent
of both Jordanians and Kuwaitis agree that maintaining order is the first
priority. In Jordan, the category receiving the second most important responses was fighting rising prices, at 20 percent. Only 4 percent believed
that reducing foreign influence should be a priority, and only another 4
percent demanded for citizens a greater role in government affairs. Kuwait
exhibits a similar trend, with 50 percent citing order as their first priority,
but respondents also showed significant support for other democratic ini-

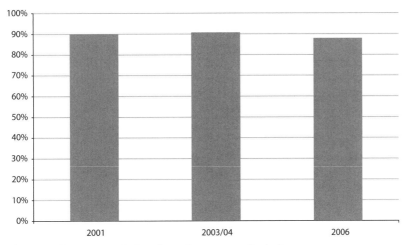

Figure 5.1a. Democracy is the best form of government (Jordan).

tiatives. Fourteen percent of Kuwaitis believed fighting corruption should also be a priority, along with another 13 percent who argued for a more meaningful citizen role in government affairs. Kuwaitis in general did not note that reducing foreign influence should be a priority.

These same concerns about security have resulted in different patterns of democratic and authoritarian preferences. Although Jordanians are favorable toward democracy, with clear majorities believing it is the best form of government, significant support for strong authoritarian leadership persists—more so in Jordan than in Kuwait. When asked whether, despite its problems, democracy is better than any other form of government, Jordanians in 2001, 2004, and 2006 agreed, with positive responses of 90 percent, 91 percent, and 88 percent, respectively. This trend also finds support in Kuwait. In 2005, 89 percent of Kuwaitis believed that democracy was the best form of government, and in 2006, 88 percent held this view (see figs. 5.1a and 5.1b).[8]

Stark variation emerged between Kuwaitis and Jordanians, however, on their support for strong leadership. When asked whether citizens supported a strong head of government that does not bother with parliament or elections, Jordanians were far more likely to agree than their Kuwaiti counterparts. Close to 40 percent of Jordanians in 2003 and 2004 held the view that strong authoritarian leadership was good for Jordan, but the proposition enjoyed only 18 percent support in Kuwait (see fig. 5.2). A Pew survey conducted

[8] Katherine Meyer, Helen Rizzo, and Ali Yousef, "Changed Political Attitudes in the Middle East: The Case of Kuwait." *International Sociology* 22, no. 3 (2007): 289–324.

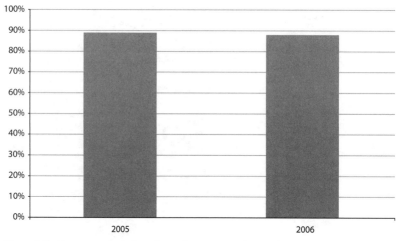

Figure 5.1b. Democracy is the best form of government (Kuwait).

in July 2005 further substantiates this finding: when asked whether citizens should rely on a democratic form of government or a leader with a strong hand to solve the country's problems, 45 percent of Jordanians agreed that a leader with a strong hand would be more beneficial than a democratic form of governance. The Pew survey was not administered in Kuwait, but other evidence from Kuwait and Jordan presented below validates these findings.

Kuwaitis were far more willing to call for the enforcement of democratic procedures and norms. Further, Kuwaitis were less willing to do away with democratic rights. For example, 80 percent of Kuwaitis agreed that the rights of the opposition should always be guaranteed, compared to 60 percent of Jordanians (see fig. 5.3).

These variations between Jordan and Kuwait are especially intriguing given that they don't conform to conventional theories derived from economic and rentier models of political development. Rentier formulations would posit that Kuwaitis should be far more likely to be supportive of their existing regimes. Given their system of rentier perks and benefits, Kuwaitis should not only embrace existing monarchical leadership but also be more wary of democracy.[9] This is not the case. Jordanians are far more likely to

---

[9]Although existing economic arguments (Boix, 2003 and Acemoglu and Robinson, 2006) suggest that a more equal distribution of wealth might lead to more demands on democracy; see Darren Acemoglu and James Robinson, *The Economic Origins of Dictatorship and Democracy* (Cambridge: Cambridge University Press, 2005); and Carles Boix, *Democracy and Redistribution* (Cambridge: Cambridge University Press, 2003). One can plausibly argue that oil facilitates equal distribution of wealth. Yet this is hard to confirm in the case of Kuwait. First, data on inequality are not available. Second, according to Boix, because oil resources are fixed assets, the incentives for elites to concede to societal demands for democracy are minimal. Thus, if oil

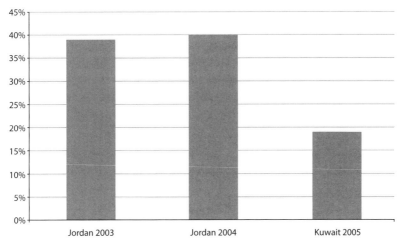

Figure 5.2. Support for strong leadership.

embrace and support existing authoritarian leadership than are their Kuwaiti counterparts.

In fact, when citizens in each country were asked whether they agreed or disagreed with the statement "People should always support the decisions of their government even if they disagree with these decisions," Jordanians were more likely to agree than Kuwaitis. Forty-nine percent of the Jordanian population says it supports its government unequivocally, where only 26 percent of Kuwaitis do. To get at the source of this variation, it is vital to comprehend the factors that structure these authoritarian and democratic dispositions in each country.

MAIN ARGUMENT: GIVEN DEPENDENCE ON THE UNITED STATES, OPPOSITION
OPINION AND MOBILIZATION STRATEGIES MATTER

I argue that the variation in levels of support for existing leadership emerging between Jordan and Kuwait is influenced by the ways citizens evaluate the essential roles existing leaderships play in maintaining an alliance with the United States. The position of a state in the international arena shapes the

were driving these findings we should see less democracy and not more democracy in a place like Kuwait. Finally, certainly oil wealth alone cannot explain democratic contestation and regime accommodation of such democratic demands. This was not clearly the case in Bahrain, during the Spring 2011 upheavals, when geostrategic concerns about the U.S. military presence and the possible close alliance between the Bahraini Shi'a and Iran stifled the democratic process. Neither is this the case in Oman, where the government engaged in greater redistribution of wealth as a means to quell democratic demands.

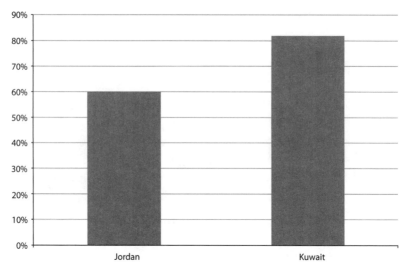

Figure 5.3. The rights of the opposition. Sources: Jordan—Tessler polls 2004; Kuwait—Tessler and Jamal poll 2005.

ways citizens engage their regimes. Those citizens who value free trade and access to a globalized economy will be more likely to worry about ensuring global access. Although they may be committed democrats, they also value the stability the regime brings—especially in guaranteeing global integration. These citizens worry about harming relations with the patron in ways that may isolate their countries. Upsetting the delicate balances of these regimes may result in a reconfiguration of trade agreements, possible sanctions, international isolation, and instability. These factors do not bode well for economic development. Witness debates in Egypt today. It is the business community that is most worried about Egypt's relationship with Israel and what this will mean for their country's economic future.[10]

This pattern extends to Jordan. More specifically, I argue that in a country like Jordan, support for the Hashemite monarchy is considerably higher when compared to levels of Kuwaiti support for the al-Sabahs because of Islamist opposition opinion. The Islamist opposition in Jordan is much more anti-American than the opposition in Kuwait. Jordanian citizens are therefore more likely to worry about the potential democratic ramifications of regime change in Jordan. The security and well-being of their country can be undermined. Maintaining the strength of the monarchy does not preoccupy Kuwaitis to the same extent that it does Jordanians. In Kuwait, Islamist opposition opinions are more favorable toward the United States. Therefore, an alteration of power structures in Kuwait through increasing

[10] Barbara Ibrahim, interview with the author, April 25, 2011.

levels of democracy will not disrupt the relationship Kuwait enjoys with the United States.

Empirical Tests

I advance a multilayered argument here. I offer the following empirical tests that aim at getting us closer to the arguments advanced in this manuscript. First, I argue that citizens of client states—especially those who value economic globalization—will want to ensure stable ties to the patron in the event of regime change. Thus, it is important to better understand the ways in which attitudes toward the patron are distributed within various societies. Primarily, it is important to determine the extent to which attitudes about economic globalization shape support or opposition toward U.S. policies in the region. In order to closely examine these questions in the context of Jordan and Kuwait, I utilize the Pew 2007 Global Attitudes Data. This survey asks a general question about support or opposition to the U.S. fight on terror. The question reads: "Which comes closer to describing your view? 'I favor the U.S.-led efforts to fight terrorism,' or 'I oppose the U.S.-led efforts to fight terrorism.'" In Kuwait, 41 percent of the public supported the so-called U.S. War on Terror. In Jordan, 19 percent lent their support. This dichotomous variable will serve as the dependent variable and serves as a proxy for support for U.S. policies.

Given the dichotomous nature of the dependent variable, I use logistic regression analysis to determine the extent to which attitudes toward economic globalization influence attitudes about the policies linked to the U.S. fight against terrorism. I anticipate that those citizens who positively evaluate economic globalization will also be more positive about U.S. policies, captured here by the question on support for the American "War on Terror." The logic of this is straightforward. Citizens who value greater economic integration also value access to the United States and the protections it affords. Thus, these citizens are also more likely to be supportive of policies that protect U.S. interests, like the War on Terror.[11]

I use two questions to tap into attitudes toward economic globalization, my main independent variable here. The first is a measure of support for free markets. Arguably, free market policies and orientations are important for greater economic openness and integration.[12] The question reads as follows: "Do you completely agree, mostly agree, mostly disagree, or completely

[11]The findings about positive assessments hold if another dependent variable were used (like U.S. favorability). I employ the dependent variable gauging support for U.S. policies because it's a more precise measure of attitudes toward U.S. influence and presence.

[12]See Kenneth Roberts, "The Mobilization of Opposition to Economic Liberalization." *Annual Review of Political Science* 11 (2008): 327–49; and Erik Gartzke, "The Capitalist Peace," *American Journal of Political Science* 51, no. 1 (2007): 166–91. See also Helen V. Milner and Bumba

disagree with the following statement? 'Most people are better off in a free market economy, even though rich and some are poor.'" The second question asks, "What do you think about the growing trade and business ties between (survey country) and other countries—do you think it is a very good thing, somewhat good, somewhat bad or a very bad thing for our country?" These two questions assess attitudes toward economic globalization. It should be noted that the analysis here concentrates on general attitudes toward economic globalization and not necessarily different economic sectors within society that stand to benefit from greater economic globalization. This is so for two reasons. First, as outlined in chapter 1, a straightforward class analysis does not illuminate who stands to benefit from greater globalization. Different members within each class or category can be globalization winners or losers. Second, even looking at the literature emerging from comparative and international political economy, there seems to be some disagreement on whether categories like "skilled" and "unskilled" labor can provide much leverage on globalization winners and losers. The Stopler Samuelson theorem, which posits that unskilled labor in developing countries is more likely to support greater economic globalization, has been substantiated in studies by Anna Maria Mayda and Dani Rodrik, Kenneth Scheve and Matthew Slaughter, and Helen Milner and Keiko Kubota. Yet, as Helen Milner and Bumba Mukerjee point out, recent survey-level evidence from Latin America (e.g., the work of Andy Baker, 2003) demonstrates that low and unskilled labor is more likely to favor protectionist policies.[13] Of course, the limited data from the Arab world does not allow for a test of the Stopler Samuelson theorem, as data on skilled versus unskilled labor are not available in any survey; however, what we can do here is look at those who positively assess policies that align with further economic integration. Basic bivariate models illustrate that those citizens who are more optimistic about the future standing of the country as a whole are also those who favor more economic globalization. These findings are substantiated in both Kuwait and Jordan.[14] Thus, assessments of global economic integration serve

---

Mukherjee, "Democratization and Economic Globalization," *Annual Review of Political Science* 12 (1999): 163–81.

[13]See Milner and Muhkerjee, "Democratization and Economic Globalization"; Helen V. Milner and Keiko Kubota, "Why the Move to Free Trade? Democracy and Trade Policy in the Developing Countries." *International Organization* 59 (2005): 107–43; Anna Maria Mayda and Dani Rodrik, "Why Are Some People (and Countries) More Protectionist Than Others?" *European Economic Review* 49, no. 6 (2005): 1393–1430 ; Kenneth Scheve and Matthew Slaughter, "What Determines Individual Trade Policy Preferences?" *Journal of International Economy* 54, no. 2 (2001): 267–92; and Andy Baker, "Why Is Trade Reform so Popular in Latin America? A Consumption-based Theory of Trade Policy Preferences," *World Politics* 55, no. 3 (2003): 423–65.

[14]Pew Global Attitudes Project, *America's Image*. Question 13 was used as a measure of optimism about the future: "When children today in [survey country] grow up, do you think they will be better off or worse off than people are now?"

as a reasonable proxy for tapping into attitudes among those who stand to benefit from economic globalization more generally.

How do attitudes about economic globalization, then, matter for evaluations of the U.S. War on Terror? Using logistic regression analysis, I examine the link between attitudes toward economic globalization and evaluations of U.S. antiterrorism policies. I also include some very important control variables. The first is satisfaction with household income, which serves here as a proxy for household income (because reliable income data is not available). I also control for a very important policy issue, which is U.S. favoritism toward Israel. Again, in order to be certain about the association between economic globalization and the U.S. fight against terrorism, it is important to control for the effect of this important U.S. policy position. Arguably, U.S. policy toward Israel is one of the issues that have earned the United States negative ratings in the region. Thus, I include this measure in the equation. The question reads, "What's your opinion of U.S. policies in the Middle East—would you say they are fair or do they favor Israel too much, or do they favor the Palestinians too much?"[15]

Another important issue to control for in the context of the Arab Muslim world is the role of religion. I include a question gauging the importance of religion in one's life. Again, this is a way of ensuring that I have a parsimonious model that controls for several dominant factors that may shape attitudes toward the United States, while focusing in on the two measures of interest—those that tap into economic globalization. Finally, I control for a host of demographic factors considered important for all individual-level surveys, including gender, employment status, age, and education.

In both Kuwait and Jordan, I find that positive evaluations about economic globalization are directly linked to positive evaluations of the U.S. War on Terror. Those citizens who are supportive of free markets and positively assess trade for their countries are also more likely to support the U.S. fight against terrorism. This finding lends credence to the argument that those citizens who value economic globalization are more likely to support U.S. policies in the region. They perhaps place a value on the role of the United States in the region, and realize that their societies might be better off with the United States than without. Examining the marginal effects of support for economic globalization on support for the U.S. fight against terrorism, one notes significant results. In Jordan, there is a 20 percent increase in probability of support between those who don't value trade and those who do; similarly, there is a 14 percent probability increase between those who believe free markets are good and those who do not. In Kuwait, I witness similar patterns, with a 30 percent probability increase between

TABLE 5.1. Logistic regression: Support for U.S. antiterrorism policies

	Favor US antiterrorism policy (Jordan)	Favor US antiterrorism policy (Kuwait)
Income satisfaction	0.438***	0.347**
	(0.110)	(0.137)
Trade	0.455***	0.502***
	(0.132)	(0.179)
Free market	0.335***	0.192**
	(0.115)	(0.096)
Religion important	0.269	0.080
	(0.225)	(0.607)
US favors Israel	−1.653***	−0.368
	(.400)	(0.350)
Employment	−0.369	0.369
	(0.265)	(0.286)
Gender	−0.258	−0.320
	(0.272)	(0.243)
Education	0.058	−0.131*
	(.043)	(0.065)
Age	0.003	0.007
	0.008	0.011
Constant	−4.11***	−3.07
	(1.19)	(2.69)
Percent predicted correctly	84%	67%
Observations	857	400

* significant at 10%; ** significant at 5%; *** significant at 1%.

supporters of trade in comparison to opponents. This pattern is also reflected among Kuwaitis who positively assess free markets. There I find a 15 percent probability increase between those who believe free markets are good and those who do not (see table 5.1).

It is important to note that a few other significant variables warrant further discussion. In Jordan, citizens who feel the United States favors Israel are less likely to approve of the U.S. War on Terror. In Kuwait, this variable is insignificant. Yet, in Jordan, people have strong positions about the Palestinian-Israeli conflict (and this is while controlling for Palestinian and Jordanian origin). However, even while controlling for this very pertinent policy issue, those Jordanian citizens who have positive economic evaluations also have positive evaluations of the United States. Thus, it is not accurate to deduce that the Palestinian-Israeli conflict trumps all else in the region; similarly, it is not accurate to argue that it does not matter. What the data reveal in the context of Jordan is that *both* matter. Citizens upset with a U.S. pro-Israeli bias are more anti-American. Yet, those citizens who are positive about economic globalization are more pro-American. That Kuwaitis were less concerned about a U.S. pro-Israeli bias in their assessments of the United States is in good part a result of the 1991 Gulf War, as outlined in chapter 2 and chapter 3. In both Jordan and Kuwait, it is also important to note that those citizens who are more satisfied with their incomes are also more likely to exhibit favorable assessments of the U.S. fight against terrorism. Thus, the economic interests matter for the ways citizens relate to the United States.

ISLAMISM AND ANTI-AMERICANISM

Having established that citizens of Kuwait and Jordan who have positive assessments of economic globalization are also those citizens who have positive assessments of U.S. policy, it is important to examine a second facet of the overall argument that this book advances. Islamists (and their supporters) are more anti-American in Jordan than they are in Kuwait. To gain leverage on this point, I turn to the Arab Barometer data. There, I rely on one key question as my dependent variable gauging anti-Americanism: "Do you agree with the following statement? 'U.S. involvement in the region justifies armed operations against the United States everywhere.'" Sixty-one percent of Jordanians either strongly agree or agree with this statement, and although Kuwaitis in general are more positive about the United States than Jordanians, I found that 58 percent either strongly agree or agree with the idea that armed operations against the United States are justified. It is also important to point out here that although support for this dimension of anti-Americanism is similar across the two states, in Jordan there is a politically organized vehicle, the Islamic Action Front (IAF), that mobilizes on anti-American viewpoints, while this is not the case in Kuwait.[16]

The key independent variable I examine here is support for political Islam. I capture this measure with a question on the Arab Barometer survey asking to what extent do respondents agree that "men of religion should have influence over the decisions of government."[17] I include several controls as

---

[16]Please note that I am not arguing that the IAF advocated violent attacks against the United States. Rather, what I demonstrate is that not only is there more support for anti-Americanism linked to Islamism in Jordan but that the IAF openly holds anti-American viewpoints and mobilizes on such platforms, as was discussed in chapter 3.

[17]Factor analysis is employed to assess the consistency among a number of survey items designed to measure judgments pertaining to political Islam. Many of these items load highly on a common factor, offering evidence of reliability and increasing confidence in validity. The item asking whether men of religion should have influence over government decisions is the

well. Two of the controls allow me to address the confluence of factors that may shape levels of anti-Americanism. First, I have maintained in this book that levels of anti-Americanism are exogenously structured. That is, levels of anti-Americanism reflect citizen dissatisfaction with U.S. policies in the region. In table 5.1, I substantiated the link between perceptions of U.S. favoritism toward Israel and negative assessments of U.S. policies in the fight against terror. Here I develop this line of argumentation. First, I include a measure of appreciation of Western culture. Often, popular critics will erroneously link anti-Americanism for a general dislike of Western norms and culture.[18] Second, I include another factor important in this analysis. Some might argue that levels of anti-Americanism are yet another dimension of authoritarianism. The argument holds that those citizens who are less democratic are also more likely to be anti-American. In order to control for these two alternative explanations, I add two questions from the Arab Barometer. The first question asks respondents to agree or disagree with the statement, "The culture of the U.S. and other Western countries has many positive attributes." The second question, tapping into support for authoritarianism, reads: "I'm going to describe various types of political systems and ask what you think about each as a way of governing [country name]. For each one, would you say it is a very good, fairly good, fairly bad, or very bad way of governing [country name]?" The possible response options included "A strong nondemocratic leader that does not bother with parliament and elections." I use this question as a measure of authoritarian support. I then run straightforward regression ordinary least squares (OLS) models and I also control for a host of other demographic variables including education, assessments of family income, religiosity (measured by frequency of Quran reading), gender, age, and national origin (Palestinian/Jordanian) in the case of Jordan.[19]

Findings

As expected, I find that supporters of political Islam in Jordan are far more likely to be anti-American than are nonsupporters. This finding is statistically significant, while controlling for a host of other variables. Also as expected, supporters of political Islam in Kuwait are not more likely than nonsupporters to be anti-American. In other words, supporters and nonsupporters of political Islam are similarly predisposed to the United States.

---

best single indicator of this dimension, and for purposes of clarity and parsimony it is used in the present analysis as a measure of support for political Islam.

[18]See, for example, Charles Krauthammer, "To Hell with Sympathy," *Time*, November 17, 2003; Jean-Francois Revel, *Anti-Americanism* (San Francisco: Encounter, 2003); and Dinesh D'Souza, *What's So Great about America* (Washington, DC: Regnery, 2002).

[19]See this chapter's appendix for all coding.

TABLE 5.2. OLS regression: Support for anti-Americanism

	Anti-Americanism (Jordan)	Anti-Americanism (Kuwait)
Education	0.027	−0.030
	(0.027)	(0.046)
Read Quran	−0.005	−0.035
	(0.317)	(0.071)
Family economic situation	0.0001	0.00003
	(0.0001)	(0.00002)
Western culture– positive	0.079	−0.075
	(0.070)	(0.206)
Religion in govt. decisions	0.159***	0.015
	(0.048)	(0.081)
Strong leader	−0.035	−0.078
	(0.042)	(0.097)
Age	0.0002	0.005
	(0.002)	(0.004)
Gender	0.048	−0.257**
	(.072)	(0.126)
Country origin Palestinian	−0.004	
	(0.061)	—
Constant	1.627***	2.800***
	(0.316)	(0.634)
R2	.03	.04
Observations	715	303

Robust standard errors in parentheses; * significant at 10%; ** significant at 5%; *** significant at 1%.

It does not appear that Islamist supporters in Kuwait pose a threat to U.S. involvement in Kuwait as they potentially do in Jordan.

Notably, support for authoritarianism and anti-Westernism are not mediating attitudes on anti-Americanism. In both Jordan and Kuwait, these two variables were statistically insignificant in explaining levels of anti-Americanism while controlling for other basic demographics.

ANTI-AMERICANISM AND SUPPORT FOR DEMOCRACY OR AUTHORITARIANISM

Thus far, I have substantiated a link between support for economic globalization and positive evaluations of the United States using the 2007 Pew Global Attitudes Survey. Relying on the Arab Barometer data, I have also demonstrated that Islamist supporters in Jordan are far more likely to be anti-American than Islamist supporters in Kuwait. Now, I turn to the last part of my empirical argument. Because the Jordanian political context has an influential anti-American opposition movement, citizens who are pro-American (those who also positively assess economic globalization) are more likely to be proregime in order to guarantee the status quo. They are more likely to be more supportive of the government and less supportive of democracy. Conversely, if they weren't worried about the implications of democracy, one would expect that they would be more supportive of democracy, since that would better serve to align their interests with the United States and in fact may be even more useful for trade and economic growth. These are the logics employed by globalization winners, those who stand to benefit from greater economic integration in Kuwait. Because the political climate of Kuwait is one marked by an influential opposition movement that is not anti-American, then pro-Americanism will not be correlated to support of the regime in power. Rather, I expect pro-Americanism to be linked to democracy.

To quantitatively test my argument, I use OLS regression models to examine the link between worries about anti-Americanism on the one hand and support for democracy and authoritarianism on the other. I employ two dependent variables to tap into attitudes about strong government and support for democracy. The first is a straightforward measure of an authoritarian predisposition. Response to one question—"People should always support the decisions of their government even if they disagree with these decisions"[20]—captures both support for government and an authoritarian disposition to allow the government to rule with little accountability. This—support for government—is the first of my dependent variables. Again, noticeable variation exists between Jordan and Kuwait, with Jordanians almost as twice as likely to support this position (49 percent to 26 percent). This variable consists of four categories, with a range of "strongly agree" to "strongly disagree."[21]

My second dependent variable is more elaborate and attempts to include simultaneous measurements of support for democracy and authoritarianism. Using the "overt support for democracy" scale developed by Ronald Inglehart and Christian Welzel,[22] I construct this index in two steps. First, I sum the respondent's support for the statements "Having a democratic political system is a good way for running a country" and "Democracy may have problems but it's better than any other form of government." This yields

---

[20]All question wording is located in this chapter's appendix.

[21]See this chapter's appendix for distributions.

[22]See Ronald F. Inglehart and Christian Welzel, "Political Culture and Democracy: Analyzing Cross-Level Linkages," *Comparative Politics* 36, no. 1 (2003): 61–79; and Christian Welzel and

a 0 to 6 scale, where 6 is the most prodemocracy.[23] Second, I add the respondents' evaluations of the statements "Having a strong leader who does not have to bother with parliament and elections" and "People should always support the decisions of their government even if they disagree with these decisions" (on a four-point scale from very good to very bad),[24] which yields a 0 to 6 proautocracy scale. I then subtract the second scale from the first, which yields an overall index of support for democracy, ranging from –6 (maximum autocracy) to 6 (maximum democracy).[25]

I employ one main explanatory variable to test my argument, one that taps into anti-Americanism. Thus far I have maintained that in Jordan, citizens who worry about the ramifications of anti-American Islamists will be more likely to cling to the status quo. To gain more leverage on this statistically, I use a question administered in the Arab Barometer survey: "Do you agree with the following statement? 'U.S. involvement in the region justifies armed operations against the United States everywhere.'" Sixty-one percent of Jordanians either strongly agree or agree with this statement. And although Kuwaitis in general are more positive about the United States than Jordanians, I found that 58 percent either strongly agree or agree that armed operations against the United States are justified. It is also important to point out here that although support for this dimension of anti-Americanism is similar across the two states, in Jordan the IAF mobilizes on an anti-American platform; as noted earlier, this is not the case in Kuwait. Hence, my expectation is that those citizens who do *not* support anti-Americanism will be more supportive of authoritarianism in Jordan. This will not be the case in Kuwait, simply because pro-American supporters are not as threatened by these tendencies in the Gulf monarchy.

I further control for competing hypotheses that can plausibly explain why citizens continue to support their regimes in Jordan and Kuwait. Specifically, I look at the effects of education, fear, clientelism and political access, patriotism, Islam, and—in the case of Jordan—national origin. These OLS models are designed to examine the ways in which anti-Americanism

Ronald F. Inglehart, "The Role of Ordinary People in Democratization," *Journal of Democracy* 19, no. 1 (2008): 126–40.

[23]Responses to the first question are coded as follows: 3 = very good; 2 = fairly good; 1 = fairly bad; 0 = very bad. Responses to the second question are coded as follows: 3 = agree strongly; 2 = agree; 1 = disagree; 0 = disagree strongly.

[24]Please note that Inglehart and Welzel, "Political Culture and Democracy," uses a different measure, "Having the army rule," which was administered on the World Values Survey. This question is not asked in the Arab Barometer, so I have replaced it with "People should always support the decisions of their government even if they disagree with these decisions" as an additional measure on support for strong authority. Support for government is measured on a four-point scale from "strongly agree" to "strongly disagree."

[25]See this chapter's appendix for the Cronbach Alpha scores.

shapes levels of authoritarian and democratic engagement while paying attention to alternative explanations.[26]

Alternative Hypotheses for Regime Support
Education and Financial Standing

Theoretical models examining the persistence of what is perceived as citizenship support for both authoritarianism and democracy have looked to socioeconomic factors emanating from modernization formulations.[27] Modernization models hold that individuals lacking basic levels of education will be less knowledgeable about and therefore lack a strong appreciation of democratic rights and responsibilities. It is hypothesized that individuals who lack education are less likely to appreciate democratic rights and responsibilities—hence, they are more likely to support authoritarianism writ large. To test this hypothesis, I examine the impact of education on support for authoritarian rule in Jordan and Kuwait. I also control for assessments of family economic standing as proxy for income.[28]

Clientelism and Political Access

Models examining continued support for authoritarianism in the Arab world have often looked at the ways citizens directly benefit from the regime in power. The logic of this argument holds that individuals engage the state through the lens of cost-benefit analyses. This strand of the literature focuses on clientelism and political access. Access to direct benefits through clientelistic or rentier channels have also been seen as a common feature sustaining authoritarian support among the population.[29] Citizens who are direct beneficiaries of the state are more likely to support it, regardless of

[26]I also replicate the models estimating the categorical variable "support for government" and "overt democracy" utilizing ordered logit. All findings are robust. I therefore present the OLS models for consistency.

[27]See Ronald Inglehart, *Culture Shift in Advanced Industrial Society* (Princeton, NJ: Princeton University Press, 1989); and Samuel Huntington, *Political Order in Changing Societies* (New Haven, CT: Yale University Press, 1964).

[28]The income data obtained in the Arab Barometer result in too many missing observations.

[29]See Amaney Jamal, *Barriers to Democracy* (Princeton, NJ: Princeton University Press, 2007); Herbert Kitschelt and Steven I. Wilkinson, *Patrons, Clients, and Policies: Patterns of Democratic Accountability and Political Competition* (New York: Cambridge University Press, 2007); Ellen Lust-Okar, "Elections under Authoritarianism: Preliminary Lessons from Jordan," *Democratization* 13, no. 3 (2006): 456–71; Giacomo Luciani, "Allocation vs. Production States: A Theoretical Framework," in *The Arab State*, ed. Giacomo Luciani (Berkeley and Los Angeles: University of California Press, 1990), 65–84; and Kiren Aziz Chaudhry, *The Price of Wealth: Economies and Institutions in the Middle East* (Ithaca, NY: Cornell University Press, 1997).

whether it is democratic or authoritarian. This line of argumentation is also closely linked to theories about the rentier state (highlighted in chapter 1) and electoral authoritarianism.

The literature on electoral authoritarianism also emphasizes the ways in which clientelism enhances support for the ruling regime in power. This literature maintains that leaders hold elections to legitimate their rule; one mechanism through which they do this is co-optation.[30] That authoritarian rulers use elections to further solidify their base of support is a finding also advanced in studies that pertain to the Arab world.[31] These scholars argue that in the context of the Arab world, elections manage political elite and voters by bringing them into the political process through the mechanism of clientelism. For authoritarian regimes, elections serve as an efficient means to distribute the spoils of office.[32] To test this alternative explanation, which straddles arguments related to both rentierism and electoral authoritarianism, I include three additional questions that gauge levels of clientelism and political access. The first looks at whether individuals have ever used a clientelistic channel or *wasta*; a second measure taps into government evaluations of existing services; and a third gauges citizen assessments of the ease of filing complaints against the government. These three variables measure citizens' perceptions about government services, the responsiveness of those services, and the extent to which citizens have access to government, respectively.[33]

---

[30]See Carles Boix and Milan Svolik, "Non-tyrannical Autocracies," paper presented at the Comparative Politics seminar, University of California–Los Angeles, 2007; Jennifer Gandhi, *Political Institutions under Dictatorship* (New York: Cambridge University Press, 2008); Jennifer Gandhi and Adam Przeworski, "Cooperation, Cooptation, and Rebellion under Dictatorship," *Economics and Politics* 18, no. 1 (2006):1–26; and Beatriz Magaloni, *Voting for Autocracy: Hegemonic Party Survival and Its Demise in Mexico* (New York: Cambridge University Press, 2006).

[31]See Lust-Okar, "Elections under Authoritarianism"; Lisa Blaydes, *Elections and Distributive Politics in Mubarak's Egypt* (Cambridge: Cambridge University Press, 2011); Marsha Pripstein Posusney, "Multi-party Elections in the Arab World: Institutional Engineering and Oppositional Strategies," *Studies in Comparative and International Development* 36, no. 4 (2002): 34–62; Tarek Masoud, "Why Islam Wins: Electoral Ecologies and Economics of Political Islam in Contemporary Egypt (PhD diss., Department of Political Science, Yale Univeristy, 2008); and Samer Shehata, "Inside an Egyptian Parliamentary Campaign," in *Political Participation in the Middle East*, ed. Ellen Lust-Okar and Saloua Zerhouni (Boulder, CO: Lynne Rienner, 2008), 95–120.

[32]See Lust-Okar, "Elections under Authoritarianism"; Blaydes, *Elections and Distributive Politics in Mubarak's Egypt*; Jennifer Gandhi and Ellen Lust-Okar, "Elections under Authoritarianism," *Annual Review of Political Science* 12 (2009): 403–22; and Kenneth F. Greene, *Why Dominant Parties Lose: Mexico's Democratization in Comparative Perspective* (New York: Cambridge University Press, 2007).

[33]These three questions do not tap into similar dimensions and their Cronbach alpha scale reliability stands at only 2741. Thus, there is ample justification to include each of these measures separately in the equation. See the appendix for question wording.

Fear

Further, models assessing citizenship in authoritarian regimes have often looked to the role of repression in stifling active forms of political engagement and contestation. Citizens fear for their everyday well-being, for their economic livelihoods, and for their loved ones.[34] Because citizens fear their regimes, they are more likely to support them not out of conviction but out of the fear of possible repercussions. Thus, any examination of continued support for regimes must look at the role of fear. In order to tap into this dimension of regime support, I examine whether citizens in Jordan and Kuwait believe they can join political parties without fear and how that impacts their support for government and democracy.[35]

Patriotism and National Pride

Patriotism and loyalty to the state may also explain regime support. The logic driving this claim is that citizens who espouse patriotic pride are more likely to support the regime. Patriotism—defined as a sense of national loyalty, a love of national symbols, and specific beliefs about a country's superiority—can significantly structure support for authoritarian rule.[36] An "unwillingness both to criticize and accept criticism of the nation,"[37] blind or "uncritical" patriotism is associated, according to Leonie Huddy and Nadia Khatib, with authoritarianism, "which is characterized, in turn, by a

[34]See Juan Linz, *Totalitarian and Authoritarian Regimes* (Boulder, CO: Lynne Rienner, 2000); Samuel Huntington, *The Third Wave: Democratization in the Late Twentieth Century* (Norman: University of Oklahoma Press, 1993); and Eva Bellin, "The Robustness of Authoritarianism in the Middle East: Exceptionalism in Comparative Perspective," *Comparative Politics* 36, no. 2 (2004): 139–57.

[35]I also substitute this question for another for robustness purposes: "Now I am going to read to you a list of statements that describe how people often feel about the state of affairs in [country name]. Please tell me whether you strongly agree, somewhat agree, somewhat disagree, or strongly disagree with each of these statements: People are free to criticize government without fear." All findings are robust.

[36]See Leonie Huddy and Nadia Khatib, "American Patriotism, National Identity, and Political Involvement," *American Journal of Political Science* 51, no. 1 (2007): 63–77; Jon Hurwitz and Mark Peffley, "Public Perceptions of Race and Crime: The Role of Racial Stereotypes," *American Journal of Political Science* 41, no. 2 (1997): 375–401; Jeff Spinner-Halev and Elizabeth Theiss-Morse, "National Identity and Self-Esteem," *Perspectives on Politics* 1, no. 3 (2003): 515–32; and John L. Sullivan, Amy Fried, and Mary G. Dietz, "Patriotism, Politics, and the Presidential Election of 1988," *American Journal of Political Science* 36, no. 16 (1992): 200–234.

[37]Robert T. Schatz and Ervin Staub, "Manifestations of Blind and Constructive Patriotism: Personality Correlates and Individual-Group Relations," in *Patriotism: In the Lives of Individuals and Nations*, ed. Daniel Bar-Tal and Ervin Staub (Chicago: Nelson-Hall), 231. See also Robert T. Schatz, Ervin Staub, and Howard Lavine, "On the Varieties of National Attachment: Blind versus Constructive Patriotism," *Political Psychology* 20, no. 1 (1999): 151–74.

tendency to defer to authority figures and support them unconditionally."[38] Do higher levels of patriotism drive support for authority in Jordan and Kuwait? I include a question from the Arab Barometer that asks whether respondents are proud of their own nationality.

Islam and Culture

In order to account for explanations that hold that the political culture of Islam is not conducive to democracy, I include one measure of Islamic religiosity as an alternative explanation. The question gauges frequency of Quran reading. If the expectation that something inherent in Islam hinders democracy is true, it should follow that those who are more committed to its theological tenets would be less democratic.

Further, another important control variable in the context of Jordan is national origin itself. It is imperative to examine whether the differences between supporters and nonsupporters of the regime are driven by differences among Palestinian and Jordanian citizens in the kingdom. Most people will expect those Jordanians of Palestinian origin to be less supportive of the government. Respondents in Jordan were asked to identify their national origin as either Jordanian or Palestinian. I include this variable as an important control.[39]

Findings and Discussion

I estimate baseline models on support for government and overt support for democracy as the dependent variables in both Kuwait and Jordan (see table 5.3). These baseline models include only demographic variables—age, gender, education, employment, and economic assessment—as well as the key explanatory variable, anti-Americanism. In both Jordanian baseline models, anti-Americanism is both statistically significant and significant in the anticipated ways—those who are less anti-American are more likely to support the existing Jordanian regime and less likely to support democracy. Further, in the baseline model on support for government, higher education is linked to less support while better economic assessments are linked to stronger support. In the overt democracy baseline model, those more educated are also more democratic.

In the full specification of the models that pay attention to alternative explanations, the key explanatory variable that sheds light on my argument remains statistically significant. Even while controlling for alternative explanations,

---

[38] Huddy and Khatib, "American Patriotism, National Identity, and Political Involvement," 64.
[39] Descriptive statistics can be found in this chapter's appendix.

anti-Americanism matters in explaining support for the existing regime and democracy in Jordan. Those citizens who harbor less anti-American sentiment are more likely to support the existing authoritarian status quo and less likely to support democracy. Other explanations also matter in both models. Citizens in Jordan tend to be more supportive of their government and less supportive of democracy when they believe the government does all that is in its power to provide services. Thus, at least at the individual level, it appears that citizens will compromise democracy for better services. Further, citizens who believe they have political access, measured here by the ease with which complaints can be filed, tend to be more supportive of the status quo and less supportive of democracy.

Fear also influences the authoritarian and democratic orientations of ordinary citizens. While one might expect those who are more fearful (measured here by whether citizens feel they can join political parties without fear) to lend support to the status quo, this is not what I find. Rather, the fearful are less supportive of the government and more in favor of democracy. National pride also matters for levels of support for government in Jordan. Those most patriotic are those most likely to support the status quo. However, patriotism has little to do with support for democracy. Notably, national origin—whether a respondent is of Palestinian or Jordanian origin—is insignificant in both equations. Further, the findings in table 5.3 remain robust when I omit national origin from these models.

In Kuwait, anti-Americanism is also significant in the baseline models (see table 5.4). However, and as anticipated, it operates in the opposite direction. Unlike their Jordanian counterparts, the less anti-American Kuwaitis are more likely to be supportive of democracy and less likely to be supportive of the regime. This substantiates my argument that the mechanisms at work in Jordan are not at play in Kuwait. More specifically, because Kuwaitis do not fear the consequences of anti-Americanism, as the ICM does not use its mobilization capabilities to advance an anti-American agenda, citizens do not worry about the consequences of more democracy. In fact, their positive orientations toward the United States also translate into stronger commitments to democracy—unlike the pro-American Jordanians, who end up clinging to the status quo.

Some other differences between the Kuwaiti and Jordanian baseline models are noteworthy as well. Education and economic assessments are not significant in Kuwait. Rather, it appears that gender and religiosity are significant variables. More specifically, men are more likely than women to support the regime, and those who read the Quran more frequently are also more likely to support the government and resist democracy. In Kuwait, it appears that politically significant religiocultural effects are at play. At least, in the case of Kuwait, there appears to be a strong linkage among gender, religiosity, and support for the existing state.

In the full models, anti-Americanism remains significant in the expected direction. Kuwaitis who are more pro-American are less in favor of the governing status quo and more in favor of democracy. As in Jordan, assessments of government provision matter in Kuwait—those citizens who believe the Kuwaiti government does everything in its power to provide services show less tolerance for democracy and a preference for the status quo. Again, the individual-level rentier mechanism appears to matter in Kuwait as well. Significantly, however, this mechanism is at play in both rich oil states like Kuwait and poorer nonoil states like Jordan.

A few more findings are noteworthy also, particularly regarding the variables of gender, fear, and patriotism. In the full model on overt support for democracy, Kuwaiti women are more likely than men to support democracy. In Kuwait, those who believe they can join political parties without fear are more likely to support democracy, while those more fearful more likely to support authoritarianism. Plausibly, the anticipated influence of fear is at work here; those citizens who are more fearful profess support for the existing regime. Finally, in the full model on support for government, Kuwaitis who are more patriotic are also more likely to support the government, a finding that is also similar to the Jordanian experience.

Since Jordanians are far more supportive of their regime than Kuwaitis, one plausible explanation is that Jordanians might hold cultural or Islamic predispositions that link up to regime support in Jordan and not Kuwait. This is not the case. At least when one looks at the frequency of reading the Quran, it is significant in Kuwait but not Jordan. Second, although it appears that a rentier mechanism is operating in both states, with those citizens evaluating service provision more positively less supportive of democracy and more supportive of the regime, it is not the only significant variable in any of the equations. Thus, my measure of rentierism matters, but it does not overshadow other competitive explanations. Further, given the dynamics of the analysis at hand, the ability of states like Jordan and Kuwait to provide for their citizens highly depends on their levels of security and economic dependency on the United States. In essence, the rentier effect is facilitated by the condition of U.S. patrimony.[40] And third, education is significant in three models from the Jordanian case, and in only one model from the Kuwaiti, with those less educated more likely to support the regime and less democracy. One can plausibly argue that the variation in levels of democratic and authoritarian engagement between the two states is driven by the fact that Jordanians might be less educated. This is not the

[40]See Eva Bellin, "Coercive Institutions and Coercive Leaders," 21–41, and Jason Brownlee, "Political Crisis and Restabilization: Iraq, Libya, Syria, and Tunisia," 43–62, in *Authoritarianism in the Middle East: Regimes and Resistance*, ed. Marsha Pripstein Posusney and Michele Angrist (Boulder, CO: Lynne Rienner, 2005); see also Lisa Anderson, "Peace and Democracy in the Middle East: The Constraints of Soft Budgets," *Journal of International Affairs* 49, no. 1 (1995): 25–45.

TABLE 5.3. Jordan: OLS models on support for government and overt support for democracy

	Support government (base model)	Support government (full model)	Overt democracy (base model)	Overt democracy (full model)
Economic situation	0.090** (0.040)	0.067 (0.045)	0.037 (0.089)	0.094 (0.098)
Age	0.034 (0.023)	0.041 (0.026)	−0.012 (0.050)	−0.044 (0.057)
Gender	−0.063 (0.067)	−0.168** (0.076)	−0.049 (0.142)	0.108 (0.163)
Education	−0.070*** (0.022)	−0.046* (0.025)	0.192*** (0.047)	0.097* (0.051)
Employed	0.059 (0.070)	−0.005 (0.075)	−0.144 (0.153)	−0.084 (0.164)
Read Quran	0.037 (0.025)	0.012 (0.029)	−0.032 (0.057)	0.053 (0.064)
Violence US	−0.086** (0.035)	−0.083** (0.040)	0.201*** (0.072)	0.175** (0.080)
Provide services		0.130*** (0.047)		−0.198* (0.102)
Wasta		0.016 (0.072)		−0.153 (0.149)
File complaint		0.113*** (0.034)		−0.267*** (0.068)
Join parties		0.152*** (0.041)		−0.411*** (0.086)
Pride		0.107** (0.054)		0.138 (0.111)
Origin		−0.096 (0.074)		0.166 (0.134)
Constant	2.405*** (0.198)	.946*** (0.342)	.832** (0.459)	2.256*** (0.747)
Adj R2	0.03	0.11	0.04	0.15
Observations	869	636	759	587

Robust standard errors in parentheses; * significant at 10%; ** significant at 5%; *** significant at 1%.

TABLE 5.4. Kuwait: OLS models on support for government and overt support for democracy

	Support government (base model)	Support government (full model)	Overt democracy (base model)	Overt democracy (full model)
Economic situation	0.007 (0.071)	0.058 (0.091)	0.132 (0.119)	0.134 (0.155)
Age	0.010 (0.030)	0.008 (0.040)	0.050 (0.062)	0.003 (0.069)
Gender	−0.152** (0.071)	−0.235** (0.096)	0.233 (0.167)	0.462** (0.201)
Education	-0.015 (0.025)	0.025 (0.031)	0.028 (0.057)	0.139** (0.055)
Employment	−0.011 (0.082)	−0.053 (0.106)	−0.085 (0.174)	0.092 (0.217)
Read Quran	0.106** (0.041)	0.144*** (0.053)	0.260*** (0.083)	−0.192* (0.099)
Violence US	0.051* (0.024)	0.118** (0.050)	−0.110* (0.058)	−0.350*** (0.088)
Government services		0.191*** (0.056)		−0.403*** (0.097)
Wasta		0.006 (0.094)		0.045 (0.200)
File complaint		0.092 (0.057)		−0.143 (0.146)
Join parties		0.019 (0.057)		0.285** (0.127)
Pride		0.286*** (0.102)		0.246 (0.263)
Constant	1.56*** (0.292)	-.824* (0.576)	3.79*** (0.521)	3.45*** (1.21)
Adj R2	0.03	0.12	0.03	0.12
Observations	585	358	525	337

Robust standard errors in parentheses; * significant at 10%; ** significant at 5%; *** significant at 1%.

case. Twenty-eight percent of Jordanians have a postsecondary education, compared to 17 percent of the Kuwaiti population.

The most pertinent finding is that the variable assessing anti-Americanism operates dissimilarly in Jordan and Kuwait. Those who are more pro-American converge toward the regime in Jordan while simultaneously supporting less democracy. The opposite is true in Kuwait. This, I maintain, is the result of the ways in which Islamist groups mobilize anti-Americanism in each setting. Given the geopolitical realities surrounding the Arab world, the ability of groups to mobilize on anti-American platforms has significant and consequential effects for democracy across various states. Qualitative analysis already presented in chapter 4 further draws out the causal logics citizens employ when they assess and calculate the strategic utility of the existing leadership for the geopolitical well-being of their country. This chapter attempts to systematically document these patterns among larger segments of the population.

APPENDIX: MACRO-MICRO SYNTHESIS—THE RELATIONSHIP BETWEEN ATTITUDES AND REGIME OUTCOMES

An important question remains. Arguably this chapter relies on attitudinal data on support for democracy. Yet, my argument has macrolevel implications. Essentially, this book offers a microfoundational account of regime outcomes in Jordan and Kuwait based on the perceptions, orientations, and causal logics citizens employ in their daily lives. What evidence do I bring that further substantiates the micro-macro synthesis? Here I rely on previous work I coconducted with Irfan Nooruddin. In our article titled "The Democratic Utility of Trust: A Cross-National Analysis,"[41] we argued the following, when addressing the issue of linkages between microlevel attitudinal data and macrolevel democratic outcomes.

Figure 5.4 plots the proportion of respondents by country in the 2002 World Values Survey who express antidemocracy attitudes, which we operationalize as a negative score on the "overt democracy" scale. By this measure, Denmark and Iceland are the most prodemocracy societies with virtually no antidemocracy respondents, and Vietnam is the least prodemocracy, with almost all citizens expressing negative views about democracy. And the expression of negative attitudes is quite common in many countries, with fifteen countries having a quarter or more of their respondents expressing mostly negative views about democracy. These countries are far more likely to be recent democratizers (Russia, Indonesia, Mexico, Romania, Macedonia, and Moldova, for instance), as are Middle Eastern states such as Jordan and Iran. By contrast, the countries with very few antidemocracy respondents are more likely to be the consolidated democracies of Western Europe. Azerbaijan, Croatia, and Bangladesh also have very small proportions of their respondents expressing antidemocracy attitudes.

Figure 5.5 provides a similar description of the distribution of the dependent variable by focusing on the proportion of each country's sample that

---

[41] Amaney Jamal and Irfan Nooruddin, "The Democratic Utility of Trust: A Cross-National Analysis," *Journal of Politics* 72, no. 1 (2010): 45–59.

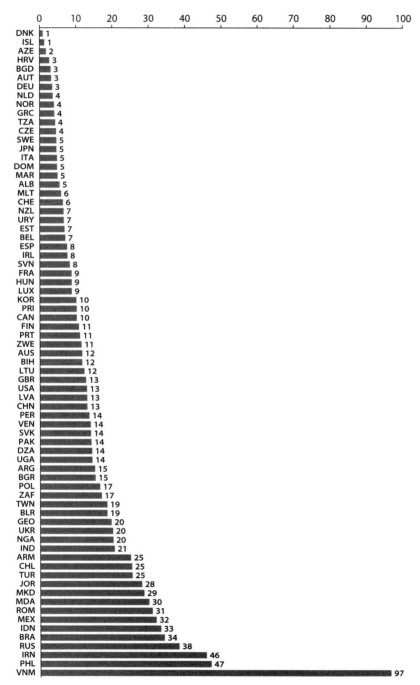

Figure 5.4. Proportion of respondents by country in the 2002 World Values Survey who express antidemocracy attitudes.

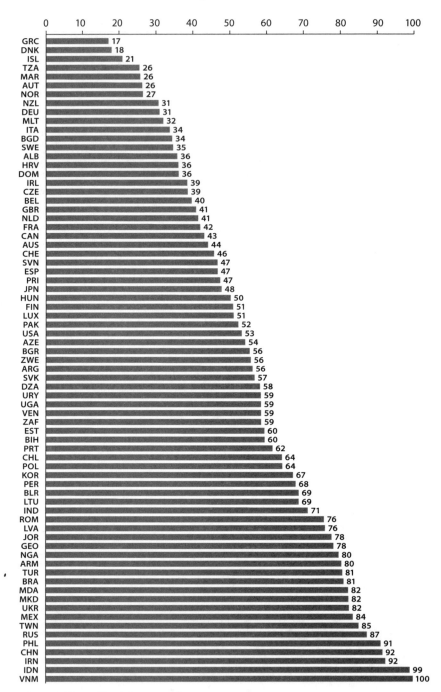

Figure 5.5. Proportion below mean democracy support.

falls below the global mean (3). Once again, the results match expectation with nondemocracies like China and Iran anchoring one end of the spectrum and consolidated democracies at the other end.

Obviously, in neither figure 5.4 nor figure 5.5 are there only democracies at one end of the graph and nondemocracies at the other end. But there exists sufficient variation across countries and enough correspondence with macrolevel outcomes to make understanding the causes of individual-level support for democracy important in its own right.[42]

The Inglehart and Welzel Index (Cronbach Alpha Scores on Index Items)

In order to ensure that the items employed here are tapping similarly into democratic and authoritarian orientations, I utilize Cronbach alpha tests to demonstrate the dimensionality of these authoritarian and democratic values. There are two "authoritarian" questions on the survey that read as follows:

1. I'm going to describe various types of political systems that exist in the Middle East and ask what you think about each as a way of governing [country name]. For each one, would you say it is a very suitable, suitable, somewhat suitable, or not suitable at all way of governing [country name]?

    A. A system with a strong president and military in which elections and competition among political parties are not important.

2. I'm going to describe various types of political systems and ask what you think about each as a way of governing [country name]. For each one, would you say it is a very good, fairly good, fairly bad, or very bad way of governing [country name]?

    A. A strong nondemocratic leader that does not bother with parliament and elections.

When I run Cronbach alpha tests on these two questions and include the support for government measure, I obtain a general alpha of 0.349 for all seven countries in the Arab Barometer. In Jordan, the alpha score is 0.45 and in Kuwait it is 0.46. These scores are quite similar to the extent that the support for democracy items correlate together.

I then took the three standard questions from the Arab Barometer survey:

1. I'm going to describe various types of political systems and ask what you think about each as a way of governing [country name]. For each

---

[42]See Jamal and Noorudin, "The Democratic Utility of Trust," web appendix, available at http://www.princeton.edu/~ajamal/JamalNooruddin.Web%20Appendix.Final.pdf.

one, would you say it is a very good, fairly good, fairly bad, or very bad way of governing [country name]?

A. The democratic political system (public freedom, equal political and civil rights, balance of power, accountability and transparency).

2. I'm going to describe various types of political systems that exist in the Middle East and ask what you think about each as a way of governing [country name]. For each one, would you say it is a very suitable, suitable, somewhat suitable, or not suitable at all way of governing [country name]?

A. A parliamentary system in which nationalist, left-wing, and Islamic political parties all compete in elections.

3. To what extent do you agree/disagree with the following statement?

A. Democracy may have its problems but is better than any other form of government.

For the entire set of cases the Cronbach alpha is 0.42; for Jordan it is 0.28 and for Kuwait it stands at 0.40. The Cronbach alphas indicate that the measures of democracy and authoritarianism are tapping into the same dimensions (with similar magnitudes) in both Kuwait and Jordan.

Arab Barometer Sampling Methods in Jordan and Kuwait

Jordan: Sample Size = 1,000 Individuals

In Jordan, we used a three-stage cluster sampling based on the 1994 national census. Jordan has been divided into several strata representing rural and urban populations within each *muhāfaza* (governorate). Also, each of the five main cities (Amman, Wadi al-Sir, al-Zarqa, Irbid, and al-Rusaifeh) represents an independent stratum. Jordan has been divided into blocs, or clusters, each containing a number of families (with an average of eighty families in each cluster). The number of families in each cluster designates the size of that cluster. The national census provided detailed data on the families as well as detailed maps showing every house in each cluster. The total number of clusters in our recently updated master sample was eight hundred.

A sample of one hundred clusters was randomly selected using probability proportionate to size. The sample was selected from our master sample. Clusters were organized according to size (number of families) and geographic location in order to insure representation of all strata and clusters of all sizes. After selecting the cluster sample, ten homes were chosen in each cluster using systemic sampling. The total size of the sample is 1,000 adults. The third stage in the sampling process occurs inside the house. Using the Kish table, our fieldworkers selected an adult (over eighteen years of age) from among the adults in the house for the interview. Interviewees were assured of complete confidentiality before starting the interview.

Kuwait: Sample Size = 750 individuals

A random sample of 750 individuals was compiled from a database of 10,000 randomly selected Kuwaiti citizens in the register of the Civil Information Authority, which issues public documentation like identification cards and keeps information about everyone living in Kuwait.

Sixty percent of the full sample were reached through this electronically randomized technique; 40 percent of the sample was reached via random door-to-door interviews within each governorate. Depending on the district size, a random technique was employed to sample every seventh house in less populated areas and every thirteenth house in more densely populated areas. At the door, a Kish table was used to select an adult over the age of eighteen to interview.[43]

Professor Ghanim al-Najjar of Kuwait University administered the surveys. He employed a two-stage area probability sample based on the most recent census, with quota sampling at the governate level for each survey. Combined, these data sources constitute the most accurate, comprehensive, and authoritative sources of public opinion data in Jordan and Kuwait.

Question Wording and Operationalization
(from the Arab Barometer)

1. Gender (0 = male; 1 = female)
2. Age/categorical variable (1 = [20; 2 = 21–30; 3 = 31–40; 4 = 41–50; 5 = 51–60; 6 = 61–70; 7 = 70])
3. Education (1 = illiterate; 2 = primary school; 3 = secondary school; 4 = college; 5 = bachelor's degree; 6 = master's degree; 7 = advanced professional)
4. How would you rate the economic situation of your family today? (1 = very bad; 2 = bad; 3 = good; 4 = very good)
5. Joining parties: People are free to join parties without fear. (1 = strongly disagree; 2 = disagree; 3 = agree; 4 = strongly agree)
6. Strong leadership: I'm going to describe various types of political systems and ask what you think about each as a way of governing

[43]This latter sampling technique yielded a skewed sample with an over-representation of educated individuals. The sample was subsequently (within a month) corrected with an additional random stratified sample of less educated individuals (N=108). The results presented here remain robust if this additional sample is removed from the dataset and weights are used instead. The results also remain robust if they rely solely on the electronically randomized technique.

Jordan. For each one, would you say it is a very good, fairly good, fairly bad, or very bad way of governing Jordan?

A. A strong nondemocratic leader that does not bother with parliament and elections. (1 = very bad; 2 = fairly bad; 3 = fairly good; 4= very good)

7. Supporting government: Do you agree or disagree with the following statement?

A. People should always support the decisions of their government even if they disagree with these decisions. (1 = strongly disagree; 2 = disagree; 3 = agree; 4 = strongly agree)

8. Democracy: Do you agree or disagree with the following statement?

A. Democracy may have its problems, but it is better than any other form of government. (1 = strongly disagree; 2 = disagree; 3 = agree; 4 = strongly agree)

9. I'm going to describe various types of political systems and ask what you think about each as a way of governing Jordan. For each one, would you say it is a very good, fairly good, fairly bad or very bad way of governing Jordan?

A. A democratic political system (public freedom, equal political and civil rights, balance of power, accountability and transparency). (1 = very bad; 2 = bad; 3 = good; 4 = very good)

10. *Wasta*: During the past five years, have you ever used *wasta* [personal connections, "pull"] to achieve something personal or family related, or to resolve a neighborhood problem? (1 = no; 2 = yes)

11. Government services: Do you agree with the following statement?

A. The government does all it can to provide citizens with all services. (1 = strongly disagree; 2 = disagree; 3 = agree; 4 = strongly agree)

12. Government access: Based on your experience, how easy or difficult is it to obtain the following administrative or social services from the government?

A. Access to individuals or institutions to file a complaint when your rights are violated. (1 = very difficult; 2 = difficult; 3 = easy; 4 = very easy)

13. Provision of services: Do you agree with the following statement?

A. The government does all it can to provide citizens with all services. (1 = strongly disagree; 2 = disagree; 3 = agree; 4 = strongly agree)

14. U.S. violence: Do you agree with the following statement?

A. U.S. involvement in the region justifies armed operations against the United States everywhere. (1 = strongly disagree; 2 = disagree; 3 = agree; 4 = strongly agree)

15. National pride: How proud are you to be [nationality]? (1 = not proud at all; 2 = not very proud; 3 = somewhat proud; 4 = very proud)

16. Religion: Do you agree with the following statement?
    A. Men of religion should have influence over the decisions of government. (1 = strongly disagree; 2 = disagree; 3 = agree; 4 = strongly agree)

17. Western culture: Do you agree with the following statement?
    A. The culture of the United States and other Western countries has many positive attributes. (1 = strongly disagree; 2 = disagree; 3 = agree; 4 = strongly agree)

18. I'm going to describe various types of political systems and what you think about each as a way of governing [country name]. For each one would you say it is a very good, fairly good, fairly bad, or very bad of governing [country name]?
    A. A strong nondemocratic leader that does not bother with parliament and elections. (1 = very bad; 2 = bad; 3 = good; 4 = very good)

19. Employment status: Are you employed? (1 = no; 2 = yes)

20. Reading the Quran: How often do you read the Quran? (1 = never; 2 = rarely; 3 = sometimes; 4 = several times a week; 5 = every day)

21. National origin (for Jordan): What is your national origin? (0 = Jordanian; 1 = Palestinian)

CHAPTER SIX

Morocco

Support for the Status Quo

ONE OF THE REASONS CITIZENS ACROSS THE ARAB WORLD RATIONALIZE THE NECESSity of supporting existing regimes (which are semidemocratic at best) is to guarantee U.S. patronage. Examining Morocco, Palestine, and Saudi Arabia provides a broader window into this dynamic. Social scientists may question the justification for comparing two states like Jordan and Kuwait that are institutionally different, especially in terms of their economic structures. This is a valid concern, and it is therefore imperative to extend these arguments to cases that are similar in structure. Thus, the Moroccan case provides an excellent comparison to that of Jordan, and the Saudi Arabian case to that of Kuwait. The inclusion of Saudi Arabia is vital because I am able to demonstrate first that variation does exist between Kuwait and Saudi Arabia and second that structural factors like Kuwait's oil rich economy cannot account for the reasons why citizens can afford to leverage more democracy. If oil-rich states are to determine citizen support and activities toward democracy, we would expect citizens of the Gulf region to be demanding democracy at startling rates. I present Saudi Arabia as a case to assess these expectations.

Further, readers may question whether strong pockets of support for the existing regimes, especially among those who should be at the forefront of democratic contestation, is a function of fear of an alternative Islamic authoritarian (nondemocratic) state or whether it is fear of an Islamist opposition movement that will undermine ties to the United States and thereby weaken the state. In chapter 5, I addressed this concern using individual-level data from Jordan; here, I continue to pay attention to this question. Morocco includes one of the most progressive Islamic movements in the region, and citizens, while applauding the movement's moderation, remain wary of its foreign intentions. Enhancing ties with the United States and maintaining ties to Europe were often cited as key reasons why the status quo was preferable to increasing levels of democracy. It became apparent that although the Islamic Party for Justice and Development (PJD) is considered moderate in terms of its internal Islamic agenda (Shari'a-oriented attitudes), many in the kingdom worried about the party's stance toward the United States. That the PJD, along with other Islamic groups, remains anti-U.S. further confirms the dynamics of state-society relations surrounding the Jordanian case. In chapter 7, I also include the Palestinian case as further evidence of the main argument here. Similar to the Algerian case in 1991, the Palestinian case of 2006 exemplifies the devastating implications of democracy for the lives of citizens when it yields undesirable results.

Moroccans are very much committed to democratic values, but worries about losing U.S. and European patronage loom large in the daily lives of ordinary citizens. Access to European markets is an important concern. In fact, many Moroccans see good ties with the Americans as necessary to ensure continued access to Europe. Like Jordanians, Moroccans also rationalized their support for the regime based on international considerations that would ensure economic progress.

Sixty-two percent of Moroccans report that they would support the government even when they don't agree with its decisions, while 92 percent of Moroccans say that democracy is the best form of government.[1] Moroccans understand that their regime is reliant on external forces for its success. Any alteration of the status quo could empower anti-American Islamists in ways that could undermine Morocco's standing with its international patrons.

MOROCCAN INTERNATIONAL CLIENTELISM

Morocco is heavily reliant on the European Union (EU) and the United States, and these are relationships that include both financial aid and military assistance. An almost equal number of Moroccans (20 percent) believe that the United States and France are Morocco's two most dependable allies.[2] The EU, especially France, aids Morocco financially, and its markets remain extremely important for Morocco. Seventy-one percent of Morocco's exports head to the EU annually;[3] in 2001, that amounted to over €12 billion in trade.[4] Morocco also receives EU funding under the Euro-Mediterranean Partnership program and since 1997 has received over 1.25 billion dollars in grants. Europe is also significant to Morocco because it is the number one immigration destination of those who leave the country; this European link provides a key source of remittances.

---

[1] Arab Baromoter 2006.

[2] See Pew Global Attitudes Project, *America's Image in the World* (Washington, DC: Pew Research Center, 2007; accessed at http://pewglobal.org/commentary/display.php?AnalysisID=1019).

[3] Melanie Claire Cammett, *Globalization and Business Politics in Arab North Africa: A Comparative Perspective* (Cambridge: Cambridge Cambridge University Press, 2007).

[4] Marvine Howe, *Morocco: The Islamist Awakening and Other Challenges* (New York: Oxford University Press, 2005), 305.

The United States is also important to Morocco, having given more aid to Morocco than to any other Arab country with the exception of Egypt (and Iraq, before the Second Gulf War). This relationship has intensified in the last two decades, but especially since 9-11. In 2007, the U.S. government-backed Millennium Challenge Corporation approved a five-year, $697.5 million economic aid package to fight poverty and promote economic growth.[5] The United States has also increased funding for education, health care, women's rights, job creation, and structural adjustment.[6] Since 1995 the regime has been trying to improve the economic climate in Morocco by enacting legislation that favors foreign direct investment. Like citizens in Kuwait and Jordan, Moroccans favor greater global integration and those who do so are also more positive toward U.S. antiterrorism policies.[7]

In 2002, U.S. president George W. Bush welcomed Morocco's King Mohammed VI to the White House, emphasizing the special friendship that exists between the two countries. According to Marvine Howe, "This meeting marked a new chapter in Morocco's foreign relations, which had been essentially Eurocentric and geared mainly to its former protectors, France and Spain. There followed flattering statements from Washington exalting the strategic relationship with Morocco."[8]

In 2004, President Bush designated Morocco as a major non-NATO ally, thereby erasing restrictions on arms sales.[9] That same year the United States adopted a free trade agreement with Morocco; this agreement aims to increase U.S. investment in the North African country. Moroccan businesspeople expressed hope that the new free trade association would contribute to economic improvements. But the agreement would not only help the kingdom economically; it also brought Morocco firmly under U.S. influence. Morocco moved ahead, solidifying its relations with the United States.

U.S. ties to Morocco have historical roots as well. Morocco had been an important historical ally to the United States during the Cold War. The United States came to Morocco's aid in the early 1980s when the Polisario had gained momentum in the disputed Western Sahara with military aid and equipment. In return, King Hassan II provided the United States access

[5]UNHCR, *World Report 2008: Morocco/Western Sahara* (Geneva: UNHCR, 2008; accessed at http://www.unhcr.org/refworld/publisher,HRW,,MAR,47a87c0cc,0.html).

[6]Jeremy M. Sharp, *U.S. Democracy Promotion Policy in the Middle East: The Islamist Dilemma*, Congressional Research Service Report, July 15, 2006 (accessed at http://www.history.navy.mil/library/online/democ%20in%20middle%20east.htm.

[7]Pew Global Attitudes Project, *America's Image*. The key independent variable that was both positive and significant in explaining support for U.S. antiterrorism policies in Morocco was a question that gauged whether Moroccans had positive or negative assessments of the influence of large external companies in Morocco.

[8]Howe, *Morocco: The Islamist Awakening and Other Challenges*, 301.

[9]"U.S. Rewards Morocco for Terror Aid," BBC News, June 4, 2004 (accessed at http://news.bbc.co.uk/2/hi/africa/3776413.stm).

to airbase facilities should the need for rapid American deployment arise. The administration of President Ronald Reagan further assured King Hassan II that the United States was committed to Morocco's Western Sahara claims. But Moroccan ties to the United States have become even stronger since 9-11, as the nation has become crucial in providing the United States with counterterrorism assistance.

Throughout Morocco, citizens voice recognition of this relationship because they realize the future of their country is tied to the maintenance of solid relations with its patrons. Yet this relationship also carries risks, especially when the United States acts aggressively in the region. Moroccan citizens took to the streets to denounce the U.S. war on Iraq, which prevented the Moroccan government from deploying any troops against Saddam Hussein's regime. Further, the government was also concerned that high levels of anti-Americanism would serve the Islamists at the ballot box.[10]

ISLAMIST POSITIONS IN MOROCCO

Like many other governments in the Arab World, King Hassan II (r. 1961–99) worked with the Islamists to curtail the influence of leftist movements in the 1970s. The assassination of Union Socialiste des Forces Populaires leader Omar Benjelloun in 1975 by an Islamist group was done with tacit regime knowledge.[11] While maintaining a firm authoritarian grip on the kingdom, Hassan II became even less tolerant of the Islamist opposition. By the late 1990s, Hassan II granted the Islamists more room in civil and political society as part of his controlled political liberalization strategies.[12] And with the ascendance of Mohammad VI to the throne, Morocco has witnessed increased liberalization measures. These measures have generally provided the Islamists with more space in civil society. The post 9-11 and 2003 Casablanca attacks, however, would witness further restrictions on their liberties.

Dating back to the 1980s, three trends characterize the political Islamic landscape of Morocco. Led by a mosque preacher in Tangiers, *al-fiqh al-zamzami*, the reformist Sunni trend focused on levels of individual piety and righteousness and was not necessarily political. Another and far more extreme trend was al-Shabiba al-Islamiyya (Islamic Youth), drawn mostly from student and high school movements that were intent on the goal of overthrowing the regime. In 1981, Abdallah Benkirane broke away from

---

[10]Howe, *Morocco: The Islamist Awakening and Other Challenges*, 303.

[11]Meir Litvak and Maddy Weitzman, "Islamism and the State in North Africa," in *Revolutionaries and Reformers: Contemporary Islamist Movements in the Middle East*, ed. Barry Rubin, 69–90 (Albany: State University of New York Press, 2003).

[12]Ibid.

al-Shabiba, adopted a more reformist stance, and followed a nonconfrontational position against the monarchy. The movement became Harakat Al-Islām wal Tajdīd (Movement for Reform and Renewal). By 1990, Benkirane became more involved in the political process, and as a result he adopted a more passive stance toward the regime. The monarchy remained cautious of allowing overtly Islamic party participation in Moroccan elections. Benkirane was ultimately incorporated into the Mouvement Populaire Democratique et Constitutionnel (MPDC), which proceeded to win nine seats (out of 325) in the 1997 elections. By 1999, the movement had become the Parti de la Justice et du Développement (Justice and Development Party, or PJD). A third movement, al-'Adl wal Ihsān (Justice and Charity Organization, or JCO) was led by 'Abdesalam Yassin, a former education ministry school inspector. Yassin's group was more radical than the PJD and still openly challenges the legitimacy of the monarchy. The strength of al-'Adl wal Ihsān was demonstrated during the First Gulf War, during which 30,000 of Yassin's followers took to the street to protest against Morocco's participation in the coalition and America's involvement in the war.[13] According to Howe, "[both] organizations condemn American [policies]—including the bombardment of Afghanistan and attacks on Iraqis—and unconditional support of Israel in the Palestinian conflict."[14] Although the PJD is Morocco's largest Islamist party represented in the 325-seat house of representatives (the lower chamber of parliament), many Moroccan specialists argue that Yassin's outlawed JCO has wider support than the PJD.[15] The JCO is by far the most influential organization in high schools and universities. Its welfare associations are impressive, and it delivers health care, literacy classes, and poverty amelioration initiatives. When popular events arise, especially those pertaining to Palestine, the JCO is able to turn out large numbers.

ANTI-AMERICAN SENTIMENT

Anti-American sentiment is strong in Morocco, especially among its Islamist groups. In a 2007 Pew survey, only 15 percent of Moroccans had favorable opinions of the United States.[16] In 2002, Moroccans adopted a boycott of U.S. goods to protest the situation in Palestine and the pending war in Iraq. The Moroccan government was ill at ease with the anti-U.S. campaign.

[13]Ibid.; see also Howe, *Morocco: The Islamist Awakening and Other Challenges.*
[14]Howe, *Morocco: The Islamist Awakening and Other Challenges,* 128.
[15]See Howe, *Morocco: The Islamist Awakening and Other Challenges*; and Alex Glennie and David Mepham, *Reform in Morocco: The Role of Political Islamists* (London: Institute for Public Policy Research, 2007; accessed at http://www.idrc.ca/uploads/user-S/12115496221reform_in_morocco [1].pdf).
[16]Pew Global Attitudes Project, *America's Image.*

Said a Moroccan government official in 2002, "Such campaigns could cause much harm to the Moroccan economy, especially since Morocco is trying to shift to a higher gear in its economic and commercial ties with the U.S."[17] This is a sentiment captured by many citizens who stand to benefit from greater economic ties across the kingdom.

Of the two main Islamic organizations, the PJD is more moderate. But many Moroccans are not truly sure about its objectives. Citizens worry that the PJD may be trying to sell itself as a moderate group in hopes of continuing its participation in the mainstream formal political process. Others believe that it is a pragmatic organization that must be moderate to ensure its success—and thus, that its moderate stances are indeed genuine. The JCO is quite clear about its objectives—it wants more Islamic rule, does not recognize the legitimacy of the monarchy, and does not support Morocco's ties to the United States, while the PJD has tried to showcase itself as both more progressive and more tolerant of the United States. Statements by the PJD, however, illustrate that the movement is not predisposed to favorable relations with America.

Palestine and Iraq remain two of the most salient issues that have galvanized anti-U.S. sentiment in Morocco. Similar to Islamists in Jordan, the PJD has joined secular coalitions, like the Association of Support to the Struggle of the Palestinian people, to voice its dissatisfaction with U.S. policies. Of more concern for citizens in Morocco are the several hardliners in both the PJD and JCO who oppose strong ties to the United States. Members of both movements are on record stating they oppose close ties to the United States.[18] In response to Bush's 2004 Greater Middle East Initiative, designed to promote more democracy in the Middle East, PJD secretary general Sa'ad al 'Othmani commented, "The current administration in the U.S. is in no position to speak of political reforms, democracy and human rights, while it violates human rights every day in Iraq."[19] In an interview in 2007, al-'Othmani reiterated his disdain for U.S. policies. Discussing the Greater Middle East initiative, he noted that it is "an American project that seeks to reshape the area in a way that would give 'Israel' political, economic and maybe even cultural domination in the whole area. This is a project that serves the interests of the ruling class in the American administration. It is a project that wants to confiscate the independence of political decisions in Middle Eastern countries, consequently dominating its fortunes and enabling the Zionist project. It is then natural that the project utilizes beautiful words like promulgation of democracy, freedom, security and peace, which practically all mean the opposite."

[17]"Call to Boycott U.S. Products Gains Momentum," May 30, 2002 (accessed at http://www .inminds.co.uk/boycott-news-0158.html). .

[18]Sharp, *U.S. Democracy Promotion Policy in the Middle East.*

[19]Pascale Harter, "Powell's Final Push for Arab Reform," BBC News (accessed at http:// news.bbc.co.uk/2/hi/africa/4085081.stm, December 2004).

The PJD remains deeply skeptical about the U.S. role in the region. When asked about the ramifications of Iran's nuclear capabilities, al-'Othmani commented, "I'd rather not focus on the positive aspects or drawbacks of nuclear possession, but on the double-standards in fully and unconditionally supporting "Israel" in possessing nuclear warheads to blackmail the countries of the region, whose intentions are severely prejudged."[20]

In a series of Institute for Public Policy Research interviews, leaders of the PJD were questioned on their attitudes toward foreign partners like the EU and the United States. The PJD on average had negative opinions about both partners. In general, the report states, the key leaders of the PJD felt that such economic initiatives as the Euro Mediterranean Partnership and the European Neighbourhood Policy—policies aimed at promoting reform in countries close to Europe—were not useful to Morocco; in fact, they felt that the Europeans were taking advantage of the people of Morocco and North Africa in general.[21] Sentiments toward the United States were much more negative, however. The PJD elite recognized that the United States wields enormous power and influence, but they were also very critical of U.S. policies in the region, especially on issues relating to Palestine and Iraq. Further, the PJD was not as favorably disposed to the free trade agreement with the United States as the general Moroccan population was; it felt that the terms of the agreement favored the United States. And while the PJD leaders had visited the United States in 2006—after Israel's invasion of Lebanon (which the United States has tacitly supported)—the PJD no longer participates in any U.S.-funded training programs or initiatives.

ISLAMIST POPULARITY AND POSITIONS

A 2007 International Republican Institute poll found that close to 47 percent of Moroccans reported that they would vote for the PJD in the upcoming election. Because the JCO is not a legal party, many of its supporters arguably back the PJD in official electoral politics.[22] The PJD has been able to secure its popularity through its moderate positions on key domestic issues. For example, after refusing to endorse the king's Moudawana (Moroccan Family Code) package, the PJD ultimately accepted it in 2003. The new gender policies, which gave women, among other things, the right to divorce and raised the age of marriage to eighteen, contradicted long-held Shari'a views. By endorsing the Moudawana, the PJD demonstrated its moderation. According to Sharp, "The PJD argued that because the family code revision

---

[20]"'Morocco's AK Party Won't Copy Turkey's," *World Bulletin* September 7, 2007 (accessed at http://www.worldbulletin.net/news_detail.php?id=10284).

[21]Glennie and Mepham, "Reform in Morocco: The Role of Political Islamists."

[22]Sharp, "U.S. Democracy Promotion Policy in the Middle East."

was democratically enacted, its members should accept it, since the party is committed to both democratic and Islamic principles."[23]

The JCO also professes moderation on issues related to Morocco's internal conditions. Nadia Yassin, the JCO's spokesperson and daughter of Shaykh Yassin, led a campaign against the Moudawana package. She argued that she supported women's rights, but would not support the reforms because they were designed to please foreign donors and did little to improve the situation of women in Morocco. Showing her commitment to women, in a speech at Georgetown University she swore by the Quran that if the JCO ever came to power they would never force women to veil and women would be even more respected under JCO rule. In fact, 30 percent of the JCO's executive body is managed by women, and nearly 15 percent of PJD candidates in the 2007 elections were women. On domestic issues like gender, it appears the JCO and PJD are improving their record.

Yet, while the JCO and PJD represent Morocco's more modern front, there remain radical elements in the kingdom. Islamist radicals have taken advantage of the more liberal environment of the 1990s and have used it to operate against the kingdom. The Casablanca bombings in 2003 and the Madrid bombings in 2004 reminded Moroccans of the harm these fringe groups are capable of. In 2002, the Moroccan security forces discovered an al-Qaeda network operating within the kingdom. These groups were linked to Salafiyya Jihadiyya, a group with close ties to al-Qaeda, and were planning attacks against American naval vessels in the Strait of Gibraltar as well as attacks on Moroccan tourist sites. Although the leaders of the conspiracy were Saudis, their accomplices were all Moroccan.[24] In May 2003, fourteen suicide bombers attacked foreign and Jewish targets in Casablanca, killing fourteen people. A year later, the Madrid bombings killed 181 and injured over 1,800. Again, most of the perpetrators were of Moroccan origin.

The coordinated offensive by Islamist extremists illustrated that a sector of the population opposed the regime and its external policies.[25] So worried was the Moroccan population that a poll indicated that 40 percent supported the banning of Islamist groups like the PJD after the bombings, while 37 percent refused to support such a ban. With such polarization on central democratic principles like the right for opposition parties to exist, key segments of the Moroccan society have galvanized their efforts behind the heavy-handed tactics of the Moroccan monarchy to counter groups that wish to undermine the interests of the regime.

Even though Mohammad VI responded aggressively to the terrorist attacks, the number of Islamist radicals has continued to surge in the kingdom. Further, with Islamist positions against the United States becoming

[23] Ibid.
[24] Howe, *Morocco: The Islamist Awakening and Other Challenges*, 140.
[25] Howe, *Morocco: The Islamist Awakening and Other Challenges*.

more intense, Mohammad VI has had to proceed cautiously in his growing relationship with the United States.[26] By 2004, it became clear that the moderate Islamist groups were also gaining momentum because of their stances against the United States. In the 2007 elections, the PJD won the most votes of any party and secured the second largest number of seats in the parliament, a pattern that repeated itself in 2011.[27] Those who are appalled by the PJD's levels of popularity point out that it continues to reject any form of normalization of relations with Israel. Further, some in the kingdom indicate that the PJD supports Hamas in Palestine and potentially rallies behind Iran. The business and intellectual sectors remain apprehensive of the potential damage the PJD can inflict on Morocco if it continues to gain momentum and popularity.[28]

VOICES FROM WITHIN: POLITICAL ENGAGEMENT AND THE REGIME IN MOROCCO

Across Morocco, concerns about U.S., and by extension, EU patronage loomed large.[29] Citizens expressed support for the regime not because it was meeting high standards but because, given the contextual dynamics of U.S. clientelism, the monarchy had an essential role to play.[30] Stronger ties to the United States were important, respondents pointed out, in improving the economic standing of the country. Moroccans, especially those who are or see themselves in the future as part of the global middle class who stand to benefit from greater economic development and globalization, deem such ties to the United States and Europe vital for the regime. Although Moroccan citizens were much more favorably disposed toward Europe, many saw that losing U.S. patronage could have an adverse effect on their European ties. Thus, many Moroccans believed the status quo was preferable to an alternative scenario in which Morocco would become internationally isolated. Moroccans were more predisposed to the Moroccan leadership, be-

[26]Ibid.

[27]Francis Dubois, "Moroccan Elections Reveal Gulf Between Regime and the Population," November 7, 2007 (accessed at http://www.wsws.org/articles/2007/nov2007/moro-n07.shtml).

[28]Naoufel Daqiqi and Mawassi Lahcen, "Morocco's PJD Confident Despite Detractors," *Magharebia*, August 31, 2007 (accessed at http://www.magharebia.com/cocoon/awi/xhtml1/en_GB/features/awi/reportage/2007/08/31/reportage-01).

[29]Note: I cannot replicate the regression tables in chapter 4 because the Interior Ministry of Morocco censored the question on anti-Americanism. In fact, the ministry was also very sensitive about allowing us to tap into anti-American sentiment more broadly. This is telling, and the fact that the question was deleted reinforces the main findings of this manuscript that anti-Americanism is an important variable influencing local political developments.

[30]Fifty-two interviews were conducted in Morocco in the fall of 2006 and winter of 2007. Alex Kobishyn and Timothy Shriver conducted these interviews. The interview schedule can be found in the appendix to chapter 5.

lieving that the key to their success was the linkage to a larger international global economy. Such support was voiced most strongly among Morocco's middle class, which was more likely to worry about the Islamist doctrine vis-à-vis the West. Those more critical of the monarchy and more supportive of democracy believed the kingdom could do without U.S. patronage.

On the ground, citizens express the possibilities that Islamist movements might jeopardize the ties between Morocco and their external patrons. Ayah, a university student, is a strong supporter of the status quo. She understands that Morocco is very much dependent on the United States. Further, she believes strong U.S. ties will potentially solve these outstanding economic issues: "We have a lot of economic problems and the free trade agreement will help us." This assistance, Ayah rationalizes, is contingent on a compliant monarchy. She understands that Morocco is micromanaged by the United States: "The Moroccan government cannot do anything unless the U.S. agrees." As such, she worries about the Islamists who can jeopardize such important ties. "Islamists in Morocco have close ties to the Islamists in Iraq who are against the U.S." Because of this and other concerns, Ayah believes Morocco should continue moving at a very gradual path toward reform and not push for democracy, which might undermine the entire regime.

Ayah's logic, which reflects the views of so many citizens in Jordan, was found throughout the Moroccan kingdom. One of the more lengthy interviews was with Hayyah, a university graduate living in the small town of Titouan, who believes in democracy but does not believe it is suitable for Morocco. The United States, she says, is only interested in pro-American democracy. Thus there is no need for Morocco to waste its time. Personally, she has no problem with Islamist groups; she believes the secular-Islamic divide is overstated: "I don't think there is anything to be afraid of. I think they are good people and want to do good things." She is not an Islamist supporter, however, but firmly believes in their inclusion. Nonetheless, she worries that their stances against the United States will become problematic: "When I think about democracy, I think about people choosing their government and that government being responsive to the people. But when I listen to the way the U.S. wants it, it seems to me it wants a government that agrees with itself." She goes on to say, "There was real democracy in Algeria in 1991, but the U.S. didn't want that government. . . . So what meaning does democracy have if we know that an elected government that does not agree with America or Israel won't be allowed to function? Do you understand why we can't support democracy? That's why the king is everything to us."

Hayyah understands that the Moroccan-American alliance is vital. "America has a good relationship with Morocco because Morocco does what America wants it to do." Doing "what America wants it do" is a way to guarantee a peaceful status quo and future prosperity. She believes the United States is not a force of good in the region. She believes that it will comfortably stand by and watch countries get destroyed. She makes a direct reference to Lebanon: "When it started to recover [from the Civil War] Israel did what it did to make sure Lebanon wouldn't become powerful. It's true! Do you think they did it [bombed Lebanon] for the sake of two kidnapped soldiers? And do you think they were just after Hizbullah? If they were just after Hizbullah then why destroy the economy of the entire country? It makes no sense unless you realize Israel has to keep all its neighbors weak. It keeps the Palestinians in prison. It bombs Lebanon once every ten years or so. And you saw what the U.S. did in Iraq?" That war and devastation loom large in Hayyah's assessment.

Hayyah is fed up with explanations that continue to paint Arab civilization as lacking in democracy. She points out that most societies in the region are democratic—even the Palestinians, who are under occupation, have proved to the world that they are democratic: "The closest thing to a democracy in the Arab world is Palestine, and they don't even have a country! So the question is where do these bad governments in the Arab world come from? From the people! People who are wise and understand Islam know that Islam is not the problem. Our people are poor, desperate, and have lost all hope in life, are angry and strongly feel the sting of injustice and want to do something to fix it." She goes on to explain that "when the U.S. wants real democracy in the Arab world, it will push for real democracy in the Arab world." For the time being, she will support the regime, because that's what the United States wants.

Miles away in another small town sits Mohammad, a nuclear physicist. His interview is also very extensive. He takes the time to explain why he supports the regime and is eager to convince the listener of the soundness of his logic. Like so many other citizens in the Arab world, Mohammad supports democracy but does not feel that it is suitable for Morocco. In fact, he believes that the United States is not justified in pretending that it is a true democracy either. "In America, you have this idea of liberty and democracy. They are just words. First, look at what the U.S. does in the world!" More important, though, Mohammad asks why democracy is more suitable in the United States than in Morocco. In the United States, people are invested in the system, and democracy won't undermine it. In Morocco, people are less invested in the system. In fact, they are invested in Islam, which *would* undermine the entire system. He meticulously tries to explain how this lack of systemic support evolved:

> In the U.S., you give freedoms to people who are invested in the system of government, because the system of government works for them. Do you understand? If you gave too many rights and freedoms to people in this area, who knows what would happen? All our political ideolo-

gies have failed after colonialism. We have nationalism and people were told to be very proud of their country, even when it is supported by someone else. So people look for nationalism and in Islam there is something people can understand. That's why Islam is political and since the revolution in Iran all the governments have feared it. Islam is extremely powerful. And if you ask most people here, they will tell you that the U.S. is working with our government to make sure Islam does not come to power. They [the United States and the Moroccan regime] actually try to convince people that Islam is bad, because it is too conservative. This is nonsense. It is harder and harder to keep people uneducated, and it is harder and harder to control populations using the tools that worked just ten or fifteen years ago. People can organize more easily using the Internet, barriers to communication have decreased; there is more information out there. And America is hypocritical when it says it wants democracy *and* it wants to eradicate the Islamic movement. The movement comes from inside the people. Do you want people to be able to express their political will or do you want to suppress an ideology that you feel is a threat to your interests? Because America is now doing both and everyone in the region sees this and it is something that makes America lose credibility.

Mohammad ridicules the way in which the United States wants to promote democracy in Morocco. Leaving the Islamists outside the political game simply won't work. Mohammad does not see Islamist movements as threats internally. He says that their conservative agenda doesn't bother him, although he himself does not support their narrow doctrine: "The Islamist groups that talk about how people should practice their religion . . . well, what of it? Nobody is forcing people to do anything. Either their ideas will be accepted or they won't be accepted, but they have the right to speak no matter what they think." But, he tells us, he also understands that Islamists have a political agenda, and this political agenda could be more harmful: "Of the political groups you will find moderate groups, like 'Adl wa Tanmiyya [the PJD] and you'll find more extreme groups like al-'Adl wal Ihsān [the JCO] and others." Both groups, he maintains, are anti-American. It is this reality that keeps citizens like Mohammad committed to the status quo.

A further illustration of the logic citizens employ for the national wellbeing of their countries is 'Alam's rationalization. 'Alam, a chemist working for an international firm in Casablanca, explains why he supports the status quo. He wants a democracy in Morocco, but he's very cautious because he believes democracy can only occur when the Islamists become more politically sophisticated. He supports Islamist movements and firmly believes that "this kind of movement is the solution of tomorrow." But this support for Islamic values and movements does not mean that he is not worried. He would like to see more democracy under certain conditions. He says, "Look at Turkey, where the Islamists work with intelligence. They find ways to succeed. They communicate well with everyone and there are few problems. America deals with the Islamists in Turkey. They have a good relationship with the movement. This needs to happen in Morocco." For 'Alam, democracy is definitely good, but only as long as the Americans are on board and in direct communication with the Islamists.

Finally, Sameh, an English teacher and tutor, is upset because he sees himself as an impotent citizen caught up in U.S. machinations in the region. Sameh has no problem with Islamist movements; he believes they can be even more democratic than non-Islamist movements. He doesn't believe, however, that the United States will allow Islamist movements to rule a country, even if these movements are democratically elected. He says, "Hamas was democratically elected but nobody gave it a chance to rule. That doesn't make sense. The U.S. encourages democracy— the U.S. doesn't like the government that is democratically elected, therefore the U.S. punishes that country for its elections? This makes no sense. So democracy and Islam can coexist only if the United States decides it will let them." Sameh understands, however, that the United States may not be interested in democracy. He argues that America is more invested in preserving the status quo:

> The U.S. looks after the interests of the Moroccan government because it wants that government to stay in place. But what the Moroccan government wants isn't good for most Moroccans. . . . The U.S. looks after the interest of stability, stability above everything, above democracy, above human rights, above development, all of those other things are used as an ends to stability—stability of a government which cooperates with the United States. Do you see? So, I say to you that stability of this government isn't in the interest of about 90 percent of the population. But that is what the U.S. guarantees.

Sameh goes on to explain how U.S. hegemony in the region has stifled the potential for democratic advancement. He believes that when the world order was structured by a bipolar distribution of power between the United States and Soviet Union, citizens had the potential to push for change. "It was different in the time of Hassan II," he says.

> Then, there was America and there was the Soviet Union, and those who wanted a change in government could find support through one or the other of those two and have a chance to get heard. And actually there were several attempts to change the government at that time, and the Soviet Union and America did send support and money and arms to one side or the other. Now, there is only America, there is nothing

else. So people who want change have no organizing force, no way to get any support or help. Any organized movement will be crushed.

Sameh is quite skeptical of the baby-step reforms that the kingdom has adopted since Mohammad VI came to power. "What does it help, for example, that people can now complain about the government in the press, or now have the right to speak about politics more freely? Nothing will come of it, it is just meaningless talk. . . . Do you see what I'm trying to say?" He goes on to say that he understands that the U.S. push for democracy and economic development are ways to improve the lives of citizens, especially the global middle class linked to such developments. But all of these reforms, he maintains, are designed with the goal of "keeping this system in power."

In fact, Sameh argues that although Moroccans enjoy more political freedoms today, it is because most Moroccans have acquiesced to a status quo dictated by the United States with the end result of keeping the Moroccan regime in power. Today, the citizens of Morocco are more dominated by the realities of U.S. hegemony in the region. Citizens know they can't contest the status quo, or they will suffer. Carefully examine his next statement: "The existing reforms [of Mohammad VI] do not matter," he says. "They are put into place when it is guaranteed not to matter." In a defeatist tone, he argues that he understands the United States will settle for nothing less than the status quo. As a result, most citizens will support the regime—thus reforms will not bring about democracy. Sameh believes if the regime were feeling threatened by society, it—along with the United States—would not allow even these little reforms. He tells us that society was more empowered when Hassan II was in power because of the bipolar world order. He says, "In the time of Hassan II, not only did the system not work in the interests of most people, but people were organized and armed and willing to do something about it, which is why you saw the abuses and why people were harshly brutalized. The more threat there is to the system, the more brutal the system will be." Thus, reforms are not reassuring; rather, for Sameh, they prove that the United States has emerged victorious in subduing Arab societies.

Sameh does not oppose ties to Western countries to further advance the interests of Morocco; he has a kinder perception of Europe. "Our dealings with the Europeans have more to do with our shared interests." He appreciates the role France and Spain play in developing Morocco's economy: "This is real politics—politics of shared interests and cooperation." This mutually beneficial relationship is not what Morocco has with the United States: "What America does is different. America adopts the politics of empire—no more and no less. It is obvious to everyone." Sameh, like so many citizens in Morocco, understands the sheer dominance of the United States in the region. While most Moroccans try to rationalize their support for the status quo as a means of improving the national well-being of their countries, Sameh's support for the status quo is more a conviction about being a conquered subject of an American empire writ large.

In contrast to these supporters of the regime, opponents of the regime take direct issue with Morocco's patron-client relationship with the United States. Such opposition is commonly found among supporters of the Islamist movements. Ahmad tells us he is a strong supporter of the JCO. Notably, however, Ahmad—like many other Moroccans who oppose their country's U.S. client status—seldom criticizes Morocco's ties to western Europe. Rather, the focus remains on the United States.

Ahmad has an engineering degree, but is unemployed and is thinking about moving to Casablanca to look for work. He is very dissatisfied with the status quo. At twenty-seven, he is not married and would very much like to be able to afford to get married. Ahmad strongly believes that an Islamic democracy is superior to American democracy. He understands that the United States is important for Morocco, but believes it only serves U.S. interests, and this disappoints him. Ahmad rejects the monarchy because of U.S. support of its authoritarian tendencies; he believes the United States is invested in destroying the lives of ordinary Muslims and set on dominating the entire region: "Iraq has now become American's new colony. America wants to control the region, the energy and oil and guarantee its place in the world. . . . There could have been more politically smart [ways to accomplish this], with less killing, murdering and destruction." As such, Ahmad is not a regime supporter. A strong advocate of democracy, he believes the route to democracy is through distancing Morocco from the United States.

Faez, who has an undergraduate degree and is working in an internet café, also supports a democratic state. But he only supports one set of politics. "The politics of the Quran is the only thing that matters," he says. Strong ties to the United States are not possible, nor is a democratic system mirrored after the United States necessary: "America ruined Iraq. They are acting like Iraq is their country. America needs to leave Iraq and the entire region." What is most upsetting to Faez is that the United States took over Iraq under the pretext of engendering democracy.

Houdaifa, a contract painter, also dislikes the United States. He is a strong supporter and member of the PJD. Houdaifa wants more democracy, opposes the regime, and believes the existing leadership "only represents the interests of the U.S." If there was more democracy, he says, they could rid Morocco of external dominance. He believes the PJD is the perfect illustration that "democracy and Islam are compatible." He argues that a real democratic government is one that "serves the needs of the people . . . not like the government we have now. We don't have democracy. This is why we need Shari'a." Hudaifa believes the United States controls Morocco's strategic standing in the world, arguing that the United States continues to meddle in the affairs of the Sahara so that Morocco will continue to rely on the United States. Further, he would love to get rid of Morocco's current leaders, "criminals who are thieves and pretend that they are democratic." He believes this status quo has been allowed to persist because the United States wants it be so.

Sana, a twenty-seven-year-old public utilities employee, joins others in her strong sentiments against the regime, attributing such disdain to U.S. patronage. With outright anger, she says, "Look at what the U.S. has done in Iraq and in Palestine!" Angered by the association the United States makes between Muslims and extremist terrorists, she says, "Ruining country after country seems more extreme to me than one or two people who blow themselves up!!" Sana is a firm supporter of Islamism, and blames the ills of Morocco on the United States. She even believes the United States and the regime orchestrated the Casablanca bombings so that both could further clamp down on the Moroccan people and convince them they aren't ready for democracy. An Islamist government, obedient to the laws of Islam, she says, "would represent the citizens of the country, help create jobs, educate the people, guard cultural values, and defend its citizens." She doesn't want American democracy or anything to do with America: "The way American democracy works is that they tell other countries how to work, imposing their will." She goes on to ask, "Why does America talk about democracy anyway? They are a dictatorship. They rule the world and attack other countries that did nothing bad to them." She believes the current government in Morocco is "worthless" and the only political party that matters is the al-'Adl wal Ihsan (JCO). "Al-'Adl wal Ihsan has some good ideas. The West will never see it that way because the West has decided that Islam is the enemy. But al-'Adl wal Ihsan wants good for the people, and wants a society in which people recognize the value of religion and are guided by the principles set out in the Quran. There is nothing wrong with that." She goes on to say that the current regime is "ruled by America and not by the people." An Islamic government, she maintains, will not be subservient to the United States.

Moroccans, like their Kuwaiti and Jordanian counterparts, understand their relationship with their regime through the lens of U.S. patronage. The suitability of democracy—indeed, the alteration of the status quo—is assessed for its strategic practicality given the international order. For its part, the United States has attempted a new model of engagement to further its interests in Morocco. Rather than declare all Islamic movements in the country as hostile to the United States, the Americans have tried to win over segments of the PJD, attempting to foment strong ties with the opposition. This would further U.S. strategic interests and the ability to promote democracy. Clearly, a pro-American opposition is important, if not a prerequisite, for further democratization.

U.S. RESPONSES TO THE ISLAMISTS IN MOROCCO

The United States has attempted to embrace the PJD in Morocco in hopes of winning it over to its side. For its part, the PJD would like stronger ties with the United States, as it understands that such relations are vital to the economic trajectory of the kingdom. Many speculate these engagements are modeled after the Turkey-U.S. relationship, where Prime Minister Recep Tayyip Erdogan's Islamic Justice and Development Party has maintained close ties to the United States. Sa'ad al-'Othmani, the PJD's general secretary, has been invited to the United States on low-level visits. The PJD believes that stimulating such ties is extremely important for the future economic progress of Morocco. According to Lahcen Daoudi, a leading member of the PJD in 2006, "It is in the interest of Morocco that the world community knows the PJD. I don't want investors to flee because of us."[31]

The United States has also allowed the JCO access to its shores. In 2005 and 2006, Nadia Yassin made several visits to America to speak on college campuses. U.S. engagement with the PJD demonstrates two important strategies. First, Islamists, whether the more moderate PJD or more conservative JCO, are willing to engage the United States in meaningful and constructive dialogue; there is nothing inherent about these Islamic movements that bars their engagement with America. Second, and more important, it appears that no amount of grooming and access can overcome the result of U.S. policies in the region, which are seen as directly undermining the Arab and Muslim nation. Absent a change of U.S. policies in the region, the United States will continue to experiment with formulas to deal with the Islamist problem and not address outstanding grievances. That the PJD has recently declared it would like to limit ties to the United States signals that open engagement will not suffice to overcome the damage of existing U.S. policies in the region.[32]

[31] Roula Khalaf, "Morocco Sees the Rise of an 'Acceptable' Islamist Party," *Financial Times of Morocco*, May 23, 2006 (accessed at http://www.iri.org/newsarchive/2006/2006-05-23-News -FinancialTimes-Morocco.asp).

[32] Judy Barsalou, *Islamists at the Ballot Box: Findings from Egypt, Jordan, Kuwait, and Turkey.* United States Institute of Peace Special Report no. 144 (Washington, DC: United States Institute of Peace, 2005; accessed at http://www.usip.org/pubs/specialreports/sr144.html).

CHAPTER SEVEN

Palestine and Saudi Arabia and the
Limits of Democracy

THE ROAD MAP FOR PEACE, ADOPTED IN 2002 BY THE QUARTET OF THE EUROPEAN Union (EU), the United States, Russia, and the United Nations, called for the necessity of Palestinian reforms in moving the peace process forward. The United States became vocal about the need for the Palestinians to reform their system of government and pushed for Palestinian elections in the early years of the new millennium. However, the United States was hoping that a pro-Fatah alliance would emerge and neglected to state publicly that it would nullify any outcome that was not favorable to its own interests. The Palestinians learned the hard way that the United States would indeed punish the entire population for exercising democracy the wrong way.

Here we have the case of the United States overturning a true democratic experiment.[1] By all accounts, the Palestinian elections were the most democratic the Arab world had ever seen. In fact, the election marks the first democratic regime change in the Arab region since World War II. After urging the Palestinians to be more democratic, a prerequisite to continue peace negotiations, the United States and the international community negated the election's outcome, declared Hamas an enemy, and then proceeded to penalize the entire Palestinian population for its democratic experiment. Economic sanctions were placed on the Palestinian government, now led by Hamas. While the aid-dependent Palestinian Authority (PA) struggled to locate alternative sources of funds, the harsh economic blockade further debilitated the Palestinian economy. Salaries could not be paid, food rotted at borders, and movement within the West Bank was further hampered. The international community didn't seem to care that the Palestinian vote was indeed a vote against a corrupt Fatah government that proved to be unable to deliver economically or on the peace front.[2]

---

[1] The other notable experiment that was overturned with tacit U.S. approval was that of Algeria in 1991.

[2] Amaney Jamal, "Security Vulnerabilities in Jordan," paper presented at the Annual Meeting of the American Political Science Association, September 2007.

All the more frustrating to the Palestinians was that they didn't even ask to hold the elections. Rather, it was Israel and the United States that demanded the Palestinians become more democratic because of the overly centralized authority of Yasir Arafat's rule. In the 1990s, Arafat was seen as instrumental to the ongoing Oslo Agreement. Thus, the West and Israel turned a blind eye to his authoritarian antics. Only when it became clear that Arafat was ineffectual and could no longer appropriate the Palestinian street did the world community, with the United States at its helm, demand more democracy. By 2001, the international community also began to hold Arafat personally accountable for the Second Intifada in 2000. Thus the push for reform, designed to limit Arafat's authority and not necessarily address the growing economic grievances of the Palestinians, grew. In fact, according to Nathan Brown, "reforms that might not weaken Arafat quickly lost the support of high-level U.S. officials."[3] One way to weaken Arafat was to weaken his grip on the executive branch and further bolster legislative powers. The American empowering of the legislative branch was completely designed with the idea of bringing Mahmoud 'Abbas to power. The Americans were banking on Mahmoud 'Abbas and his Fatah party remaining in power. They did not methodically examine other scenarios that would not result in a Fatah victory. Thus, the legislative branch, the branch that Hamas would gain control of in 2006, was given more democratic power, reducing the executive role in Palestinian affairs. Again, all of this was intended to limit Arafat's rule.

Leading up to these democratic reforms, U.S. policy makers were convinced that the Oslo process had failed because the Palestinians were not democratic enough. During her confirmation hearings in 2005, incoming secretary of state Condoleezza Rice said, "The establishment of a Palestinian democracy will help to bring an end to the conflict in the Holy Land."[4] Little analytical insight backed such proclamations. Surely Jordan and Egypt were able to uphold peace treaties with Israel under severe authoritarian circumstances. Neither does it appear that Syria's rogue status as a supplier of Hizbullah weaponry and entrenched authoritarian standing hindered the ongoing Israel-Syrian bilateral talks. According to Brown, "Lacking sovereignty, freedom of movement, fiscal autonomy, and basic security, Palestinians were still supposed to forge ahead with building accountable, professional, and efficient governmental structures operating in accordance with the standards of first world states."[5] For Palestinians—who

---

[3] Nathan J. Brown, *Requiem for Palestinian Reform: Clear lessons from a Troubled Record*, Carnegie Paper no. 81 (Washington DC: Carnegie Endowment for International Peace, 2007), 7.

[4] "Transcript: Confirmation Hearing of Condoleezza Rice," *New York Times*, January 18, 2005 (accessed at http://www.nytimes.com/2005/01/18/politics/18TEXT-RICE.html?pagewanted =print).

[5] Brown, *Requiem for Palestinian Reform*, 11.

never really had a state, were segregated by over seven hundred checkpoints on the West Bank, and were enclosed with barbed wire in the desert strip of Gaza—democracy would become a precondition for moving the peace effort forward.

So vocal was the international push for Palestinian democracy that the internal discourse in Palestine soon shifted to a "democracy now, statehood later" mantra. In fact, when interviewing one of the leading Palestinian negotiators in 2004, I was informed that the peace talks had failed because Palestinians were not democratic enough. As he noted, "We have to be democratic to prove to the U.S. and Israel that we can lead a state."[6] The Palestinian leadership had apparently embraced the notion, either through choice or circumstance, that it was the democratic inferiority of Palestinians that justified their continued occupation by Israel.

In 2005, the Palestinians elected Mahmoud 'Abbas to a now-weakened executive post. Legislative elections followed in the winter of 2006. Comparing the percentage of Arab citizens who believed their legislative elections were free and fair to those who believed the elections encountered serious problems, the Palestinians give the highest rankings to their own elections: 90 percent of Palestinians felt that their elections were free and fair, compared to an average of 60 percent across Arab states for which data is available—30 percent above the mean (see table 7.1).[7]

Not only did the Palestinians rate their electoral experience positively, but they also showed the highest levels of voter turnout in the entire region—72 percent of the population came out to vote in the 2006 elections. The total average generally for Arab countries is 57 percent (see table 7.2).[8] Hamas's electoral victory cannot be explained away by nondemocratic practices, vote buying, or a dismal turnout; it apparently had a significant electoral mandate.

FATAH'S DECLINE AND THE VICTORY OF HAMAS

To understand Hamas's success, one must understand Fatah's disintegration as a mass political party. Citizens voted for Hamas because of its political stances vis-à-vis Fatah and because of their dissatisfaction with the gradual pace of the peace process. Citizens—secular and religious, Muslim and Christian—turned out to vote. Entire Christian towns on the West Bank turned out in Hamas's favor. Hamas did not win solely because it appealed to Islamists.

[6] Anonymous, interview with the author, summer 2004.

[7] Arab Barometer 2005-6 (principal investigators: Mark Tessler and Amaney Jamal; accessed at http://www.arabbarometer.org/survey/survey.html).

[8] The Kuwaiti percentage is so low because women had not been enfranchised when the survey was conducted.

TABLE 7.1. Logistic regression:Support for Fatah (PSR data)

	Support for Fatah
US aid important	0.520***
	(0.072)
Refugee status	0.088
	(0.124)
Age	−0.014***
	(0.005)
Education	0.035
	(0.050)
Income	0.038
	(0.032)
Constant	−2.053***
	(0.429)
Observations	1237
	66% predicted correctly

Source: PSR Survey Research Unit, Poll No. 19 (Ramallah, West Bank: Palestinian Center for Policy and Survey Research, 2006; accessed July 2008 at http://www.pcpsr.org/survey/polls/2006/p19etables1.html). See this chapter's appendix.

Robust standard errors in parentheses; * significant at 10%; ** significant at 5%; *** significant at 1%.

Several factors explain Fatah's unraveling. First and foremost, the isolation and then death of Arafat removed the symbolic figure who had not only united Fatah as a party but also united Fatah with those structures of the PA. Frictions within Fatah exploded dramatically after Arafat's death. First, this internal factionalism was reflected in party and candidate electoral lists. The sheer number of Fatah candidates dispersed across localities diluted the Fatah vote. While Hamas only received 44 percent of the popular vote, Fatah—combined with other nationalistic/secular groups—received 56 percent. These results, however, were not reflected in legislative seat allocations due to the number of Fatah candidates on electoral lists. Hamas ended up with 56 percent of the seats in parliament because it had run a limited number of candidates in each district. Second, persistent corruption in the ranks of Fatah and the PA depressed their popular standing. Third, limited sources of funding tremendously weakened Fatah's effective, albeit patrimonial, presence in the civic sector. Fourth, international scrutiny of Arafat's financial accounts made it difficult for Fatah to continue to support its expanded clientelistic base. And fifth, support for the peace process not only decreased but it became all too clear that with the Israeli unilateral

TABLE 7.2. Evaluations of elections in
the Arab world, 2005–6

All Arab countries	60%
Jordan	71%
Palestine	90%
Algeria	50%
Morocco	36%
Kuwait	46%
Lebanon	66%
Yemen	48%

disengagement of Gaza there was less need for a compliant Palestinian leadership. Sadly, in the fall of 2005, Saeb 'Erakat, senior Palestinian negotiator, admitted that over six months had passed without any direct talks with the Israelis.[9] With growing anti-American sentiment in the region, a U.S. endorsement of Fatah on the eve of the elections only hurt the fragile party, if anything.[10] Hamas's electoral slogan—"Israel and the U.S. want Fatah . . . what do you think?"—resonated strongly with Palestinian voters, even Palestinian Christian voters.

Together these factors explain the decline in support for Fatah and the successive vote for Hamas. At the very least, Hamas had made strong promises to counter Fatah's corruption and to rule justly. And 43 percent of those who voted for Hamas believed those promises, voting on the basis that Hamas would fight corruption. Hamas also promised to deliver on the peace process, provided Israel recognized a Palestinian state based in the West Bank and Gaza, including East Jerusalem. Sixty-seven percent of Palestinians surveyed believed Hamas should continue with the peace process. Therefore, the vote for Hamas was not a vote *against* a two-state solution but a vote *for* it.

Immediately after assuming the reins of power, however, Hamas was confronted with a bitter reality: Fatah, Israel, and the international community wanted it out of power. Fatah would not join a Hamas-led government, and international forces, along with Israel, rejected the idea of unity government between Hamas and Fatah. Competition between Fatah and Hamas over key governmental portfolios like finance and security effectively led to tense internal conflict. Internationally, foreign donors declared that they would

[9]See Ken Ellingwood, "Abbas, Sharon Hope to Avoid Repeating Past," *Los Angeles Times*, February 5, 2005 (accessed at http://articles.latimes.com/2005/feb/05/world/fg-summit5).
[10]Erica Silverman, "Fatah's U.S. Savior," *Al-Ahram Weekly*, October 19–25, 2006 (accessed at http://weekly.ahram.org.eg/2006/817/re52.htm).

not deal with Hamas—and more important, they would suspend all their funding to a government led by Hamas's Ism'ail Haniyya. In actuality, this meant that the tens of thousands of teachers, security officers, and government employees who relied on their monthly checks from the PA would be left without any means of subsistence. The PA was the largest employer of Palestinian labor, with some 120,000 people depending on wages from the government; 80 percent of the Gaza population was already living under the $2.70-per-day poverty level, and the unemployment rate was at 40 percent. It was no exaggeration to state that sanctions would devastate the civic sector. The PA's annual budget was estimated at between $1.5 and $1.7 billion, with $790 million coming from customs revenue held by Israel, $360 million from internal taxes, and the rest from donor monies—that is, the United States and the EU.[11] By the end of 2006, the already crippled Palestinian economy had shrunk another 21 percent due to the sanctions.[12] In 2006, the overall Palestinian gross domestic product was 40 percent lower than that of 1999.[13] In 2007, United Nations Relief and Works Agency for Palestine Refugees in the Near East reported that "46 percent of Palestinians do not have enough food to meet their needs. The number of people in deep poverty, defined as those living on less than 50 cents a day, nearly doubled in 2006 to over 1 million."[14]

As tensions mounted in Palestine between Fatah and Hamas, Fatah was able to gain control over the West Bank in 2007, even as Hamas solidified its control over Gaza.[15] While Gaza remained under lock and key, with its population—according to several rights groups[16]—on the verge of a humanitarian catastrophe, the West Bank performed better due to the donor aid to Mahmoud 'Abbas's PA.[17] The humanitarian situation in Gaza drastically worsened after the Israeli campaign on the Gaza Strip in December 2008,

---

[11]For U.S. donor restrictions on Palestine, see Christopher M. Blanchard and Jeremy M. Sharp, *U.S. Foreign Aid to the Palestinians*, Congressional Research Service Report, July 27, 2006 (accessed at http://fpc.state.gov/documents/organization/68794.pdf). See also Wendy Kristiansen, "Palestine: Hamas Besieged," *Le Monde*, June 3, 2006 (accessed at http://mondediplo .com/2006/06/03hamas).

[12]Associated Press, "Palestinian Economy Shrinks 21% in Fourth Quarter of 2006," February 2, 2007 (accessed at http://www.haaretz.com/hasen/spages/830389.html).

[13]Emad Mekay, "Palestinian Economy Tumbles under Sanctions," March 26, 2007 (accessed at http://ipsnews.net/news.asp?idnews=37093).

[14]"Palestine Monitor Fact Sheet: Poverty," *Palestine Monitor*, December 18, 2008 (accessed at http://www.palestinemonitor.org/spip/spip.php?article13); see the link for more information on the impact of the economic blockade and sanctions.)

[15]Brown, "Requiem for Palestinian Reform."

[16]Ian Black, "Sanctions Causing Gaza to Implode, Say Rights Groups," *Guardian*, March 6, 2008 (accessed at http://www.guardian.co.uk/world/2008/mar/06/israelandthepalestinians .humanrights).

[17]See Paul Morro, *U.S. Foreign Aid to Palestinians*, Congressional Research Service Report, October 9, 2007 (accessed at http://www.usembassy.it/pdf/other/RS22370.pdf).

which witnessed over a month of continued bombardment. Across the Arab world there is firm conviction that this is the price of democracy if it does not result in partners that the United States deems appropriate.[18]

This strategy certainly influenced the Palestinians. A population already deprived and traumatized by war and instability has come to terms with the fact that democracy may be an ideal form of governance, but it is probably not the best system of governance for them. This reality is captured in public opinion polls conducted by the Palestine Survey Research Center under Dr. Khalil Shikaki's direction. On the eve of Palestinian elections, 60 percent of Palestinians believed that democracy was suitable for their country, a view they shared with the international community that demanded more democracy. By 2008, after two years of brutal sanctions that rendered 80 percent of Palestinians in Gaza dependent on donor aid rations, that percentage had fallen to 40 percent. Support for Hamas had also fallen, and just before Israel's assault on Gaza in December 2008, support for Hamas was higher on the West Bank (at 51 percent) than it was in Gaza (37 percent).

Another poll further documents how Palestinians understand that their national well-being is linked to the United States and the Western world more generally. In March 2006, 60 percent of the Palestinian people believed that the PA could not do without Western donor aid, and another 52 percent worried that the PA would collapse if that aid were cut off.[19] By September 2006, 77 percent of the Palestinian people reported that they needed "the support and understanding of the international community." In the March 2006 poll, the Palestine Survey Research Center included a question worded as follows: "The Western Donor Community provided the PA with assistance; can the PA do without this assistance?"[20] Sixty-eight percent of the Palestinians reported that their government could not. In fact, in logistic regression analysis (see table 7.3)—controlling for other demographic variables as refugee camp residence, education, age, and gender—those Palestinians who believed that their government was reliant on Western funds were 32 percent more likely to report that they supported Fatah.[21] Gradually, Palestinians began expressing a desire to return to the nondemocratic Fatah as a means of appeasing the donor community—especially the United States. Whereas support for Hamas was at 47 percent in the wake of the Palestinian elections, its popularity had fallen to 31 percent by June 2008.

[18]"Gaza Humanitarian Plight 'Disastrous,' U.N. Official Says," December 28, 2008 (accessed at http://www.cnn.com/2008/WORLD/meast/12/28/gaza.humanitarian/).

[19]PSR Survey Research Unit, *Palestinian Public Opinion Poll*, Poll no. 19 (Ramallah, West Bank: Palestinian Center for Policy and Survey Research, 2006; accessed at http://www.pcpsr.org/survey/polls/2006/p19e.html).

[20]Ibid.

[21]Substantive effects calculated by the first difference method while controlling other independent variables at their means

TABLE 7.3. Votes in the elections, 2005–6

All Arab Countries	57%
Jordan	60%
Palestine	72%
Algeria	51%
Morocco	58%
Kuwait	24%
Lebanon	64%
Yemen	58%

Amira Haas captures this situation well in "Missing the Government of Thieves," where she describes Palestinian protests in November 2006 against the PA. During these riots, and in reference to Hamas leader Ism'ail Hanniyya, Palestinians shouted the slogan, "Not Ism'ail, not Haniyya, we want back the government of haramiyya [thieves]." Not having received their salaries for the prior seven months, government workers went to the street demanding pay.[22] Those who felt vulnerable to variances in aid, those more vulnerable to the security and stability considerations of the nation, and those who needed desperately to feed their children chose to support the authoritarian Fatah government, demonstrating what citizens have always worried about—any movement toward democracy in the Arab world must be aligned with U.S. preferences.[23] Otherwise, states will suffer as a result of democracy.

THE U.S. RESPONSE TO HAMAS

Unlike the U.S. response to the Parti de la Justice et du Développement (PJD) in Morocco, Hamas was refused outright, then banned, and then sanctioned.

[22]Amira Hass, "Missing the Government of Thieves," November 11, 2006 (accessed at http://www.haaretz.com/hasen/spages/767581.html).

[23]I do not employ the similar models that I use in the Jordan and Kuwait sections because of the volatile situation of "regime transition" during the time of administering the Palestine survey—early 2006. In Palestine it is not clear whether the question that gauges "support of government" refers to the Hamas government or the Fatah government. Thus, to avoid this confusion, I utilize a different data set from the PSR Survey Research Unit in Ramallah, which allows for a precise testing of my hypothesis. However, when the dependent variable is "overt democracy" the findings are consistent with the Jordanian case. Pro-American Palestinians are more likely to have *less* support for democracy.

For the entire year after the elections, the international community boycotted the government and blocked any private or public party from providing financial assistance. The international community also publicly supported Fatah, and as it became clear that the two sides, Hamas and Fatah, were coming closer to confrontation, international actors continued to bolster Fatah by providing it with financial and military assistance. Along with the United States, the EU also stood behind Fatah.

Significantly, not only did the international community reject Hamas but in essence it also undermined the numerous democratic reforms adopted from the early years of the new millennium in preparation for the election. Much of the U.S. reform effort had focused on removing the security forces from direct control of the executive to the control of the cabinet. Further, payments of the security services would occur from the treasury and not the executive. All of these factors were designed to weaken the executive position (which Arafat had assumed) and strengthen parliamentary oversight. With Hamas at the helm, however, the United States reversed track, freezing all security payroll under Hamas's governance and only legitimizing security payments that emanated from the executive branch now assumed by 'Abbas.[24]

More important, however, is what Hamas's punishment—the punishment of a democratically elected government—signaled to the Palestinian people. Their desire and effort to clean up their own society and sanction a corrupt leadership would entail huge economic losses and suffering. Democracy would only suit Palestinians if they practiced pro-American democracy.[25]

WHY DID THE PALESTINIANS VOTE FOR HAMAS?

That the Palestinians voted for Hamas may, on the surface, seem to undermine the argument of this book. After all, Palestinians did vote Hamas into power. Yet it is important to note that my argument suggests that citizens will support less democracy, and be more willing to tolerate authoritarian abuses, in order to prevent or limit Islamist access to power. In a sense, the Palestinians were doing just that before the Hamas elections—until the administration of U.S. president George W. Bush stepped in with its strategy of implementing reforms to limit Arafat's rule, subsequently pushing a Fatah government that had lost legitimacy because of its internal corruption and the failed peace talks to hold elections. Independents and supporters of Fatah worried about the consequences of elections; they would have

[24]Brown, "Requiem for Palestinian Reform."
[25]Ibid.

liked to see more "controlled" or managed elections, perhaps by excluding Hamas or at least creating a "code" that would guide Hamas's behavior if it were to access power. In many instances, these negotiations about managed elections and controlled Islamist participation resemble ongoing discussions in Egypt on the role of the Muslim Brotherhood in the Fall 2011 elections.

The Palestinians fell under considerable pressure to democratize their institutions and bureaucracy. According to Nathan Brown, "by the summer of 2003, Palestine had perhaps the most transparent and efficient fiscal apparatus of any Arab state."[26] The Palestinian Basic Law was amended in a clear tactic to limit executive authority and place more power with the prime minister and the cabinet. This also included transferring powers of the internal security away from the executive office to parliament. Thus, the international community pushed its reform agenda in the belief that limiting Arafat's power would be useful to the peace process.

There were also discussions among particular nongovernmental organizations (like the National Democratic Institute and the International Republican Institute) and USAID that concentrated on the risk of Hamas's participation in the election. These organizations recommended that the Palestinians develop a code of conduct to guide the behavior of parties entering the electoral process—with a specific recommendation that parties that did not disavow violence should not be allowed to participate. Yet it was difficult to justify this recommendation with existing Palestinian law. Domestically, Hamas was seen as a legitimate political entity. Thus, the United States postponed the idea of elections. It wasn't until after Arafat's death that discussions about the elections would emerge again. Yet when they emerged in late 2004, the code of conduct dealt with only internal campaigning procedures and not the issue of violence toward Israel. Hence, Hamas was allowed to participate.[27] The organized and well-disciplined Hamas carefully managed the quality and quantity of candidates running in each district, while Fatah was tarnished by internal squabbling, infighting, competition, and chaos. Fatah ran far too many candidates in districts where they could have won, and as a result of this disorganized display, the party ended up diluting its own vote. Hence, Hamas won, and won handsomely. With a plurality of the vote, Hamas ended up with the majority of seats in parliament.[28]

Immediately, though, the issue of Western donor assistance emerged. With the imposed "democratic" elections, and then the unanticipated vic-

[26] Ibid.
[27] Ibid.
[28] Nathan J. Brown, *Aftermath of the Hamas Tsunami* (Washington, DC: Carnegie Endowment for International Peace, 2006).

tory of Hamas, Palestinians began planning for the inevitable—the cessation of aid from Western donor countries. Hamas began looking to Iran, Saudi Arabia, and other Gulf countries for foreign contributors. Israel made it clear that it would not allow Palestinians to carry monies into the embattled Gaza, and Hamas officials tried to transport funds in suitcases. Wire transfers and other forms of monetary exchange became heavily monitored as Gaza fell under complete economic blockade.[29]

The Hamas vote wouldn't have happened had the international community not pushed for it. The backing of the international community seemed to signal that it would honor the outcome of that election. Further, Hamas never really won the majority, yet the Palestinians found themselves penalized for carrying out the wishes of the international order. Had the international community not pushed for the elections, it's unclear if the Palestinians would have done so on their own—especially given the stakes.

With Hamas fully in control of Gaza, and the PA in the West Bank, the Palestinians of the West Bank under Prime Minister Salam Fayyad have been investing in building stronger political institutions. Fayyad's new vision for Palestine—building the institutions of the state now and ending occupation later—has won broad international support. Yet this international applause for Fayyad ignores a gradual yet pervasive and palpable development. With the tacit approval of the PA, the United States, and Israel, and with the Palestinians who fear Hamas coming to power, the West Bank has increasingly become authoritarian since 2006. The opposition is fiercely harassed by the PA; political opponents are detained without charges and basic laws and court orders are not enforced.[30] The United States has increased its security funding to the PA, and under the command of Lieutenant General Keith Dayton, the U.S. security coordinator for the Palestinians, four Palestinian security battalions were trained in the Jordan International Police Training Center in 2008 and 2009. Since 2009, new U.S. funding has been allocated to the construction of a police base and a Presidential Guard Training Center in Jericho. President Barack Obama stepped up funding for what is currently called the Security Sector Reform and Transformation Program, part of the Palestinian Reform and Development Plan. Palestinians continue to blame Dayton's security reforms for the deterioration of human rights. Yet in reality the human rights abuses are handled by the Palestinian intelligence communities, which are in direct relations with the U.S. Central Intelligence Agency and not Dayton per se.[31]

[29] Ibid.

[30] Nathan J. Brown. *Are Palestinians Building a State?* (Washington, DC: Carnegie Endowment for International Peace, 2010).

[31] Yezid Sayigh, *"Fixing Broken Windows": Security Sector Reform in Palestine, Lebanon, and Yemen* (Washington, DC: Carnegie Endowment for International Peace, 2009).

The West Bank has become more stable now than in the aftermath of the Hamas election. These levels of stability have been accompanied by significant economic growth rates. In 2009, the growth rate was at 8 percent. However, these numbers don't capture the economic realities on the ground: the PA is still very dependent on foreign assistance and restrictions on Palestinian mobility still make long-term economic growth difficult. When I visited the West Bank in both 2009 and 2010, these authoritarian developments were noticeable across the spectrum of political life. I posed the following question to a leading academic in Nablus: "You say the situation has improved—but doesn't it feel more repressive and more authoritarian today than in 2006?" He replied, "Democracy brought us sanctions—at least things are improving now. There's a good section of the population that is willing to tolerate this for these improvements."[32]

That Palestinians are willing to accept the authoritarian abuses linked to Fayyad's "reforms" is witnessed in his growing approval ratings. Yet one must be wary of these ratings; they are less about outright support for the authoritarian bureaucracy, which is becoming firmly entrenched in the West Bank, and more a means to get on with life in accordance to the preferences of the United States and Israel. If democracy was rejected, then authoritarianism might be the only route to pursue. As Nathan Brown cautions, "U.S. officials who take comfort in these polls [Fayyad's approval ratings] are missing some other critical developments, such as the deepening despair and cynicism in Palestinian society and the corrosive long-term effects of the Ramallah government's reputation for human rights abuses."[33] This sentiment is also captured well in an International Crisis Group Report: "The undeniable success of the reform agenda has been built in part on popular fatigue and despair—the sense that the situation had so deteriorated that Palestinians are prepared to swallow quite a bit for the sake of stability, including deepened security cooperation with their foe. Yet, as the situation normalizes over time, they could show less indulgence."[34] Indeed, trading democracy for authoritarianism might appear to be a necessary bargain on the immediate horizon. Yet, as the developments in Egypt and elsewhere have shown, these equilibria are fragile at best, and show the capacity to tip. Given the fact that with authoritarian repression grievances grow, one cannot rely on repression as a long-term strategy.

[32]Personal interview with the author, summer 2009. The Pew Global Attitudes data also show that Palestinians more supportive of free markets and the influence of big external companies are also more favorable of the policies linked to the U.S. War on Terror (a pattern found in Kuwait, Jordan, Morocco, and Egypt as well).

[33]Brown, "Are Palestinians Building a State?"

[34]International Crisis Group, quoted in Nathan Brown, *Fayyad Is Not the Problem, but Fayyadism Is Not the Solution to Palestine's Political Crisis* (Washington, DC: Carnegie Endowment for International Peace, 2010), 7.

SAUDI ARABIA AND ITS STATUS QUO ADVANTAGE

The arguments of this book also extend to the case of Saudi Arabia. Although Saudi Arabia, like Kuwait, is an oil-rich state, it nevertheless houses anti-American Islamist movements. Thus, in many ways Saudi Arabia mirrors the experiences of non–oil-rich states that are captured in this manuscript. Significant segments of the Saudi public recognize the importance of the Saudi regime in maintaining close alliances with the United States.

In November 1995, a bomb destroyed the Riyadh office of the American training mission working with the Saudi National Guard, killing five Americans and two Indian employees. Four Saudis were arrested for the bombing and confessed on television to being members of the Islamist opposition. The Saudi government executed them in May 1996. Less than a month later, in June 1996, a car bomb exploded in front of an apartment building housing U.S. Air Force personnel in Dhahran. The bombings were carefully orchestrated to go off at noon, while Muslims were at prayer, thus targeting only non-Muslims. Nineteen Americans died and nearly four hundred Americans, Saudis, and others were wounded. The American personnel, most of whom were involved in maintaining air reconnaissance of the no-fly zone in southern Iraq, were subsequently moved from Dhahran to an isolated desert airbase south of Riyadh.

These violent responses to the high-profile U.S. role in Saudi Arabia rattled the Saudi monarchy, Saudi citizens, and the United States itself.[35] The U.S.-Saudi alliance has historically been a strong one. In fact, the legitimacy of the al-Saud family as the chief leaders and "owners" of Saudi Arabia is in good part due to U.S. efforts to bolster the country's security after World War II. The United States has sold the Saudis vital military equipment, including AWACS airborne radar aircraft and F-15 combat aircraft. These military sales were complemented by a major modernization program for the Saudi Arabia National Guard, the establishment in 1951 of the U.S. Military Training Mission for the training of Saudi forces, and the transfer of a dozen F-86 fighters to the kingdom in 1957. Further, the United States has also stationed its military personnel in Saudi Arabia in times of need. When Egypt intervened in the Yemeni civil war (1963–64), the United States directly stated to Egyptian president Gamal Abdel Nasser that it would protect Saudi Arabia. The United States was also available, as it was for Kuwait, to protect Saudi tankers during the Iran-Iraq War.

[35] Mamoun Fandy, *Saudi Arabia and the Politics of Dissent* (New York: Palgrave Macmillan, 1999) and F. Gregory Gause III, "'Over the Horizon' to 'Into the Backyard': The Saudi-American Relationship and the Gulf War," in *The United States and the Middle East: A Historical Reassessment*, 4th ed., ed. David W. Lesch (Boulder, CO: Westview, 2007), 380–90.

Three regional events gave cause for worry to the Saudi regime. The Islamic Revolution in Iran proved not only to be unfriendly to the United States but also threatening to those Muslim regimes, including Saudi Arabia, that maintained close ties to the Americans. After the revolution the new government in Iran often verbally attacked Muslim countries with significant Shiʿa populations, like Saudi Arabia and Kuwait. Such anti-Saudi rhetoric inspired the Shiʿa in the eastern province of the country to riot against the regime. Iranian pilgrims would also protest against the Saudi royal family during the annual hajj to the kingdom; in 1985, more than 400 people were killed, including 275 Iranians, when Iranians protested against the Saudi regime.[36] The Iran-Iraq War was a second source of worry. The war could potentially destabilize the entire region and bring out a clear and mighty victor that could later pose a threat to the country. Finally, the Soviet invasion of Afghanistan was also extraordinarily worrisome to the kingdom.[37] There were fears in both Washington, D.C., and Jeddah that the Soviets could expand their campaign into the Persian Gulf.

These regional vulnerabilities lay behind attempts by King Fahd to strengthen relationships with the United States during the administration of U.S. president Ronald Reagan. More than any other Saudi leader, Fahd pursued a special relationship with the United States, despite growing criticism of such strong ties. By the 1990s and the time of Iraq's occupation of Kuwait, the Americans had a visible presence in the oil kingdom. The Saudis asked the United States for assistance to withstand Saddam Hussein's threat, exposing the kingdom's dependency on the United States. Both the Americans and the Saudis were worried that Saddam would launch an attack on the oil fields of the eastern province. The United States responded immediately to Saudi Arabia's invitations, supplying close to 600,000 troops and dispatching both naval and air forces to the Persian Gulf.[38]

On the eve of the First Gulf War, the American military buildup in the Gulf proceeded very quickly, shocking the Saudi population and leading to a period of intensive public debate. The autumn of 1990 witnessed unprecedented discussions that in the past had been confined to private domains, revolving around issues directly related to the Gulf War and touching on the very foundation of the Saudi political system and the legitimacy of the ruling group. One of the most heated issues was the presence of American troops on Saudi soil and the dependence of Saudi Arabia on the United States for security. While Saudis were aware of their country's tight rela-

[36] Madawi al-Rasheed, *A History of Saudi Arabia* (Cambridge: Cambridge University Press, 2002).
[37] Ibid.
[38] Lousia Dris-Ait-Hamadouche and Yahia H. Zoubir, "The U.S.-Saudi Relationship and the Iraq War: The Dialectics of a Dependent Alliance," *Journal of Third World Studies* 24, no. 1 (2007): 109–35.

tionship with the United States, not many had anticipated the arrival of such massive numbers of American military personnel—a humiliating blow to significant pockets of the Saudi population. While the majority accepted American military support as a necessary strategy—Saudis had never thought of defending themselves against anything as large as the threat posed by Saddam—a substantial minority regarded it as a violation of Islamic principles. The strongest criticism of the government over this issue originated from the rank and file of young religious scholars. Mosque preachers used their Friday sermons to criticize the government's decision to invite "infidel" Americans to defend the land of Islam.

The U.S. troops' presence on Saudi soil prompted one hundred religious clerics to circulate a memorandum of advice in 1992 to the ruling family, calling on the regime to be more self-reliant in its defense and to be less dependent on the United States. The signers of the petition also cautioned the Saudi regime about conducting their business according to the preferences of the United States, which meant aiding other infidel regimes like that in Egypt and moving toward a peace process with Israel.[39] But Saudi dependence only grew during this critical time period. Between 1950 and 1998, the kingdom received a staggering $93.8 billion in military and economic assistance. Arms agreements alone from 1991 to 1998 totaled $22.8 billion. To put it simply, as Louisa Dris-Ait-Hamadouche and Yahia Zoubir do, "the kingdom has no real alternative to the United States for its security needs."[40]

U.S. interest in Saudi Arabia is driven by Saudi oil reserves and production. The U.S. Department of Energy estimates that the global economy will require Gulf oil production to increase from 22.4 million barrels a day to 45.2 by 2025. To meet this demand, Saudi production alone has to reach 23 million barrels a day (up from 10.2 in 2001). These levels of oil production require increasing levels of security commitments from the United States and massive foreign direct investment in order to meet the demands of such production.[41] That is, the Saudi regime will be dependent for its security (and by implication its economy) on the United States for the next several years.[42]

A point may illustrate the degree to which the U.S.-Saudi relationship is influenced by the stronger power in the international arena. When Saudi Arabia was deemed uncooperative in the War on Terror in 2002, a RAND

[39]Gause "'Over the Horizon' to 'Into the Backyard': The Saudi-American Relationship and the Gulf War," 389.
[40]Dris-Ait-Hamadouche and Zoubir, "The U.S.-Saudi Relationship and the Iraq War."
[41]Ibid.
[42]Demographically, the population has increased from 6 million in 1970 to 22 million in 2004. Even if birth rates decline, the estimated total population in 2030 is expected to be at 55 million. This means that the Saudi regime (especially with the forecast of decreasing oil revenues) must diversify its economy.

briefing described the kingdom as an enemy, and requested that Saudi Arabia stop supporting terrorists or "risk seizure of the oil fields and all financial assets in the U.S."[43] This is an argument that William Quandt also advances when he discusses oil prices, noting, "Refusal to increase production, especially in times of crisis, could produce a sharp U.S.-Saudi confrontation, inevitably leading to talk of military action to seize Saudi oil fields."[44] Whether the United States will occupy Saudi oil fields is not the point of debate here; rather, that it is topic that can be openly discussed illustrates Saudi Arabia's unique dependency on the United States.

The Saudi regime for its part has tried to keep the strong ties with the United States a secret from its citizens, especially during times of war. Like King Abdullah in Jordan, Saudi officials in 2003 denied that they would allow the United States to launch military assaults into Iraq from Saudi Arabia. However, U.S. commanders reported they were given private assurances that they would be allowed to lead an air war from the command center at Prince Sultan Airbase—the same airbase where the Afghanistan-led offensive had been carried out a year earlier. In fact, elite U.S. troops were flown to airbases in northwest Saudi Arabia and carried out missions against Iraq from there.[45]

The United States has also been instrumental in training Saudi troops. After the First Gulf War, the United States maintained close to five thousand U.S. troops at the Prince Sultan Airbase. However, the U.S. presence was much deeper than the actual presence of troops. The United States has established a state-of-the-art command center on the same base, with capabilities to cover the entire Middle East, Central Asia, and Gulf regions. Such presence has served to further galvanize and augment anti-U.S. radicalism in the kingdom. In fact, the transfer of these five thousand troops to Qatar in 2003, to quell al-Qaeda concerns that U.S. troops were stationed in the holy Islamic lands of Mecca and Medina, does not reflect the actual number of U.S. military personnel and civilian contractors on the ground, which is estimated at over 30,000.[46] The military transfer to Doha was at best cosmetic, designed to appease anti-American sentiment in the kingdom. The

---

[43]Joseph A. Kéchichian, "Democratization in Gulf Monarchies: A New Challenge to the GCC," *Middle East Policy Council Journal* 11, no. 4 (2004): 37–58 (accessed at http://www.mepc .org/journal_vol11/0412_kechichian.asp).

[44]William Quandt, *Saudi Arabia in the 1980s: Foreign Policy, Security, and Oil* (Washington, DC: Brookings Institution, 1981), 64. See also Shibley Telhami, Fiona Hill, et al., "Does Saudi Oil Still Matter? Differing Perspectives on the Kingdom and Its Oil," *Foreign Affairs* 81, no. 6 (2002): 167–73 (accessed at http://www.foreignaffairs.com/articles/58444/shibley-telhami-fiona-hill -et-al/does-saudi-arabia-still-matter-differing-perspectives-on-the-kin

[45]Dris-Ait-Hamadouche and Zoubir, "The U.S.-Saudi Relationship and the Iraq War."
[46]Ibid.

ultimate culmination of the degree of anti-Americanism was witnessed with Osama bin Laden's attack on the United States in 2001.

Saudi public opinion continues to support strong ties with the United States. In 2007, 69 percent of Saudis supported strong and close relations between the two countries. These attitudes were also coupled with strong support of the monarchy: 79 percent supported an absolute monarchy, with another 88 percent saying that terrorism against the West is extraordinarily problematic for the kingdom.[47] Absent individual-level data to probe these relationships further, one can confidently say that the majority of Saudis are concerned about anti-American Islamist groups, do believe ties to the United States are important, and lend their support to an existing authoritarian monarchy. For now, suffice it to say that these trends mirror patterns of political engagement that have emerged in other client regimes across the Arab region.

At the domestic level, the Saudi regime has been trying to create a more hospitable environment for investors even while extremists are a major issue to contend with. In April 2000, the Saudi legislature adopted a new FDI law allowing international investors to hold full ownership of projects, and reduced corporate taxes from 45 percent to 30 percent. Thus, the 2002 Arab Peace Initiative advanced by King Abdullah in Beirut was seen as a major initiative to enhance regional stability in ways that would bode well for higher levels of FDI.[48]

Sine the war in Iraq began in 2003, anti-U.S. sentiment among extreme and moderate Islamist groups alike, among the new generation of Saudis, and among women in particular, has increased. They object to U.S. involvement in Afghanistan and Iraq, the tendency of the United States to side with Israel, the perceived U.S. attack on Islam, and U.S. collusion with Arab authoritarian regimes. Saudi women in the early years of the new millennium led the boycott efforts against U.S. products like McDonald's, Pampers, and Coca Cola—a potentially significant action given the fact that 40 percent

---

[47]Center for Public Opinion, *Terror Free Tomorrow: Nationwide Public Opinion Survey of Saudi Arabia* (Washington, DC: Center for Public Opinion; accessed at http://www.terrorfreetomorrow .org/upimagestft/TFT%20Saudi%20Arabia%20Survey.pdf). These findings are also substantiated in Zogby International, *Arabs: What They Believe and What They Value Most* (Ithaca, NY: Zogby International, 2002; accessed at http://aai.3cdn.net/7b568f016f6ad3a301_b5m6be8kr .pdf), where 70 percent believe that relations with non-Arab countries are extremely important for the kingdom. However, U.S. policies received less support with only 25 percent favorable of the U.S. liberation efforts in Kuwait; 35 percent in favor of the U.S. War on Terror; 5 percent favorable toward the way the United States handles Palestine; and 80 percent of Saudis saying their impression would be more favorable if the United States would apply pressure to create an independent Palestinian State.

[48]Dris-Ait-Hamadouche and Zoubir, "The U.S.-Saudi Relationship and the Iraq War."

of the wealth of Saudi Arabia is in female hands and over 70 percent of all bank accounts are held by women.⁴⁹

Anti-U.S. Islamists make securing these goals that much more difficult, even as they make the democratic option for potential reformers all the more elusive. As Shibley Telhami argues, "Rapid radical transitions from authoritarianism to democracy in places such as Saudi Arabia are unlikely, but were they to occur, the resulting instability or unpredictable outcomes, such as the possibility of a militant Islamists regime being democratically elected, may seem even more threatening to American interests that then status quo."⁵⁰ This is a reality understood by the United States, the regime, and the reform movement internally.

Islamist Positions in Saudi Arabia

After the series of attacks inside the Saudi kingdom in the 1990s, the regime realized that the Islamist threat was growing and vowed to confront it. On the one hand, citizens rallied the government to confront the domestic terrorist problem, arguing that it could destabilize the monarchy. On the other hand, among powerful Islamists there emerged strong voices demanding that the regime distance itself from the United States. Several prayer leaders opted to resign their posts in early 2002 to protest their government's ties to the United States. The regime was also unnerved by the overwhelming showing of citizens in the funeral procession of Shaykh Hamud bin Uqla al-Shu'aybi, who authored a fatwa (Islamic edict) against the al-Saud family for its ties to the United States. This showing prompted the monarchy to warn the Islamists and the citizens of Saudi Arabia that the negative rhetoric against the United States and the regime was causing a lot of commotion in Washington, D.C.⁵¹

According to Gwenn Okruhlik, there are only two historic moments of opposition that resemble the current Islamist movements. The first is the Ikhwan Rebellion of 1929, the second is the 1979 seizure of the great mosque in Mecca by a Saudi Islamist, Juhayman al-'Utabi. At both historical junctures, the opposition forces accused the regime of deviating from Islam and of collusion with and dependence on the West.⁵²

Historically, the regime has responded to accusations of collusion by adopting even more conservative Islamic policies to bolster its commitment

⁴⁹Ibid.
⁵⁰Shibley Telhami, "The Role of the Persian Gulf," in *The Contemporary Middle East*, ed. Karl Yambert (Boulder, CO: Westview Press, 2005), 183.
⁵¹Kéchichian, "Democratization in Gulf Monarchies."
⁵²Gwenn Okruhlik, "Making Conversation Permissible: Islamism and Reform in Saudi Arabia," in *Islamic Activism A Social Movement Theory Approach*, ed. Quintan Wiktorowicz (Bloomington: Indiana University Press, 2004), 250–69.

to Islam. Women, increasingly restricted, were the targets of such policies. According to Okruhlik, "Working women lost their jobs in shops, salons and at Aramco."[53] A segregated public space where women did not enjoy equal access to the polity emerged, while a very narrow and intolerant Wahhabi doctrine (an ultraconservative branch of Islam) dominated political and social life.

There are several Islamic currents in Saudi Arabia. By the 1990s the Islamist scene was dominated by two main strains. In one, political Islamist reformers sought to modernize the religion. This group included Sunnis, Shi'is and intellectuals. This camp has also tried to envelop the more conservative sector of the Sahwa (revival) movement. The Sahwa movement, galvanized in the 1980s, is more traditional, adopting a conservative Wahhabi vision on social issues but a more Ikhwan (Muslim Brotherhood) stance on political matters, especially on anti-U.S. matters. The other major Saudi Islamist group is the jihadi movement, which is more violent and dedicated to harming Western interests—U.S. interests, in particular. Saudi jihadists were allowed to travel back and forth to Afghanistan during the Soviet occupation of that country; subsequently, they became politically mobilized and militarily trained. Indeed, they began to make up a significant presence in Saudi Arabia; as the International Crisis Group notes, "By the end of the Afghan war against the Soviet Union, an international jihadist culture had already spread to many Saudi Islamist circles."[54]

The First Gulf War was the most critical event in the history of Saudi Islamism and helps explain the later domestic politics. The regime's invitation of the U.S.-led coalition set off the Sahwa's further politicization. The Sahwa began targeting its criticism toward the regime. Two of the Sahwa's main clerics, Salam al-'Awda and Safar al-Hawali, delivered damning sermons against the Sauds for allowing the Americans to stay in the cradle of Islamic civilization.[55] Al-Hawali, whose books and sermons were extraordinarily well received, gained popularity during the Gulf War. Of particular focus were his sermons on the role of the United States in the region. According to al-Hawali, the most pernicious threat facing Saudi Arabia and the Muslim world is the "imposition of Israeli and American hegemony over the

[53]Ibid., 254.
[54]International Crisis Group, *Saudi Arabia Backgrounder: Who Are the Islamists?* Middle East Report no. 31 (Amman, Jordan, and Brussels: International Crisis Group, 2004; accessed at http://www.pbs.org/wgbh/pages/frontline/shows/saud/themes/backgrounder.pdf), 4. see also Sherifa Zuhur, *Saudi Arabia: Islamic Threat, Political Reform, and the Global War on Terror* (Carlisle, PA: Strategic Studies Institute 2005; accessed at http://www.strategicstudiesinstitute.army.mil/pubs/display.cfm?pubID=598); Fandy, *Saudi Arabia and the Politics of Dissent*; and Madawi al-Rasheed, *Contesting the State: Islamic Voices from a New Generation* (Cambridge: Cambridge University Press, 2007).
[55]International Crisis Group, *Can Saudi Arabia Reform Itself?* ICG Middle East Report 28 (Cairo and Brussels: International Crisis Group, 2004; accessed at http://www.pbs.org/wgbh/pages/frontline/shows/saud/themes/canreform.pdf).

whole area."[56] As if he were well-versed in David Lake's international hierarchy operationalization, al-Hawali identifies the root weaknesses of the Arab and Muslim world in its military and economic dependence on the United States.

Palestine is central to al-Hawali's rationale, and the U.S. support for the Israeli Occupation of Palestinian lands is evidence to al-Hawali and his followers that the Christian world is inherently anti-Islamic.[57] He is also displeased with the nature of U.S. dominance of the Gulf region, arguing that because Iran poses a threat to the United States, the United States must dominate the entire Gulf region to secure its own oil interests. In his view, the Americans orchestrated the First Gulf War to assert control over the oil fields of the Persian Gulf, with the 2003 war on Iraq as the natural culmination of these imperial ambitions. With effective oratory, al-Hawali reminds his followers, "Do you think that the West came to this region to defend us? . . . By God no! They have never wanted any good to happen to us."[58]

The stationing of U.S. troops in Saudi Arabia after the First Gulf War ushered in a new era of opposition against the Saudi regime. New political voices called for the overthrow of the regime and the removal of U.S. troops. This Islamic awakening (Sahwa) resulted in a memorandum of advice (MOA) to Shaykh Abd al-Aziz ibn Baz (the highest state cleric, who died in 1999), drafted in 1992 by religious leaders around the country. The memorandum expressed the anger of the religious leaders for not being allowed to participate in politics. It called for greater human rights and an independent judiciary.[59] In addition to internal reforms, the MOA called for the establishment of an Islamic army. The MOA outlined the signatories' disappointment over the inability of Saudi Arabia to defend itself against a country like Iraq. Its dependence on the United States was embarrassing to many in the kingdom. Not only were the authors of the memorandum disappointed that the country could not defend itself but they were equally upset that other Muslim countries were not called on to defend Saudi Arabia. Further, the MOA urged the monarchy to adopt an Islamic foreign policy, one calling for the defense of Islamist movements in countries like Algeria and Sudan where the United States had already declared such movements "terrorist."[60]

More compelling was the surging popularity of these critics, with their tapes, books, and sermons circulating across the kingdom. Drawing on

---

[56] Fandy, *Saudi Arabia and the Politics of Dissent*, 63.

[57] See International Crisis Group, *Saudi Arabia Backgrounder*; and Zuhur, "Saudi Arabia: Islamic Threat, Political Reform, and the Global War on Terror."

[58] Fandy, *Saudi Arabia and the Politics of Dissent*, 71.

[59] Al-Rasheed, *A History of Saudi Arabia*; Zuhur, "Saudi Arabia: Islamic Threat, Political Reform, and the Global War on Terror."

[60] Al-Rasheed, *A History of Saudi Arabia*.

ample support from university students, the Sahwa movement was growing in strength and momentum, and in 1994 it formed the Committee for Defense of Legitimate Rights to demand more political and civil rights. The regime clamped down and arrested members of the group. Since this direct confrontation with the regime in the 1990s, the movement has become a little more moderate; nevertheless, it remains committed to some of its core values, especially regarding its stance against the United States.[61] However, the jihadi tide continues to grow.

Osama bin Laden, too, had been able to galvanize al-Qaeda sympathizers with his disdain for the role of the United States in the kingdom. He accused the regime of being a branch of the U.S. government. The First Gulf War further mobilized Bin Laden; as an International Crisis Group report notes, "Criticizing individual regimes no longer sufficed; by the mid-1990s he concluded that a direct, global confrontation with the U.S. was needed. In short, the Gulf war triggered a process whereby jihadists became both more critical of the Saudi regime and more openly hostile to the U.S."[62] According to Gregory Gause, "The fact that Bin Laden made his opposition to the U.S. military presence in Saudi Arabia a centerpiece of his propaganda unnerved the Saudi rulers. They knew this issue resonated with their public."[63]

The willingness and ability of Saudi Islamists to harm U.S. interests was demonstrated during the attacks on the United States on September 11, 2001. Fifteen of the nineteen hijackers were Saudi. The attacks were followed by a series of attacks in Saudi Arabia, all aimed at harming American interests. Saudi Islamists, especially since the Gulf War of 1991, have remained firmly opposed to U.S. intervention in the region and vehemently resistant to the deployment of the U.S. military in the kingdom; they further see the regime's relationship with the United States as inherently exploitative. Many Islamists in the kingdom openly call for severing ties with the United States and the establishment of an Arab Islamic order that would rid the region of U.S. involvement.

REGIME RESPONSES, THE REFORM MOVEMENT, AND THE UNITED STATES

The First Gulf War segmented Saudi society. Reformers, moderate Islamists, and liberals found themselves in confrontation with the radical extremists, who were increasingly infuriated by their government and its growing alliance with the United States. In 1992, the regime responded to this emerging

[61] See International Crisis Group, *Saudi Arabia Backgrounder.*
[62] Ibid.
[63] Gause, "'Over the Horizon' to 'Into the Backyard': The Saudi-American Relationship and the Gulf War," 391.

polarization in society by accommodating some of the internal demands of the reform movements. While it chose not to reconfigure its dependent relationship with the United States, it offered some domestic changes. Three reforms capture these changes: the Basic Law of Government, the Law of Consultative Council, and the Law of the Provinces. These laws allowed for the creation of a consultative council, which aimed to discuss social and political matters but played no legislative role. Further, in 1993, municipal councils were created in Saudi Arabia to allow local communities to monitor their own progress and report to national authorities.

Reformers opted to continue to work carefully with the government, pushing for gradual change in an attempt not to overempower the extremists. Thus, in its moment of desperation, the regime realized that in order to counter the radical tide it must win over the reformers, and it embarked on reform agendas. These agendas might give the reform establishment both the necessary maneuverability to gradually advance their own cause and, more important from the perspective of the regime, a critical voice to counterbalance the efforts of the extremists. The reformers also agreed, out of both conviction and circumstance, to work with the government and not to push the reform agenda too far so as not to overempower the extremists in ways that would harm the standing of the kingdom.[64]

Several recent developments show that the reform movement, which includes business leaders, intellectuals, and more liberal religious scholars, is willing to express its desire for democracy without undermining the authority of the monarchy, which the reformers see as necessary not only to ensure internal cohesion but also to maintain external links to the United States. In January 2003, 104 reform-minded leaders signed a petition to Crown Prince Abdullah. The leader of this group of reformers—dubbed the "Petition Lobby"—is Dr. Abdullah al-Hamed, an Islamist from Riyadh who was active in the Committee for the Defense of Legitimate Rights. His goal in the reform movement is simultaneously to counter the extremist threat and to enhance the legitimacy of the al-Saud monarchy. These reformers believe it is vital to deal with the Islamist problem before further democratization takes root. They advocate moving toward a constitutional monarchy, but they also argue that the extremist tendency in Saudi Arabia can undermine the interests of the country as a whole. Thus, the reform movement finds itself working closely with the regime, supporting the monarchy as a first-order priority while carefully working to deal with the Islamist issue. This model of reformers, liberals, and intellectuals taking on the work of

---

[64]Amr Hamzawy, *The Saudi Labyrinth: Evaluating the Current Political Opening*, Carnegie Paper no. 68 (Washington, DC: Carnegie Endowment for International Peace, 2006); al-Rasheed, *Contesting the Saudi State*; and International Crisis Group, *Can Saudi Arabia Reform Itself?*

winning over the Islamists so that they are less prone to violence is a path endorsed by the regime.

The regime has also engaged the reformers, who include moderate Islamists, in a series of national dialogues aimed at exploring options for countering Islamist radicalism in the kingdom. These dialogues also addressed issues of greater participation, the loosening of restrictions on civil society, and more executive accountability. From the regime's perspective, these national dialogues will allow the liberal and democratic movements the space and effort to counter the Islamist radical tide and break down the monopoly on civil society Islamists had attained.[65] Five rounds of these dialogues have taken place, and in each, reformers have been given more freedom to voice their concerns and desires for future reforms.[66] Through these dialogues, the regime has been better able to solidify its ties with the reform movement; in turn, the reform movement vows to deal with the issue of radicalization as well.[67] Saudi Arabia's stability will depend on its ability to keep the reform movement on board and further marginalize the extremists. Whatever its success with the regime and the Islamist groups, the reform movement won't be able to overcome the extent to which the Islamist radical tendencies in the Saudi Kingdom are fueled by American policies.

In recent years, what has emerged in Saudi Arabia is a very controlled and managed reform process that aims at bringing the reform movement on board as part of a governing coalition against extremist Islamists who may harm the standing of the kingdom as a whole. This strategy is receiving direct backing from the United States. Yet the United States continues to bank on the assumption that its policies will *not* one day lead to the alienation of reformers as well. If all of the efforts toward reform only add up to so much talk because the United States feels that it can't have true democracy, they may very well drive the reformers out of their camp. The status quo is fragile and can easily be altered. If U.S. policies do not change, it is doubtful whether those reformers will aid the regimes they are now

[65] International Crisis Group, *Can Saudi Arabia Reform Itself?*

[66] These initiatives have resulted in a strengthening of the Shura Council, Saudi Arabia's consultative institution that has no oversight or legislative powers. In 2005, the Shura Council stood at 150 members—composed half of Wahhabi conservative elements and half of technocrats, professors, and members of the business community. The council has gradually been given more authority to discuss pertinent political issues relating to the kingdom. Further, in 2005 the monarchy allowed partial elections. Saudis were allowed to vote for half of the 178 municipal council seats, while the monarchy appointed the other half. Turnout was not necessarily high, ranging between 25 percent and 35 percent in most districts. These lower levels of turnout could suggest that although the reform movement is committed to working with the regime, the Saudi population remains skeptical.

[67] Hamzawy, "The Saudi Labyrinth"; International Crisis Group, *Can Saudi Arabia Reform Itself?*

willing to tolerate for the overall well-being of the country. Furthermore, the direct goal of the reform effort, as commissioned by the United States and the Saudi regime, is to deter the growth of extremism in the country. By embracing the reformers in a more open and direct manner, similar to what King Abdullah in Jordan has done, the regime's goal has become to weaken the Islamists rather than democratization per se. Indeed, reform is designed to preserve the status quo. If the reform effort proves that it cannot accomplish the goals demanded by both the United States and the Saudi regime, it may also lose its instrumentality to both actors. For now, democrats and reformers across the region will cling to existing authority because it is the only legitimate channel for their existence.

THE ROLE OF THE UNITED STATES

The initial U.S. response to 9-11 was a demand that Saudi Arabia change its religious curriculum and crush its fundamentalist problem, a policy that would have further reduced political and civil liberties across the entire kingdom and completely undermined the regime and the reformist movement.[68] The jihadist problem was far more complicated; the arrest of a few militants would not effect any real change. Rather, the problem was with the potential sympathizers of these movements, which included clergymen, an estimated 20,000 veterans of the Afghanistan campaign against the Soviet Union, and the ever-larger pool of those who perceived America as holding double standards in its Middle East foreign policy.[69]

Refusing to seriously reexamine its own policies in the region, aside from relocating five thousand troops from Saudi Arabia to Doha, the United States has also been vigorously promoting reform in education in the desert kingdom. In fact, it has insisted that the educational curriculum is a root cause of Saudi extremism. Some of the reforms that the United States is currently backing include the introduction of English-language curriculum at the primary school level; more tolerance of Shi'as in the education curriculum; and an increase in the number of nonreligious credit hours dedicated to the sciences.[70] It is speculated that such measures will enhance tolerance and pluralism in ways that will bode well for reducing terrorism. The assumption driving such reforms is that Saudi citizens disdain the United States because of what they are taught by a Wahhabi curriculum and not necessarily their lived experiences in the region. What's more troubling in

---

[68]Ali Alyami, "Saudi Arabia: The Gathering Storm," *The Journal of International Security Affairs* 15 (2008): n.p. (accessed at http://www.securityaffairs.org/issues/2008/15/alyami.php).

[69]International Crisis Group, *Can Saudi Arabia Reform Itself?*

[70]Hamzawy, "The Saudi Labyrinth."

this analysis is the overall tone of the discourse; the United States firmly believes it is religious education that has led to such displeasure on the ground. Yet history does not support such claims. The secular educational systems under Nasser's Egypt or Iraq's Ba'thist regimes did not produce friends of the United States nor a curriculum that showcased America in a more positive light. While placing the blame for existing anti-American stances on the shoulders of regimes in the Arab World, the United States will indeed be prescribing solutions that do not address the root causes of the trouble. And all the while, Islamists criticize the United States for insisting that their own history pages and curricula be rewritten to serve the interests of external actors.[71]

The future prospects of democrats and reformers will be contingent on levels of anti-Americanism in the region and the ability of Islamists to continue mobilizing on such anti-American platforms. Islamic groups across the region have shown their propensity to change on internal debates ranging from human rights and women's issues to matters relating to democratic governance. A multitude of examples emerge from across the region. Hamas promised not to impose Islamic laws in its electoral platforms; the Moroccan PJD became a chief endorser of the liberal Moudawana (women's reform policy) package; the Jordanian Islamic Action Front has become increasingly more liberal on domestic initiatives in the last several years; finally, the Sahwa movement in Saudi Arabia has shown remarkable evolution on its social contract, especially in its treatment of Shi'as. Where Islamist movements have been more stubborn is in their sheer disdain for the dominant role the United States continues to play in the region. Even the most moderate PJD shows its reluctance to wholeheartedly embrace the United States.

Some scholars, like Amr Hamzawy, accuse the Saudi regime of playing up the Islamist threat to maintain the status quo.[72] Again, regardless of whether the regime, along with the United States, orchestrates such machinations, the fact of the matter is that this triangulated (or two-stage) model of state-society relations—through which citizens look not only to their own regimes but also to the preferences of the external patron—demonstrates the inefficacy of bottom-up democratization mechanisms in the client states of the Arab world. For the present situation, Saudi reformers are shouldering the burden to deradicalize Saudi society. Complicating these efforts, U.S. policy in the region has remained pretty much consistent. The United States has tried different strategies to deal with the Islamist problem. In Palestine, it rejected any ties to Hamas and shunned them as a governing authority, reversing the engine of democracy and attempting to rebuild Fatah,

---

[71]Hamzawy, "The Saudi Labyrinth"; International Crisis Group, *Can Saudi Arabia Reform Itself?*
[72]Hamzawy, "The Saudi Labyrinth."

even if it meant a return to authoritarianism. In Morocco, it has embraced the PJD and tried to win it over through a strategy of dangling carrots. Yet concerns remain that the PJD is inherently anti-American and can cause the country serious harm. Thus, reform efforts stagger along in Morocco. Finally, in Saudi Arabia the United States has blamed the regime and places its trust in reform efforts to alter the extremist tide. Whether such strategies will succeed has yet to be determined. What is clear from my analysis, however, is that the preferences of the United States matter for the ways citizens rationalize the utility of democracy. The keystone of democracy is not only in the hands of Arab societies, but it also appears to be in the hands of the United States itself. And so long as U.S. policies are seen as undermining citizen interests, neither reforms nor curricular changes can lead to real movements toward democracy.

The cases of Morocco, Palestine, and Saudi Arabia illustrate that the realities surrounding support for the authoritarian status quo in Jordan extend to these countries as well. Morocco, growing in its dependency on the United States, exhibits similar state-society relations as does Jordan. Even while their country enjoys considerable ties to the EU, Moroccans systematically explained how upsetting the United States could entail a loss of EU favor as well. Further, although Moroccan Islamists have shown moderation on internal issues, they remain sources of skepticism due to their anti-American stances.

Structural similarities, like the oil rentier economies of Kuwait and Saudi Arabia, do not determine similar patterns of regime engagement. In the end, because Kuwaiti Islamists are more pro-American, we have witnessed pressures for more democracy in Kuwait. In Saudi Arabia, democratic or reform momentum has been accompanied by cautious measures so as to not overempower radical elements. Unfortunately, among Arab client states there is not another example to extend the Kuwaiti argument. I therefore look outside the Arab region to the larger Muslim world. There, two extensions to the Kuwaiti case study are Turkey and Indonesia. In both places, the major Islamist movements have proven to be more hospitable toward the U.S. government and less likely to mobilize on anti-American platforms. Indonesia, the largest Muslim country, has several mainstream Muslim movements as well as a few radical fringe Islamist groups; Laskar Jihad and the Islamic Defenders Front are the two most popular of the more radical groups, although in general the radical fringe has little support.[73] Mainstream Islamist parties like the Prosperous Justice Party, the National Mandate Party, the United Development Party, and the National Awakening Party have shown remarkable levels of tolerance toward the United

[73]Howard M. Federspiel, "Indonesia, Islam, and U.S. Policy," *Brown Journal of World Affairs* 9, no. 1 (2002): 107–14.

States. Like the Justice and Development Party (Adalet ve Kalkınma Partisi, or AKP) of Turkey, these Islamists seek closer ties to the United States and believe that it will enhance the economic standing of their country.[74] In fact, under the AKP's rule the country has pursued a stronger record on democratization and integration into the world economy. Annual growth rates in Turkey have averaged 7.3 percent between 2002 and 2006. Further, foreign direct investment has increased from $1.14 billion in 2002 to $20 billion in 2006.[75] The AKP has worked with the International Monetary Fund, and the business elite of Turkey largely share the AKP's economic goals as well.[76] The AKP has successfully portrayed integration with the West as compatible with the Muslim identity of Turkey.[77]

The pro-American positions of these Islamist groups are perhaps a result of multiple issues at play. First, the sources that have exacerbated anti-U.S. opinion in the Arab world may be less salient in these countries. For example, although Turks stood against the Iraq War and their parliament blocked the use of Turkey for U.S. forces to launch the war in Iraq, the AKP deputies in parliament voted in favor of allowing U.S. access to Iraq via Turkey, arguing vehemently about the need to secure the interests of their major ally.[78] Further, the AKP still showed a remarkable willingness to work with the Bush administration during the Iraq War (2003) and its aftermath.[79] According to Joshua Walker, the AKP "has guarded the alliance and tried to work with the Bush administration."[80] The AKP was actively involved in the rebuilding efforts in Iraq; it even authorized a peacekeeping contingency of 10,000 Turkish soldiers to be sent to Iraq in October 2003. In 2005, Turkey served 60 percent of the logistical support to U.S. ground troops in Iraq.[81] And since the war, U.S.-Turkish relations have even grown stronger.[82] According to Haste Dikici Bilgin, "the party has never

[74]Mohammad Ayoob, *The Many Faces of Political Islam: Religion and Politics in the Muslim World* (Ann Arbor: University of Michigan Press, 2008); Murat Somer, "Moderate Islam and Secularist Opposition in Turkey: Implications for the World, Muslims and Secular Democracy," *Third World Quarterly* 28, no. 7 (2007): 1271–89.

[75]Somer, "Moderate Islam and Secularist Opposition in Turkey"; Ionnis Grigoriadis and Antnis Kamaras, "Foreign Direct Investment in Turkey: Historical Constraints and the AKP Success Story," *Middle Eastern Studies* 44, no. 1 (2008): 53–68.

[76]Grigoriadis and Kamaras, "Foreign Direct Investment in Turkey."

[77]Ihsan Dagi, "Turkey's AKP in Power." *Journal of Democracy*, 19, no. 3 (2008): 25–30.

[78]Joshua Walker, "Re-examining the U.S.-Turkish Alliance," *Washington Quarterly* 31, no. 1 (2007–8): 93–109.

[79]Dagi, "Turkey's AKP in Power"; Aylin Guney, "Anti-Americanism in Turkey: Past and Present," *Middle Eastern Studies* 44, no. 3 (2008): 471–87.

[80]Walker, "Re-examining the U.S.-Turkish Alliance," 100.

[81]Walker, "Re-examining the U.S.-Turkish Alliance."

[82]Hasret Dikici Bilgin, "Foreign Policy Orientation of Turkey's Pro-Islamist Parties: A Comparative Study of the AKP and Refah," *Turkish Studies* 9, no. 3 (2008): 407–21.

taken a consistently negative attitude towards Western countries."[83] The AKP also draws considerable support from Müstakil Sanayici ve İşadamları Derneği (MUSIAD), which is a Muslim business organization that provides businessmen with an Islamic platform. MUSIAD supports closer ties to the West and is very much supportive of economic globalization.[84]

In Indonesia, citizens showed similar dismay at the U.S. war in Iraq; however, the war did little for the mobilization tactics of extreme Islamist movements. Demonstrations against the war were relatively calm, and when radical Islamist groups called for Indonesians to join in defending Saddam Hussein, few turned out.[85] According to the Pew Global Attitudes Project, views on the United States have fluctuated drastically from year to year (or rather from event to event). In 2002, 61 percent of Indonesians had a favorable view of the United States, but in 2003 (after the invasion of Iraq), only 15 percent held that view.[86] Then, after American aid following the tsunami in 2004, favorable attitudes rose significantly. In several cases, it is only the United States' actions against Muslim countries that have prompted the mainstream Muslim organizations to become anti-American. For instance, after the United States invaded Afghanistan, an organization of Muslim scholars from groups like the Muhammadiyya and Nahdlatul Ulama called for a jihad. At the same time, however, these leaders opposed violence against tourists and explained that a jihad could take many forms. The mainstream groups tend to support or oppose the United States depending on current U.S. actions such as aid or invasion rather than having a long-term anti- or pro-American viewpoint.[87] Further, the Palestinian-Israeli issue may also be less salient in Indonesia and Turkey than in Arab states. For example, a Pew survey found that while 68 percent of Egyptians and 67 percent of Jordanians viewed the Arab-Israeli conflict as a major danger to world peace, only 44 percent of Turks and 33 percent of Indonesians held this view.[88] It appears that Turks and Indonesians, while passionate, are not as passionate as other Arabs about the hot topics in the Arab world. Further, there are fewer movements to operate against U.S. interests in these countries.

[83]Ibid.
[84]E. Fuat Keyman, and Berrin Koyuncu, "Globalization, Alternative Modernities, and the Political Economy of Turkey," *Review of International Political Economy* 12 (2005): 105-28.
[85]Greg Fealy, "Islamic Radicalism in Indonesia: The Faltering Revival," *Southeast Asian Affairs* 2004 (2004): 104-21.
[86]Richard Wike, *Indonesia: the Obama Effect* (Washington, DC: Pew Research Center, 2010; accessed at http://pewresearch.org/pubs/1529/indonesian-views-america-image-president-obama-trip.
[87]Bowen, John R. 2007. "Anti-Americanism as Schemas and Diacritics in France and Indonesia." In *Anti-Americanisms in World Politics*, ed Peter J. Katzenstein and Robert O. Keohane (Ithaca, NY: Cornell University Press), 227-50.
[88]Pew Global Attitudes Project. *America's Image in the World* (Washington, DC: Pew Research Center, 2007; accessed at http://pewglobal.org/commentary/display.php?AnalysisID=1019).

CONCLUSION

This book has focused on the cases of Jordan, Kuwait, Morocco, Saudi Arabia, and Palestine, but several other cases have not entered my analysis—Egypt is certainly one of them.[89] The client regime of Egypt serves three interrelated and vital functions for the Americans. First, Egypt is absolutely essential to the peace treaty with Israel. Second, the Suez Canal provides a direct access route to the U.S. military in the Gulf region. Third, Egypt is important for countering the Islamist tide.[90] As Egypt begins to chart its new democratic trajectory, will it confront realities similar to those encountered by the Palestinians? Only time will tell. The concessions the Muslim Brotherhood made about capping the percentage of seats it would contest, for example—a self-imposed concession that strikes at the heart of "true" democracy—is seen as a strategy to avoid Hamas's predicament. With Egyptian Islamists securing close to 65 percent of the popular vote in the winter of 2011, the future of democracy in Egypt seems precarious at best.

Other countries in the region led by authoritarian regimes have increasingly become clients of the United States. Pakistan under Pervez Musharaf and then Asif Ali Zardari, Afghanistan under Hamid Karzai, and several republics in Central Asia like Azerbaijan and Kyrgyzstan are now U.S. client regimes beginning to mirror the state-society nexus of the Arab region. These countries will gradually become more authoritarian in the upcoming years if Islamism and anti-Americanism continue to grow.

The cases at hand illustrate that the U.S. presence looms large in the minds of ordinary citizens. Certainly, the role of the United States is not the only factor that has shaped debates about regime stability and democratization. But certainly it is a factor that matters. The U.S. presence in the Arab world has increased since the Cold War. And although there is variation across the region, the average citizen understands the U.S. presence as overwhelming. Future research should examine, more precisely, the relationship between the degree of international hierarchy and domestic democratic developments. While the current data used for this book are not sufficient to employ hierarchical models to assess domestic democratization trajectories, they should suggest future avenues for research that will move in this very direction.[91] Models assessing the effectiveness of economic development, democracy promotion, and political development should begin to

[89]After one full year of waiting to obtain government clearance to administer our survey in Egypt (which also resulted in two rounds of question item deletions), the government turned down our request to conduct the survey. Notably, questions gauging support for political Islam and questions gauging anti-Americanism were deleted before the survey was rejected.

[90]Naiem A. Sherbiny, "America: A View form Egypt." *Social Research* 72, no. 4 (2005): 1–26.

[91]See, for example, Amaney Jamal and Irfan Nooruddin. "Trust in Cross-National Perspective," *Journal of Politics* 72, no. 1 (2010): 45–59.

employ hierarchical models to capture power relations in the international arena and their immediate effects on domestic developments.

The questions herein are from the PSR Poll,[92] the data from which are given in table 7.2.

1. The Western donor community provides the Palestine Authority (PA) economic and financial assistance reaching about one billion dollars every year. Do you think the PA can or cannot do without this assistance?
   A. It certainly can do without it: 7.5%
   B. It can do without it: 23%
   C. It cannot do without it: 40.1%
   D. It certainly cannot do without it 27.8%
   E. Don't know/no answer: 1.7%
2. Which political parties do you support?
   A. Fatah: 35%
   B. Others: 65%
3. Refugee Status
   A. Refugee: 47%
   B. Nonrefugee: 53%
4. Education
   A. Illiterate: 6.32%
   B. Elementary school: 13.60%
   C. Preparatory school: 24.51%
   D. Secondary school: 34.70
   E. Some college: 7.91%
   F. Bachelor's degree: 11.54%
   G. Master's Degree: 1.42%
5. Income, in new Israeli shekels:
   A. Under 600: 20.30%
   B. 601–1200: 20.14%
   C. 1801–2400: 16.43%
   D. 2401–3000: 8.93%
   E. 3001–3600: 2.69
   F. 3601–4200: 2.79%
   G. 4201–4800: 1.6%
   H. Over 4800: 4.11%

[92] PSR Survey Research Unit, *Palestinian Public Opinion Poll.*

The Influence of International Context on Domestic-Level Models of Regime Transition and Democratic Consolidation

> Question: What do you think is the root cause of anti-American sentiment sweeping the nations of the world?
>
> John Bolton [U.S. ambassador to the United Nations, 2005–7]: "I don't think there's anti-American sentiment sweeping the world. The U.S. is most responsible for peace and security in the world. We didn't ask for that [role]. But I would say to people who hold that view, 'Be careful what you ask for.' Because if you say, 'America, go home,' at some point, we may just do that."
>
> —"10 Questions for John Bolton," *Time*, November 26, 2007

THE DYNAMICS SURROUNDING THE ARAB WORLD FOLLOWING THE COLD WAR ARE unique. Most notable is the persistence of authoritarianism in the Arab region—a state of affairs that was and remains perplexing. The explanation for this authoritarian durability rests in the relationship among Arab states, indigenous prodemocracy movements and their levels of pro- and anti-Americanism, and the United States. While the end of the Cold War reduced superpower hegemony in many parts of the developing world, the Arab region saw an increase. In fact, the Arab world is one of the only regions across the globe that witnessed an increase in both security and economic dependence on the United States. Acknowledging this international climate, citizens rationalized their preferences for the status quo as a function of U.S. geostrategic priorities in the region. One cannot understand support for the authoritarian status quo in some cases, and a willingness to compromise on core democratic principles in other parts of the Arab world, without taking into account how the U.S. presence intersects with popular anti-Americanism to weaken democratic voices.

The international context—and more specifically, patron-client relations in the international system—shape domestic debates about regime stability, transition, and, by extension, democratization and democratic consolidation. In U.S. client regimes, like many of those states in the Arab world, domestic levels

222 | CHAPTER EIGHT

of anti-Americanism among organized and influential opposition movements can lead to a bias that reinforces regime stability.

My argument advances a model that examines individual-level strategic interactions, within the framework of U.S. clientelism that looms large in the everyday calculations citizens make. Similar to other microfoundational accounts that model regime outcomes as equilibria based on elite-society negotiations over redistribution,[1] this book advances an important additional variable: the preferences of the external patron in shaping domestic-level negotiations. People who believe that the current regime has privileged, stabilizing, and beneficial relationships with external patrons may come to support a regime even when it is otherwise not in their apparent interest. These levels of stability subsequently shape debates about whether democracy should be extended to an opposition that may jeopardize ties to the external patron.

This book not only questions the mechanisms that induce bottom-up approaches to democratization that dominate studies of comparative development, but also advances a model of state-society relations that takes into account the location of states within international hierarchal networks. This location diffuses direct accountability mechanisms between subordinate states and their societies. The theoretical arguments the present study advances are thus located at the intersection of comparative politics and international relations.

Although my findings highlight how the benefits from the external patron shape societal debates about regime stability and the prospects for democracy, this is but one of many factors that will shape the future of democratization trajectories in the Arab world. Certainly, oil revenues and other rents continue to supply many regimes with both the cooptation and coercive capabilities to repress societies. Yet it is increasingly becoming clear that sometimes the external patron may sanction government repression. This was the case in Bahrain's recent experiment, where the regime overturned a transitory revolution. That Bahrain remains geostrategically important, that Saudi Arabia objected to an expanded civil revolution that would have considerably empowered the Bahraini Shi'a population, and Iran's proximity to Bahrain were all key factors shaping the Bahraini regime's repressive crackdown on the revolution. And although the United States will probably not back all its other clients (it certainly did not do so in the case of Egypt, and President Barack Obama sent clear signs to the regime of Husni Mubarak not to exercise violence against protestors), its position on Bahrain nevertheless sent a signal to Arab citizens that the

---

[1] See Darren Acemoglu and James Robinson, *The Economic Origins of Dictatorship and Democracy* (Cambridge: Cambridge University Press, 2005); and Carles Boix, *Democracy and Redistribution* (Cambridge: Cambridge University Press, 2003).

TABLE 8.1. Client states versus nonclient states

	Globalization winners	Globalization losers
Client states: No anti-Americanism	Will support more democracy	Will prefer status quo
Client states: Anti-Americanism	Will prefer status quo	Will support more democracy
Nonclient states	Will support more democracy	Will prefer status quo

United States does not uniformly apply its policies and its ideals where it has strong geostrategic interests. This signal serves as an important reference point when citizens consider the benefits of existing regimes for the well-being of their nations.

THEORIZING ABOUT NONCLIENT REGIMES

What of the nonclient states of the Arab World? How can one explain Syrian, Iranian, or Libyan authoritarian durability in the absence of U.S. patronage? The lack of a scope condition of international clientelism should shape domestic-level engagements as well. In the absence of the scope condition of U.S. patronage, domestic debates about regime durability will involve different mechanisms. First, countries that are not clients of the United States—like Syria, Iran, and Libya—already have regimes that are less cooperative with the United States and Europe. Therefore, these regimes and their supporters do not rely on external patronage to sustain their rule. The existing regime is not central to gaining access to global benefits. Therefore, those who demand a change in regimes (including democratizers) stand to benefit from more democracy for both ideological and economic reasons. They perhaps see benefits in greater global integration and believe that their systems of government have prevented greater economic integration. Lacking a patron, democratizers will not fear negative consequences of the patron regardless of outcome.

In many ways then, domestic debates about regime stability mirror developments in client states with pro-American opposition movements. In these environments, domestic level factors, including ideological orientations, shape debates about regime stability (see table 8.1).

In the case of the Arab Spring, nonclient states like Syria and Libya have been far more willing to exercise violence against their own populations precisely because they are not client states. Thus, the repressive capacity of a state unchecked by an external patron stifles democratization. However, the United States did not invoke that mandate in Bahrain either. So while it is not clear if client states will be more cautious about exercising violence in the future, it is certainly becoming more difficult to do so. Certainly when Egypt's citizens took to Tahrir Square in January 2011, President Obama issued a stern warning to the Mubarak regime against the use of violence. And while the firm stance may have saved hundreds of lives, the ongoing status of Egypt as a client of the United States may very well be a key factor shaping Egypt's future democratic trajectory.

EGYPT'S FUTURE DEMOCRATIC CONSOLIDATION

Arguably, several factors will shape Egypt's democratic consolidation. Certainly stabilizing the Egyptian economy and creating jobs will be a top priority for the new regime. Addressing the sources of deep grievances of Egyptians, like the unapologetic levels of corruption, inequality, and outright poverty, will also be important tasks for any new regime. Finally, holding free and fair elections will serve as an obvious step toward democracy. As the electoral process is unfolding in Egypt during the winter of 2012, the Islamists have already secured an impressive and commanding majority, securing close to 65 percent of the popular vote. We had initially (as of fall 2011) witnessed much trepidation about the role of the Muslim Brotherhood, prompting many liberals, including Mohamed El-Barradei, to support the postponement of elections until liberal parties could mount a significant opposition. Many of the concerns emerging from liberal sectors have to do with domestic-level issues, like the future of women's rights, the role of Islam in society, and relations with Egypt's Coptic community. Yet international and regional considerations are also important factors shaping debates about the elections. Will the Muslim Brotherhood jeopardize ties or relations with regional and international partners?

In fact, during the protests, these issues *did* surface in Tahrir Square. A brief glimpse of the ways that the protests were projected to the international order—especially the United States—mattered. So as not to upset the United States or Israel, protests linking the liberation of Jerusalem and Palestine to Egyptian self-determination were held away from the eyes of the international media, in certain quarters of Tahrir Square. To calm anxieties about the Islamist presence, a common unsubstantiated claim emerged during the protests: the Muslim Brotherhood was not involved (or their influence was minimal) even when it became obvious that their presence was in fact substantial. Indeed, it was the Muslim Brotherhood, with years of experience dealing with regime harassment, that stood up and defended the protesters against Mubarak's thugs on one of the most violent days of protest on February 2, 2011.[2]

[2]Barbara Ibrahim, interview with the author, April 2011.

We also see that the Muslim Brotherhood is aware that there are those in Egypt who will "postpone" democracy to limit the Brotherhood's influence. This is perhaps why, even after its overwhelming show of popularity at the polls, the Muslim Brotherhood continues to work very closely with the Egyptian military. The Muslim Brotherhood is concerned that it might be penalized for its overwhelming show of support. It also understands that its policy positions (both domestic and international) are under heavy scrutiny.

In addition to liberals, there are other sectors—like the business community—that are worried about the Muslim Brotherhood destabilizing Egypt vis-à-vis Israel and the United States.[3] The military, despite its good ties to the Muslim Brotherhood, is prepared to insert a clause into any new constitution that it will take over control of the state if any party causes the state instability. It appears this nondemocratic clause is also finding support in the United States and among Egyptians who remain concerned about the Brotherhood.[4] Although the vast majority of Egyptians are upset with Israeli policies in Palestine, some Egyptians see the peace treaty as important to the maintenance of U.S. security and aid commitments. According to a recent Pew Global Attitudes survey, 54 percent of Egyptians want the peace treaty with Israel annulled, with another 39 percent saying they do not. And despite the prodemocracy nature of the Tahrir Square events, when asked would they support democracy over a strong leader, 64 percent said yes with 32 percent opposing. Of those asked if they would prefer democracy at the risk of instability, 54 percent agreed with another 32 percent saying they would choose stability even if the government were not fully democratic.[5] In fact, in the second wave of the Arab Barometer surveys (2011), 88 percent of the Egyptian public wants political reform to proceed at a gradual pace. Sizable numbers also want to preserve close ties with the United States, with 40 percent saying they want to keep ties as they are and another 15 percent saying they want to enhance such ties. However, another 43 percent would prefer a more distant relationship.[6]

One of the key questions looking forward is what role the Muslim Brotherhood will play in either stabilizing or destabilizing ties to the United States or its ally, Israel. It appears that the Muslim Brotherhood is divided between a younger and an older guard. Although opposition to the peace treaty is common in Egypt, whether the Brotherhood will use its newfound position to influence policy vis-à-vis the Israelis is uncertain. The Brotherhood has been

---

[3]Ambassador Daniel Kurtzer, interview with the author, May 2011; Ibrahim interview, April 2011.

[4]Kurtzer interview, May 2011.

[5]Pew Global Attitudes Project, *U.S. Wins No Friends, End of Treaty with Israel Sought* (Washington, DC: Pew Research Center, 2011; accessed at http://www.pewglobal.org/2011/04/25/egyptians-embrace-revolt-leaders-religious-parties-and-military-as-well/).

[6]Ibid.

inconsistent. For example, in February 2011, Mahmoud 'Ezzat, the Brotherhood's deputy supreme guide, was reported as saying that the Muslim Brotherhood "will respect the peace treaty with Israel as long as Israel shows real progress on improving the lot of the Palestinians."[7] Yet a deputy leader, Rashad al-Bayoumi, was quoted as saying, "There is a need to dissolve the peace treaty with Israel."[8] The Muslim Brotherhood's general guide, Muhammad Badi, recently said that a new Egyptian parliament should revise the Camp David Accords.[9]

More recently, Essam El-'Erian, senior leader of the Muslim Brotherhood and its new political arm, the Freedom and Justice Party, expressed his hope that the United States would continue to support the country financially. Yet he also made clear that U.S. aid should not come with political conditionality: "If the Americans are ready to support a democratic government in Egypt, this means a lot [so long as the aid is] without political pressure."[10] He then added that it was time for Israel "to understand the implications of the democratic openings of the Arab Spring . . . which have given new voice to Arab anger at Israel's occupation of the Palestinian territories."[11] The fact of the matter is that the Muslim Brotherhood will most likely try to maintain peaceful ties with Israel to ensure U.S. aid. However, the Brotherhood, compared to the Mubarak regime, will be far less compliant on issues like the Palestine question. This may cause many in Washington, D.C., and on the streets of Egypt to worry about the future course of democracy in the country.[12]

It appears that the Muslim Brotherhood is also concerned about what it perceives as a U.S. double standard on Iran and Hamas. In March 2011 it issued a statement that read, "The U.S. is concerned that Iran is expanding its influence in the Middle East, while Hamas remains vigilant against Israeli occupation and the Brotherhood continues to commit itself to peace-

---

[7]Eli Lake, "Muslim Brother Seeks End to Israel Treaty," *Washington Times*, February 3, 2011.
[8]Ibid.
[9]Tarek Masoud, "The Road to and from Liberation Square." *Journal of Democracy* 22, no. 3 (2011): 20–34.
[10]Essam El-'Erian, quoted in David Kirkpatrick, "Islamists in Egypt Back Timing of Military Handover," *New York Times*, January 8, 2012; accessed at http://www.nytimes.com/2012/01/09/world/middleeast/muslim-brotherhood-backs-egyptian-militarys-transition-date.html?pagewanted=all).
[11]Ibid.
[12]The Pew Global Attitudes Project, *America's Image in the World* (Washington, DC: Pew Research Center, 2007, accessed at http://pewglobal.org/commentary/display.php?AnalysisID=1019), also demonstrates that Egyptians who thought more positively of trade and free markets were also more positive about U.S. policies on fighting terrorism. Hence, one can also hypothesize that in the conundrum of uncertainty looking forward, potential globalization winners are also worried about Islamist majority access to parliament.

ful democratic change in Egypt. Perhaps the U.S. fails to understand why a variety of nations, with obviously different trends, would loosely affiliate with each other for a common goal; the end to occupation. Indeed, a democratic goal."[13]

What role the Muslim Brotherhood will play if it *actually* seizes significant power in Egypt's parliament is unclear. But it *is* clear that the debates now surrounding the continued and influential role of the military in Egyptian political life are designed to take into account the potential "threat" the Brotherhood could play in the future of Egyptian domestic and international affairs.

THE CLASH OF CIVILIZATIONS AND THE SEARCH FOR LIBERAL AND SECULAR DEMOCRATS

> They hate what we see right here in this chamber—a democratically elected government. . . . They hate our freedoms— our freedom of religion, our freedom of speech, our freedom to vote and assemble.
>   —President George W. Bush, September 20, 2001, quoted in Shibley Telhami, *The Stakes: America in the Middle East*

Perhaps nothing is more insulting to Arab societies than U.S. claims that America values freedoms in ways that ordinary Muslim and Arab citizens don't—or even worse, can't. It is one thing to claim that the United States has strong geostrategic interests in the region that render democracy inconsequential; it is another altogether to sell such interest, which has resulted in authoritarian durability, as the result of something inherently undemocratic among the people of the region. Not only has the United States continued to invest in the myth of a civilizational divide but it now designs policies to remedy this clash that miss the root cause of the problem and, indeed, perpetuate it.

Because democratic inferiority is the policy theory du jour, we are now confronted with a new set of policies aimed at addressing it. The United States is currently engaged in bolstering liberal and secular elements of Arab societies as a means to counter the influence of Islamists. This strategy does little to address the sources of anti-Americanism in the region. But describing the problem as an ideological one exonerates the United States from culpability because this strategy implies that Islamists are problematic because of their Islamic belief systems and not their anti-Americanism.

---

[13]Muslim Brotherhood, *Muslim Brotherhood, Hamas and Iran*, March 14, 2011 (accessed at http://www.ikhwanweb.com/article.php?id=28217).

In fact, commentators often assume that Islamists are anti-American by default, failing to recognize the significant variation that exists among Islamists in their anti-American sentiments. While Islamists have shown significant levels of moderation on domestic political issues relating to Islam, whether it is human rights, women's rights, or democracy (as documented in chapter 6), they have been less compromising on the issues that they are most passionate about, like foreign policy. Islamist groups have shown a remarkable willingness to play within the rules of democratic elections—in part because they can be confident about the level of their support among the voters. According to Muriel Asseburg, "The democratic openings that have been achieved, albeit limited, have encouraged many Islamists to pursue their agendas through the ballot box rather than violence; when and where Islamists have been allowed to do so, they have started to work for change within the political systems."[14]

The United States understands that Islamists, especially those in the Arab world, will not turn a blind eye toward American power in the region. Since the Algerian elections of 1991, which would have brought the Islamic Salvation Front to power, the United States has made clear its stance. According to Fawaz Gerges, "The U.S. administration understood that the Islamist tide emerging in the region was one that pitted future governments in that region against the geostrategic priorities of the United States."[15] Public discourse, however, equated political Islam with hatred for Western culture, a hatred of Christianity, and a hatred of Judaism. This discourse never reflexively analyzed the important role of Christians and Jews as "People of the Book" in these Islamic movements, nor the quite positive outlooks many Islamist movements have for Western European countries like France. Masking the problem as "Islam versus the West" ignored the root cause of anti-Americanism in the region—and continues to do so. By reducing the real grievances of the citizens as delusional constructs incapable of appreciating the civilized norms of the West, the United States continues to inflame the sensibilities of ordinary citizens.

The Algerian (1991) and Palestinian (2006) elections showed that clients not in line with U.S. preferences can suffer unpleasant consequences. There are a multitude of incidents in recent years in which the United States has sanctioned client regimes, including Yasir Arafat's Palestine after the al-Aqsa Intifada, the economic sanctions against Jordan for not joining the Iraq coalition in 1991, hostility toward the al-Sauds for not doing more to counter

[14]Muriel Asseburg and Daniel Brumberg, eds., *The Challenges of Islamists for EU and US Policies: Conflict, Stability, and Reform* (Washington, DC: Stiftung Wissenschaft und Politik/United States Institute of Peace, 2007; accessed at http://www.swp-berlin.org/fileadmin/contents/products/research_papers/2007_RP12_ass_brumberg_ks.pdf).

[15]Fawaz Gerges, *America and Political Islam: Clash of Cultures or Clash of Interests?* (Cambridge: Cambridge University Press, 1999), 77.

the radical anti-American tide, and strong language against Mubarak's regime to do more about anti-Americanism in the Egyptian Republic.

So worried are the actors in the Arab world about the ways in which the United States might respond to Islamist victories that Islamist movements themselves sometimes worry about the consequences of their own success. When a 2007 International Republican Institute poll revealed that Morocco's PJD was set to win 47 percent of the vote, the senior deputy, Abdallah Kiran, appeared on Al Jazeera TV's *Wara' al-Khabar* (Behind the News). In his interview, he proclaimed it wasn't in the PJD's or Morocco's interest to have such an overwhelming show of support for his own movement. He cautioned that the PJD and Morocco could suffer the fate of other Islamist movements that had made gains through democracy.[16] These same concerns are structuring the strategies of the Muslim Brotherhood in Egypt as well.

Yet key American analysts and policy makers continue to argue that secular and liberal forces have to be encouraged to counter the Islamists.[17] These policies seldom address the issue of implementing strategies that would lessen anti-Americanism. Rather, they appear to be designed to address the problem *despite* levels of anti-Americanism. Delaying democracy until the right liberal and secular conditions emerge on the ground is a remarkably unrealistic strategy, one that reinforces the status quo even as it misses its realities. Gregory Gause, for example, calls for the United States to hold back its efforts on promoting democracy. Gause writes, "The United States should instead focus its energy on encouraging the development of secular, nationalist, and liberal political organizations that could compete on an equal footing with Islamist parties. Only by doing so can Washington help ensure that when elections finally do occur, the results are more in line with U.S. interests."[18] The assumption here is that secular and liberal forces will necessarily be more pro-American than the Islamists. But this begs the question of why a secular group would be any more pro-American than an Islamist group. Historical and contemporary records show that this is not the case. Secular forces have rarely been pro-American. As Timothy Mitchell reminds us, "As a rule, the most secular regimes in the Middle East have been those most independent of the United States. . . . Egypt under Nasser,

[16]Carnegie Endowment for International Peace, "Debate over Electoral Survey," April 2006 (accessed at http://www.carnegieendowment.org/arb/?fa=show&article=20933).

[17]F. Gregory Gause III, "Can Democracy Stop Terrorism?" *Foreign Affairs*, September–October 2005 (accessed at http://fullaccess.foreignaffairs.org/20050901faessay84506/f-gregory -gause-iii/can-democracy-stop-terrorism.html?mode=print); Judy Barsalou, *Islamists at the Ballot Box: Findings from Egypt, Jordan, Kuwait, and Turkey*, United States Institute of Peace Special Report no. 144 (Washington, DC: United States Institute of Peace, 2005; accessed at http:// www.usip.org/pubs/specialreports/sr144.html).

[18]Gause, "Can Democracy Stop Terrorism?"

republican Iraq, the Palestine national movement, post-independence Algeria, the Republic of South Yemen, and Ba'thist Syria all charted courses of independence from the United States."[19] Representing the national sentiments of their people, all these countries turned to the Soviet Union for assistance during the Cold War. Shibley Telhami concurs: "In the 1960's, '70s, and '80s, the U.S. saw secular movements as more threatening to U.S. geostrategic interests than Islamic groups and governments."[20] So when and how, and under what conditions, did secularism become pro-American?

This also raises the question of why liberalism should be a precondition to democratic transitions. Liberal values, at least in the Western experience, emerged as a result of democracy; they were not conditions of democracy. Women's rights, gay rights, and the emancipation of the enslaved all occurred more than a hundred years after the democratic experience in the United States. This is not to justify the lack of liberal values in the Arab world but instead to question their usefulness for democracy. On this same point, even if the Arab world were to become a beacon of liberal values, what would guarantee that these liberal values would be accompanied by pro-American opinions? As policy makers continue to figure out how to liberally reform Islam, they should also be aware that no amount of reform will alter the image of the United States in the region without a direct change of U.S. policies.

To that point, none of America's friends in the region are models of secular and liberal leaderships. For example, Jordan continues to sanction honor killings, and Saudi Arabia's record on human rights is astonishingly bad. The Fatah leadership has become more pro-American, but this is not because it has become more secular or democratic—it has become so because of U.S. aid and security arrangements. There was no miraculous liberal or secular transformation in the ranks of Fatah when it became a pro-American client.

The shortsightedness of the American quest for liberal and secular friends is similar to the debates about whether to accommodate or confront Islamist actors. Advocates of engagement believe Islamists can be won over, while opponents believe that engagement only harnesses support for the movements and that only moderation will leave the requisite room for their accommodation. However, the dilemma is clear: the moderation of Islamist stances doesn't necessarily mean that citizens will follow suit. Engaging elite decision makers by either accommodation or confrontation is a strategy of co-optation. Even if Islamic movements were to moderate their politics, it does not follow that their societies would stay on board.

---

[19]Timothy Mitchell, "McJihad: Islam in the U.S. Global Order," *Social Text* 20, no. 4 (2002): 1 (accessed at http://muse.jhu.edu/journals/social_text/v020/20.4mitchell.html).

[20]Shibley Telhami, *The Stakes: America in the Middle East* (Boulder, CO: Westview, 2002), 27.

Consider Fatah before the Oslo Accords. Moderation was an Israeli and American precondition to engagement of the Palestine Liberation Organization. Fatah conceded and recognized Israel, and the vast majority of Palestinians supported the decision, even while Hamas enjoyed minority support among the population. When the rewards for moderation were not granted—the peace process did not end with the creation of a Palestinian state—Palestinians gradually moved their support to Hamas. Even Hamas could quickly lose its support from the public if it turned to support U.S. preferences on foreign policy. These strategies of cooptation have worked to ensure the status quo but have done little to address the roots of daily grievances.

Another U.S. strategy is to either rid the region of its Islamist problem or shun the Islamists until they acquiesce, but that, too, is limited in its analytical rigor. The Islamist movement is a social movement. Not only is it legitimated by Islamic doctrine but its strength is its nationalist core. So long as Arab citizens think the United States rules their world, Islamism will continue to serve as the vehicle through which citizens voice their protest and their dissent. No amount of U.S. shunning will destroy the movement; if anything, this will only strengthen it. Today's Islamism is yesterday's pan-Arabism. Nationalist movements are difficult to defeat and they are intolerant of collective punishments. Shunning such movements only strengthens their support base. Further, if Islamists like the Egyptian Muslim Brotherhood are believed to have become too compliant with U.S. geostrategic interests while ignoring Arab public opinion, then surely there will be other movements that will grow to champion the voices of Arab citizens. These new movements may be religious, secular, or liberal in orientation.

IRAN'S INFLUENCE

Some see Iran's rise to power as a threat to U.S. geostrategic interests in the region. If Iran is able to fortify strong alliances with Russia and China, then the geostrategic map in the Arab world would be dramatically altered. If Arab (non-Islamist) democracy supporters come to believe that an empowered Iran can protect them, that may serve as an alternative to winning U.S. favor. Currently, the non-Islamist democrats support the status quo because they understand the influence of the United States is paramount for their national well-being. However, the possibility of turning to an alternative powerhouse, one that is sympathetic to Islamist movements, may reduce the desire and the ability of reformers to maintain the status quo. Reformers may begin looking eastward rather than westward for greater economic integration and globalization. Already, Islamic movements across the region look to Iran and Hizbullah as inspirational forces of power, and Arab states that house large Islamist opposition movements are also concerned about Iran. However, the lack of a resolution on the Palestinian-Israeli front has hurt the ability to forge a common alliance between Israel and other Arab countries against Iran.[21]

Realistically, though, Iran is not going to replace U.S. hegemony in the region. Yet the United States must tread carefully; it must not put itself in direct confrontation with Iran. Most important, it mustn't alienate the reform movements in Iran that desire stronger ties to the United States. Any attack on Iran, whether by the United States or its allies, will blur the line between reformers and nonreformers. In the face of external aggression, Iranians will unite as one people. There is no quicker way to destroy Iranian democratic gains than for an external power to attack the country.

POSSIBLE PATHS FORWARD

Because U.S. hegemony will remain paramount, the route to more democracy is to lessen anti-Americanism and to compete for Arab audiences. One possible path, some argue, would be rapid economic development that could serve as a means of winning over Arab publics, even while U.S. policies remain unpopular. If economic growth and development expanded in ways that benefit larger sectors of Arab societies, it could drastically reduce the Islamist audience effect—that is, the ability of Islamists to win over popular support in Arab societies. Nevertheless, the key to economic prosperity in the Arab region rests on its ability to attract FDI. FDI inputs to jump start these economies could also prove tremendously beneficial to the reformist coalitions. If these coalitions are strengthened and empowered in ways that allow them to outgrow Islamists, then a democratic current might arise among this sector of society; such a democratic current may be more tolerant of U.S. hegemony and demand more accountability and representation from existing states.

The success of this scenario would depend on the willingness and desire of regimes to allow expanded economic growth. If the regimes forecast future instability, they may choose to delay the rate of economic growth. Further, the political instability of the region, the numerous wars, the ongoing Palestinian-Israeli conflict, the authoritarian stalemate, the rise of Islamists, and the reliance of the economies on oil have not created a hospitable environment to FDI projections. Neither are economic forecasts promising. As an Economist Intelligence Unit report argues, "Foreign investors will be

---

[21] Marina Ottaway, *Iran, the United States, and the Gulf: The Elusive Regional Policy* (Washington, DC: Carnegie Endowment for International Peace, 2009).

discouraged by poor business environments and regional political tensions. Investor sentiment and tourism could be adversely affected by a deterioration of the security environment. Apart from the possibility of a general rise in terrorist attacks against local and Western targets across the region, there are specific risks associated with the security situation in Iraq, political turmoil in Lebanon and concerns about Iran's nuclear program."[22]

As a result, the Middle East is expected to attract no more than 2.6 percent of the world's FDI.[23] Ironically, many analysts doubt that the Arab world can make the necessary economic leaps without further advancements in its democratic trajectory.[24] Democratic development of the Arab world is normatively significant, and the livelihoods of millions of citizens will depend on the economic trajectories in years to come. Peace and stability are also mandatory for future economic progress. Already, unemployment rates (holding in some countries near 30 percent), the "youth bulge," and rising expectations depict a region in dire need of economic and political reform.

IGNORING ARAB PUBLIC OPINION AND THE ISLAMIST RESPONSE

> In foreign and security policy, when you deal with a country, you deal with the government of that country. What are we supposed to do? Deal with the man on the street?
> —James Baker, U.S. Secretary of State, interview, *PBS Frontline*

A sounder approach to the U.S. problem with Islamists would involve reducing levels of anti-American sentiment across the region more generally. The United States needs to compete directly for the hearts and minds of ordinary Arab citizens, and should premise its engagements with Islamists on winning over the supporters of these movements and not simply their elite decision-makers.

The United States will probably not be able to alter the political worldviews of Islamist movements. But it can compete with Islamists to win the

[22]Economist Intelligence Unit/Columbia Program on International Investment, *World Investment Prospects to 2011: Foreign Direct Investment and the Challenge of Political Risk* (London: Economist Intelligence Unit, 2007; accessed at http://graphics.eiu.com/upload/WIP_2007_WEB .pdf).

[23]Ibid.

[24]Robert Beschel, Nadereh Chamlou, Dipak Dasgupta, and Tarik Yousef, *Unlocking the Employment Potential in the Middle East and North Africa: Toward a New Social Contract* (Washington, DC: World Bank, 2004); Pete Moore, "The Newest Jordan: Free Trade, Peace and an Ace in the Hole," *Middle East Report Online*. June 26, 2003 (accessed at http://www.merip.org/mero/ mero062603.html).

Arab street—which is not a monolithic mass whose attitudes are fixed in stone. Reducing levels of anti-Americanism in this way will directly mitigate the audiences of these Islamist groups. With a friendly street, real democratic reform becomes possible. The current status quo does not serve this objective. The United States today is at an important juncture—it can no longer only rely on Arab states to win the so-called War on Terror, and it needs the help of the population, which is alienated from U.S. policies to begin with; therefore, it must constructively reevaluate the way it conducts its business in the region.

Even while the United States has proclaimed more commitment toward democracy as part of its Greater Middle East Initiative of 2004 (dubbed the Freedom Agenda), such pronouncements were accompanied by war, devastation, occupation, and authoritarian consolidation. As a result, Islamism has grown in strength. Given these dynamics, many in the policy establishment believed that democratic elections were the route to pro-American democracy. In the current climate of anti-Americanism, free and democratic elections cannot return pro-American platforms. Wars are not conducive to winning support from ordinary people. Citizens reinforce the status quo.

Graham Fuller had noticed growing political apathy in the Arab world that is utterly alarming. Before the Arab Spring of 2011 he wrote:

> This greater surface political passivity in the face of growing U.S. interventionism and imposition of unpopular policies represents a disturbing new trend—the concealment of anger, frustration, and impotence. . . . Part of the quiescence can be attributed to regime skills in managing repression. . . . But part of it too represents a bitter fatalism that resistance is so essentially futile, that the domestic and international order is so arrayed as to make protest both impotent and impossible. The United States is observed by Muslims to have irrevocably turned a corner in the embrace of naked hostility to Muslims, their interests, honor and dignity. . . . The silent impassiveness is the newest and most disturbing feature of anti-American sentiment. It is dangerous to assume that such Muslim anger is basically transient, manageable, and basically irrelevant to U.S. global strategy and deeper U.S. interests in the region.[25]

The verdict is still out on how the Arab Spring might change these realities. But it is clear that Arab public opinion shouldn't be ignored. However, U.S. policies have done precisely that—they have overlooked the sentiments of ordinary citizens.

---

[25]Graham Fuller, *The Future of Political Islam* (New York: Palgrave MacMillan, 2003), 160.

The idea that authoritarian tactics could either ignore or manipulate Arab public opinion firmly guided the first Camp David Talks in the 1970s, when key policy makers decided to disregard Arab sentiment. This approach was again adopted in 1991 by the United States as it established its coalition of Arab leaders to attack Saddam Hussein in Iraq.[26] In order for several Arab countries to satisfy U.S. geostrategic priorities, they have had to ignore their own publics and repress public sentiment. It is no wonder that all the major U.S. and Israeli interventions in the region—the First Gulf War in 1991, the War on Terror from 2001 onward, the Iraq War of 2003, Israel's reoccupation of the West Bank in 2000, Israel's Lebanon incursion of 2006, and its attack on Gaza in 2008—witnessed reversals in levels of political and civil liberties across the region.

This raises the question of where Arab public opinion stands on issues related to the United States. Significantly, the crux of Arab resentment for America relates to U.S. policies in the region. Arab citizens have little faith in the United States and believe that it will never advance the interests of the people. A Program of International Policy Attitudes survey of citizens around the world found the Middle East region to have the lowest levels of enthusiasm for Obama's presidency.[27] In fact, a Pew 2008 poll found very small percentages across the region had confidence that Obama would do the right thing in international affairs.[28] According to that poll, only 7 percent in Pakistan and Turkey, 23 percent in Egypt, 20 percent in Jordan, and 22 percent in Lebanon believed that Obama would do what they thought was right in international affairs. Arab citizens feel threatened by U.S. military power, and significant majorities are uneasy with the hegemonic domination the United States now has in the region.

A 2007 Pew poll found that majorities in eight Middle Eastern countries were worried that the United States could become a military threat.[29] In fact, significant majorities in a World Public Opinion poll showed that large numbers support the United States removing its military bases from all Islamic countries; 72 percent supported this view in Morocco, 92 percent

[26]Telhami, *The Stakes: America in the Middle East*, 68.

[27]Steven Kull, Clay Ramsay, Stephan Weber, and Evan Lewis, *America's Global Image in the Obama Era* (Washington, DC: Program on International Policy Attitudes, 2009; accessed at http://www.worldpublicopinion.org/pipa/pdf/jul09/WPO_USObama_Jul09_packet.pdf).

[28]Michael Remez and Richard Wike, "Global Media Celebrate Obama Victory—But Cautious Too: A Changed View of American Democracy" (Washington, DC: Pew Research Center Publications, 2008; accessed at http://pewresearch.org/pubs/1033/global-media-celebrate-obama-victory-but-cautious-too).

[29]Pew Global Attitides Project, *Global Unease with Major World Powers: Rising Environmental Concern in 47-Nation Survey* (Washington, DC: Pew Research Center, 2007; accessed at http://pewglobal.org/reports/display.php?ReportID=256).

in Egypt, and 71 percent in Pakistan.[30] Another World Public Opinion poll found that majorities across the region supported the following statement: "America pretends to be helpful to Muslim countries, but in fact everything it does is really part of a scheme to take advantage of people in the Middle East and steal their oil." This statement found support with 87 percent of Egyptians, 62 percent of Moroccans, and 56 percent of Pakistanis. Further majorities believe that the U.S. goal in the region is to maintain control over Middle Eastern oil, with 91 percent of Egyptians, 82 percent of Moroccan, 68 percent of Pakistanis, 87 percent of Jordanians, 89 percent of Palestinians, and 89 percent of the Turks supporting this assessment of U.S. influence in the region.[31]

Attitudes toward the United States are also structured by the Palestinian-Israeli conflict. When Telhami conducted a six-country poll in 2008, he found that the most-often cited response to improving the U.S. image in the region was finding a resolution to the Arab-Israeli conflict.[32] Majorities across the region—86 percent of Egyptians, 77 percent of Palestinians, and 58 percent even in Azerbaijan—felt that the United States was not doing its part to resolve the conflict. Further, majorities in Arab states don't even believe the United States is genuinely seeking the creation of an independent, economically viable Palestinian state. Ninety-one percent of Egyptians, 64 percent of Moroccans, 63 percent of Jordanians, and 52 percent of Turks support this position.[33] In Saudi Arabia, which witnesses some of the most vehement anti-American stances, a poll of elites found that 66 percent said their frustrations with the United States would be significantly reduced if they were able to strike a peace deal between Israel and the Palestinians.[34] Telhami puts it concisely when he writes, "Only peace between Israelis and Arabs can significantly reduce the challenge to America's interests in the region."[35]

In the spring of 2011, Fatah and Hamas signed a reconciliation agreement paving the way to a unified government, central for advancing the case

[30]"Poll Finds Widespread International Opposition to U.S. Bases in Persian Gulf," December 15, 2008 (accessed at http://www.worldpublicopinion.org/pipa/articles/international_security_bt/579.php?lb=btvoc&pnt=579&nid=&id=).

[31]Steven Kull, "Can Obama Restore the U.S. Image in the Middle East?" *Harvard International Review*, December 19, 2008 (accessed at http://hir.harvard.edu/can-obama-restore-the-us-image-in-the-middle-east).

[32]Shibley Telhami with Zogby International, *2008 Arab Public Opinion Poll* (Washington, DC: Brookings Institution, 2008; accessed at http://www.brookings.edu/~/media/Files/events/2008/0414_middle_cast/0414_middle_east_telhami.pdf).

[33]Steven Kull, Clay Ramsay, Stephen Weber, Evan Lewis, Ebrahim Mohseni, Mary Speck, Melanie Ciolek, and Melinda Brouwer, *Muslim Public Opinion on U.S. Policy, Attacks on Civilians, and al Qaeda* (Washington DC: Program on International Policy Attitudes, 2007; accessed at http://www.worldpublicopinion.org/pipa/pdf/apr07/START_Apr07_rpt.pdf).

[34]Telhami, *The Stakes: America in the Middle East*, 98.

[35]Ibid., 178.

of Palestinian statehood at the United Nations General Assembly in September 2011. Accordingly, the unity government, important for bypassing the political impasse that has plagued the Palestinians since Hamas's election in 2006, and necessary to move both the peace process and more transparent and accountable governance forward, raised concerns in Washington, D.C. It appears that the United States will not tolerate the inclusion of Hamas in any official governing capacity. Furthermore, the United States finds itself in a bind as it prepares to vote against Palestinian statehood while simultaneously paying lip service to democratic and self-determination movements in some Arab countries. The ability of the United States to support democracy and self-determination *only sometimes* has not served its legitimacy and credibility problems in the Arab world. These inconsistencies suggest why Arab citizens question United States's commitment to democracy in cases when it does not yield pro-American outcomes.

Citizens' worries about the consequences of democracy are again captured in public opinion surveys. They believe the United States is not committed to democracy per se but only to pro-American democracy. A World Public Opinion survey in 2009 found that a mere 8 percent of Egyptians, 13 percent of Indonesians, 10 percent of Pakistanis, 6 percent of Jordanians, 11 percent of Palestinians, 7 percent of Turks, and 9 percent of Azerbaijanis support the claim that the "U.S. favors democracy in Muslim countries, whether or not the government is cooperative with the U.S." Significant pluralities in all countries, however, support the claim that the "U.S. favors democracy in Muslim countries only if the government is cooperative with the U.S." This opinion enjoys support from 42 percent in Egypt, 44 percent in Indonesia, 36 percent in Pakistan, 40 percent in Jordan, and 38 percent in Palestine; 40 percent of Jordanians believe this claim, as well as 49 percent of Turks, and 59 percent of Azerbaijanis.[36] A Gallup Poll in 2005 found similar results, with majorities believing that the United States was not interested in the establishment of democratic systems in the region; 66 percent in Jordan, 64 percent in Egypt, 56 percent in Iran, 54 percent in Pakistan, 59 percent in Turkey, and 58 percent in Lebanon didn't believe the United States was genuinely committed to democracy in the area.[37]

Those citizens who positively assess the role of the United States in its democracy-promotion efforts are more likely to be supportive of the existing regime. One would expect citizens who are supportive of U.S. democracy promotion to be less committed to authoritarian leadership. But as the find-

[36] Steven Kull, Evan Lewis, Ebrahim Mohensi, Clay Ramsay, and Stephen Weber, *Public Opinion in the Islamic World on Terrorism, al Qaeda, and U.S. Policies* (Washington DC: Program on International Policy Attitudes, 2009; accessed at http://www.worldpublicopinion.org/pipa/pdf/feb09/STARTII_Feb09_rpt.pdf).

[37] Kull, "Can Obama Restore the U.S. Image in the Middle East?"

ings presented here have shown, the given international dynamics have aligned reformers into the pro–status quo camp. Fifty-five percent of those in Jordan who believe U.S. democracy-promotion initiatives are positive are more likely to support the regime. Those who believe that U.S. democracy promotion is lacking are more likely to be less supportive of their government. This is not the case in Kuwait, where assessments of U.S. democracy-promotion initiatives have little impact on the support for government. Similar percentages, 25 percent of positive evaluators and 29 percent of negative evaluators of U.S. democracy-promotion initiatives, are supportive of their government in Kuwait.[38]

The Lesson of Latin America

This stands in sharp contrast to the development of the patron-client relationship between the United States and Latin American states after the end of the Cold War. Latin America, too, remains an economic client of the United States, although its status as a security client ended with the dissolution of the Soviet Union. Yet Latin America witnessed an increase in pro-Americanism that accompanied its democratic trajectory more generally. Put simply, Latin American democratic forces were and currently are far friendlier toward the United States than those forces demanding democracy in the Arab region.

This was not always the case. Take, for example, Chile's democratically elected Salvador Allende in 1970. U.S. president Richard Nixon authorized the Central Intelligence Agency to block Allende's confirmation as president out of fear of a strong Soviet-Chilean alliance. Subsequently, the United States supported Augusto Pinochet, despite his repressive tactics, because he was pro-American.[39] In the 1980s, President Ronald Reagan's stance against Nicaragua's Sandinista government followed a similar path. The United States feared that these less friendly governments would undermine U.S. geostrategic interests in the region, even while these movements enjoyed popular legitimacy.[40]

Following the Cold War, anti-Americanism declined in Latin America, primarily because with the collapse of the Soviet Union the United States in-

---

[38]Arab Barometer 2005–6, principal investigators Mark Tessler and Amaney Jamal; accessed at http://www.arabbarometer.org/survey/survey.html.

[39]See Grace Livingstone, *America's Backyard: The United States and Latin America from the Monroe Doctrine in the War on Terror* (New York: Zed, 2009).

[40]Jorge Dominguez, "U.S. Latin American Relations during the Cold War and Its Aftermath" (unpublished manuscript, Weatherhead Center for International Affairs, Harvard University, January 1999).

tervened less in the politics of Latin America. Further, because U.S. policies became less interventionist, precipitating the decline in anti-Americanism, the United States became more serious about democracy promotion. According to Kurt Weyland, "Since the end of the Cold War, the United States and other First World countries have put much more emphasis on preserving pluralistic, civilian rule in the region."[41] Since the communist threat has dissipated, the U.S. support for democracy has only increased in Latin America.

Thus, the reduction of U.S. intervention has resulted in pro-American outcomes. For example, the 1990 election of the more pro-American Violeta Barrios de Chamorro in Nicaragua dampened U.S. anxiety. Honduras witnessed a similar decline in anti-Americanism as the U.S. military presence decreased in that country.[42] Panama's anti-Americanism has gradually declined since the 1990s as well.[43] In fact, between 1995 and 2005, Latin America became one of the most pro-American regions of the world.[44] The decline in U.S. intervention coupled with aid, remittances, trade, and migration all promoted a more pro-American climate. [45] In the case of Latin America, the United States has been able to secure its interests by simultaneously promoting democracy, not authoritarianism.

REASSESSING U.S. POLICIES IN THE ARAB WORLD

> For 60 years, the United States pursued stability at the expense of democracy . . . and we achieved neither. Now, we are taking a different course. We are supporting the democratic aspiration of all people.
> —Secretary of State Condoleezza Rice, speech at American University in Cairo, June 20, 2005

Stability will remain the central concern of the United States in the Arab world for the foreseeable future. The global economy will continue to rely

[41]Kurt Weyland, "Neoliberalism in Latin America: A Mixed Record," *Latin American Politics and Society* 46, no. 1 (2004): 135–57.

[42]Livingstone, *America's Backyard.*

[43]Alan McPherson. *Yankee No! Anti-Americanism in U.S. Latin American Relations* (Cambridge, MA: Harvard University Press, 2003).

[44]Andy Baker and David Cuorey, "Understanding Anti-Americanism in Latin America: The Influence of Economic Exchange and Foreign Policy Legacies on Mass Attitudes toward the U.S.," paper presented at Workshop on Anti-Americanism, Princeton University, May 2011.

[45]Ibid. See also Devra Moehler and Nicolas Van de Walle, "Pro- and Anti-Americanism in Sub-Saharan Africa" paper presented at the Workshop on Anti-Americanism, Princeton University, May 2011, which finds that support for the United States is driven by those who support free market economic policies and argues that, in general, Africans are more pro-American because the United States does not militarily intervene in the region.

on Middle Eastern oil for several decades into the future. Oil accounts for 40 percent of the world's energy consumption, and its levels will not fall in the next twenty years. It is estimated that the European Union (EU) will need to import 70 percent of its energy needs by 2025. In 2008, it imported 50 percent. The United States will also be importing 60 percent of its energy needs, mostly from the Persian Gulf. Further, estimates hold that by 2035, the global energy consumption will be double of what it was in 2005, with China and India demanding larger stakes of the world's energy reserves.[46]

These realities make the geostrategic utility of the Arab world indispensable to the global economy and will structure U.S. engagement with the region. Islamists could harm U.S. energy interests by disrupting oil flow to the United States,[47] but they could also favor other countries, like China. China now imports 60 percent of its oil from the Persian Gulf. In the next two decades, that number is likely to climb to 90 percent.[48] Islamists have threatened to sabotage oil fields as a means of retaliating against the United States. The Saudi government spent a billion dollars to protect its oil fields from Islamist extremists right after the Iraq War of 2003 began, and it then deployed 30,000 Saudi troops to protect the oil infrastructure. Another concern is the potential Islamist access to the oil fields of the Persian Gulf. Many analysts worry that if Islamists were to seize control of the oil they would be less likely to adjust production to keep prices low, as do many current Gulf leaders.

Recognizing the increasing need for security, between 2000 and 2003 the Bush administration increased military aid to the top twenty-five oil suppliers in the world, including Saudi Arabia, Qatar, Kuwait, Oman, and Iraq. Central Asia is also a growing region coming firmly under U.S. patronage, with Uzbekistan, Kyrgyzstan, and Azerbaijan receiving large amounts of military aid. The EU has signed bilateral energy partnerships with Azerbaijan and Kazakhstan that circumvent the democracy and human rights strictures of the European Neighborhood Policy. In fact, the 2001 Defense Review (a panel established by President Bush to evaluate U.S. energy security) explicitly noted the possible deployment of U.S. armed forces where energy supplies might be impeded. In 2007, the Bush administration established a new Africa command for the sizable relocation of naval forces to protect Nigerian oil fields, and defined Western African oil as a "strategic national interest." As the United States protects its oil needs, so does it compromise its stances on democracy.[49]

---

[46]Richard Youngs, *Energy: A Reinforced Obstacle to Democracy?* (Madrid: Fundación para las Relaciones Internacionales y el Diálogo Exterior, 2008; accessed at http://www.fride.org/publi cation/467/energy-a-reinforced-obstacle-to-democracy).

[47]Ibid.

[48]Telhami, *The Stakes: America in the Middle East*, 135.

[49]Youngs, *Energy: A Reinforced Obstacle to Democracy?*

The heavy buildup of the U.S. military in the Gulf is not simply to maintain U.S. access to oil supplies but also to guarantee that enemies do not seize these fields. According to Telhami, for more than half a century a central drive behind the American military strategy in the oil-rich region is "to deny control of these vast resources to powerful enemies."[50] This was the logic that the United States employed against Saddam Hussein's Iraq when it invaded Kuwait. If Saddam were not pushed out of Kuwait, the reasoning went, he would have doubled the capacity of Iraq's oil supply and would have become the most significant power in the Middle East.[51] Since Iraq's foreign policy was radically at odds with that of the United States, there was all the more reason for the United States to sanction Iraq.[52]

FROM BUSH TO OBAMA

> We seek broad engagement based upon mutual interests and mutual respect. We will listen carefully, bridge misunderstanding, and seek common ground. We will be respectful, even when we do not agree.
> —President Barack Obama, speech in Ankara, Turkey, April 6, 2009

President Barack Obama may work for a better Middle East strategy, yet there are reasons to remain skeptical. The same strategic facts remain in play now as under the adminsitrations of former presidents George W. Bush and Bill Clinton. The Obama administration is preoccupied with Afghanistan and Pakistan, as the fear of those states turning Islamist is paramount—all the more so because Pakistan possesses nuclear capabilities.

But studying the trajectory of Middle East foreign policy from Clinton to Bush makes clear that in many ways Bush was simply continuing a U.S. foreign policy that very much characterized the Clinton years. True, Clinton and Obama are savvier interlocutors than was Bush. Nevertheless, Clinton's policies can't be seen as improving the position of the United States in the region. The Clinton administration placed the devastating sanctions on Iraq, resulting in the suffering of ordinary citizens. With children denied basic medicines like antibiotics, the death toll mounted in Iraq prior to the U.S. invasion of 2003. The Clinton administration shunned the Palestinians after the Camp David fiasco and the subsequent international condemnation of Arafat and the Palestinians for not accepting a peace treaty that would

---

[50]Telhami, *The Stakes: America in the Middle East*, 140.
[51]Ibid., 148.
[52]Ibid.

not have guaranteed a territorially contiguous Palestinian state on the West Bank. The Clinton administration enacted democratization reversals, and U.S. policy became readily clear about its refusal to deal with Islamists—all while the sources of anti-Americanism continued to grow.

Officials in the Clinton administration admitted that if the Islamists did not have an international agenda, the United States would not resist their coming to power. In other words, the theological or potentially non-democratic character of the Islamists is not the driving force behind U.S. rejection of them. The United States rejects Islamists because they are anti-American. According to Fawaz Gerges, "The Clinton administration would not oppose Islamists if they . . . kept their focus on domestic issues."[53] In other words, it appears that the United States is far more likely to tolerate conservative, nondemocratic rulers, like the monarchy in Saudi Arabia and the Taliban in Afghanistan (before they became more internationalized through al-Qaeda), than a democratic state that is not friendly toward the United States.

One official affiliated with Clinton's administration was more blunt: "We are prepared to live with Islamic regimes as long as they not endanger or be hostile to our vital interests."[54] Under Clinton, U.S. policy toward Islamists became more crystallized. Government officials worried about the implications of Islamists because of their foreign policy agendas. And while it is not necessarily the place for the world's superpower to take this stance, the rhetorical commitment to democracy makes the democracy-promotion establishment seem hypocritical at best. Worse, however, this hypocrisy injures the potential for democracy in the region.

Where Do We Go Next?

Bottom-up approaches to democracy remain the cornerstone of U.S. democracy-promotion initiatives and inform models of comparative political development. Yet in the context of the Arab world these approaches are remarkably flawed. Existing state-society models assume states enjoy full autonomy and are shielded from the international political environment. But Arab democratization has never been and will never be a completely indigenous process. Given U.S. hegemony in the region, U.S. investment shapes the democratization process in profound ways that simultaneously undermine democratic forces and bolster the authoritarian status quo. While the findings of this book offer some hope, they also forecast demo-

---

[53] Gerges, *America and Political Islam*, 102.
[54] Ibid.

cratic despair. The most immediate mechanism of facilitating the path to democracy is to reduce anti-American sentiment across the region. Under those circumstances, the potential that democracy will yield pro-American friends would be that much higher.

Policy makers often argue that there is little room for winning the hearts and minds of ordinary Arab citizens. Yet the substantial variation in evaluations of the United States within and across states tells us that Arab anti-American sentiment is not monolithic. Demonstrating a commitment to the citizens in the region and including them as part of U.S. geostrategic strategies could win the United States significant favor in the region—gains vital to the democratization process. The United States was able to win over the allegiance of the Kuwaiti Islamic Constitutional Movement and Turkey's Justice and Development Party not because it simply engaged them and allowed them space and recognition as political parties but because U.S. policies were seen as benefiting the citizens of these two countries.

The United States can no longer afford to talk about democracy while turning a blind eye to democratic and human rights abuses. It is not sufficient to withdraw from Iraq without a firm commitment to Iraqis that they will not become yet another Arab country with an authoritarian leader who is friendly toward the United States. Nor is it sufficient to talk about a peace process when the future Palestinian state is shrinking. A whole generation has come to political consciousness since the commencement of the "peace process," and yet no firm dates have been established to end this long-winded progression of negotiations. The cycle of violence between Israel and its neighbors has to end, and working toward a comprehensive peace agreement that ensures Israel's security along with Palestinian sovereignty is the only viable route.

Islamists draw their support only in part from strong theological commitments to Shari'a-oriented policies that will reintroduce a myriad of conservative policies. The average man or woman is not well versed in the machinations of a complicated *fiqh*-based Islamic constitutional system of governance. Rather, the Islamist movement derives its popularity from its authentic message of resistance to external forces. As Lisa Wedeen emphatically states, "Islamism has become a coherent anti-imperialist doctrine."[55] Citizens of the Arab world see these movements as authentic nationalist vehicles that stand against foreign occupation. Until the United States understands that its wars in Iraq and Afghanistan, its applause for cosmetic Arab reform efforts while civil and political liberties dissipate, and its ongoing support for the Israeli occupation have galvanized political national consciousness

---

[55] Lisa Wedeen, "Beyond the Crusades: Why Huntington and Bin Laden Are Wrong," *Middle East Policy* 10, no. 2 (2003): 56.

in the Arab world—until the United States understands that its policies form the cornerstone of Islamism—then it will continue to invest in policies that miss their targets. Given the conditions of the U.S. presence in the Arab world, the road to democracy must address and mitigate the root causes of anti-Americanism.

BIBLIOGRAPHY

Abou El Fadl, Khaled. *Islam and the Challenge of Democracy*. Princeton, NJ: Princeton University Press, 2003.

Acemoglu, Darren, and James Robinson. *The Economic Origins of Dictatorship and Democracy*. Cambridge: Cambridge University Press, 2005.

Adorno, Theodor W. *The Authoritarian Personality*. New York: Harper and Brothers, 1950.

Adserà, Alícia, and Carles Boix. "Trade, Democracy, and the Size of the Public Sector: The Political Underpinnings of Openness." *International Organization* 56, no. 2 (2002): 229–62.

El-Affendi, Abdelwahab. "The Elusive Reformation." *Journal of Democracy* 24, no. 2 (2003): 34–39.

Afoaku, Osita G. *Explaining the Failure of Democracy in the Democratic Republic of Congo: Autocracy and Dissent in an Ambivalent World*. Lewiston, NY: Mellen, 2005.

———. "U.S. Foreign Policy and Authoritarian Regimes: Change and Continuity in International Clientelism." *Journal of Third World Studies* 17, no. 2 (2000): 13–40.

Almond, Gabriel, Samuel Huntington, and Myron Weiner. *Understanding Political Development: An Analytic Study*. Boston: Little, Brown, 1987.

Almond, Gabriel, and Sidney Verba. *The Civic Culture: Political Attitudes and Democracy in Five Nations*. Princeton, NJ: Princeton University Press, 1963.

Alt, James E., and Michael Gilligan. "The Political Economy of Trading States: Factor Specificity, Collective Action Problems and Domestic Political Institutions." *Journal of Political Philosophy* 2, no. 2 (1994): 165–92.

Alyami, Ali. "Saudi Arabia: The Gathering Storm." *Journal of International Security Affairs* 15 (2008): n.p. Accessed January 2009 at http://www.securityaffairs.org/issues/2008/15/alyami.php.

AME Info. "Jordan Looks Near and Far for Economic Growth." February 2007. Accessed January 2008 at http://www.ameinfo.com/110694.html.

———. "Kuwait: 2002 Economic Data." July 2003. Accessed January 2008 at http://www.ameinfo.com/25866.html.

Anderson, Betty S. *Nationalistic Voices in Jordan*. Austin: University of Texas Press, 2005.

Anderson, Lisa. "Arab Democracy: Dismal Prospects." *World Policy Journal* 18, no. 3 (2001): 53–60.

———. "Peace and Democracy in the Middle East: The Constraints of Soft Budgets." *Journal of International Affairs* 49, no. 1 (1995): 25–45.

———. "The State in the Middle East and North Africa." *Comparative Politics* 20, no. 1 (1987): 1–18.

Andoni, Lamis. "Has Jordan Turned Its Back on Pan-Arabism?" *Middle East International* 573 (1998): 18–19.

Andoni, Lamis. "King Abdallah: In His Father's Footsteps?" *Journal of Palestinian Studies* 29, no. 3 (2000): 77–89.

Arab Barometer 2005–6. Principal Investigators Mark Tessler and Amaney Jamal. Accessed January 2012 at http://www.arabbarometer.org/survey/survey.html.

Arab Barometer 2011. Principal Investigators Mark Tessler and Amaney Jamal. Accessed January 2012 at http://www.arabbarometer.org/survey/survey.html.

Arkin, William M. "Keeping Secrets in Jordan." *Washington Post*, November 16, 2005. Accessed January 2008 at http://www.informationclearinghouse.info/article11031.htm.

Asseburg, Muriel, and Daniel Brumberg, eds. *The Challenges of Islamists for EU and US Policies: Conflict, Stability, and Reform*. Washington, DC: Stiftung Wissenschaft und Politik/United States Institute of Peace, 2007. Accessed December 2011 at http://www.swp-berlin.org/fileadmin/contents/products/research_papers/2007_RP12_ass_brumberg_ks.pdf.

Associated Press. "Kuwait to Give $500M for Katrina Relief." September 4, 2005. Accessed December 2011 at http://www.foxnews.com/story/0,2933,168443,00.html.

———. "Palestinian Economy Shrinks 21% in Fourth Quarter of 2006." February 2, 2007. Accessed December 2007 at http://www.haaretz.com/hasen/spages/830389.html.

Awadallah, Bassem. "Jordan's Economic Miracle." February 3, 2003. Accessed December 2011 at http://www.jordanembassyus.org/new/events/event_02032003.htm.

Ayoob, Mohammad. *The Many Faces of Political Islam: Religion and Politics in the Muslim World*. Ann Arbor: University of Michigan Press, 2008.

Baker, Andy, and David Cuorey. "Understanding Anti-Americanism in Latin America: The Influence of Economic Exchange and Foreign Policy Legacies on Mass Attitudes toward the U.S." Paper presented at the Workshop on Anti-Americanism, Princeton University, May 2011.

Baker, James. Interview, *PBS Frontline*. October 2001. Accessed August 2008 at http://www.pbs.org/wgbh/pages/frontline/shows/saudi/interviews/baker.html.

Baldwin, Peter. *The Politics of Social Solidarity*. Cambridge: Cambridge University Press, 1990.

Barari, Hassan. "Elections in Jordan: Poor Showing for Islamists." December 13, 2007. Accessed December 2011 at http://www.ikhwanweb.com/Article.asp?ID=14866&SectionID=0.

Barsalou, Judy. *Islamists at the Ballot Box: Findings from Egypt, Jordan, Kuwait, and Turkey*. United States Institute of Peace Special Report no. 144. Washington, DC: United States Institute of Peace, 2005. Accessed December 2007 at http://www.usip.org/pubs/specialreports/sr144.html.

Bates, Robert. "The Impulse to Reform." In *Economic Change and Political Liberalization in Sub-Saharan Africa*, ed. Jennifer Widner, 13–28. Baltimore: Johns Hopkins University Press, 1994.

Beblawi, Hazem. "The Rentier State in the Arab World." In *The Arab State*, ed. Giacomo Luciani, 85–98. Berkeley and Los Angeles: University of California Press, 1990.

Beehner, Lionel. *The Effects of the Amman Bombings on US-Jordanian Relations*. New York: Council on Foreign Relations, 2005. Accessed October 2007 at http://www.cfr.org/publication/9200/.

Bellin, Eva. "Coercive Institutions and Coercive Leaders." In *Authoritarianism in the Middle East: Regimes and Resistance*, ed. Marsha Pripstein Posusney and Michele Penner Angrist, 21–41. Boulder, CO: Lynne Rienner, 2005.

——. "The Politics of Profit in Tunisia: Utility of the Rentier Paradigm?" *World Development* 22, no. 3 (1994): 427–36.

——. "The Robustness of Authoritarianism in the Middle East: Exceptionalism in Comparative Perspective." *Comparative Politics* 36, no. 2 (2004): 139–57.

——. *Stalled Democracy: Capital, Labor and the Paradox of State-Sponsored Development.* Ithaca, NY: Cornell University Press, 2002.

Bermeo, Nancy. "Myths of Moderation: Confrontation and Conflict during Democratic Transitions." *Comparative Politics* 29, no. 3 (1997): 305.

——. *Ordinary People in Extraordinary Times: The Citizenry and the Breakdown of Democracy.* Princeton, NJ: Princeton University Press, 2003.

Beschel, Robert, Nadereh Chamlou, Dipak Dasgupta, and Tarik Yousef. *Unlocking the Employment Potential in the Middle East and North Africa: Toward a New Social Contract.* Washington, DC: World Bank, 2004.

Bilgin, Hasret Dikici. "Foreign Policy Orientation of Turkey's Pro-Islamist Parties: A Comparative Study of the AKP and Refah." *Turkish Studies* 9, no. 3 (2008): 407–21.

Black, Ian. "Sanctions Causing Gaza to Implode, Say Rights Groups." *Guardian*, March 6, 2008. Accessed August 2008 at http://www.guardian.co.uk/world/2008/mar/06/israelandthepalestinians.humanrights.

Blanchard, Christopher M., and Jeremy M. Sharp. *U.S. Foreign Aid to the Palestinians.* Congressional Research Service Report, July 27, 2006. Accessed December 2011 at http://fpc.state.gov/documents/organization/68794.pdf.

Blaydes, Lisa. *Elections and Distributive Politics in Mubarak's Egypt.* Cambridge: Cambridge University Press, 2011.

Boix, Carles. *Democracy and Redistribution.* Cambridge: Cambridge University Press, 2003.

Boix, Carles, and Luis Garicano, "Democracy, Inequality, and Country-Specific Wealth." Unpublished manuscript, 2002.

Boix, Carles, and Milan Svolik. "Non-tyrannical Autocracies." Paper presented at the Comparative Politics seminar, University of California–Los Angeles, 2007.

Bookmiller, Robert. "Abdullah's Jordan: America's Anxious Ally." *Alternatives: Turkish Journal of International Relations* 2, no. 2 (2003): 174–95.

Boulby, Marion. *The Muslim Brotherhood and the Kings of Jordan, 1945–1993.* Lanham, MD: Rowman and Littlefield, 1999.

Bowen, John R. 2007. "Anti-Americanism as Schemas and Diacritics in France and Indonesia." In *Anti-Americanisms in World Politics*, ed. Peter J. Katzenstein and Robert O. Keohane, 227–50. Ithaca, NY: Cornell University Press.

Brand, Laurie A. "The Effects of the Peace Process on Political Liberalization in Jordan." *Journal of Palestine Studies* 28, no. 2 (1999): 52–67.

——. *Jordan's Inter-Arab Relations: The Political Economy of Alliance Making.* New York: Columbia University Press, 1995.

——. "Palestinians and Jordanians: A Crisis of Identity." *Journal of Palestine Studies* 24, no. 4 (1995): 46–61.

Brinks, Daniel, and Michael Coppedge. "Diffusion Is No Illusion: Neighbor Emulation in the Third Wave of Democracy." *Comparative Political Studies* 39, no. 4 (2006): 463–89.

Brown, Nathan J. *Aftermath of the Hamas Tsunami.* Washington, DC: Carnegie Endowment for International Peace, 2006.

——. *Are Palestinians Building a State?* Washington, DC: Carnegie Endowment for International Peace, 2010.

Brown, Nathan J. *Fayyad Is Not the Problem, but Fayyadism Is Not the Solution to Palestine's Political Crisis.* Washington, DC: Carnegie Endowment for International Peace, 2010.

———. *Jordan and Its Islamic Movement: The Limits of Inclusion?* Carnegie Paper no. 74. Washington, DC: Carnegie Endowment for International Peace, 2006.

———. *Pushing Toward Party Politics: Kuwait's Islamic Constitutional Movements.* Carnegie Paper no. 79. Washington, DC: Carnegie Endowment for International Peace, 2007.

———. *Requiem for Palestinian Reform: Clear Lessons from a Troubled Record.* Carnegie Paper no. 81. Washington DC: Carnegie Endowment for International Peace, 2007.

Brownlee, Jason. "Political Crisis and Restabilization: Iraq, Libya, Syria, and Tunisia." In *Authoritarianism in the Middle East: Regimes and Resistance*, ed. Marsha Pripstein Posusney and Michele Angrist. Boulder, CO: Lynne Rienner, 2005.

Bruh, Kathleen, and Daniel Levy. *Mexico: The Struggle for Democratic Development.* Berkeley and Los Angeles: University of California Press, 2001.

Brynen, Rex. "Economic Crisis and Post-Rentier Democracy in the Arab World: The Case of Jordan." *Canadian Journal of Political Science* 25, no. 1 (1992): 69–97.

Calhoun, Craig, Frederick Cooper, and Kevin W. Moore, eds. *Lessons of Empire: Imperial Histories and American Power.* New York: New Press, 2006.

"Call to Boycott U.S. Products Gains Momentum," May 30, 2002. Accessed May 2008 at http://www.inminds.co.uk/boycott-news-0158.html.

Cammett, Melanie Claire. *Globalization and Business Politics in Arab North Africa: A Comparative Perspective.* New York: Cambridge University Press, 2007.

Caparico, Sheila. "Foreign Aid and Promoting Democracy in the Middle East." *Middle East Journal* 56, no. 3 (2002): 379–95.

Cardoso, Fernando Henrique. *Dependency and Development in Latin America.* Berkeley and Los Angeles: University of California Press, 1979.

Carnegie Endowment for International Peace. "Debate over Electoral Survey in Morocco." *Saba*, April 2006. Accessed April 2007 at http://www.carnegieendowment.org/arb/?fa=show&article=20933.

Carter, Jimmy. *Palestine: Peace Not Apartheid.* New York: Simon and Schuster, 2007.

Center for Public Opinion. *Terror Free Tomorrow: Nationwide Public Opinion Survey of Saudi Arabia.* Washington, DC: Center for Public Opinion. Accessed December 2011 at http://www.terrorfreetomorrow.org/upimagestft/TFT%20Saudi%20Arabia%20Survey.pdf.

Center for Strategic Studies in Jordan. *Revisiting the Arab Street: Research from Within.* Amman: Center for Strategic Studies in Jordan, 2005.

Chaudhry, Kiren Aziz. *The Price of Wealth: Economies and Institutions in the Middle East.* Ithaca, NY: Cornell University Press, 1997.

Clark, Ian. *The Hierarchy of States: Reform and Resistance in the International Order.* New York: Cambridge University Press, 1989.

Clark, Janine A. "The Conditions of Islamist Moderation: Unpacking Cross-ideological Cooperation in Jordan." *International Journal of Middle East Studies* 38, no. 4 (2006): 539–60.

———. *Islam, Charity, and Activism: Middle-Class Networks and Social Welfare in Egypt, Jordan, and Yemen.* Indiana Series in Middle East Studies. Bloomington: Indiana University Press, 2003.

Clement, Henry. "The Clash of Globalizations in the Middle East." *Review of Middle East Economics and Finance* 1, no. 1 (2007): 104–28.

Clement, Henry, and Robert Springborg. *Globalization and the Politics of Development in the Middle East*. Cambridge: Cambridge University Press, 2001.

Cleveland, William L. *A History of the Modern Middle East*. Boulder, CO: Westview, 2004.

Cohen, Amnon. *Political Parties in the West Bank under the Jordanian Regime, 1949–1967*. Ithaca, NY: Cornell University Press, 1982.

Cohen, Benjamin. "The Revolution in Atlantic Economic Relations: A Bargain Comes Unstuck." In *The United States and Western Europe: Political, Economic, and Strategic Perspectives*, ed. Wolfram Hanrieder, 106–33. Cambridge, MA: Winthrop, 1974.

Cohen, Shana. *Searching for a Different Future: The Rise of a Global Middle Class in Morocco*. Durham, NC: Duke University Press, 2004.

Cole, Juan. "A 'Shiite Crescent'? The Regional Impact of the Iraq War." *Current History* 105, no. 687 (2006): 20–26.

Crystal, Jill. *Oil and Politics in the Gulf: Rulers and Merchants in Kuwait and Qatar*. New York: Cambridge University Press, 1995.

Crystal, Jill, and Abdallah al-Shayeji. "The Pro-democratic Agenda in Kuwait: Structures and Contexts." In *Political Liberalization and Democratization in the Arab World*, vol. 2, *Comparative Experiences*, ed. Bahgat Korany, Rex Brynen, and Paul Noble, 101–25. Boulder, CO: Lynne Rienner, 1998.

Dagi, Ihsan. "Turkey's AKP in Power," *Journal of Democracy* 19, no. 3 (2008): 25–30.

Dahl, Robert. *Polyarchy*. New Haven, CT: Yale University Press, 1970.

Daqiqi, Naoufel, and Mawassi Lahcen, "Morocco's PJD Confident Despite Detractors." *Magharebia*, August 31, 2007. Accessed May 2008 at http://www.magharebia.com/cocoon/awi/xhtml1/en_GB/features/awi/reportage/2007/08/31/reportage-01.

Darwish, Adel. "Kuwait: Kuwait Goes to the Polls." *Middle East*, August–September 2003. Accessed December 2011 at http://findarticles.com/p/articles/mi_m2742/is_337/ai_n25072206.

Dashti, Rola. Personal interview with the author, winter 2006.

Davis, Christina. *Why Adjudicate? Enforcing Trade Rules in the WTO*. Princeton, NJ: Princeton University Press, 2012.

Dawisha, Adeed. "The United States in the Middle East: The Gulf War and Its Aftermath." *Current History* 91, no. 561 (1992): 1–5.

Deutsch, Karl W. "Social Mobilization and Political Development." *American Political Science Review* 55 (1964): 634–47.

Diamond, Larry. "Toward Democratic Consolidation." In *The Global Resurgence of Democracy*, ed. Larry Diamond and Marc Plattner, 228–40. Baltimore: John Hopkins University Press, 1996.

Diamond, Larry, Juan Linz, and Seymour Martin Lipset. "What Makes for Democracy?" In *Politics in Developing Countries: Comparing Experiences with Democracy*, 2nd ed., ed. Larry Diamond, Juan Linz, and Seymour Martin Lipset, 1–66. Boulder, CO: Lynne Rienner, 1995.

Dominguez, Jorge. "U.S. Latin American Relations during the Cold War and Its Aftermath." Unpublished manuscript, Weatherhead Center for International Affairs, Harvard University, January 1999.

Donno, Daniela, and Bruce Russett. "Islam, Authoritarianism, and Female Empowerment: What Are the Linkages?" *World Politics* 56 (2004): 582–607.

Doyle, Michael W. *Empires*. Ithaca, NY: Cornell University Press, 1986.

Dris-Ait-Hamadouche, Louisa, and Yahia H. Zoubir, "The U.S.-Saudi Relationship and the Iraq War: The Dialectics of a Dependent Alliance," *Journal of Third World Studies* 24, no. 1 (2007): 109–35.

D'Souza, Dinesh. *What's So Great about America.* Washington, DC: Regnery, 2002.

Dubois, Francis. "Moroccan Elections Reveal Gulf between Regime and the Population," November 7, 2007. Accessed May 2008 at http://www.wsws.org/articles/2007/nov2007/moro-n07.shtml.

Dunne, Michele. "Getting Over the Fear of Arab Elections." *Daily Star* (Beirut), October 2, 2007.

Economist Intelligence Unit/Columbia Program on International Investment. *World Investment Prospects to 2011: Foreign Direct Investment and the Challenge of Political Risk.* London: Economist Intelligence Unit, 2007. Accessed December 2011 at http://graphics.eiu.com/upload/WIP_2007_WEB.pdf.

Eichengreen, Barry, and David Leblang. "Democracy and Globalization." Unpublished manuscript, Department of Political Science, University of Colorado–Boulder, 2007.

Ellingwood, Ken. "Abbas, Sharon Hope to Avoid Repeating Past." *Los Angeles Times*, February 5, 2005. Accessed April 2008 at http://articles.latimes.com/2005/feb/05/world/fg-summit5.

Embassy of the Hashemite Kingdom of Jordan. *U.S.-Jordan Relations.* Washington, DC: Embassy of the Hashemite Kingdom of Jordan. Accessed January 2012 at http://www.jordanembassyus.org/new/aboutjordan/uj1.shtml.

Esposito, John, and John Voll. *Islam and Democracy.* Oxford: Oxford University Press, 1996.

Evans, Peter. *Dependent Development: The Alliance of Multinational, State and Local Capital in Brazil.* Princeton, NJ: Princeton University Press, 1979.

Fandy, Mamoun. *Saudi Arabia and the Politics of Dissent.* New York: Palgrave Macmillan, 1999.

Fealy, Greg. "Islamic Radicalism in Indonesia: The Faltering Revival." *Southeast Asian Affairs* 2004 (2004): 104–21.

Federation of American Scientists, Arms Sales Monitoring Project. "U.S. Arms Clients Profiles—Kuwait," February 2002. Accessed March 2007 at http://www.fas.org/asmp/profiles/kuwait.htm.

Federspiel, Howard M. "Indonesia, Islam, and U.S. Policy." *Brown Journal of World Affairs* 9, no. 1 (2002): 107–14.

Fischbach, Michael. *State, Society, and Life in Jordan.* Leiden, Netherlands: Brill, 2000.

Fish, Steven. "Islam and Authoritarianism." *World Politics* 55 (2002): 4–37.

Frieden, Jeffry A. "Invested Interests: The Politics of National Economic Policies in a World of Global Finance." *International Organization* 45 (1991): 425–51.

Fuller, Graham E. *The Future of Political Islam.* New York: Palgrave Macmillan, 2003.

———. *Islamists in the Arab World: The Dance around Democracy.* Carnegie Paper no. 49. Washington, DC: Carnegie Endowment for International Peace, 2004.

Fukuyama, Francis. *The End of History and the Last Man.* New York: Free Press, 1992.

Gallup Organization. *The 2002 Gallup Poll of the Islamic World.* Princeton, NJ: Gallup Organization, 2002.

Gandhi, Jennifer. *Political Institutions under Dictatorship.* New York: Cambridge University Press, 2008.

Gandhi, Jennifer, and Ellen Lust-Okar. "Elections under Authoritarianism." *Annual Review of Political Science* 12 (2009): 403–22.

Gandhi, Jennifer, and Adam Przeworski. "Cooperation, Cooptation, and Rebellion under Dictatorship." *Economics and Politics* 18, no. 1 (2006): 1–26.

Gartzke, Erik. "The Capitalist Peace," *American Journal of Political Science* 51, no. 1 (2007): 166–91.

"Gaza Humanitarian Plight 'Disastrous,' U.N. Official Says," December 28, 2008. Accessed February 2009 at http://www.cnn.com/2008/WORLD/meast/12/28/gaza .humanitarian/.

Gause, F. Gregory III. "Can Democracy Stop Terrorism?" *Foreign Affairs*, September–October 2005. Accessed July 2007 at http://fullaccess.foreignaffairs.org/20050901 faessay84506/f-gregory-gause-iii/can-democracy-stop-terrorism.html?mode=print.

———. *Oil Monarchies: Domestic and Security Challenges in the Arab Gulf States.* New York: Council on Foreign Relations, 1994.

———. " 'Over the Horizon' to 'Into the Backyard': The Saudi-American Relationship and the Gulf War." In *The United States and the Middle East: A Historical Reassessment,* 4th ed., ed. David W. Lesch, 380–90. Boulder, CO: Westview, 2007.

Gerges, Fawaz. *America and Political Islam: Clash of Cultures or Clash of Interests?* Cambridge: Cambridge University Press, 1999.

Ghabra, Shafeeq N. "Balancing State and Society: The Islamic Movement in Kuwait." In *Revolutionaries and Reformers: Contemporary Islamist Movements in the Middle East,* ed. Barry Rubin, 105–24. Albany: State University of New York Press, 2003.

———. "Closing the Distance: Kuwait and the United States in the Persian Gulf." In *The Middle East and the United States: A Historical and Political Reassessment,* 4th ed., ed. David W. Lesch, 332–50. Boulder, CO: Westview, 2007.

Ghalioun, Berhan. "The Persistence of Arab Authoritarianism." *Journal of Democracy* 15, no. 4 (2004): 126–32.

El-Ghobashy, Mona. "Constitutionalist Contention in Contemporary Egypt." *American Behavioral Scientist* 51, no. 11 (2008): 1590–1610.

Gilpin, Robert. *U.S. Power and the Multinational Corporation.* New York: Basic Books, 1975.

Glennie, Alex, and David Mepham. *Reform in Morocco: The Role of Political Islamists.* London: Institute for Public Policy Research, 2007. Accessed December 2011 at http://www.idrc.ca/uploads/user-S/12115496221reform_in_morocco[1].pdf.

Gourevitch, Peter. *Politics in Hard Times: Comparative Responses to International Economic Crises.* Ithaca, NY: Cornell University Press, 1986.

———. "The Second Image Reversed." *International Organization* 32, no. 4 (1978): 881–912.

———. "Squaring the Circle: The Domestic Sources of International Cooperation." *International Organization* 50, no. 2 (1996): 349–73.

Gowa, Joanne. *Allies, Adversaries and International Trade.* Princeton, NJ: Princeton University Press, 1995.

Greene, Kenneth. *Why Dominant Parties Lose: Mexico's Democratization in Comparative Perspective.* New York: Cambridge University Press, 2007.

Greenwood, Scott. "Bad for Business? Entrepreneurs and Democracy in the Arab World." *Comparative Political Studies*, 41, (2008): 837–60. Accessed December 2011 at http://cps.sagepub.com/cgi/reprint/41/6/837.pdf.

———. "Jordan, the al-Aqsa Intifada and America's 'War on Terror' " *Middle East Policy* 10, no. 3 (2003): 90–111.

Grigoriadis, Ionnis, and Antnis Kamaras. "Foreign Direct Investment in Turkey: Historical Constraints and the AKP success Story." *Middle Eastern Studies* 44, no. 1 (2008): 53–68.

Guney, Aylin. "Anti-Americanism in Turkey: Past and Present," *Middle Eastern Studies* 44, no. 3 (2008): 471–87.

Haddad, Yvonne Yazbeck. "Islamist Perceptions of U.S. Policy in the Middle East." In *The Middle East and the United States: A Historical and Political Reassessment*, 4th ed., ed. David W. Lesch, 467–90. Boulder, CO: Westview, 2007.

Hafner-Burton, Emilie M. "Trading Human Rights: How Preferential Trade Arrangements Influence Government Repression." *International Organization* 59, no. 3 (2005): 593–629.

al-Hamdi, Mohaned, and Mohamed Mostafa. "Political Islam, Clash of Civilization, U.S. Dominance and Arab Support of Attacks on American: A Test of a Hierarchical Model." *Studies in Conflict and Terrorism* 30, no. 8 (2007): 723–36.

Hamzawy, Amr. *The Saudi Labyrinth: Evaluating the Current Political Opening*. Carnegie Paper no. 68. Washington, DC: Carnegie Endowment for International Peace, 2006.

Harter, Pascale. "Powell's Final Push for Arab Reform," BBC News, December 10, 2004. Accessed March 2009 at http://news.bbc.co.uk/2/hi/africa/4085081.stm.

Hass, Amira. "Missing the Government of Thieves," November 11, 2006. Accessed November 2008 at http://www.haaretz.com/hasen/spages/767581.html.

Hawthorne, Amy. "Can the United States Promote Democracy in the Middle East?" *Current History*, January 2003, 21–26.

Herb, Michael, *All in the Family: Absolutisms, Revolution, and Democratic Prospects in the Middle Eastern Monarchies*. SUNY Series in Middle Eastern Studies. Albany: State University of New York Press, 1999.

Heston, Alan, Robert Summers, and Bettina Aten. Penn World Table Version 6.2, Center for International Comparisons of Production, Income and Prices at the University of Pennsylvania, 2006.

Hinnebusch, Raymond. "The Iraq War and International Relations: Implications for Small States." *Cambridge Review of International Affairs* 19, no. 3 (2006): 451–63.

Hirschman, Albert. *The Passions and the Interests: Political Arguments for Capitalism before Its Triumph*. Princeton, NJ: Princeton University Press, 1977.

Hiscox, Michael. "Class versus Industry Cleavages: Inter-industry Factor Mobility and the Politics of Trade." *International Organization* 55 (2001): 1–46.

Hofmann, Steven. "Islam and Democracy: Micro-level Indications of Compatibility." *Comparative Political Studies* 37, no. 6 (2004): 652–76.

Holmes, Stephen. "The Secret History of Self-Interest." In *Beyond Self-Interest*, ed. Jane Mansbridge, 267–86. Chicago: University of Chicago Press, 1990.

Howe, Marvine. *Morocco: The Islamist Awakening and Other Challenges*. New York: Oxford University Press, 2005.

Huddy, Leonie, and Nadia Khatib. "American Patriotism, National Identity, and Political Involvement." *American Journal of Political Science* 51, no. 1 (2007): 63–77.

Hudson, Michael. *The Search for Legitimacy*. New Haven, CT: Yale University Press, 1979.

Huntington, Samuel. *Political Order in Changing Societies*. New Haven, CT: Yale University Press, 1968.

——. *The Third Wave: Democratization in the Late Twentieth Century*. Norman: University of Oklahoma Press, 1993.

Hurwitz, Jon, and Mark Peffley. "Public Perceptions of Race and Crime: The Role of Racial Stereotypes." *American Journal of Political Science* 41, no. 2 (1997): 375–401.

Ikenberry, John. *Reasons of State: Oil Politics and the Capacities of American Government.* Ithaca, NY: Cornell University Press, 1988.

Inglehart, Ronald. *Culture Shift in Advanced Industrial Society.* Princeton, NJ: Princeton University Press, 1989.

———. *Modernization and Post-modernization.* Princeton, NJ: Princeton University Press, 1997.

Inglehart, Ronald, and Pippa Norris. *Sacred and Secular-rational: Religion and Politics Worldwide.* New York: Cambridge University Press, 2004.

Inglehart, Ronald F., and Christian Welzel. "Political Culture and Democracy: Analyzing Cross-Level Linkages." *Comparative Politics* 36, no. 1 (2003): 61–79.

International Crisis Group. *Can Saudi Arabia Reform Itself?* Middle East Report 28 (Cairo and Brussels: International Crisis Group, 2004). Accessed December 2011 at http://www.pbs.org/wgbh/pages/frontline/shows/saud/themes/canreform.pdf.

———. *The Challenge of Political Reform: Jordanian Democratization and Regional Instability.* Middle East Briefing no. 10. Amman, Jordan, and Brussels: International Crisis Group, 2003. Accessed January 2012 at http://www.crisisgroup.org/~/media/Files/Middle%20East%20North%20Africa/Iran%20Gulf/Jordan/B010%20The%20Challenge%20of%20Political%20Reform%20Jordanian%20Democratisation%20and%20Regional%20Instability.pdf.

———. *Jordan's 9/11: Dealing with Jihadi Islamism.* Middle East Report no. 47. Amman, Jordan, and Brussels: International Crisis Group, 2005. Accessed December 2011 at http://www.crisisgroup.org/en/regions/middle-east-north-africa/iraq-iran-gulf/jordan/047-jordans-9-11-dealing-with-jihadi-islamism.aspx.

———. *Saudi Arabia Backgrounder: Who Are the Islamists?* Middle East Report no. 31. Amman, Jordan, and Brussels: International Crisis Group, 2004. Accessed December 2011 at http://www.pbs.org/wgbh/pages/frontline/shows/saud/themes/backgrounder.pdf.

International Monetary Fund, Statistics Department. *International Financial Statistics Yearbook.* Washington, DC: International Monetary Fund, 1996. Accessed December 2011 at http://www.imf.org/external/pubs/cat/longres.cfm?sk=410.

Jabhat al-'Amal al-Islāmī [Islamic Action Front]. *Al-Barnāmij al-Intikhābī l-murashahīn Hizb Jabhat al-'Amal al-Islāmī (1993–1997)* [The Electoral Platform of the Islamic Action Front (1993–1997)]. Amman, Jordan: Jabhat al-'Amal al-Islāmī, 1993.

———. *Al-Barnāmij al-Intikhābī l-murashahīn Hizb Jabhat al-'Amal al-Islāmī (2003–2007)* [The Electoral Platform of the Islamic Action Front (2003–2007)]. Amman, Jordan: Jabhat al-'Amal al-Islāmī, 2003.

———. *Al-Barnāmij al-Intikhābī l-murashahīn Hizb Jabhat al-'Amal al-Islāmī (2007–2011)* [The Electoral Platform of the Islamic Action Front (2007–2011)]. Amman, Jordan: Jabhat al-'Amal al-Islāmī, 2007.

Jamal, Amaney. *Barriers to Democracy: The Other Side of Social Capital in Palestine and the Arab World.* Princeton, NJ: Princeton University Press, 2007.

———. "Security Vulnerabilities in Jordan." Paper presented at the Annual Meeting of the American Political Science Association, September 2007.

Jamal, Amaney, and Vickie Langohr. "Gender Status as an Impediment to Democracy in the Muslim World: What Does Gender Explain and Not Explain?" Unpublished manuscript, 2008.

Jamal, Amaney, and Irfan Nooruddin. "The Democratic Utility of Trust: A Cross-National Analysis." *Journal of Politics* 72, no. 1 (2010): 45-59.

———. "United States Military Intervention and the Status of Women in the Arab World." Unpublished manuscript, 2011.

Kanet, Roger E. "The Superpower Quest for Empire: The Cold War and Soviet Support for Wars of National Liberation." *Cold War History* 6, no. 3 (2006): 331-52.

Kanovsky, Eliyahu. *The Middle East Economies: The Impact of Domestic and International Politics.* Mideast Security and Policy Studies no. 31. Ramat Gan, Israel: Begin-Sadat Center for Strategic Studies, Bar-Ilan University, 1997. Accessed December 2011 at http://www.biu.ac.il/SOC/besa/publications/kanov/index.html.

Katzenstein, Peter J. *Small States in World Markets: Industrial Policy in Europe.* Ithaca, NY: Cornell University Press, 1985.

Katzenstein, Peter J., ed. *Between Power and Plenty: Foreign Economic Policies of Advanced Industrial States.* Madison: University of Wisconsin Press, 1977.

Katzenstein, Peter J., and Robert O. Keohane, eds. *Anti-Americanisms in World Politics.* Ithaca, NY: Cornell University Press, 2007.

Katzmann, Kenneth. *Kuwaiti Security, Reform, and U.S. Policy.* Congressional Research Service Report RS21513, July 5, 2006. Accessed December 2011 at http://digital .library.unt.edu/gov docs/crs/permalink/meta-crs-9890:1.

Kaufmann, Daniel, Aart Kraay, and Massimo Mastruzzi. "Governance Matters III: Governance Indicators for 1996, 1998, 2000, and 2002." *World Bank Economic Review* 18, no. 2 (2004): 253-87. doi:10.1093/wber/lhh041.

al-Kazi, Lubna. Personal interview with the author, winter 2006.

Kéchichian, Joseph A. "Democratization in Gulf Monarchies: A New Challenge to the GCC." *Middle East Policy Council Journal* 11, no. 4 (2004): 37-58. Accessed June 2008 at http://www.mepc.org/journal_vol11/0412_kechichian.asp.

Keck, Margaret E., and Kathryn Sikkink. 1998. *Activists beyond Borders.* Ithaca, NY: Cornell University Press.

Kedourie, Elie. *Democracy and Arab Political Culture.* Washington DC: Washington Institute for Near East Policy, 1992.

Kelley, Judith. "International Actors on the Domestic Scene: Membership Conditionality and Socialization by International Institutions." *International Organization* 59, no. 3 (2004): 425-57.

Keohane, Robert O., and Helen V. Milner. *Internationalizaton and Domestic Politics.* Cambridge: Cambridge University Press, 2005.

Keohane, Robert O., and Joseph S. Nye Jr., eds. 1972. *Transnational Relations and World Politics.* Cambridge, MA: Harvard University Press.

Keyman, E. Fuat, and Berrin Koyuncu. "Globalization, Alternative Modernities, and the Political Economy of Turkey." *Review of International Political Economy* 12 (2005): 105-28.

Khalaf, Roula. "Morocco Sees the Rise of an 'Acceptable' Islamist Party." *Financial Times of Morocco,* May 23, 2006. Accessed May 2008 at http://www.iri.org/news archive/2006/2006-05-23-News-FinancialTimes-Morocco.asp.

Khalidi, Rashid. *Resurrecting Empire.* Boston: Beacon, 2004.

Kitschelt, Herbert, and Steven I. Wilkinson. *Patrons, Clients, and Policies: Patterns of Democratic Accountability and Political Competition.* New York: Cambridge University Press, 2007.

Kohli, Atul. "Democracy Amid Economic Orthodoxy: Trends in Developing Countries." *Third World Quarterly* 14, no. 4 (1993): 671–89.

———. *State-Directed Development*. Cambridge: Cambridge University Press, 2004.

Kornbluth, Danishai. "Jordan and the Anti-Normalization Campaign, 1994–2001." *Terrorism and Political Violence* 14, no. 3 (2002): 80–108.

Krämer, Gudrun. "Good Counsel to the King: The Islamist Opposition in Saudi Arabia, Jordan, and Morocco." In *Middle East Monarchies: The Challenge of Modernity*, ed. Joseph Kostiner, 257–87. Boulder, CO: Lynne Rienner, 2000.

Krasner, Stephen. *Sovereignty*. Princeton, NJ: Princeton University Press, 1989.

Krauthammer, Charles. "To Hell with Sympathy." *Time*, November 17, 2003.

Kristianasen, Wendy. "Palestine: Hamas Besieged." *Le Monde*, June 3, 2006. Accessed November 2008 at http://mondediplo.com/2006/06/03hamas.

———. "We Don't Want to Box Islam In," *Le Monde*, June 4, 2002. Accessed January 2008 at http://mondediplo.com/2002/06/04kuwait.

Kubba, Laith. "Faith and Modernity." *Journal of Democracy* 14, no. 2 (2003): 45–49.

Kull, Steven. "Can Obama Restore the U.S. Image in the Middle East?" *Harvard International Review*, December 19, 2008. Accessed December 2011 at http://hir.harvard.edu/can-obama-restore-the-us-image-in-the-middle-east.

Kull, Steven, Evan Lewis, Ebrahim Mohensi, Clay Ramsay, and Stephen Weber. *Public Opinion in the Islamic World on Terrorism, al Qaeda, and U.S. Policies*. Washington DC: Program on International Policy Attitudes, 2009. Accessed March 2009 at http://www.worldpublicopinion.org/pipa/pdf/feb09/STARTII_Feb09_rpt.pdf.

Kull, Steven, Clay Ramsay, Stephan Weber, and Evan Lewis, *America's Global Image in the Obama Era*. Washington, DC: Program on International Policy Attitudes, 2009. Accessed January 2012 at http://www.worldpublicopinion.org/pipa/pdf/jul09/WPO_USObama_Jul09_packet.pdf.

Kull, Steven, Clay Ramsay, Stephen Weber, Evan Lewis, Ebrahim Mohseni, Mary Speck, Melanie Ciolek, and Melinda Brouwer. *Muslim Public Opinion on U.S. Policy, Attacks on Civilians, and al Qaeda*. Washington DC: Program on International Policy Attitudes, 2007. Accessed December 2011 at http://www.worldpublicopinion.org/pipa/pdf/apr07/START_Apr07_rpt.pdf.

Lake, David A. "Escape from the State of Nature: Authority and Hierarchy in World Politics." *International Security* 32, no. 1 (2007): 47–79.

Lake, Eli. "Muslim Brotherhood Seeks End to Israel Treaty." *Washington Times*, February 3, 2011.

Lerner, Daniel. *The Passing of Traditional Society*. Glencoe, IL: Free Press, 1958.

Lesch, David W., ed. *The Middle East and the United States: A Historical and Political Reassessment*. 4th ed. Boulder, CO: Westview, 2007.

Leveau, Remy. "The Moroccan Monarchy: A Political System in Quest of a New Equilibrium," in *Middle East Monarchies: The Challenge of Modernity*, ed. Joseph Kositner, 117–30. Boulder, CO: Lynne Rienner, 2000.

Levitsky, Steven, and Lucien Way. "International Linkage and Democratization." *Journal of Democracy* 16, no. 3 (2005): 20–34.

Lewis, Bernard. "Free at Last? The Arab World in the Twenty-First Century." *Foreign Affairs*, March–April 2009. Accessed May 2009 at http://www.foreignaffairs.com/articles/64830/bernard-lewis/free-at-last.

Lindblom, Charles. *Politics and Markets: The World's Political Economic Systems*. New York: Basic Books, 1977.

Linz, Juan. *Totalitarian and Authoritarian Regimes*. Boulder, CO: Lynne Rienner, 2000.

Lipset, Seymour Martin. *Political Man: The Social Bases of Politics*. Garden City, NY: Doubleday, 1960.

———. "Some Social Requisites of Democracy." *American Political Science Review* 53, no. 1. (1959): 69–105.

Litvak, Meir, and Maddy Weitzman. "Islamism and the State in North Africa." In *Revolutionaries and Reformers: Contemporary Islamist Movements in the Middle East*, ed. Barry Rubin, 69–90. Albany: State University of New York Press, 2003.

Livingstone, Grace. *America's Backyard: The United States and Latin America from the Monroe Doctrine to the War on Terror*. New York: Zed, 2009.

López-Córdova, J. Ernesto, and Christopher M. Meissner. "The Globalization of Trade and Democracy." Unpublished manuscript, 2005.

Lucas, Russell E. *Institutions and the Politics of Survival in Jordan: Domestic Responses to External Challenges, 1988–2001*. SUNY Series in Middle Eastern Studies. Albany: State University of New York Press, 2006.

———. "Jordan: The Death of Normalization with Israel." *Middle East Journal* 58, no. 1 (2004): 93–111.

Luciani, Giacomo. "Allocation vs. Production States: A Theoretical Framework." In *The Arab State*, ed. Giacomo Luciani, 65–84. Berkeley and Los Angeles: University of California Press, 1990.

Lust-Okar, Ellen. "Elections under Authoritarianism: Preliminary Lessons from Jordan." *Democratization* 13, no. 3 (2006): 456–71.

———. *Structuring Conflict in the Arab World: Incumbents, Opponents, and Institutions*. New York: Cambridge University Press, 2007.

Lust-Okar, Ellen, and Amaney Jamal. "Rulers and Rules: Reassessing the Influence of Regime Type on Electoral Law Formation." *Comparative Political Studies* 35, no. 3 (2002): 337–66.

Lust-Okar, Ellen, and Saloua Zerhouni, eds. *Political Participation in the Middle East*. Boulder, CO: Lynne Rienner, 2008.

Lynch, Marc. "Anti-Americanism in the Arab World." In *Anti-Americanism in World Politics*, ed. Peter J. Katzenstein and Robert O. Keohane, 196–224. Ithaca, NY: Cornell University Press, 2007.

———. "Jordan's King Abdallah in Washington," *Middle East Report Online*, May 8, 2002. Accessed December 2011 at http://www.merip.org/mero/mero050802.

———. "No Jordan Option." *Middle East Report Online*, June 21, 2004. Accessed December 2011 at http://www.merip.org/mero/mero062404.html on.

———. *State Interests and Public Spheres: The International Politics of Jordan's Identity*. New York: Columbia University Press, 1999.

MacFarquhar, Neil. "Anti-U.S. Feeling Leaves Arab Reformers Isolated." *New York Times*, August 9, 2006.

Magaloni, Beatriz. *Voting for Autocracy: Hegemonic Party Survival and its Demise in Mexico*. New York: Cambridge University Press, 2006.

Mansfield, Edward D., Helen V. Milner, and Peter B. Rosendorff. "Why Democracies Cooperate More: Electoral Control and International Trade Agreements." *International Organization* 56, no. 3 (2002): 477–513.

Mares, Isabela. "Firms and the Welfare State: When, Why and How Does Social Policy Matter to Employers?" In *Varieties of Capitalism*, ed. Peter Hall and David Soskice, 184–212. Oxford: Oxford University Press, 2001.

Margalit, Yotam. "Commerce and Oppositions: The Political Responses of Globalization's Losers." Unpublished manuscript, 2010.

Martin, Patrick. "Adding Fuel to the Mid-East Fire: U.S. Unveils Huge Arms Package." August 1, 2007. Accessed December 2011 at http://www.wsws.org/articles/2007/aug2007/mide-a01.shtml.

Masmoudi, Radwan. "The Silenced Majority." *Journal of Democracy* 14, no. 2 (2003): 40–44.

Masoud, Tarek. "The Road to and from Liberation Square." *Journal of Democracy* 22, no. 3 (2011): 20–34.

——. "Why Islam Wins: Electoral Ecologies and Economics of Political Islam in Contemporary Egypt." PhD dissertation, Yale University, 2008.

Mayda, Anna Maria, and Dani Rodrik. "Why Are Some People (and Countries) More Protectionist Than Others?" *European Economic Review* 49, no. 6 (2005): 1393–1430.

McGirk, Tim. "How to Deal with Hamas." *Time*, June 21, 2007. Accessed August 2007 at http://www.time.com/time/magazine/article/0,9171,1635824,00.html.

McPherson, Alan. *Yankee No! Anti-Americanism in U.S.–Latin American Relations*. Cambridge, MA: Harvard University Press, 2003.

Mecham, Quinn. "Islamist Mobilization in Turkey: A Study in Vernacular Politics." *Political Science Quarterly* 118, no. 3 (2003): 526–27.

Mekay, Emad. "Palestinian Economy Tumbles under Sanctions." *IPS News*, March 26, 2007. Accessed November 2008 at http://ipsnews.net/news.asp?idnews=37093.

Meyer, Katherine, Helen Rizzo, and Ali Yousef. "Changed Political Attitudes in the Middle East: The Case of Kuwait." *International Sociology* 22, no. 3 (2007): 289–324.

Milner, Helen V. *Interests, Institutions, and Information*. Princeton, NJ: Princeton University Press, 1987.

Milner, Helen V., and Keiko Kubota. "Why the Move to Free Trade? Democracy and Trade Policy in the Developing Countries." *International Organization* 59 (2005): 107–43.

Milner, Helen V., and Bumba Mukherjee. "Democratization and Economic Globalization." *Annual Review of Political Science* 12 (1999): 163–81.

Mitchell, Timothy. "McJihad: Islam in the U.S. Global Order." *Social Text* 20, no. 4 (2002): 1–18. Accessed September 2008 at http://muse.jhu.edu/journals/social_text/v020/20.4mitchell.html.

Moaddel, Mansoor. "Religion and the State: The Singularity of the Jordanian Religious Experience." *International Journal of Politics, Culture, and Society* 15, no. 4 (2004): 527–68.

Moehler, Devra, and Nicolas Van de Walle. "Pro and Anti-Americanism in Sub-Saharan Africa." Paper presented at the Workshop on Anti-Americanism, Princeton University, May 2011.

Moore, Barrington. *Social Origins of Dictatorship and Democracy: Lord and Peasant in the Making of the Modern World*. Boston, MA: Beacon, 1993.

Moore, Pete. "The Newest Jordan: Free Trade, Peace and an Ace in the Hole." *Middle East Report Online*, June 26, 2003. Accessed May 2007 at http://www.merip.org/mero/mero062603.html.

Moore, Pete W. *Doing Business in the Middle East: Politics and Economic Crisis in Jordan and Kuwait.* Cambridge Middle East Studies. Cambridge: Cambridge University Press, 2004.

"Morocco's AK Party Won't Copy Turkey's." *World Bulletin*, September 7, 2007. Accessed May 2008 at http://www.worldbulletin.net/news_detail.php?id=10284.

Morro, Paul. *U.S. Foreign Aid to Palestinians.* Congressional Research Service Report, October 9, 2007. Accessed December 2011 at http://www.usembassy.it/pdf/other/RS22370.pdf.

Mufti, Malik. "A King's Art: Dynastic Ambition and State Interest in Hussein's Jordan." *Diplomacy and Statecraft* 13, no. 3 (2002): 1–22.

al-Mughni, Haya. *Women in Kuwait: The Politics of Gender.* London: Saqi, 2000.

al-Mughni, Haya, and Mary Ann Tetreault. "Modernization and Its Discontents: State and Gender in Kuwait." *Middle East Journal* 49, no. 3 (1995): 403–17.

Murdock, Heather. "Muslim Brotherhood Sees Opportunity in Jordan." *Washington Times*, March 1, 2011.

Musallam, Ali Musallam. *The Iraqi Invasion of Kuwait: Saddam Hussein, His State and International Politics.* New York: British Academic Press, 1996.

Muslim Brotherhood. *Muslim Brotherhood, Hamas and Iran.* March 14, 2011. Accessed at http://www.ikhwanweb.com/article.php?id=28217.

"Muslims Positive about Globalization, Trade." 2008. Accessed January 2012 at http://worldpublicopinion.org/pipa/articles/btglobalizationtradera/528.php?lb=brme&pnt=528&nid=&id=.

al-Najjar, Ghanim. "Challenges of Security Sector Governance in Kuwait." Unpublished manuscript, 2004.

———. "Kuwait: Struggle over Parliament." *Arab Reform Bulletin* 4, no. 5 (2008). Accessed December 2011 at http://www.carnegieendowment.org/files/najjar_june06.pdf.

Nasr, Vali. *Forces of Fortune: The Rise of the New Muslim Middle Class and What It Will Mean for Our World.* New York: Free Press, 2009.

National Agenda Steering Committee, *The National Agenda: The Jordan We Strive for 2006–2015.* Amman, Jordan: National Agenda Steering Committee, n.d. Accessed January 2012 at http://www.nationalagenda.jo/Portals/0/EnglishBooklet.pdf.

National Bank of Kuwait. "Doing Business in Kuwait." Accessed January 2012 at http://www.kuwait.nbk.com/investmentandbrokerage/researchandreports/doingbusinessinkuwait_en_gb.aspx.

Niblock, Tim, ed. *State, Society and Economy in Saudi Arabia.* London: Croom Helm/Centre for Arab Gulf Studies, 1982.

Norton, Augustus Richard. "The Puzzle of Political Reform in the Middle East." In *International Relations of the Middle East*, ed. Louise Fawcett, 131–50. Oxford: Oxford University Press, 2005.

Nye, Joseph. *Soft Power: The Means to Success in World Politics.* New York: Public Affairs Press, 2004.

O'Donnell, Guillermo, and Phillipe Schmitter. *Transitions from Authoritarian Rule*, vol. 4, *Tentative Conclusions about Uncertain Democracies.* Baltimore: Johns Hopkins University Press, 1986.

Okruhlik, Gwenn. "Making Conversation Permissible: Islamism and Reform in Saudi Arabia." In *Islamic Activism: A Social Movement Theory Approach*, ed. Quintan Wiktorowicz, 250–69. Bloomington: Indiana University Press, 2004.

——. "Rentier Wealth, Unruly Law, and the Rise of the Opposition: The Political Economy of Rentier States." *Comparative Politics* 31, no. 3 (1999): 295–315.

O'Reilly, Marc J., and Wesley B. Renfro. "Evolving Empire: America's 'Emirates' Strategy in the Persian Gulf." *International Studies Perspectives* 8, no. 2 (2007): 137–51.

Organisation for Economic Co-operation and Development. *SourceOECD International Development Statistics*; accessed December 2011 at http://lysander.sourceoecd .org/vl=92415576/cl=13/nw=1/rpsv/ij/oecdstats/16081110/v77n1/s4/p1.

Ottaway, Marina. *Democracy Promotion in the Middle East: Restoring Credibility.* Policy Brief no. 60. Washington, DC: Carnegie Endowment for International Peace, 2008. Accessed December 2011 at http://www.carnegieendowment.org/files/pb_ 60_ottaway_final.pdf.

——. *Iran, the United States, and the Gulf: The Elusive Regional Policy.* Washington, DC: Carnegie Endowment for International Peace, 2009.

——. *Promoting Democracy in the Middle East and the Problem of U.S. Credibility.* Carnegie Paper no. 35. Washington, DC: Carnegie Endowment for International Peace, 2003.

Ottaway, Marina, and Thomas Carothers. *Greater Middle East Initiative: Off to a False Start.* Carnegie Policy Brief no. 29. Washington, DC: Carnegie Endowment for International Peace, 2004.

——. "Middle East Democracy (Think Again)." *Foreign Policy*, November–December 2004, 22–24, 26–28.

"Palestine Monitor Fact Sheet: Poverty." *Palestine Monitor*, December 18, 2008. Accessed December 2011 at http://www.palestinemonitor.org/spip/spip.php?article13.

Pastor, Robert. *Exiting the Whirlpool: U.S. Foreign Policy toward Latin America and the Caribbean*, 2nd ed. Boulder, CO: Westview, 2001.

Pelham, Nicolas. "Jordan's Balancing Act." *Middle East Report Online*, February 22, 2011. Accessed October 2011 at http://www.merip.org/mero/mero022211.

Perry, Glenn. "The Arab Democracy Deficit: The Case of Egypt." *Arab Studies Quarterly* 26, no. 2 (2004): 91–107.

Perthes, Volker, ed. *Arab Elites: Negotiating the Politics of Change.* Boulder, CO: Lynne Rienner, 2004.

Pevehouse, Jon. *Democracy from Above: Regional Organization and Democratization.* Cambridge: Cambridge University Press, 2005.

——. "Democracy from the Outside In? International Organizations and Democratizations." *International Organization* 56, no. 3 (2002): 515–49.

Pew Global Attitudes Project. *America's Image in the World.* Washington, DC: Pew Research Center, 2007. Accessed May 2009 at http://pewglobal.org/commentary/ display.php?AnalysisID=1019.

——. *Global Unease with Major World Powers: Rising Environmental Concern in 47-Nation Survey.* Washington, DC: Pew Research Center, 2007. Accessed August 2008 at http://pewglobal.org/reports/display.php?ReportID=256.

——. *U.S. Wins No Friends, End of Treaty with Israel Sought.* Washington, DC: Pew Research Center, 2011.

——. *World Publics Welcome Global Trade but Not Immigration: 47-Nation Pew Global Attitudes Survey.* Washington, DC: Pew Research Center, 2007. Accessed December 2011 at http://pewglobal.org/reports/pdf/258.pdf.

Pfeifer, Karen. "How Tunisia, Morocco, Jordan and Even Egypt Became IMF 'Success Stories' in the 1990s." *Middle East Report* 210 (1999): 23–27.

Pfeifer, Karen. "Kuwait's Economic Quandary." *Middle East Report Online* 223 (2002). Accessed January 2012 at http://www.merip.org/mer/mer223/kuwaits-economic -quandary.

Phillips, James. *The U.S. Stake in Post-Hussein Jordan.* Executive Memorandum no. 574. Washington, DC: Heritage Foundation, 1999. Accessed December 2011 at http:// www.heritage.org/Research/MiddleEast/EM574.cfm.

Pipes, Daniel. *In the Path of God: Islam and Political Power.* New York: Basic Books, 1983.

Plattner, Marc. "The Democratic Moment." In *The Global Resurgence of Democracy,* ed. Larry Diamond and Marc Plattner, 36–48. Baltimore: John Hopkins University Press, 1996.

"Poll Finds Widespread International Opposition to U.S. Bases in Persian Gulf." December 15, 2008. Accessed March 2009 at http://www.worldpublicopinion.org/ pipa/articles/international_security_bt/579.php?lb=btvoc&pnt=579&nid=&id=.

Posusney, Marsha Pripstein. "Multi-party Elections in the Arab World: Institutional Engineering and Oppositional Strategies." *Studies in Comparative International Development* 36, no. 4 (2002): 34–62.

PSR Survey Research Unit. Poll no. 19. Ramallah, West Bank: Palestinian Center for Policy and Survey Research, 2006. Accessed July 2008 at http://www.pcpsr.org/ survey/polls/2006/p19etables1.html.

Putnam, Robert. 1998. "Diplomacy and Domestic Politics: The Logic of Two-Level Games." *International Organization* 43, no. 2 (1998): 427–60.

———. *Making Democracy Work: Civic Traditions in Modern Italy.* Princeton, NJ: Princeton University Press, 1993.

Pye, Lucien. "Political Science and the Crisis of Authoritarianism." *American Political Science Review* 84 (1990): 3–19.

Quandt, William. *Saudi Arabia in the 1980s: Foreign Policy, Security, and Oil.* Washington, DC: Brookings Institution, 1981.

al-Rasheed, Madawi. *Contesting the State: Islamic Voices from a New Generation.* Cambridge: Cambridge University Press, 2007.

———. *A History of Saudi Arabia.* Cambridge: Cambridge University Press, 2002.

Ravid, Barak, and Yoav Stern. "Israel: Erdogan's Davos Behavior May Ruin Turkey's EU Chances." February 2, 2009. Accessed March 2009 at http://www.haaretz. com/hasen/spages/1060369.html.

Remez, Michael, and Richard Wike. "Global Media Celebrate Obama Victory—But Cautious Too: A Changed View of American Democracy." Washington DC: Pew Research Center Publications, 2008. Accessed March 2009 at http://pewresearch .org/pubs/1033/global-media-celebrate-obama-victory-but-cautious-too.

Remmer, Karen. "Elections and Economics in Contemporary Latin America." In *Poststabilization Politics in Latin America: Competition, Transition, Collapse,* ed. Carol Wise and Riordan Roett, 31–55. Washington, DC: Brookings Institution Press, 2001.

"Report: Radical Kuwaiti Imams Drowned Out in Pro-American Protests by Local Worshippers." *Al-Siyasa,* July 9, 2005.

Revel, Jean-Francois. *Anti-Americanism.* San Francisco: Encounter, 2003.

Richards, Alan, and John Waterbury. *A Political Economy of the Middle East.* Boulder, CO: Westview, 2007.

Richards, David, Ronald Gelleny, and David Sacko. "Money with a Mean Streak? Foreign Economic Penetration and Government Respect for Human Rights in Developing Countries." *International Studies Quarterly* 45, no. 2 (2001): 219–39.

Roberts, Kenneth. "The Mobilization of Opposition to Economic Liberalization." *Annual Review of Political Science* 11 (2008), 327–49.

Robins, Philip. *A History of Jordan*. Cambridge: Cambridge University Press, 2004.

Robinson, Glenn E. "Defensive Democratization in Jordon." *International Journal of Middle East Studies* 30, no. 3 (1998): 387–410.

Rogoff, Kenneth, Ethan O. Ilzetzki, and Carmen M. Reinhart. "Exchange Rate Arrangements into the 21st Century: Will the Anchor Currency Hold?" *Quarterly Journal of Economics* 119, no. 1 (2004): 1–48.

Rogowski, Ronald. *Commerce and Coalitions: How Trade Affects Domestic Political Alignments*. Princeton, NJ: Princeton University Press, 1989.

——. "Trade and the Variety of Democratic Institutions." *International Organization* 41, no. 2 (1987): 203–23.

Rosefsky, Carrie. *Mobilizing Islam*. New York: Columbia University Press, 2002.

Ross, Michael. "Does Oil Hinder Democracy?" *World Politics* 53, no. 3 (2001): 325–61.

Rotberg, Robert. *When States Fail: Causes and Consequences*. Princeton, NJ: Princeton University Press, 2003.

Rubin, Michael. "Iran against the Arabs." *Wall Street Journal*, July 19, 2006. Accessed September 2008 at http://proquest.umi.com/pqdweb?did=1079537721&sid=1&Fmt=3&clientId=17210&RQT=309&VName=PQD.

Rubinstein, Alvin. "Soviet Client-States: From Empire to Commonwealth." *Orbis* 35, no. 1 (1991): 69–78.

Rudra, Nita. "Globalization and the Strengthening of Democracy in the Developing World." *American Journal of Political Science* 49 (2005): 704–30.

Rueschemeyer, Dietrich, Evelyn Huber Stephens, and John Stephens. *Capitalist Development and Democracy*. Chicago: University of Chicago Press, 1992.

Ryan, Curtis R. *Jordan: Islamic Action Front Presses for Role in Governing*. Washington, DC: Carnegie Endowment for International Peace, 2006. Accessed June 2007 at http://www.carnegieendowment.org/arb/?fa=show&article=20919.

——. "Jordan and the Rise and Fall of the Arab Cooperation Council." *Middle East Journal* 52, no. 3 (1998): 386–401.

——. "Jordan First: Jordan's Inter-Arab Relations and Foreign Policy under King Abdullah II." *Arab Studies Quarterly* 26, no. 3 (2004): 43–62.

——. "Reform Retreats Amid Jordan's Political Storm." *Middle East Report Online*, June 10, 2005. Accessed December 2011 at http://www.merip.org/mero/mero061005.

Safi, Omid, ed. *Progressive Muslims: On Justice, Gender and Pluralism*. Oxford: Oneworld, 2003.

Saikal, Amin. "The United States and Persian Gulf Security." *World Policy Journal* 9, no. 3 (1992): 515–32.

Salabi, Kamal. *The Modern History of Jordan*. London: I. B. Tauris, 1995.

Salah, Mohamad Ahmad. *"Athr al-Maʿawanāt al-Māliyya al-Britāniyya fi al-Wadʿa al-Māli fi Sharq al-Urdun 1921–1925"* [Effect of British Aid on the Financial Situation of Trans-Jordan 1921–1925]. *Arab Journal for the Humanities* 80 (2002): n.p..

Satloff, Robert. *From Abdullah to Husssein: Jordan in Transition*. New York: Oxford University Press, 1994.

Sayigh, Yezid. *"Fixing Broken Windows": Security Sector Reform in Palestine, Lebanon, and Yemen*. Washington, DC: Carnegie Endowment for International Peace, 2009.

Schatz, Robert T., and Ervin Staub. "Manifestations of Blind and Constructive Patriotism: Personality Correlates and Individual-Group Relations." In *Patriotism:*

In the Lives of Individuals and Nations, ed. Daniel Bar-Tal and Ervin Staub, 229–45. Chicago: Nelson-Hall, 1997.

Schatz, Robert T., Ervin Staub, and Howard Lavine. "On the Varieties of National Attachment: Blind versus Constructive Patriotism." *Political Psychology* 20, no. 1 (1999): 151–74.

Scheve, Kenneth F., and Matthew J. Slaughter. "Economic Insecurity and the Globalization of Production." *American Journal of Political Science* 48, no. 4 (2004): 662–74.

——. "What Determines Individual Trade-policy Preferences?" *Journal of International Economics* 54, no. 2 (2001): 267–92.

Schmitz, Hans Peter. "Transnational Perspectives on Democratization." *International Studies Review* 6, no. 3 (2002): 403–26.

Schwedler, Jillian. "Democratization, Inclusion and the Moderation of Islamist Parties." *Development* 50, no. 1 (2007): 56–61.

——. "Don't Blink: Jordan's Democratic Opening and Closing." *Middle East Report Online*, July 3, 2002. Accessed December 2011 at http://www.merip.org/mero/mero070302.

——. *Faith in Moderation: Islamist Parties in Jordan and Yemen*. New York: Cambridge University Press, 2007.

——. "Occupied Maan: Jordan's Closed Military Zone." *Middle East Report Online*, December 3, 2002. Accessed May 2007 at http://www.merip.org/mero/mero120302.

Scott, James C. *Domination and the Arts of Resistance: Hidden Transcripts*. New Haven, CT: Yale University Press, 1992.

——. *Weapons of the Weak: Everyday Forms of Peasant Resistance*. New Haven, CT: Yale University Press, 1987.

Sharabi, Hisham. *A Theory of Distorted Change in America*. Oxford: Oxford University Press, 1992.

Sharp, Jeremy M. *Jordan: Background and U.S. Relations*. Congressional Research Service Report, October 17, 2008. Accessed December 2011 at http://ftp.fas.org/sgp/crs/mideast/RL33546.pdf.

——. *U.S. Democracy Promotion Policy in the Middle East: The Islamist Dilemma*. Congressional Research Service Report, July 15, 2006. Accessed November 2007 at http://www.history.navy.mil/library/online/democ%20in%20middle%20east.htm.

Shehata, Samer. "Inside an Egyptian Parliamentary Campaign." In *Political Participation in the Middle East*, ed. Ellen Lust-Okar and Saloua Zerhouni, 95–120. Boulder, CO: Lynne Rienner, 2008.

Sherbiny, Naiem A. "America: A View from Egypt." *Social Research* 72, no. 4 (2005): 1–26.

Sick, Gary. "The United States in the Gulf: From Twin Pillars to Dual Containment." In *The Middle East and the United States: A Historical and Political Reassessment*, 4th ed., ed. David W. Lesch, 315–31. Boulder, CO: Westview, 2007.

Silverman, Erica. "Fatah's U.S. Savior." *Al-Ahram Weekly*, October 19–25, 2006. Accessed November 2008 at http://weekly.ahram.org.eg/2006/817/re52.htm.

Singerman, Diane. *Avenues of Participation: Family, Politics, and Networks in Urban Quarters of Cairo*. Princeton, NJ: Princeton University Press, 1996.

Skocpol, Theda. *States and Social Revolutions: A Comparative Analysis of France, Russia, and China*. Cambridge: Cambridge University Press, 1979.

Smith, Benjamin. *Hard Times in the Land of Plenty: Oil Politics in Iran and Indonesia*. Ithaca, NY: Cornell University Press, 2007.

Somer, Murat. "Moderate Islam and Secularist Opposition in Turkey: Implications for the World, Muslims and Secular Democracy." *Third World Quarterly* 28, no. 7 (2007): 1271–89.

Spinner-Halev, Jeff, and Elizabeth Theiss-Morse. "National Identity and Self-Esteem." *Perspectives on Politics* 1, no. 3 (2003): 515–32.

Spruyt, Hendrik. *Ending Empire: Contested Sovereignty and Territorial Partition.* Ithaca, NY: Cornell University Press, 2005.

Stallings, Barbara. *Economic Dependency in Africa and Latin America.* Stanford, CA: Stanford University Press, 1972.

Stallings, Barbara, and Robert Kaufman, eds. *Debt and Democracy in Latin America.* Boulder, CO: Westview, 1989.

Stenner, Karen. *The Authoritarian Dynamic.* New York: Cambridge University Press, 2005.

Stokes, Susan C. "Public Opinion of Market Reforms: A Framework." In *Public Support for Market Reforms in New Democracies,* ed. Susan C. Stokes, 1–27. Cambridge: Cambridge University Press, 2001.

Stork, Joe. "The Gulf War and the Arab World." *World Policy Journal* 8, no. 2 (1991): 365–74.

Sullivan, John L., Amy Fried, and Mary G. Dietz. "Patriotism, Politics, and the Presidential Election of 1988." *American Journal of Political Science* 36, no. 16 (1992): 200–234.

Susser, Asher. "The Jordanian Monarchy: The Hashemite Success Story." In *Middle East Monarchies,* ed. Joseph Kositner, 87–116. Boulder, CO: Lynne Rienner, 2000.

Takeyh, Ray. "Uncle Sam in the Arab Street." *National Interest,* April 1, 2004. Accessed May 2007 at http://www.allbusiness.com/government/3584148-1.html.

Telhami, Shibley. "Arab Public Opinion on the United States and Iraq: Postwar Prospects for Changing Prewar Views." *Brookings Review* 21 (2003): 24–27.

———. "The Role of the Persian Gulf." In *The Contemporary Middle East,* ed. Karl Yambert, 171–84. Boulder, CO: Westview, 2006.

———. *The Stakes: America in the Middle East.* Boulder, CO: Westview, 2002.

Telhami, Shibley, Fiona Hill, et al. "Does Saudi Oil Still Matter?" *Foreign Affairs,* November–December 2002. Accessed January 2012 at http://www.foreignaffairs.com/articles/58444/shibley-telhami-fiona-hill-et-al/does-saudi-arabia-still-matter-differing-perspectives-on-the-kin.

Telhami, Shibley, with Zogby International. *2008 Arab Public Opinion Poll.* Washington, DC: Brookings Institution, 2008. Accessed January 2012 at http://www.brookings.edu/~/media/Files/events/2008/0414_middle_east/0414_middle_east_telhami.pdf.

"10 Questions for John Bolton," *Time,* November 26, 2007. Accessed December 2007 at http://www.time.com/time/magazine/article/0,9171,1684527,00.html.

Terrill, W. Andrew. *Kuwaiti National Security and the US-Kuwaiti Strategic Relationship after Saddam.* Carlisle, PA: Strategic Studies Institute, 2007). Accessed December 2011 at http://www.strategicstudiesinstitute.army.mil/pdffiles/pub788.pdf.

Tessler, Mark. "Assessing the Influence of Religious Predispositions on Citizen Orientations Related to Governance and Democracy: Findings from Survey Research in Three Dissimilar Arab Societies." *Taiwan Journal of Democracy* 1, no. 2 (2005): 139–49.

———. "Islam and Democracy in the Middle East: The Impact of Religious Orientations on Attitudes toward Democracy in Four Arab Countries." *Comparative Politics* 34 (2002): 337–54.

Tetreault, Mary Ann. "Autonomy, Necessity and the Small State: Ruling Kuwait in the Twentieth Century." *International Organization* 31, no. 4 (1991): 565–91.

——. "Designer Democracy in Kuwait." *Current History* 96, no. 606 (1997): 36–39.

——. "A Global Affairs Commentary: Frankenstein's Lament in Kuwait." November 29, 2001. Accessed December 2011 at http://www.fpif.org/pdf/gac/0111kuwait.pdf.

——. "Kuwait's Annus Mirabilis." *Middle East Report Online*, September 7, 2006. Accessed December 2011 at http://www.merip.org/mero/mero090706.

——. "Kuwait's Parliament Considers Women's Political Rights, Again." *Middle East Report Online*, September 2, 2004. Accessed December 2011 at http://www.merip.org/mero/mero090204.

——. "Kuwait's Unhappy Anniversary." *Middle East Policy* 7, no. 3 (2000): 67–77. Accessed December 2011 at http://www.thefreelibrary.com/KUWAIT'S+UNHAPPY+ANNIVERSARY.-a063564934.

——. *Stories of Democracy: Politics and Society in Contemporary Kuwait.* New York: Columbia University Press, 2000.

——. "Three Emirs and a Tale of Two Transitions." *Middle East Report Online*, February 10, 2006. Accessed December 2011 at http://www.merip.org/mero/mero021006.

——. "Women's Rights and the Meaning of Citizenship in Kuwait." *Middle East Report Online*, February 10, 2005. Accessed December 2011 at http://www.merip.org/mero/mero021005.

Timmerman, Kenneth R. "The Gulf Monarchies: Kutwait's Real Elections." *Middle East Quarterly* 3, no. 4 (1996): 53–58. Accessed December 2011 at http://www.meforum.org/article/425.

Tolchin, Martin. "After the War: Congress Withholds $55 Million in Aid to Jordan." *New York Times*, March 23, 1991.

Toqueville, Alexis de. *Democracy in America.* Edited by Richard D. Heffner. New York: New American Library, 1956.

"Transcript: Confirmation Hearing of Condoleezza Rice." *New York Times*, January 18, 2005. Accessed January 2009 at http://www.nytimes.com/2005/01/18/politics/18TEXT-RICE.html?pagewanted=print.

Tristam, Pierre. "Jordan: Country Profile," About.com, 2008. Accessed December 2011 at http://middleeast.about.com/od/jordan/p/me071114.htm.

Tsai, Kellee S. "Capitalists without a Class: Political Diversity among Private Entrepreneurs." *Comparative Political Studies* 38, no. 9 (2005): 1130–58.

Tucker, Robert W. *The Inequality of Nations.* New York: Basic Books, 1977.

UNHCR. *World Report 2008: Morocco/Western Sahara.* Geneva: UNHCR, 2008. Accessed June 2008 at http://www.unhcr.org/refworld/publisher,HRW,,MAR,47a87c0cc,0.html.

U.S. Central Intelligence Agency. *The World Factbook: Kuwait.* Accessed January 2012 at https://www.cia.gov/library/publications/the-world-factbook/geos/ku.html.

U.S. Commercial Service. *Doing Business in Jordan: 2010 Country Commercial Guide for U.S. Companies.* Washington, DC: U.S. Department of Commerce, 2010. Accessed January 2012 at http://export.gov/jordan/doingbusinessinjordan/eg_jo_038317.asp.

"U.S. Rewards Morocco for Terror Aid." BBC News, June 4, 2004. Accessed December 2011 at http://news.bbc.co.uk/2/hi/africa/3776413.stm.

U.S. State Department. *Middle East and North Africa Overview*, 2005. Accessed December 2011 at http://www.state.gov/documents/organization/65472.pdf.

Vandewalle, Dirk. *Libya Since Independence: Oil and State-Building*. Ithaca, NY: Cornell University Press, 1998.

Walker, Joshua. "Re-examining the U.S.-Turkish Alliance." *Washington Quarterly* 31, no. 1 (2007–8): 93–109.

Washington Institute for Near East Policy. *Hamas Weapons in Jordan: Implications for Islamists on the East Bank*. PolicyWatch no. 1098. Washington, DC: Washington Institute for Near East Policy, 2006.

Weber, Max. *From Max Weber: Essays in Sociology*. Edited by Hans Heinrich Gerth; translated by Hans Heinrich Gerth and C. Wright Mills. London: Routledge, 2009.

Wedeen, Lisa. "Beyond the Crusades: Why Huntington and Bin Laden Are Wrong." *Middle East Policy*, 10, no. 2 (2003): 54–61.

——. *Peripheral Visions: Publics, Power, and Performance in Yemen*. Chicago: University of Chicago Press, 2008.

Welzel, Christian, and Ronald F. Inglehart. "The Role of Ordinary People in Democratization." *Journal of Democracy* 19, no. 1 (2008): 126–40.

Weyland, Kurt. "Neoliberalism in Latin America: A Mixed Record." *Latin American Politics and Society* 46, no. 1(2004): 135–57.

——. *The Politics of Market Reform in Fragile Democracies*. Princeton, NJ: Princeton University Press, 2004.

Wike, Richard. "Indonesia: The Obama Effect." Washington, DC: Pew Research Center, 2010. Accessed January 2012 at http://pewresearch.org/pubs/1529/indonesian-views-america-image-president-obama-trip.

Wiktorowicz, Quintan. "Civil Society as Social Control: State Power in Jordan." *Comparative Politics* 33, no. 1 (2000): 43–61.

——. "Islamists, the State and Cooperation." *Arab Studies Quarterly* 21, no. 4 (1999): 4–12.

Williams, David. "Political Islam's Opportunity in Jordan." *Washington Post*, April 13, 2006. Accessed December 2011 at http://www.washingtonpost.com/wp-dyn/content/article/2006/04/12/AR2006041201897_pf.html.

World Values Survey 2002. Accessed January 2012 at http://www.wvsevsdb.com/wvs/WVSData.jsp.

Yacoubian, Mona. *Engaging Islamists and Promoting Democracy: A Preliminary Assessment*. United States Institute of Peace Special Report no. 190. Washington, DC: United States Institute of Peace, 2007. Accessed December 2007 at http://www.usip.org/pubs/specialreports/sr190.html.

Yetiv, Steve. "Kuwait's Democratic Experiment in Its Broader International Context." *Middle East Journal* 56, no. 2 (2002): 257–62.

Youngs, Richard. *Energy: A Reinforced Obstacle to Democracy?* Madrid: Fundación para las Relaciones Internacionales y el Diálogo Exterior, 2008. Accessed February 2009 at http://www.fride.org/publication/467/energy-a-reinforced-obstacle-to-democracy.

Zogby International. *Arabs: What They Believe and What They Value Most*. Ithaca, NY: Zogby International, 2002. Accessed January 2012 at http://aai.3cdn.net/7b568f016f6ad3a301_b5m6be8kr.pdf.

Zuhur, Sherifa. *Saudi Arabia: Islamic Threat, Political Reform, and the Global War on Terror*. Carlisle, PA: Strategic Studies Institute 2005. Accessed August 2008 at http://www.strategicstudiesinstitute.army.mil/pubs/display.cfm?pubID=598.

INDEX

‘Abbas, Mahmoud, 192–93, 196, 199
‘Abd al-Jaber, Salah, 93
Abdul Aziz, King of Saudi Arabia, 44
Abdullah, King of Saudi Arabia, 207, 212–14
Abdullah I, King of Jordan, 41–44, 68
Abdullah II, King of Jordan, 49–52; marriage of, 135; national cohesion campaigns of, 80–83, 110n; public opinion of, 104–5, 112, 121; relationship with the Islamist groups of, 76, 83–84; role in U.S.-Iraq War of, 92
Abulhassan, Mohammad Abbas, 100
Abu-‘Odeh, ‘Adnan, 77
Abu Rumman, Hussein, 71
Abu-Sukkar, ‘Ali, 77
Acemoglu, Darren, 13, 14, 16
al-‘Adl wal Ihsān (JCO) (Morocco): anti-Americanism of, 179; domestic polices of, 181; public support of, 178, 180; U.S. engagement with, 190
Adserà, Alícia, 14
Afghanistan: Soviet invasion of, 56, 204, 214; Taliban rule of, 242; U.S. war in, 24, 206, 207, 218, 241, 243
Afoaku, Osita, 19n53
Africa, 1, 2t, 4
Ahmedinejad, Mahmoud, 24
al-‘Akayilah, Abdallah, 75
AKP. See Justice and Development Party
Algeria, 191n1, 210, 228–29
Allende, Salvador, 238
Almond, Gabriel, 7
Anderson, Betty, 53–54
Andoni, Lamis, 85
Anglo-Transjordan Agreement, 42–43
Anglo-Transjordan Treaty, 43–44
anti-Americanism, 2, 4, 29–36, 214–22; in Egypt, 66, 229; exogenous origins of, 154–55; in Indonesia, 34, 218; in Jordan, 48, 63–64, 66–69, 74, 76, 78, 88–89; in

Latin America, 238–39; in Lebanon, 66; in Morocco, 33, 34, 66, 177, 178–80, 182n29; multilayered analysis of, 147–69; in Palestine, 33, 34, 195; pro-democracy links with, 143–44; reduction of, 233–38; role of education in, 214–15; in Saudi Arabia, 33, 34, 66, 101, 203, 206–8, 229. See also Islamist movements; public opinion
anti-patron interests, 18–19
al Aqsa Intifada. See Second Intifada
Arab Barometer survey, 6n9, 34, 35, 142, 153, 155–56, 169–73
Arabic language transliteration, xv
Arab-Israeli conflict, 152–53; impact on public opinion of, 236–37; War of 1956 in, 45; War of 1973 in, 56
‘Arabiyat, ‘Abd al-Latif, 78
Arab League, 1n1, 55–56, 60
Arab Legion, 41–45
Arab Peace Initiative of 2002, 207
Arab Spring, xi–xii, 2, 6, 234; in Bahrain, 146n, 222–23; in Egypt, xi, 18–19, 48, 222, 224; Islamist participation in, 224–26; in nonclient states, 223–24; Palestinian cause in, 224, 226
Arab world: civil liberties in, 1, 2t; client relationships of, 19–21; definition of, 1n1; democracy in, 1, 2t; economic development in, 6–7; modernization indicators for, 1, 3f; nonclient regimes in, 223–24; political culture in, 6–9; secular regimes of, 229–31; U.S. entrenchment in, 2–3, 26–29
Arafat, Yasir, 59, 94, 228; centralized authority of, 192, 199, 200; in Clinton's Camp David negotiations, 241–42; death of, 194
al-Assaf, Nimer, 78
Asseburg, Muriel, 228

authoritarian regimes, 8–9, 219–20; acceptance of the status quo in, 21, 35–36, 174–75, 189, 221–23; in nonclient states, 223–24; public opinion on, 35, 80–83
al-'Awadi, Nabil, 92
al-'Awda, Salam, 209
Azerbaijan, 219, 240

Badi, Muhammad, 226
Baghdad Pact of 1955, 45
Bahrain: government repression in, 146n, 222–23; Islamist movement in, 70, 87n72
Baker, James, 233
al-Bakhit, Marouf, 70n22
al-Banna, Hasan, 64
Barsalou, Judy, 70n24
Basha, Glubb, 45
Basic Law of Government (Saudi Arabia), 212
al-Bayoumi, Rashad, 226
Beblawi, Hazem, 11
Bellin, Eva, 10, 16
Benjelloun, Omar, 177
Benkirane, Abdallah, 177–78
Bilgin, Haste Dikici, 217–18
Bin Arshaid, Zaki, 78
Bin Laden, Osama, 211
Boix, Carles, 13, 146n
Bolton, John, 221
Bookmiller, Robert, 53
bottom-up models of democracy, 6–12, 215, 222, 242–44; political culture of, 6–9; political economy of, 6–7, 9–11
Brand, Laurie A., 42, 76, 83n60, 134–35
British patronage, 65n3; of Kuwait, 54–55; of Transjordan, 41–46, 67
Brown, Nathan, 101, 192, 200, 202
Bush, George H. W., 58
Bush, George W., 78; Greater Middle East Initiative of, 179, 234; Jordan policies of, 53, 67, 110; Kuwait policies of, 59; military aid policies of, 240–41; Morocco policies of, 176; Palestine policies of, 199; statement on Arab values by, 227. See also U.S.-Iraq War (2003–)

Cammett, Melanie Claire, 10
Camp David Accords of 1979, 67, 226, 235
Carter, Jimmy/Carter Doctrine, 56–57
Casablanca attacks of 2003, 177, 181–82
causal logics of citizens, 104–6, 143, 166, 222

Central Asia, 240
Chamorro, Violeta Barrios de, 239
Chaudhry, Kiren Aziz, 7n12, 10
Chile, 238
China, 240
civil liberties, 1, 2t, 14, 230, 243
civil society, 7–8
The Clash of Civilizations (Huntington), 8
Cleveland, William L., 41–44
client states/clientelism, 19–21; acceptance of the status quo in, 21, 35–36, 174–75, 189, 221–23; altered state-society relations in, 19–21, 35, 104–6, 143, 166, 221–23; definition of, 19n53; emergence of, 35, 38–62; feedback mechanisms in, 20–21; in Latin America, 238–39; patrons as barriers to democracy in, 18, 64, 219–20; public opinion of, 104–6, 113–16, 129–33, 143; societal agency in, 21; vs. nonclient states, 223–24. See also geostrategic patron-client relationships
Clinton, Bill, 86, 241–42
Cold War, 6, 38–39, 44–47, 176–77
Committee for Defense of Legitimate Rights (Saudi Arabia), 211, 212
Committee for Protecting the Country (Jordan), 73n33
Committee for Resisting Submission and Normalization (Jordan), 73–74
Correlates of War data, 24, 26t
Cox, Henry, 42–43
Cronbach Alpha Scores, 169–70
Crystal, Jill, 10
Cultural Social Society, 89, 90
currency exchange rates, 26n67

Dahl, Robert, 13
Daoudi, Lahcen, 190
al-Dashti, Rola, 96, 97
Davis, Christina, 15n40
Dayton, Keith, 201
democracy promotion, 5
democratic inferiority policy, 227–31
democratic reformers, 5n
"The Democratic Utility of Trust" (Jamal and Nooruddin), 166–69
democratization, 1–3; bottom-up approaches to, 6–12, 215, 222, 242–44; global increases in, 1, 2f; impact of international organization membership on, 31n81, 93; Jordan's fears of, 33, 35–36,

63–64, 71–72, 76, 79–86, 108–13; Kuwait support for, 33, 35–36, 64, 92–100; public attitudes toward, 33, 35–36, 63–64; Saudi Arabia's fears of, 135; secular contexts for, 229–31; U.S. strategic approaches to, 3–7, 18–19, 214–20, 227–31, 239–44

Deutsch, Karl, 10

Diamond, Larry, 7

differentiated markets, 17–18

domestic democratization debates, xi–xii, 12–19, 222–23; class contexts of, 16–18; on income inequality, 13–14; individual cost-benefit analysis in, 13; mobile assets in, 13–14; on patron-client relationships, 18–19; on trade openness, 14–15. *See also* anti-Americanism; public opinion

Donno, Daniela, 9

Doyle, Michael W., 28n72

Dris-Ait-Hamadouche, Louisa, 205

East Asia, 2t

Eastern Europe, 1, 2t

al-Ebrahim, Yousef, 99–100

economic development, 6–7, 13–15, 23–24, 40, 232–33; foreign direct investment in, 7, 17, 207, 232–33; link with democracy of, 6n8, 10n23; growth of middle class in, 10–11, 16. *See also* political economy

economic sanctions: in Iraq, 135, 241; in Palestine, 191, 196–201, 215–16, 226–27

Egypt, xi–xii, 19, 219; anti-Americanism in, 66, 229; and Camp David Accords of 1979, 67, 226, 235; demonstrations of 2011 in, xi, 18–19, 48, 222, 224; economic development in, 32–33, 106; economic inequality in, 14; future democratization in, 224–27; military governance in, 19, 225; Muslim Brotherhood of, 19, 68, 219, 224–27; nonalignment under Nasser of, 45; relationship with Israel of, 148; secularism in, 215, 229; survey data from, 219n89; treaty with Israel of, 192, 225–26; U.S. development aid to, 24n61; War of 1956 of, 45

Eisenhower Doctrine, 38–39, 40, 45–46

El-Barradei, Mohamed, 224

El-'Erian, Essam, 226

empire (definition), 28n72

England. *See* British patronage

Erdogan, Recep Tayyip, 190

Euro Mediterranean Partnership, 180

European Neighbourhood Policy, 180, 240

European Union (EU), 175; energy needs of, 240; Palestine policies of, 191, 199

exchange rates, 26n67

Fahd, King of Saudi Arabia, 204

Faruq, King of Egypt, 44

Fatah Party (Palestine), 94, 191–93, 230–31; decline of, 193–98; electoral support of, 194f; international support of, 199–200, 215–16; recognition of Israel by, 231; unity government with Hamas of, 236–37

Fayyad, Salam, 201

al-fiqh al-zamzami, 177

First Gulf War, 25, 33, 49, 57–59, 92, 235; Iraqi occupation of Kuwait in, 40, 57–58, 90; Islamist responses to, 209–11; Jordan's support of Iraq in, 47, 48, 51–52; Moroccan activism against, 178; Saudis' role in, 25, 58–59, 204–5, 209–12; U.S. role in, 55

First Reform Act/Britain, 16

Fischbach, Michael, 53

Fish, Steven, 9

Foley, Laurence, 79

foreign direct investment (FDI), 7, 17, 207, 232–33

France, 65n3, 175

Freedom and Justice Party (Egypt), 226

Freedom House measures, 1, 2t, 86, 95

Fukuyama, Francis, 8

Fuller, Graham, 65, 234

Gallup Poll, 66, 237

Gause, Gregory, 59, 69n20, 87, 211, 229

Gaza, 194–97, 201, 228, 235

George-Picot, François, 65n3

geostrategic patron-client relationships, xi–xii, 2–7, 13–14; altered state-society relations in, 19–21, 35, 104–6, 143, 166, 221–23; Arab dependence in, 26–29, 35, 38–40; barriers to democracy in, 18–19, 64, 219–20, 239–44; containment goals in, 4–5, 38–39, 40; Lake's security/economy hierarchy of, 24–26, 38n1, 39, 210; regime clientelism in, 19n53; U.S. dominance in, 23–29, 38–40; winners and losers in, 30, 35, 40, 107–8, 223t. *See also* client states/clientelism

Gerges, Fawaz, 228, 242

Gerschenkron, Alexander, 30

Ghabra, Shafeeq, 55, 59, 89–90

globalization, 14–15, 40; public opinion of, 32–33, 67, 85; U.S. support for, 88; winners and losers in, 30, 35, 40, 107–8, 223*t*

Gourevitch, Peter, 30

Greater Middle East Initiative, 86–87, 234

Gulf Cooperation Council, 93

Gulf War of 1990–91. *See* First Gulf War

Haas, Amira, 198

HADAS. *See* Islamic Constitutional Movement (ICM)

Haddad, Yvonne Yazbeck, 65

H-5 Airbase, 53

Hamas (Palestine), 3, 29, 231; control of Gaza of, 194–97, 201; electoral victory of, 85, 94, 191, 193–202; IAF support for, 72, 77, 78, 85, 88, 93–94; international sanctions of, 191, 196–201, 215–16, 226–27; public opinion of, 116; repression in Jordan of, 76; unity government with Fatah of, 236–37

al-Hamed, Abdullah, 212

Hamzawy, Amr, 215

Haniyya, Ism'ail, 196

Harakat al-Islām wal Tajdīd, 178

Hashemite monarchy. *See* Jordan

Hassan II, King of Morocco, 176–77

al-Hawali, Safar, 209–10

hegemony (definition), 28n72

Heritage (al-Turāth) organization (Kuwait), 89

Higher Committee for the Coordination of National Opposition Parties (HCCNOP) (Jordan), 73n33

Hizb al-Istiqlal (Independence Party) (Jordan), 43

Hizb al-Umma (Kuwait), 90

Hizbullah (Lebanon), 232; IAF support for, 72, 77, 94; Kuwait's condemnation of, 94; public opinion of, 116; Syrian support for, 192

Hizb ul-Tahrīr (Jordan), 79

Howe, Marvine, 176, 178

Huddy, Leoni, 160–61

Human Development Index scores, 1n2, 3*f*, 36*t*

human rights, 1, 2*t*, 14, 230, 243

Huntington, Samuel, 3, 7, 8, 10

Hurricane Katrina, 59

Hussein, King of Jordan, 44–49; Civil War of 1970 of, 46, 67n11; in First Gulf War, 47, 48, 51–52; relationships with the Islamists of, 68–69, 76; treaty with Israel of, 48–52, 68–69, 73–78. *See also* Jordan

Hussein, Saddam, 23, 58–59; Arafat's support for, 59, 94; international sanctions against, 135, 241; Muslim Brotherhood support for, 92. *See also* Iraq

IAF. *See* Islamic Action Front (IAF)

ibn Baz, Shaykh Abd al-Aziz, 210

ICM. *See* Islamic Constitutional Movement (ICM)

Ikhwan Rebellion of 1929, 208

income inequality, 13

individual interviews, 34–35, 103, 137–41

individualism, 7n12

Indonesia: anti-Americanism in, 34, 218; Islamist movements in, 33, 216–17; on Palestinian-Israeli conflict, 218; tsunami of 2004 in, 218

Indyk, Martin, 86

informal empire, 27–28

Inglehart, Ronald, 7; on economic development and democracy, 6n8; "overt support for democracy" scale of, 156–57, 169–70

internal negotiations. *See* domestic democratization debates

International Crisis Group, 209, 211

International Monetary Fund (IMF), 49

international political economy (IPE), 14–15

Iran, 223, 231–32; anti-Saudi rhetoric in, 204; Islamic Revolution in, 38, 40, 46, 56–57, 204; in Nixon's Twin Pillar Policy, 40; U.S. containment strategy for, 4–5, 38–39, 226–27

Iran-Iraq War, 40, 46, 203–4

Iraq: attitudes on Kuwait in, 54–55; Cold War relationship with the U.S. of, 45; international sanctions on, 135, 241; occupation of Kuwait by, 40, 57–58, 90, 92, 241; secularism in, 215, 230; trade with Jordan of, 46n38; U.S. containment strategy for, 38–39. *See also* First Gulf War; U.S.-Iraq War (2003-)

Islam: compatibility with authoritarianism of, 8–9; compatibility with democracy of, 8n18; mosque activity in, 68, 70–71, 92, 93; Shari'a doctrines of, 72, 79, 101, 129–34, 243; status of women in, 9, 208, 209, 230

Islamic Action Front (IAF) (Jordan), 33, 35, 215; anti-Americanism of, 63–64, 66–69, 74, 76, 78, 88–89, 102, 153; anti-globalization in, 67, 85; anti-Israeli policies of, 72–78, 93–94; associational networks of, 69–73; blacklist of, 77; Committee for Resisting Submission and Normalization of, 73–74; domestic agenda of, 91; parliamentary seats of, 72, 75–76, 87n72; political influence of, 83–86; public opinion of, 66, 70, 85n68, 116–17, 121; regime's response to, 79–86

Islamic Constitutional Movement (ICM) (Kuwait), 33, 35; coalition partners of, 91; democratization support of, 92–94, 98–102; domestic agenda of, 90–92; gender segregation policies of, 91; parliamentary seats of, 91–92; pro-Americanism of, 63–64, 89–92, 100–101, 162, 243; regional policies of, 92–94; women's suffrage debates of, 95, 97

Islamic Defenders Front (Indonesia), 216

Islamic Justice and Development Party (Turkey), 190

Islamic National Alliance (Kuwait), 90

Islamic Party for Justice and Development (PJD) (Morocco). See Parti de la Justice et du Développement (PJD)

Islamic Popular Alliance (Kuwait), 90

Islamic Salvation Front (Algeria), 228

Islamist Islah (Yemen), 70, 87n72

Islamist movements, 2, 63–66, 230–31; anti-Americanism in, 5, 28–29, 39–40, 63–69, 101–2, 215, 228, 242; anti-globalization in, 32, 67, 85; Arab Spring roles of, 224–26; in civil society, 69–73; as democratic reformers, 5n; electoral successes of, 68–69, 72, 75–76, 85, 87n72, 91–92, 94, 182, 191, 193–202, 228; fears of success within, 229; Iran's Islamic Revolution, 38, 40, 46, 56–57, 204; moderation of, 215, 228–31; in Morocco, 174–75, 177–78; mosque activity in, 68, 70–71, 92, 93; as nationalist movements, 243–44; Palestinian cause of, 65, 67–69, 178–79, 210; public opinion of, 69–70,

86n70, 105, 106, 108, 116–28; radical jihadism in, 203, 209–12, 214, 218, 240; U.S. policies toward, 4–5, 86–89. See also Islamic Action Front (IAF); Islamic Constitutional Movement (ICM); Muslim Brotherhood

Israel: Arab boycotts of, 55–56, 60; Camp David Accords of, 67, 226, 235; confiscation of Arab lands by, 76; Gaza policies of, 194–97, 201, 235; invasions of Lebanon by, 46, 94, 180, 235; Islamist responses to, 65, 67–69, 178–79, 209–10; occupation of the West Bank by, 235; Oslo Agreement of, 76; Road Map for Peace of, 191; treaty with Egypt of, 192, 225–26; treaty with Jordan of, 48–52, 68–69, 72–78, 192; U.S. support for, 4–5, 38, 45, 65–66. See also Arab-Israeli conflict; Hamas (Palestine)

al-Jaber, Shaykh Sabah al-Ahmad, 97

Jamal, Amaney, 21n, 142, 166–69

JCO. See al-'Adl wal Ihsān (JCO)

Jordan, 2–3, 21–23, 28–29, 34, 216; anti-Americanism in, 29, 33, 34f, 35, 48, 63–64, 66–69, 78–79, 153; anti-globalization in, 32, 67, 85; barriers to democracy in, 64; Civil War of 1970 in, 46, 67n11; democracy scores of, 22n55, 86; economic reforms in, 7n10, 31–33, 49–52, 80–83; economic status of, 14, 36t, 46–48, 67; electoral reforms in, 69; emergence of regime clientelism in, 35, 38–54; fear of democracy and deliberalization in, 33, 35–36, 63–64, 71–72, 76, 79–86, 108–13, 142–43; honor killings in, 230; Islamist movements in, 33, 67–69, 79; national cohesion campaigns in, 80–83, 110n; Palestinian-Jordanian relations in, 46n38, 49, 54, 66, 67, 73, 75, 82–83, 134–35; political opposition in, 22, 73n33, 74, 75–76, 83–86, 87n72; press freedoms in, 22; role in U.S. wars of, 50–53, 84–85, 92, 228; state-society relations in, 35; treaty with Israel of, 48–52, 68–69, 72–78, 192; tribal population of, 82, 83; U.S. development aid in, 24n61, 46, 47n40, 50–51, 52t, 110; U.S. military aid in, 50–51, 52t, 53. See also Islamic Action Front (IAF)

Jordan First campaign, 79–80, 81, 82, 110n

Jordan's public opinion: anti-Americanism in, 143–44, 153–55, 161–62; of authoritarianism, 144–47, 156–66; of democracy/liberalization, 116–21, 143–46, 161–62, 163; economic status factors in, 107–8, 128–29, 134–35; of economic ties to the West, 106; education factors in, 163–65; fear factors in, 161–62; of free trade, 149–51; of Islamist opposition movements, 105, 106, 108, 116–21, 143–44, 153–55, 161–62; of Israel, 73, 152–53; of Jordan's client status, 104–6, 129–32; of the monarchy, 104–5, 106–13; multilayered analysis of, 147–69; patriotism and loyalty factors in, 162; political access factors in, 162; pro-Americanism in, 165–66; religiosity factors in, 163; of Shari'a, 128–32, 135–36; of stability and security, 108–13, 136, 137, 144–47; of U.S. policies, 105, 149, 151–53, 157

Justice and Charity Organization (JCO) (Morocco). See al-'Adl wal Ihsān (JCO)

Justice and Development Party (AKP) (Turkey), 217–18, 243

Karzai, Hamid, 219
Kaufmann, Daniel, 22n55
Kazakhstan, 240
al-Kazi, Lubna, 96
Keohane, Robert O., 15n40
Khatib, Nadia, 160–61
King Abdullah II Center for Special Operations Training, 53
Kiran, Abdallah, 229
Kohli, Atul, 15
Kraay, Aart, 22n55
Krasner, Stephen, 23
Kubota, Keiko, 150
Kuwait, 2–3, 21–23, 28–29, 34, 216; barriers to democracy in, 64; democracy scores of, 22n55, 95; economic reforms in, 60–61, 93, 99–100; emergence of regime clientelism in, 35, 38–41, 54–62; gender segregation in, 91; Iraqi occupation of, 40, 57–58, 90, 92, 241; Islamist movements in, 87n72, 89–93; oil production of, 54–55, 57, 61, 135, 146n; Palestinian workers in, 49; pan-Arabism in, 55–56, 59–60, 89, 92; political opposition in, 100–102; pro-Americanism in, 29, 33, 34f, 35, 63–64, 89–92; redistricting/

desertization reforms in, 22, 89–90, 95n96, 98–100; rentier status of, 21, 34, 61, 146; state-society relations in, 35; succession crisis in, 22, 97–98; tribal population of, 89–90, 91, 96, 98; U.S. presence in, 58–60, 92, 93, 238; women's suffrage in, 22, 95–97. See also First Gulf War; Islamic Constitutional Movement (ICM)

Kuwait's public opinion: anti-Americanism in, 153–55; of authoritarianism, 144–47, 156–66; of democracy/liberalization, 33, 35–36, 64, 92–100, 121–28, 135, 143–46, 163, 165–66; of economic reforms, 32–33, 149–51; economic status factors in, 162; of economic ties to the West, 106; education factors in, 162; fear factors in, 162; of Islamist movements, 106, 122–28, 153–55; of Israel, 152–53; of Kuwait's client relationship, 104–6, 113–16, 133; of the monarchy, 113–16; multilayered analysis of, 147–69; pro-Americanism in, 143–44, 165–66; religiosity factors in, 162, 163; of Shari'a, 133–34; of stability and security, 144–47; of U.S. policies, 101, 105–6, 121–22, 149, 151–53, 157

Kyrgystan, 219, 240

Lake, David, 23; on informal empire, 27–28; security/economy hierarchy of, 24–29, 38n1, 39, 210
Laskar Jihad (Indonesia), 216
Latin America, 1, 2t, 4, 238–39
Law of Consultative Council (Saudi Arabia), 212
Law of the Provinces (Saudi Arabia), 212
Lebanon: anti-Americanism in, 66; Civil War of the 1970s in, 46; economic ties to the West of, 106; Hizbullah in, 72, 77, 94; Israeli invasions of, 46, 94, 180, 235
Lerner, Daniel, 10
liberal values, 230
Libya, 223–24
Lindblom, Charles, 10
Linz, Juan, 7
Lipset, Seymour Martin, 7, 10
Lust-Okar, Ellen, 83n60
Lynch, Marc, 76

Madrid bombings of 2004, 181–82
managed elections, 199–200

Margalit, Yotam, 30
Marxism/Marx, 16–17
Mastruzzi, Massimo, 22n55
Mayda, Anna Maria, 150
Meccan mosque seizure of 1979, 208
middle classes (bourgeoisie), 10–11, 16
Middle East Free Trade Agreements, 88
military intervention, 23, 25, 27–28f
Millennium Challenge Corporation, 176
Milner, Helen, 15, 30, 150
Misha'al, Khalid, 72, 76
"Missing the Government of Thieves"
    (Haas), 198
Moaddel, Mansoor, 42
mobile assets, 13–14
modernization models, 158
Moehler, Devra, 239n46
Mohammed VI, King of Morocco, 176, 177,
    180–82
Moore, Barrington, 10, 16
Moore, Pete, 10, 88
Morocco, 3, 29, 174–90, 215, 216; anti-
    Americanism in, 33, 34, 66, 177–80,
    182n29; client relationships of, 175–77,
    189–90; counterterrorism assistance
    of, 176–77; economic ties to the West
    of, 32–33, 106, 175–76, 180; moderate
    Islamist movements in, 33, 70, 87n72,
    174–75, 177–82, 215, 216, 229; Mou-
    dawana (Family Code) reforms of, 180–
    81, 215; public opinion in, 36, 182–89;
    radical Islamism in, 177, 181–82; U.S.
    aid to, 176. See also Parti de la Justice et
    du Développement (PJD)
Mouvement Populaire Democratique et
    Constitutionnel (Morocco), 178
Mubarak, Husni: corruption of, 19; demon-
    strations against, 18–19, 224; resignation
    of, xi, 222
Mufti, Malik, 47
Mukherjee, Bumba, 15, 150
al-Mulla, Lulwa, 96
Musharaf, Pervez, 219
Muslim Brotherhood, 64–65, 92; on 2011
    Arabic protests, 18n51; in Egypt, 19, 68,
    219, 224–27; in Jordan, 67–69; in Kuwait,
    89–90, 92–93; parliamentary roles of,
    68–69; in Saudi Arabia, 209; support for
    Saddam Hussein by, 92
Müstakil Sanayici ve İşadamları Derneği
    (MUSIAD), 217–18

Nabulsi, Suleiman, 45
al-Nashi, Badr, 97
Nasser, Gamal Abdel, 45, 203, 229
National Agenda campaign, 80, 81
National Mandate Party (Indonesia), 216–17
natural resources, 11. See also oil
Nayef, Prince of Jordan, 44
neodependency, 31
Netanyahu, Benjamin, 76
Nicaragua, 238
Nigeria, 240
Nixon, Richard/Nixon Doctrine, 40, 238
nonclient states, 223–24
Nooruddin, Irfan, 21n, 166–69

Obama, Barack, 78, 201; Middle East poli-
    cies of, 241–42; public opinion of, 235;
    responses to Arab Spring of, 222–24
'Obaydat, Ahmad, 76
Office of the Boycott of the League of Arab
    States against Israel, 55–56
oil, 11, 239–40; impact in rentier states of,
    21, 34, 61, 174, 222; in Kuwait, 54–55, 57,
    61, 135, 146n; OPEC's price policies for,
    56; in Saudi Arabia, 203, 205; U.S. poli-
    cies on, 4–5, 24, 38, 40. See also rentierism
Okruhlik, Gwenn, 208–9
Oman, 146–47n
Operation Desert Shield. See First Gulf War
Operation Desert Storm. See First Gulf War
Operation Earnest Will, 57
Organization of the Petroleum Exporting
    Countries (OPEC), 56
Oslo Agreement, 76, 192
al-'Othmani, Sa'ad, 179–80, 190
Ottoman Empire, 65n3
"overt support for democracy" scale (Ingle-
    hart and Welzel), 156–57, 158n26,
    164–65t, 166, 169–70

Pakistan, 219, 241
Palestine, 3, 29, 175, 216; anti-American-
    ism in, 33, 34, 195; Arafat's centralized
    authority in, 192, 199, 200; client status
    of, 197; Clinton's Camp David negotia-
    tions of, 241–42; democratic elections
    in, 191–93, 200–201; economic ties to
    the West of, 106; Fatah Party of, 94,
    191–98; free-market reforms in, 32–33;
    Hamas victory in, 85, 94, 191, 193–202;
    international sanctions in, 191, 196–201,

Palestine *continued*
215–16, 226–27; Islamist movements in, 33; Israeli occupation in, 235; Oslo Agreement for, 76; Road Map for Peace for, 191; Second Intifada of, 69, 88, 192, 228; security and authoritarianism in, 36, 201–2; statehood petition of, 237; status of Gaza in, 194–97, 201, 235; unity government in, 236–37. *See also* Hamas (Palestine)

Palestine Liberation Organization (PLO), 231

Palestine Survey Research Center poll, 197, 198n23, 220

Palestinian Authority (PA), 194, 196–97, 201

Palestinian Basic Law, 200

Palestinian cause, 218; impact on public opinion of, 236–37; Islamist support of, 65, 67–69, 178–79, 210; secularism in, 230. *See also* Arab-Israeli conflict

Palestinian residents: in Jordan, 46n38, 49, 54, 66, 67, 73, 75, 82–83, 134–35; in Kuwait, 49

Panama, 239

pan-Arabism, 231; under British rule, 43, 47; in Jordan, 71, 80–81, 111; in Kuwait, 55–56, 59–60, 89, 92, 105, 115

Paris Club for Jordan, 51

Paris Commune/France, 16

Parti de la Justice et du Développement (PJD) (Morocco), 70, 174–75, 178, 215, 216; anti-Americanism of, 179–80; moderate stance of, 179, 180–81; parliamentary seats of, 182, 229; pro-Palestinian work of, 179; U.S. engagement with, 190

patron-client relationships. *See* geostrategic patron-client relationships

Pew Global Attitudes Survey, 142–43, 149, 150n14, 155

Pinochet, Augusto, 238

PJD (Morocco). *See* Parti de la Justice et du Développement (PJD)

political culture, 6–9, 12; compatibility with democracy in, 8–9; role of civil society in, 7–8; role of modernization in, 7

political economy, 6–7, 9–11, 12; of global trade, 14–15; link with democracy of, 6n8; rentierism in, 11, 146, 216, 222; role of modernization in, 9–11

political Islam. *See* Islamist movements

Polyarchy (Dahl), 13

pro-Americanism, 4–5, 229–30; in Jordan, 165–66; in Kuwait, 29, 33, 34f, 35, 63–64, 89–92, 143–44, 165–66, 243

Program of International Policy Attitudes survey, 235

Prosperous Justice Party (Indonesia), 216–17

public opinion, 6, 35; anti-Americanism in, 143–44, 153–55, 161–62, 182n29; of authoritarianism, 35, 80–83, 144–47, 155–66, 165–66; causal logics of citizens in, 104–6, 143, 166, 222; of client relationships, 104–6, 113–16, 129–33, 143; of democracy/liberalization, 116–28, 135, 143–46, 163, 165–69; economic status factors in, 107–8, 128–29, 134–35, 143, 158–59, 162; educational level factors in, 158, 162; fear factors in, 160; of free trade, 32–33, 67, 85, 106, 143, 148, 149–51; gender factors in, 163; of Islamist opposition movements, 105, 106, 108, 116–28, 143–44, 153–55, 161–62; of Israel, 152–53; macrolevel implications of, 166–69; of monarchy, 104–16; multilayered analysis of, 147–69; "overt support for democracy" scale in, 156–57, 164–65t, 166, 169–70; Palestinian-Israeli conflict in, 236–37; patriotism and loyalty factors in, 160–61, 162; political access factors in, 158–59, 162; pro-Americanism in, 165–66; reducing anti-Americanism in, 233–38; religiosity factors in, 161, 162, 163; of Shari'a, 128–34, 135–36; of stability and security, 108–13, 136, 137, 143–47; of U.S. policies, 105–6, 121–22, 149, 151–53, 157, 176–77. *See also* Jordan's public opinion; Kuwait's public opinion

Putnam, Robert, 7, 30

al-Qaeda, 51, 211

Qatar, 206–7

Quandt, William, 206

Rabin, Yitzhak, 76

Radical Party revolts/Argentina, 16

al-Ramleh Society (Jordan), 70, 72

Rania, Queen of Jordan, 135

Reagan, Ronald, 57, 177, 204, 238

regime clientelism, 19n53

relative trade dependence, 26n69

rentierism, 11, 216, 222; distribution of wealth in, 146n; of Kuwait, 21, 34, 61; of Saudi Arabia, 174, 203, 205; support for the status quo in, 146, 174

research methods, 34–36; individual interviews in, 103, 137–41; in Morocco, 182nn29–30; multilayered analysis in, 147–69; "overt support for democracy" scale in, 156–57, 158n26, 164–65t, 166, 169–70; sampling methods in, 170–71; "support for government" scale in, 157n24, 161, 162, 164–65t; survey data analysis in, 142–43, 198n23; survey questionnaire in, 171–73

resource wealth. See rentierism

Revisiting the Arab Street report, 106

Rice, Condoleezza, 192, 239

Road Map for Peace, 191–93

Robins, Philip, 43, 45–46, 49, 51

Robinson, James, 13, 14, 16

Rodrik, Dani, 150

Rogowski, Ronald, 14

Rueschmeyer, Dietrich, 16

Russett, Bruce, 9

Russsia, 1, 2t, 4. See also Soviet Union

Ryan, Curtis, 52

Sa'ad, Zaki, 72–73

al-Sabah, Abdullah, 55

al-Sabah, Jaber III al-Ahmad al-Jaber, 22, 89–90, 97

Sabah monarchy (Kuwait), 62, 89

Sadat, Anwar, 68

Sahwa movement (Saudi Arabia), 209–11, 215

Salabi, Kamal, 44

Salafi movement (Kuwait), 89, 90, 95

Salafiyya Jihadiyya (Morocco), 181–82

al-Salim, Shaykh Sa'ad al-Abdallah, 22, 97–98

al-San'a, Nasser, 93, 97

Sandinista regime (Nicaragua), 238

al-Saud family (Saudi Arabia), 203–4

Saudi Arabia, 3, 29, 203–16; anti-Americanism in, 33, 34, 66, 101, 203, 206–8, 229; democracy and authoritarianism in, 36, 135; educational reforms in, 214–15; and First Gulf War, 25, 58–59, 204–5, 209–12; foreign direct investment law in, 207; human rights record of, 230; Islamist movements in, 33, 87n72, 203, 208–11, 240; in Nixon's Twin Pillar Policy, 40;

oil wealth of, 174, 203; political reforms in, 211–14, 215; population growth of, 205n42; public opinion in, 36, 135, 207–8; rentier status of, 34, 205; Shura Council of, 213n66; status of women in, 208, 209; U.S. role in, 203–8, 214–16

Scheve, Kenneth, 150

Schwedler, Jillian, 69n20, 75

Second Gulf War. See U.S.-Iraq War (2003–)

"The Second Image Reversed" (Gourevitch), 30

Second Intifada (Palestine), 69, 88, 192, 228

sector-based class interests, 17n48

secularism, 215, 229–31

security/economy hierarchy (Lake), 24–29, 38n1, 39, 210

Security Sector Reform and Transformation Program (Palestine), 201

September 11, 2001, attacks, 50, 51, 211

al-Shabiba al-Islamiyya, 177–78

Shahid Muwaffiq Airbase, 53

Shari'a law, 72, 79, 101, 128–36, 243

Sharp, Jeremy M., 180–81

Shati, Ismail, 92

Shikaki, Khalil, 197

al-Shu'aybi, Shaykh Hamud bin Uqla, 208

Shubaylat, Layth, 75, 76

Shura Council (Saudi Arabia), 213n66

Sick, Gary, 38, 40

Slaughter, Matthew, 150

Smith, Benjamin, 10

Social Reform Society, 89

socioeconomic class, 16–18; Marxist classifications of, 16–17; Weber's differentiation of, 17–18

South Asia, 2t

Soviet Union: Afghanistan war of, 56, 204, 214; collapse of, 38, 66; as potential patron, 38, 47, 230; U.S. containment policies toward, 38–39

Special Operation Command and Anti-Terrorism Center, 53

Stephens, Evelyn Huber, 16

Stephens, John, 16

Stopler Samuelson theorem, 150

sub-Saharan Africa, 1, 2t, 4

Sudan, 210

Suez Canal, 45, 219

support for democracy, 21n

"support for government" scale, 157n24, 161, 162, 164–65t

Sykes, Mark, 65n3
Sykes-Picot Agreement, 65
Syria, 31n79, 223–24; Hamas in, 72; secularism in, 230; talks with Israel of, 192

Talal, King of Jordan, 44
Tarawnah, Fayez, 77
al-Tawhīd wal-Jihād (Jordan), 79
Telhami, Shibley, 66, 208, 230, 236, 241
Tessler, Mark, 142
Tetreault, Mary Ann, 54, 90, 97
The Third Wave (Huntington), 3, 10n23
third wave of democratization, 6, 10–11
transition to democracy. See democratization
Transjordan, 41–43. See also Jordan
transliteration of Arabic, xv
Tsai, Kellee, 16
Tunisia, 31n79
Turkey: anti-Americanism in, 34; economic inequality in, 14; Islamist movement in, 33, 190, 216–18; on Palestinian-Israeli conflict, 218; role in U.S.-Iraq War of, 217–18
Twin Pillar Policy, 40, 55, 56

UAE, 66
United Development Party (Indonesia), 216–17
United States, 2–3, 23–29, 35; Afghanistan war of, 56, 206, 207, 218, 241, 243; Arab Spring responses of, 18–19, 222–24; Carter Doctrine of, 56–57; economic development aid from, 24, 25t, 46, 47n40, 50–51, 52t, 110, 176; Eisenhower Doctrine of, 38–39, 40, 45–46; energy needs of, 240; geostrategic goals of, 4–5, 24, 38–40, 57; Hamas policies of, 191, 196, 198–99, 226–27; Islamist movement policies of, 86–89, 190; Israel policies of, 4–5, 38, 45, 65–66; Middle East Free Trade Agreements of, 88; military aid from, 50–51, 52t, 53, 240–41; Nixon's Twin Pillars Policy of, 40, 55, 56; oil production in, 56–57; Persian Gulf role of, 38n2, 40–41; reduction of anti-Americanism by, 233–38; relationship with Morocco of, 176–77, 190; September 11, 2001,

attacks in, 50, 51, 211; strategic approach to democracy of, 3–7, 18–19, 214–18, 222–23, 227–31, 239–44; War on Terror of, 53, 63, 69, 84–85, 101, 176–77, 205–6, 235. See also anti-Americanism; First Gulf War
U.S.-Iraq War (2003–), 23, 24, 47–48, 69, 235; Jordan's support of, 50, 51–53; Kuwait's role in, 58–59; occupation of Iraq in, 65, 101; Saudi opinion on, 207–8, 240; U.S. withdrawal from, 243
U.S.S.R. See Soviet Union
al-'Utabi, Juhayman, 208
Uzbekistan, 240

values. See political culture
Van de Walle, Nicolas, 239n46
Verba, Sidney, 7

Wahhabism (Saudi Arabia), 209, 214–15
Walker, Joshua, 217
War on Terror, 63, 69, 235; Jordan's support of, 53, 84–85; Kuwait's support of, 101; public opinion of, 149; response to radical jihadism of, 203, 209–12, 214; Saudi participation in, 205–6
"We are all Jordan" campaign, 80, 81
Weber, Max, 17–18
Wedeen, Lisa, 243
Welzel, Christian, 156–57, 169–70
Weyland, Kurt, 239
women, 9; honor killings of, 230; Saudi Arabia's treatment of, 208, 209; suffrage in Kuwait of, 22, 95–97
World Public Opinion poll, 235–36, 237
World Trade Organization (WTO), 49, 60
World Values Survey, 6n9, 143, 166–69
World War II, 43–44

Yacoubian, Mona, 86n70
Yassin, 'Abdesalam, 178, 181
Yassin, Nadia, 181, 190
Yemen, 70, 203

Zardari, Asif Ali, 219
al-Zarqawi, Abu Musa'ab, 77, 79
Zoubir, Yahia, 205